TIRPITZ

TIRPITZ

The Life and Death of
Germany's Last Super Battleship

Niklas Zetterling & Michael Tamelander

CASEMATE PUBLISHERS
Philadelphia & Newbury

Published in the United States of America in 2009 by
CASEMATE
908 Darby Road, Havertown, PA 19083

and in the United Kingdom by
CASEMATE
17 Cheap Street, Newbury, Berkshire, RG14 5DD

ISBN 978-1-935149-18-7

Cataloging-in-publication data is available from the Library of
Congress and from the British Library.

Printed and bound in the United States of America.

10 9 8 7 6 5 4 3 2 1

For a complete list of Casemate titles, please contact

United States of America
Casemate Publishers
Telephone (610) 853-9131, Fax (610) 853-9146
E-mail casemate@casematepublishing.com
Website www.casematepublishing.com

United Kingdom
Casemate-UK
Telephone (01635) 231091, Fax (01635) 41619
E-mail casemate-uk@casematepublishing.co.uk
Website www.casematepublishing.co.uk

Contents

GREENLAND

Reykjavik•
Hyal Fjord

ICELAND

Jan Mayen
Island

ATLANTIC OCEAN

Seydis Fjord

NORWEGIAN SEA

ARCTIC CIRCLE

Faroe
Islands

Orkney
Islands
Kirkwall•
Moray Firth
•Lossiemouth
•Milltown
•Aberdeen

SCOTLAND

*Scapa
Flow*

Shetland
Islands
•Sumburg

Fætten Fjord

Trondheims Fjord

Mosjøen

•Namso

Ålesund•
Trondheim•
Vaernes

Bergen•

NORWAY

Stavanger•

Oslo•

SWEDEN

Kristiansand•

N

Is Fjord

Grön Fjord

Barentsburg • •Longyearbyen

Svalbard

Bell Strait

Hopen

Bear Island

Stjern Strait

Langfjord

Lyngen Fjord

Altafjord

Bals Fjord Tromso

Bogen Bay

•Hammerfest

Alta

•Bardufoss •Banak

Ofot Fjord

•Narvik

Kaafjord

•Bodø

Lake Torne

Vest Fjord

•Porjus

BARENTS SEA

•Kirkenes

Petsamo•

Murmansk• •Vaenga

•Ponoy

GULF of
BOTHNIA

•Uleåborg

WHITE
SEA

FINLAND

Jagodnik•

SOVIET
UNION
•Archangelsk

The launch of the *Tirpitz* on April 1, 1939.

Preface

When working on our previous book about the battleship *Bismarck*, whose career turned out to be as brief as it was dramatic, it was impossible not to make comparisons with the fate of her sister ship, the *Tirpitz*. The latter—commissioned after the destruction of the *Bismarck* and despite being Germany's largest warship—remained stationary and unharmed for most of her service. As the fates of the two ships differed considerably, the way we approached the story of the *Tirpitz* also differs significantly from the way we approached *Bismarck*. The latter was the focal point of a highly dramatic week in May 1941. Of course, there was the bigger picture in which she temporarily played a part, but the narrative was built around the battleship herself, the fate of the crew manning different battle stations, and also around the commanders who made decisions that would have important implications for maritime strategy in the later parts of the Second World War.

In a sense, the *Tirpitz* was a focal point too, but rather as a piece in a broader game played by actors located very far from the battleship herself. The drama of the *Tirpitz* did not to the same extent take place on the bridge or at the battle stations of the ship. Instead, several dramatic episodes unfolded around her, as she was continuously regarded as a major threat by the Allies. Most of these episodes took place in one of the most inhospitable parts of the earth—the Arctic Sea. During the summer months, this region could offer spectators a scenery as tranquil as it was dazzling. The winters, though, could be very severe. Despite the harsh climate, many merchant ships were sent to Murmansk and Archangelsk, bringing vital armaments and other important cargo from the Western Allies to the Soviet Union. The *Tirpitz* constantly threatened these convoys, and innumerable attempts were therefore made to destroy her. The German battleship, however, long defied these efforts.

There are many very good sources if one wants to study the history of the *Tirpitz*. Most of her war diary still remains, as do many relevant documents from the Luftwaffe and various German naval staffs. Also, a large part of her crew and many additional eyewitnesses survived the war. With so many sources available, priorities have to be made in order to produce a readable account. We have chosen not to describe the *Tirpitz* from a technical point of view, since we have already discussed her almost identical sister ship in our previous work. Instead we have focused upon the war in the Arctic, the convoys and the Allied efforts to destroy the battleship. No warship presents an isolated history. Not until the full picture is clear, can the importance of the *Tirpitz* be judged. With this book we hope to assist the reader in attaining a better understanding of the war in the Arctic, as well as the *Tirpitz's* role in it. This was our main objective.

Prologue

Despite his warm clothes, Lieutenant Commander Sommer suffered from the bitter cold. It penetrated his boots and proceeded up his legs until his entire body felt frozen. Already as a young cadet, he had learned how to relax to ignore the cold, but this technique seemed to be ineffective as he stood on the pier and gazed upon the huge battleship lying at anchor in the roadstead.

At this time of the year the days were very short, with late mornings and the dusk coming early. Presently, the sun had risen above the white mountains. It made the trees cast shadows and created a yellowish glow on the battleship. The asymmetric camouflage, which was intended to break up the contours of the ship, had been painted over. Instead, the hull and parts of the superstructure had been dyed dark grey, while higher parts had been given a lighter grey surface, to blend with the snow-clad mountains slopes surrounding the battleship's mooring place. Despite the distance, Sommer could also discern the many buoys on the water above the torpedo nets.

With a length of 251 meters, the *Tirpitz*—like her almost identical sister ship *Bismarck*, which had been sunk on the Atlantic in May 1941—was an impressive spectacle, even though the majestic mountains surrounding Tromsø diminished her appearance by comparison. Since she had been accepted by the German Navy on 25 February 1941, the British had feared her, but she had seldom been allowed an opportunity to fire with her eight 38cm guns upon an enemy. Rather, she had long been a hunted prey, subjected to innumerable British attacks. Except for an air attack in April 1944, her complement of more than 2,000 had always escaped virtually unharmed.

The latest air attacks however had damaged the battleship significantly. In fact, she could no longer be regarded as fit for action. She had been lying in Kaafjord and been given superficial repairs, but the damage to her bow did not allow speed much in excess of ten knots. In such circumstances, it was utterly unthinkable to challenge the Allied command of the seas. She was still a weapon, though, and had thus been sent to her mooring near Kvaløya, to assume the role of a floating battery. To the crew of what was deemed to be one of the world's most powerful battleships, it was an ignominious task, but it was no fault of theirs.

As the battleship was no longer expected to sail on the open seas, some 600 of the crew, mainly from the machinery, had been transferred to land duties and were commanded by Sommer. They were to establish anti-aircraft cover, operate fog projectors, and ensure that the ship was protected by nets to ward off torpedoes and submarines. Still, some 1,700 men remained on board—gun crews, electricians, sailors, and officers—to perform duties whose significance had paled. When Germany still had some sort of chance to win the war, which had begun in Poland in 1939, the struggle in the Arctic Ocean had been part of the conflict, in which the *Tirpitz* significantly influenced the decisions taken on both the German and the Allied sides. Now she had been reduced to a static role in a remote area of little significance. Soviet forces were already on the German eastern borders, as were Allied troops in the west. There was nothing the crew could do about it, stuck as they were in the crippled battleship far up in the north. Sommer shivered. In the battleship it was at least warmer. He really yearned for the warmth on board.

The Norwegian harbour master left his hut and approached. His face was serious-minded. Sommer sighed imperceptibly. For how long would he have to stand here in the cold?

"I am afraid you will have to wait for awhile," the harbour master replied, precisely as Sommer suspected.

"So that's how it is, is it? Do you know why?"

"We have received a report on enemy aircraft near Bodø, they may be on the way to Tromsø."

"I see." Sommer gazed toward the battleship and despite the distance, he could make out the air raid warning flag. It was mainly intended to alert the anti-aircraft batteries located on the surrounding islands. Sommer mused on how long the flag had been visible. He could not recall seeing it being hoisted. "Well," he said, as much to himself as to the harbour master, "It seldom lasts long."

"In any case, you will have to wait until it is over before I can provide you with a boat," the Norwegian said. "Wait here in the meantime."

Sommer decided to take up a higher position to better see what transpired. Half walking, half running, he moved up the trail to an anti-aircraft battery situated on a low hill. He found an army lieutenant who was busy making his guns ready for action.

"Do you believe the battleship to be the target?" Sommer asked, still breathing heavily.

"Probably." The lieutenant looked toward the horizon in the south with his binoculars. "Unless they intend to attack Bardufoss."

Sommer used his hand to protect his eyes from the sun, but still had to screw up his eyes as he looked at the snow-clad mountains. Above Tromsdalstind, the highest summit in the area, he could barely discern six small glimmering objects. "Twin engine?" he suggested. "Probably Bostons. And only six of them. If so they will not even order action stations on board."

"I am afraid it is worse," said the lieutenant, who could see better with his binoculars. "I can see at least 18 aircraft and a second wave is following. And they are not twin engine. They are Lancasters." He lowered his field glasses and turned his head toward the battery, which was protected by sandbags and concealed by a camouflage net. "Have you obtained the range?" he yelled.

"Just a moment, lieutenant," the NCO operating the range finder replied.

Anxiously, Sommer observed the approaching aircraft with mounting apprehension. During all previous air attacks, he had been on board the ship, below deck and unable to see anything outside the ship. He had experienced the air alarm, the thunder, and the vibrations caused by the firing guns. That had been all. But this was something very different: the majestic ship lying in anchor at the roadstead with guns trained south, the dazzling scenery, and the lieutenant who had hastily taken up his position at the battery and shouted instructions to the crew. It was like a drama directed specifically for the benefit of Sommer.

While the enemy aircraft approached, Sommer looked for other objects in the sky. Surely the German fighters at Bardufoss must have been alerted? But where were they? Soon it would be too late to attack the British aircraft before they had released their bombs.

He was brusquely interrupted by the flashing forward guns on the battleship. A few seconds later, the shells burst ahead of the enemy aircraft and turned into brown smoke clouds. Sommer had expected the enemy aircraft to make some kind of evasive maneuver, but they maintained a steady course, seemingly oblivious to the firing German guns.

The thunder from the battleship's artillery had already passed the hill where Sommer keenly observed the spectacle, when the crackling sound from the battery revealed that the lieutenant had ordered it to open fire. The lighter guns on the battleship joined in. Behind Grindøya, tracer from an anti-aircraft ship raced toward the enemy. Sommer could not see the vessel, but he knew where it was stationed.

In the blue sky, the Lancaster bombers had reached close enough for Sommer to clearly observe their silhouettes. He could see the four engines and the characteristic tail, despite all the shells bursting around the aircraft. Astoundingly, none of the shells hit, and even more remarkably, the air crews did not seem to bother about the fire. Did they think themselves invulnerable, these Britons?

Sommer saw the first bomb tumble from the aircraft leading the formation. Within seconds, the other aircraft also released their bombs, until 18 huge devices could be seen between the aircraft and the battleship. Sommer shuddered from dread as he saw that the bombs were well aimed—far too well aimed.

Within a fraction of a second, Sommer imagined how the section of the catapult, which protruded on the port side, was crushed beneath the weight of the bomb before it disappeared below the main deck, close to the bridge. A violent flame followed almost instantly and the deck was split open as if it had been made from paper. At the same moment, two more bombs hit the surface. One of them landed in the water on the starboard side of battleship, outside the torpedo nets, throwing up an enormous fountain of water. The other bomb hit Haakøya, where it threw a cascade of earth and snow toward the blue sky.

While Sommer remained motionless, almost as if he were petrified, the battleship received another hit, this time between the aft turrets and the superstructure. The ship was engulfed in a thick smoke cloud, as bomb after bomb splashed into the water around her.

Then the sound waves from the explosions hit Sommer and he instantly covered his ears with his hands.

It was almost a quarter to ten on the beautiful Sunday of 12 November 1944—the morning that witnessed the destruction of the battleship *Tirpitz*.

Tirpitz during sea trials in the Baltic Sea, summer 1941.

Nordmeer

In the afternoon of 6 March 1942, the commander of the British submarine *Seawolf* raised his periscope above the surface to watch the estuary of the Trondheimsfjord. The weather permitted good visibility, and the mild southwesterly breeze only occasionally caused the waves to moisten the periscope's lens.

Lieutenant Raikes swiftly turned the periscope to watch the entire horizon, to see if there was any menace from enemy warships or aircraft. While the commander's attention was focused on the periscope, the Chief Engineer, Navigation Officer, and other men in the control room eyed him intensely. As the commander was the only person who could see what transpired above the sea, the other men watched for any sign in his behaviour that could reveal something.

The war was into its fourth year, and nothing suggested that it would soon come to an end. The conflict, which in the beginning had befallen only four European countries, had expanded to consume most of the world. Italy had entered the war, then the Soviet Union had been attacked. Now even Japan and the United States had become warring states, along with China, thereby making the conflict the most extensive ever fought. Battles were raging in Europe, Africa, and the Far East, but to the crew of the *Seawolf*, the strategic perspective of the war was remote. The men on the submarine were encased in their crammed metal coffin, where sweat, humidity, bad air—and not least the gloominess and hopes for something different to occur—were the most common elements of everyday life.

The day before, the First Sea Lord, Admiral Dudley Pound, had been replaced by General Alan Brooke as chairman of the British Chiefs of Staff Committee. Perhaps this change would eventually mean changes even to Raikes and his crew, since Pound had been a proponent of schemes in which the Royal Navy held a prominent role. Now a representative of the ground forces had taken the seat. But even if the crew of *Seawolf* had known what was taking place in their home country, they probably would not have been bothered. Their concern was first and foremost to survive. When Raikes again turned the periscope, to take a final look at the area near the fjord estuary, the crew returned to their normal duties.

Raikes had assumed command of the *Seawolf* in 1941, but neither he nor his predecessor had experienced anything remarkable. During the German invasion of Norway in 1940, the *Seawolf* had sunk one merchant ship, but for the most part her crew had vainly searched for the enemy while performing the many monotonous duties necessary to keep the submarine in working order. This day wasn't any different. In daylight, it was prudent to remain submerged, or else German aircraft or warships sailing into or out of the fjord might easily see the sub. Also, the water was much calmer a few meters below the surface, something that made life easier to put up with. By listening in the hydrophones and occasionally poking the periscope above the surface, the *Seawolf* had every chance of detecting German ships in the area.

Nothing of importance had happened as the sun began to set. March 6 seemed to be just one in an apparently endless range of uneventful days. Raikes, however, decided to reconnoitre the sea surface one more time. He strained his eyes and this time he really saw something important—a very large warship. It was difficult to identify the vessel, but clearly it was a heavy cruiser or a battleship, sailing on a northerly course. Also, Raikes saw that the huge ship was escorted by several destroyers.[1]

The enemy ships were too distant to allow the *Seawolf* to attack them, but at last a wave of excitement swept across the submarine. Clearly, this might be an observation of great significance. It was tempting to surface and transmit a report, but such a decision had to be carefully considered. On the one hand, if the Admiralty was informed immediately, countermeasures to the enemy movement could quickly be organized. On the other hand, it was risky to surface until the darkness of night provided concealment, especially as the enemy squadron might well enjoy air support. Furthermore, if the Germans located a wireless signal from the submarine, they might well realize that it had something to do with the large warship leaving Trondheim. Hence, they might recognize that their plans had been discovered. Raikes decided to wait a few hours. In the dark night, he surfaced and sent the radio message. He had not been able to identify the enemy warship, but the information he provided was combined with other pieces of information available to the British. They realized what had happened: the *Tirpitz* had put to sea.

In the winter months, the Arctic Ocean is among the planet's most forbidding areas. The rays of the sun cannot be seen for many months, while the pack ice gradually creeps south. Time and again, icebergs break loose from the pack and drift south, melting slowly in the cold water. The crews of the few ships that moved in the area 60 years ago had to be very vigilant to avoid the fatal consequences of a collision with an iceberg. In the low temperature, men did not survive long if their ship sunk. As few ships traveled in the area, and visibility was often poor, chances of rescue were slim. Had it not been for the Gulf Stream—whose warm water flows along the Norwegian coast even in the darkest of winter nights—the Arctic Ocean would probably not have been navigable at all. However, the warm water flowing along the coast of Norway keeps the coastal area free of ice, even as far away as the Russian port of Murmansk, despite the severe winter.

The stern climate did not allow a large population to live in the Arctic region. Most of the inhabitants in the northern parts of Norway dwelled on the coast. Perhaps it is symptomatic that the only real towns—Hammerfest and Tromsø— were both situated on islands. Thus the sea water could more easily keep the climate reasonably mild during the winter. Also, the location allowed quick access to the sea, an important circumstance to a population that was dependent on fishing. Farther east was the Kola peninsula. Except for the important port of Murmansk, it was very sparsely populated. There were also a few smaller villages, for example Petsamo, where limited actions had been fought during the Finnish "Winter War" of 1939, but the area was almost untouched by the initial period of World War II. In 1940, during the German invasion of Norway, battles had been fought around Narvik, but not farther north, and not in the arctic seas above the Norwegian coast.

When Hitler decided to invade the Soviet Union, this would all change. At the end of June 1941, two German mountain divisions attacked across the tundra on the Kola peninsula, along the northern coast. They aimed for Murmansk, but the task was difficult. The rugged terrain combined with Soviet defences to resist the attackers. There were hardly any roads. Large quantities of ammunition, fuel, and reinforcements could only be brought to the area by sea, but the few harbours were very small. The German advance came to a halt about halfway to Murmansk. With hindsight, this is hardly surprising. The sparsely populated, rugged area did not lend itself to major ground operations. The only transport route on land was the railway that connected Murmansk with the other parts of the Soviet Union. As the Red Army firmly controlled the railway, it could more easily bring in reinforcements and supplies. Already in September 1941, the German mountain troops had to assume defensive positions and begin to prepare for surviving the coming winter.[2]

No naval battles had been fought on the surface of the Arctic Ocean. Rather, the struggle for control of the sea routes had been raging on the Atlantic and in the Mediterranean. During previous wars, the Arctic Ocean had usually been untouched by combatants. The history of these waters had mainly been about daring voyages of discovery rather than dueling warships. The latter usually engaged each other at latitudes farther south, where port facilities were closer.

During the first week of March 1942, the severe winter firmly held its grip on northern Europe, and the Arctic Ocean was no exception; but the days had finally become longer. This was of great significance, particularly to air units, as they depended on daylight for most of their missions. It was still unclear what effect this would have on the military operations soon to unfold.

The Fættenfjord is a part of the larger Trondheimsfjord, located in the central part of Norway. In this area, the sun rose above the horizon even during the darkest days of the winter, but on 5 March it was hidden behind thick clouds. It was still cold. The thermometer showed minus eight degrees Celsius (18 Fahrenheit), but as the clouds were high, the outlooks on the *Tirpitz* had to endure the cold wind as they searched the sky for enemy aircraft. The battleship had been carefully camouflaged in the small fjord, but as she had been moored for almost seven weeks, the British were fully aware of the need to keep an eye on her. The crew had experienced numerous air alerts during the period in the Fættenfjord, and this day was no exception. Just before noon, a Spitfire was sighted about ten kilometers west of the battleship. None of the guns of the *Tirpitz* opened fire, but soon the bursting shells from land based anti-aircraft guns could be heard over the Trondheimsfjord, while German fighters scrambled to intercept the intruder.[3]

Two hours later, there was yet another air alert. This time, an unidentified aircraft was observed at such great distance that no engagement occurred. To the men serving on the *Tirpitz*, air alerts had become part of the daily routine, and the crew quickly settled back when the intruder had disappeared. In the evening, however, something unusual happened. The clattering teleprinter on the *Tirpitz* conveyed an important message from Marinegruppe Nord, which oversaw the German naval forces in Norway. A reconnaissance aircraft had reported a British convoy south of the Jan Mayen Island. It consisted of 15 merchant ships and sailed on a northeasterly course, which suggested that it was bound for Murmansk. According to the report, it had an escort of one cruiser and two destroyers.[4]

The message was immediately forwarded to Captain Karl Topp, who had commanded the *Tirpitz* since 26 February 1941, and Vice Admiral Otto Ciliax, who was in overall command of the German heavy ships stationed in Norway. The former, Captain Topp, was a big man whose appearance betrayed his true character—a sailor who knew his profession inside and out. During World War I, he had commanded submarines and destroyers, and then served as navigation officer on board the cruiser *Emden*. Reputedly, he could manoeuvre the *Tirpitz* with a certainty and precision more akin to a light vessel. When its sister ship *Bismarck* and the heavy cruiser *Prinz Eugen* left Gdynia to conduct Operation Rheinübung in May 1941, Topp had felt envious. The loss of the *Bismarck*—which followed an unfortunate torpedo hit that destroyed her rudder—did not diminish his confidence in the *Tirpitz*. If he found a British convoy, he would do his utmost to inflict disastrous losses; if he had to duel with Allied surface forces, he would show what the *Tirpitz* could accomplish against heavy enemy warships.[5]

While Topp was responsible for everything that happened on the *Tirpitz*, Vice Admiral Ciliax, who's flag flew on the battleship, commanded the German warships as a unit. He had assumed a position which would probably have been predestined for Admiral Lütjens, had the latter not perished with the *Bismarck* almost a year ago. Ciliax had previously commanded the *Admiral Scheer* and the *Scharnhorst*, and he had subsequently been Chief of Staff, Marinegruppe West. In February 1942, he had been in overall command of operation Cerberus when the *Scharnhorst*, *Gneisenau*, and *Prinz Eugen* dashed through the English Channel and reached German ports. Now he was entrusted with the German naval forces in the north.

Ciliax and Topp agreed that the reported British convoy was a worthwhile target. The warships were ordered to raise steam. Such an order was uncomplicated, but there were more difficult issues to consider.[6] To begin with, the future course of the convoy had to be considered. As it had been observed by the reconnaissance aircraft, it could not be excluded that someone on board the ships in the convoy had also seen the German plane. Indeed, the convoy might have been ordered to turn back to Britain. If the German ships steamed north to search for a convoy no longer on it's way to Murmansk, precious fuel oil would be consumed, and without any tangible results to show. It was, however, not very likely that the convoy would turn back. A more plausible alternative was that it would change to a new course, but one that would still ultimately bring it to Murmansk. But there was a problem for the merchant ships, as the convoy was close to Jan Mayen: They did not have much room for maneuver farther north, as the pack ice was very close.[7]

Ciliax and Topp had to carefully consider the proper moment to sail from Trondheim. Secrecy was of utmost importance. It was preferable to put to sea in darkness. Of course, a delay might compromise the chances to catch the convoy, but if the convoy sailed at six knots, as reported by the German aircraft, it would hardly get very far away. The German warships possessed a substantial speed advantage compared to the merchant ships. No undue risk would have to be incurred by weighing anchor in the evening of 6 March.[8]

The resources available to Ciliax in Trondheim were limited. In addition to the *Tirpitz*, he had the heavy cruiser *Admiral Scheer*, the 5th Destroyer Flotilla, and the 2nd Torpedo Boat Flotilla. The small vessels of the latter were not suitable for the open seas of the Arctic Ocean, and the other ships were of dissimilar character. The destroyers were better suited to the harsh conditions of the northern seas, but their endurance was limited. Furthermore, the *Admiral Scheer*, which Ciliax had commanded at the time of the Spanish Civil War, had serious limitations. She could not do more than 26 knots, which was less than Ciliax desired, and also less than the other ships available to him. In fact, the cruiser *Prinz Eugen* had been sent to Trondheim to reinforce Ciliax. However, on 26 February, while on her way to Trondheim, Lieutenant Commander Geoffrey Sladen, on board the British submarine *Trident,* caught sight of the German cruiser and torpedoed it. The *Prinz Eugen* was hit in the stern. Nobody was killed by the torpedo hit, but the damage was so serious that she had to be towed to Trondheim. In the Norwegian port, provisional repairs were made that allowed the cruiser to return to Germany for more thorough repairs. She would be absent from the German order of battle for almost a year.[9]

The resources available to Ciliax left him with few options, and he was not even allowed to choose freely among the few alternatives he had. After a brief deliberation, the supreme Naval Command in Berlin ordered Ciliax not to include the *Admiral Scheer* in the forthcoming "Operation Nordmeer."[10] He had to rely on the *Tirpitz* and his destroyers.[11]

While the men on board the ships strived to make them ready for action, Ciliax and his staff worked out an operations order for Nordmeer. Four ships would take part: the *Tirpitz*, and the destroyers Z25, *Herrmann Schoemann,* and *Friedrich Ihn.* The destroyer *Paul Jacobi* and two torpedo boats would initially accompany the task force; however, they were supposed to return to Trondheim quite soon. The Luftwaffe would provide fighter cover and reconnaissance, and the floatplanes on the *Tirpitz* would be on 30 minutes alert.[12]

Endurance was of paramount importance. While the *Tirpitz* by a wide margin possessed sufficient fuel oil for the forthcoming operation, the destroyers were much less fortunate in this respect. Ciliax decided that they would have to be refuelled at sea. As no tankers would be available, they would have to receive fuel oil from the battleship. He made a preliminary decision to refuel the destroyers at about 04.00 on 7 March, approximately eight hours after leaving Trondheim.[13]

Several German submarines had been positioned in the Arctic Ocean with orders to attack Allied convoys sailing to or from

Murmansk. To minimize the risk of friendly-fire incidents, it had been decided that the submarines would operate east of the 28th meridian and the surface ships to the west. Thus Ciliax would have to find his prey before it passed the 28th meridian. If luck accompanied him, he could attack the convoy just before it passed east of the dividing line, allowing the submarines to attack ships of a presumably decimated and scattered convoy.[14]

At 04.00 on 6 March, the *Tirpitz* left the Trondheimsfjord, accompanied by the six smaller vessels. Despite brighter weather, nothing suggested that British reconnaissance aircraft had detected the German squadron. Ciliax could confidently set a northerly course, while the ships raised steam for 25 knots in fairly calm sea. As planned, the *Paul Jacobi* and the two torpedo boats returned to Trondheim, after escorting the main force during the first four hours of the operation.[15]

Vice Admiral Ciliax and his staff had prepared guidelines on how to engage the enemy. The main task for the *Tirpitz* was to destroy the convoy's escort, in particular the cruiser which had been reported by the German reconnaissance aircraft. The German destroyers would initially prevent British destroyers from attacking the battleship with torpedoes. When the British escort had been neutralized, the merchant ships could be attacked by all the German warships. Because of the shortage of torpedoes, they would only be fired at short range. These guidelines were valid only if superior enemy forces were not encountered. However, action against a strong enemy force should be avoided.[16]

During the night the sea became rougher and the destroyers were hard-pressed to maintain 25 knots. Ciliax ordered his squadron to proceed at 21 knots, a measure that in no way jeopardized the operation, as the convoy was plodding east at a much lower speed. However, something much more serious took place south of Ciliax's present position. The *Seawolf*'s Lieutenant Raikes decided to transmit a report on his sighting. The radio waves were not received by the commander of Home Fleet, Admiral John Tovey, but the Admiralty in London intercepted the signal and relayed it to Tovey soon after midnight.[17]

Admiral John Cronin Tovey had, as commander of the destroyer *Onslow*, participated in the Battle of Jutland during World War I. In the interwar years he had held numerous positions. His career path climbed sharply. Four years before World War II broke out, he was promoted to Rear Admiral. He was soon given the command over British destroyer forces in the Mediterranean and was then promoted to Vice Admiral. As commander of the 7th Cruiser Division he took part in the battle at Punta Stilo in June 1940, which was the first major engagement between British and Italian naval forces. Later in 1940, Tovey was appointed to command the Home Fleet, and was responsible for chasing the German battleship *Bismarck* in May 1941. He hoped to repeat this success against the *Tirpitz*.

In fact, Tovey had already put out to sea. His ships were farther north than Ciliax's, and the British Admiral had impressive might at his disposal. In addition to his flagship, the *King George V*, he was accompanied by her sister ship, the *Duke of York,* and the older battle-cruiser *Renown*. Also included in his force were the cruiser *Berwick*, 12 destroyers, and—perhaps most important of all—the aircraft carrier *Victorious*. Both the *King George V* and the *Victorious* had participated in the chase of the *Bismarck* in 1941. With such an impressive force to rely on, Tovey did not fear engaging the German battleship.[18]

Tovey also had to protect the merchant ships, and although his orders allowed him to perform the mission at a considerable distance from the convoy, he could not just plunge away to search for a presumed German battleship. The convoy found by the German reconnaissance aircraft was called PQ12 by the British, and it was sailing to Murmansk. The German report was almost perfectly accurate. The escort consisted of the light cruiser *Kenya,* and the destroyers *Oribi* and *Offa,* as well as a few smaller escort vessels. The only error in the German report was the number of merchant ships, as PQ12 consisted of 16 rather than 15 ships, an insignificant inaccuracy.[19]

The Germans, however, were unaware of something that Tovey knew and which the British Admiral had to consider carefully. Another convoy—QP8—had sailed from Murmansk on 1 March with 15 empty merchant ships heading for ports in Britain. The escort was very small, only two minesweepers and two corvettes, utterly insufficient for the German force reported to be heading north. Tovey had previously suggested that the convoys to and from Murmansk should be scheduled in such a way that he could initially follow the eastbound. When it met the westbound convoy, his ships would simply switch and escort the ships heading back to British ports. The benefits of the proposal included reduced consumption of fuel, reduced wear and tear on the ships, and the crews would experience less hardships. Furthermore, the Arctic Ocean was dangerous, although Tovey's warships usually sailed south of the convoys, thus facing less risk of colliding with icebergs.

There were also disadvantages with Tovey's proposal. As the merchant ships travelled slowly—usually five to ten knots—many days passed before the ships that sailed from Murmansk reached the area where they could rendezvous with Tovey. There was also the harsh weather. It often forced the ships to alter course or speed. Weather, in the form of humid air or large waves splashing over the ships, also caused another problem: accumulated ice. Large amounts of frozen water could cover the ships and make them top heavy, endangering their stability. Ships had been lost due to excessive amounts of ice. Such perils, in addition to the obvious dangers to the sailors, made it difficult to estimate how quickly the convoys could travel. On top of all this, strict radio silence was usually adhered to, as the Germans could take bearings and locate a convoy transmitting signals. Hence, Tovey might very well find himself in a position where he only had scant knowledge of the whereabouts of the westbound convoy.

On the other hand, Ciliax was woefully short of information on Tovey's situation. Certainly the German Admiral could suspect that a convoy had departed from Murmansk, but he had no solid facts to base his decisions upon. No intelligence suggested that the Home Fleet had put to sea—and already on a more northerly latitude than his own squadron. The harsh reality was that Ciliax was forced to grope in the darkness, but he hoped more information would become available next day, in particular from aerial reconnaissance. Unfortunately, the weather forecast received on the evening on 6 March did not bode well. It predicted increasing wind and more clouds farther north, although visibility at the surface of the sea was expected to vary between ten and twenty miles.[20]

As the wind grew stronger, the sea got rougher. In particular, the destroyers rolled violently. They disappeared in the troughs of the sea and then suddenly appeared again on the crests, where they briefly remained until they again fell down. The bitterly cold water flushed the decks and trickled into corridors, cabins, and messes; the sailors strained their muscles to avoid falling. It was not only the men on board the destroyers who suffered; even the big battleship was heaving in the rough sea. Many sailors on the *Tirpitz* suffered from seasickness, among them the seaman Herbst. Overcome by his feeling of sickness, he unfortunately went astray on the wrong side of a 15cm gun turret, where a huge wave swept him overboard. Such dangers were unfortunately common on the warships. Far to the north, the hazards were even more serious, especially during the long, dark, and cold winter days. A man did not live long in the icy water. Darkness and rough seas combined to make it very difficult to find those in distress. One example is the British destroyer *Matabele*, which was escorting the convoy PQ8 when she was torpedoed off Murmansk by a German submarine commanded by Lieutenant Burckhard Hackländer. Within a few minutes, the *Matabele* had disappeared from the surface of the ocean. Within short notice a rescue ship arrived to help, but even though many of the destroyermen wore life vests, it was too late for most. While bobbing up and down in the black water they had frozen to death, their empty eyes staring at their would-be rescuers. Only two men from the *Matabele* were still alive and saved.[21]

At 04.00 on 7 March, Ciliax's four ships were at the level of the Lofoten Islands and continuing north. By this time, he appears to have shelved his plan to refuel the destroyers from the *Tirpitz*. Rather, his ships steamed at 25 knots. As no intelligence reports had reached the Admiral, he decided to form a screen of his ships. Thus he hoped to find the convoy that had not been seen by German eyes for almost two days. The *Tirpitz* altered course to the northwest while the destroyers continued north for an hour, when they also turned northwest and assumed a wider formation.[22]

The weather—which was of paramount importance to Ciliax's plans—continued to deteriorate. A strong northwesterly wind brought a succession of snow squalls into the area where his ships searched for the convoy. Visibility changed dramatically from minute to minute. Plans to launch two floatplanes from the battleship had to be cancelled, as it would be virtually impossible for them to land on the rough sea. An alternative discussed was to send the floatplanes to Tromsø after completing their reconnaissance missions. It was rejected, however, as it was doubted that the aircrews would find the northern Norwegian town in the poor visibility. [23]

The decision to refrain from using the floatplanes turned out to be wise, as the weather deteriorated further. At about 2:00 p.m. it began to snow continuously, and visibility fell to less than 2,000 meters. Drifting ice was soon encountered, but worse was to come. The sea turned out to be so cold that a crust of ice lay ahead of the *Tirpitz*. However, it was brittle and presented little hindrance to the battleship. The very poor visibility was a graver problem. It would require a great deal of luck to find a convoy. Also, if by chance enemy warships were encountered, the short range would deprive the *Tirpitz* of many of her advantages.[24]

So far the Germans had not used their radar sets, as it was feared that the British might detect the radar waves and locate the German battleship. However, at 14.40, the radar was switched on for a two-minute period, but the operators found nothing on their screens. Soon afterwards it ceased snowing, but the ocean around the *Tirpitz* turned out to be empty. She continued at 27 knots on a northwesterly course for an hour, whereupon she altered course to east-northeast.[25]

After the German reconnaissance aircraft detected PQ12 on 5 March, the convoy had continued its east-northeasterly course until the evening of 6 March, when it encountered ice. Some of the smaller escort ships were damaged. The convoy altered course to southeast and thus avoided further mishaps. At 08.00 on 7 March, it resumed the east-northeasterly course. These maneuvers brought the convoy within a

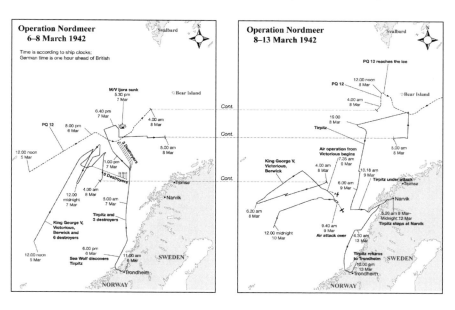

distance of less than 100 kilometers from the *Tirpitz*, which passed behind PQ12. The German destroyers got even closer, but neither of them saw anything of the convoy. The poor visibility saved the merchant ships from being found by the German warships.[26]

It was a close shave for PQ12, but in fact it was even closer for QP8. On the morning of 7 March it was sailing on a course exactly opposite to PQ12, and at noon the two convoys passed each other. QP8 was still heading west-southwest, unaware of the German warships' presence. Fortunately for the convoy, the *Tirpitz* steamed at such high speed that she crossed the convoy's course ahead of it at a distance of 80 kilometers. However, one of the destroyers was only 20 kilometers away. Had the convoy not been concealed by the heavy snow, it would almost certainly have been found by the Germans.[27]

Ciliax could not know it, but the *Tirpitz* was in fact using a speed too high to encounter QP8, but slightly too low to find PQ12. Nevertheless, he was first and foremost prevented from finding at least one of the convoys because of the atrocious weather.

Ciliax's ignorance wasn't limited to the British convoys. He had still not received any information suggesting that the Home Fleet was close. Luck had not betrayed him altogether, though, as Tovey was not much better informed of the true situation. During much of 6 March, he had patrolled the area south of PQ12, but at about 12.00, he turned and set a south-southwesterly course. However, at midnight he received the information originating from the *Seawolf* and promptly turned to north-northeast. Also, he ordered the *Victorious* to prepare a reconnaissance mission at dawn.[28]

The fickle weather upset Tovey's plans too. As dawn broke, he could see that the weather precluded air operations. Snow squalls and rain showers superseded each other at irregular intervals. The moisture assembled as ice on the aircraft, and Tovey had no choice but to postpone the reconnaissance flights. He ordered a turn to starboard, bringing his ships on a southeasterly course. He did not know it, but the distance to the *Tirpitz* was rapidly shrinking. Had he maintained this course, he stood a fair chance to find the German battleship, but after about an hour he turned northeast, thus increasing the distance again.[29]

Not only was Tovey lacking information on the position of the German ships, the whereabouts of the two convoys were unclear. For some reason, he believed that the QP8 was farther east than its true position. Accordingly, he ordered a new sharp turn to port and set a southwesterly course. Thus, he quickly increased the distance from the *Tirpitz*, as well as the convoys. At 17.00 Tovey still sailed southwest, while Ciliax headed northeast at 20 knots. For the moment, almost 300 kilometers separated the two commanders.[30]

On board the *Tirpitz*, there was a small group of men called the "B-Dienst."[31] They were experts in the field of cryptography and worked on decoding intercepted Allied radio messages. Until 5 p.m. they'd had no success to boast of, simply because there were hardly any radio messages to decipher. However, at this moment a message was unexpectedly intercepted, and it was soon clear that it originated from a Soviet merchant ship under fire from German warships. It was immediately handed over to Ciliax and Topp, who understood that the German destroyers had found a merchant ship.[32]

The German B-Dienst had interpreted the message correctly. It had been transmitted by the *Ijora*, which had been part of QP8. However, on 6 March a gale had partly scattered the convoy, and the *Ijora* lagged behind. Her misfortune was not over when the storm abated, as she was found by Ciliax's destroyers on the evening of 7 March. After a brief, one-sided fight, the defenseless merchant ship disappeared beneath the surface.[33]

The distress signal from the *Ijora* was also received by Tovey, but unlike the German B-Dienst, the British radio operators could not establish the position of the Soviet merchant ship. Tovey hesitated, but after an hour a radio message was intercepted from a ship whose bearing could be established. Was it the *Tirpitz*? Tovey gambled and assumed it was. He set a southeasterly course. If his assumption was correct, he would position himself between the German battleship and Trondheim.[34]

Admiral Ciliax realized that the signal from the *Ijora* might also have been received by the British, prompting a decision to alter the convoy's course. Even more important, the Home Fleet would most likely put to sea, especially as spies in the Trondheim area had probably reported that the German battleship had left its moorings. Evidently, Ciliax was presuming that the Home Fleet had remained at Scapa Flow until now. He would soon realize the magnitude of his error.[35]

For a while, the *Tirpitz* continued on her easterly course. Nothing particular occurred, until at 18.00, when faint smoke clouds could be discerned. A few minutes later, the silhouettes of three ships appeared. On the Admiral's bridge, it was assumed that the destroyers were approaching. Ciliax and his staff officer's assumption turned out to be correct, and he ordered the smaller vessels to join the battleship and set a southeasterly course.[36]

Ciliax had originally planned to refuel the destroyers before dawn on 7 March, but he postponed it and the destroyers were very low on fuel oil in the evening. Shortly after 19.00, Ciliax gave orders to prepare for refuelling and, about an hour later, an attempt was made. But in the darkness and the rough sea, it proved too difficult. After half an hour, the refuelling was cancelled. It was disappointing, as Ciliax might soon be forced to send the destroyers to ports in northern Norway.[37]

To rub salt in Ciliax's wounds, a breakdown occurred in one of the port engine rooms on the *Tirpitz*. The necessary spare parts were available on the battleship, but the components to be replaced were far too hot to allow repairs. Until the *Tirpitz* returned to port she would be limited to 29.5 knots.[38]

The German misfortunes were not over. The commander of the

Hitler visits the *Tirpitz* in Gotenhafen (Gdynia) on May 5, 1941.

destroyer flotilla, Captain Berger on board the *Friedrich Ihn*, fell seriously ill. Ciliax decided to send the *Friedrich Ihn* to Harstad. There Berger could be transferred ashore and its fuel oil could be replenished. For the time being, the other destroyers remained with the flagship. Ciliax hoped that it would be possible to refuel in the morning.[39]

After the loss of the *Ijora*, QP8 continued on its westerly course, thus increasing the distance from the German force. Simultaneously, the Home Fleet moved toward a position between the *Tirpitz* and QP8, as Tovey had decided to make a turn to port, bringing his ships on a north-westerly course. He did detach six destroyers, however, and gave them the mission to watch the possible German routes to Trondheim. At the time, nobody realized that QP8 was no longer endangered by the *Tirpitz*. On the morning of 8 March, a distance of about 500 kilometers separated the convoy from the German battleship.[40]

At this stage of the operation, the PQ12 convoy faced a greater hazard than the convoy sailing toward Britain. The convoy bound for Murmansk continued on its east-northeasterly course, which almost coincided with the course maintained by Ciliax. As the German warships were much faster, the convoy depended entirely on poor visibility and its course to escape from the Germans. Later in the night, the Admiralty sent an order to the convoy to proceed north of Bear Island. Accordingly, PQ12 changed course before dawn on 8 March. [41]

While the ships of PQ12 ploughed the icy water of the Arctic Ocean, Tovey fumbled in the darkness. He had far too little information to act upon and seldom left his bridge, although the crew could occasionally see him walk back and forth on the deck, repeatedly searching the dark waves in his binoculars. Since his ships had turned north-northeast during the evening of 7 March, he had adhered to the course until midnight. Nothing noteworthy occurred, and Tovey gradually began to believe that the enemy had escaped him. At the same time he had deprived himself of a significant part of his destroyer force, which made his heavy ships more vulnerable as they proceeded into areas believed to be infested with German submarines. The British commander decided to turn south at midnight and regain contact with his dispatched destroyers. Thus he quickly began to increase his distance from PQ12, and after turning to an almost westerly course at 05.00, the gap increased even more rapidly. In the afternoon of 8 March, almost 800 kilometers separated the Home Fleet from PQ12.

Tovey's warships would have to steam hard for the better part of a day to reach the convoy.[42]

The menace to PQ12 had not diminished. On board the *Tirpitz*, it was decided to launch aircraft as soon as daylight permitted air operations, but when dawn broke the weather turned out to be so poor that flying was precluded. Snow squalls plastered the battleship, whose forecastle became covered by thick ice. The airmen were allowed to return to normal readiness. Weather was not the only impediment to Ciliax's plans. The destroyers were so low on oil that he could no longer refrain from sending them to Tromsø where they could refuel. Still, Ciliax was not prepared to break off the operation. The battleship would continue searching for the convoy until dusk, and then set course for Trondheim. Since he now wanted air cover, he broke radio silence and informed Marinegruppe Nord about his intentions. Thereafter, Ciliax ordered a northerly course, but proceeded at fairly low speed to facilitate his hydrophone operators' work as they listened for propeller noise from other ships.[43]

The German efforts met with no success. A drifting mine was encountered, but passed at a distance of 150 meters. Also, German submarines were stumbled upon, but no trace of the convoy was found. The *Tirpitz* maintained her northerly course while zigzagging 20° to either side. When the battleship was engulfed in snow squalls, speed was reduced to improve the chances for the hydrophone operators to detect any ships. The lookouts strained their eyes to find anything, while the First Gunnery Officer, Commander Robert Weber, received permission to open fire at any target found. The guns of the battleship remained silent, but at noon the air-raid alarm reverberated through the ship. After a few tense minutes, the lookout could identify the aircraft as a Focke-Wulf 200, a German long-range reconnaissance aircraft. Ciliax sent a message to the aircrew instructing it to search farther west, while a bank of fog approached.[44]

At this moment PQ12 had reached a point approximately 160 kilometers northwest of the German battleship, i.e. slightly west of Bear Island, as it had previously made a turn according to the orders received from the Admiralty. However, the limit of the pack ice turned out to be farther south than estimated by the Admiralty. There was no alternative but to proceed south of Bear Island. At noon the convoy set a south-easterly course and attentively followed the edge of the ice. Thus, without anybody being aware of it, the convoy began to close its distance to the *Tirpitz*, while the Home Fleet was still far away and opening the gap, as it followed a southwesterly course. In fact, at this stage the convoy was completely dependent on its own means. To the north, the ice was an impenetrable barrier; to the south, a roving enemy battleship menaced. Still, the only realistic option was to proceed toward Murmansk, while all available eyes searched the horizon for any sign of danger. Before dusk, the men on board the merchant ships could discern the barren summits of the Bear Island.[45]

After he had communicated with the Focke-Wulf, Ciliax decided to set a westerly course, still zigzagging, as he wanted to search an area as large as possible. His speed varied from 15 to 25 knots, depending on visibility and the work of the hydrophone operators. At 13.30, smoke clouds became visible on the horizon, and soon the radar detected three objects at a range of 8,000 meters. The mood on the bridge vacillated between exultation at finding the convoy and fear of encountering enemy warships. However, it turned out that no ships were in the vicinity. Probably the alleged smoke clouds had just been thick snow squalls, which caused the illusion of ships and smoke. As the staff pondered the event, the air-raid alarm resounded. However, the intruder turned out to be the German reconnaissance aircraft, which once again approached.[46]

The afternoon of 8 March remained uneventful, and in the evening Ciliax received a weather forecast. As it indicated that fickle weather would prevail, he decided to break off the operation and turn south. In fact, the *Tirpitz* had now increased its distance from PQ12 and had by the evening reached a point more than 200 kilometers from the convoy. It was by no means an insurmountable distance—the battleship could cover it in five or six hours—but this presupposed that the position and course of the PQ12 was known. At this stage, Ciliax and his staff had every reason to suspect that the British were aware that enemy warships were searching for the convoy; still, the Germans had no indications on where to find it. It was not even evident that the *Ijora* had sailed with a convoy, although it was more likely that she was a straggler rather than a ship sailing alone. In any case, it was clear that the risk of encountering the Home Fleet increased as time elapsed.[47]

Ciliax was not far from the truth when he presumed that the Home Fleet was approaching. Although Tovey had proceeded southwest during the afternoon, thus distancing himself from the center of events, in the evening he received an important message from the Admiralty. It informed him briefly that the enemy was to be found northeast of Bear Island. Tovey turned northeast and for the first time broke radio silence, as he informed London that he was operating without anti-submarine capabilities. To his good fortune, the message was not intercepted by the Germans. To the ships nearby he signalled: "We are close on their heels."[48]

The excitement mounted on the bridge of the British flagship. Did they still have a chance to intercept the *Tirpitz*? Tovey asked the Admiralty to assume control over the detached cruisers and destroyers, as he could no longer reliably communicate with them.[49]

During the evening before 9 March—after Ultra had broken some German radio messages—the Admiralty was convinced that the *Tirpitz* was heading toward Trondheim. At 02.30 the radio operators on board the *King George V* received the short message: "Enemy heading south."

After receiving the message, Tovey ordered a course to east-southeast, changing his ships' bearing toward Bodø on the Norwegian coast. The Ultra codebreakers had provided Tovey with a golden opportunity, contrasting starkly with the fumbling that had character-ized the previous days.[50]

Would he be able to repeat the success achieved against the *Bismarck* in 1941?

"A Wonderful Opportunity"

The *Tirpitz* maintained her southerly course during the night of 8–9 March, and only a series of messages from Marinegruppe Nord interfered with the routine work. At eight in the morning, the destroyer *Friedrich Ihn*, which had put to sea from Harstad, appeared before the battleship. The rendezvous occurred about 300 kilometers west of Narvik, and the two ships could either proceed to Trondheim or set course for Narvik, depending on how the situation unfolded. The prospects of air cover would improve as the distance to the Norwegian coast diminished.[51]

Ciliax did not know how dearly he needed air cover, but farther west, Tovey noted how the weather that prevented the *Victorious* from launching reconnaissance aircraft had gradually improved. Soon after 03.00 he sent a report to Captain Henry Bovell on the carrier. It said that the *Tirpitz* would probably reach the Lofoten Islands at about 07.00. This information was provided to Tovey by the Admiralty, but it originated from Ultra. He concluded with an exhortation: "Report proposals."[52]

Two hours later a reply was sent from the *Victorious*: "Recommend launching six reconnaissance aircraft at 06.30." According to Bovell, the aircraft should search the area west of the Lofoten Islands and immediately report any contact with the enemy. Meanwhile, an attack force should be prepared. It consisted of five Albacores from 817th Squadron, commanded by Lieutenant Commander P.G. Sugden, and another seven Albacores from 832nd Squadron, led by Lieutenant Commander W.J. Lucas. The latter would be in command of the attack on the *Tirpitz*.[53]

At 06.45, as occasional showers of rain washed the flight deck, the six reconnaissance aircraft were launched from the *Victorious*. About half an hour later, a message from Tovey was received: "A wonderful opportunity which may produce remarkable results," it said. "May God be with you."

The Albacores, armed with torpedoes, were prepared. From 07.35 they were launched one by one. Bovell watched them as they formed and set off on a southeasterly course. He knew this was a chance the Admiralty had dreamt of; he also knew it might never recur. For the moment he was unable to influence the course of events—he could only wait and see what the reconnaissance yielded. When Lieutenant T.T. Miller, pilot on one of the reconnaissance aircraft, reported at 08.15 that he had located the *Tirpitz*, Bovell instantly felt satisfied. The British pilot followed the German battleship and regularly reported its position.[54]

On board the *Tirpitz*, the excellent visibility was noted. Clearly, this was advantageous to the enemy. Second gunnery officer Albrecht Schnarke considered it ideal weather for carrier aircraft. During the days that had just passed, the Germans would have desired such weather. But now, when all hopes of finding the convoy had been relinquished and the only aim was to reach port safely, good visibility was a liability. It was still bitterly cold, and the strong wind caused the battleship to roll and heave in the waves. This was yet another advantage to the enemy, as it would render anti-aircraft fire less accurate. All available eyes were prying for signs of the enemy. An air-raid alarm at 09.05 produced anxiety, but it turned out to be a German aircraft, a Heinkel 115 seaplane. However, the joy caused by the sighting of the German plane turned out to be short-lived.[55]

Lieutenant Commander Bidlingmaier, Navigation Officer on board the *Tirpitz*, was in the chart house when he heard the shout: "Two aircraft astern!"

Bidlingmaier dashed to the bridge: "Report to the Captain," he said, and ordered full speed. The aircraft were no floatplanes. Undoubtedly they were hostile, as no single-engine aircraft could operate so far from the coast. There was only one possible conclusion: an enemy carrier could not be far away. "Turn east," Bidlingmaier said, "and prepare to launch the Arado aircraft."[56]

Soon Topp arrived at the bridge, followed by Ciliax a few moments later. They approved the actions ordered by Bidlingmaier and followed the aircraft with their binoculars. Evidently the enemy aircrews had no intention of getting close to the battleship. Rather they stayed at a range that was prudent enough, but which still allowed them to monitor the battleship's speed and course. At that distance, it was difficult for the Germans to establish the type of aircraft, but it was correctly guessed that the disturbers were of the type Fairey Albacore. Soon a third aircraft of the same type was seen. There could be no doubt that an enemy carrier had found the battleship.[57]

There was little more the Germans could do, except what Bidlingmaier had already ordered. The *Tirpitz* had been sailing at 25 knots, and gradually increased speed to 29 knots. At such high speed no British battleship could catch up with her, but aircraft was another matter. As the German warship had already reached a point on the same latitude as the southern part of the Lofoten Islands, she could turn east toward Narvik. At her present speed, she could reach the port in seven hours.[58]

A few minutes later, the B-Dienst on board the *Tirpitz* broke a few intercepted British messages. The first was a report from the aircraft, which transmitted the speed and course of the German battleship, but it contained an error, as it indicated a position 35 kilometers west of the true position. The second message was of greater importance to the Germans, as it informed them about a British naval force, 160 kilometers west-northwest and sailing at 26 knots with an east-south-easterly course.[59]

Air cover was urgently needed. The distance to airfields in Norway was not overwhelmingly great, but a few hours would pass before any friendly aircraft reached the German battleship. Until then the *Tirpitz* would be on her own, as the destroyer *Friedrich Ihn* provided little protection against enemy torpedo planes. The only alternative left to Topp and Ciliax was the Arado floatplane, which was being prepared according to instructions issued by Bidlingmaier. The Arado would also be useful to search for enemy submarines, which might be lurking at the entrance to Narvik. Furthermore, it could engage enemy aircraft, although the situation would probably not allow the plane to be brought back on board the *Tirpitz*. The pilot would simply have to fly to Narvik or Bodø when running low on fuel. The Arado pilot took off and promptly attacked each British reconnaissance aircraft, but none of them were shot down, although one crew member was wounded in his legs. When the German pilot had used up all his ammunition, he set course for the naval base at Bodø.[60]

The approaching British air unit also had its share of difficulties. Burdened with the weight of a torpedo, the aircraft could not fly fast. The headwind was also strong, and as the *Tirpitz* and *Friedrich Ihn* sailed at almost maximum speed, the aircraft had an advantage of only 30 knots. This speed edge was not expected, and the Albacores had to struggle hard to maneuver into a suitable attack position. In an attempt to surprise the Germans, the British commander ordered his aircraft to fly into the clouds. However, a gap in the clouds opened up and exposed the aircraft to the German lookouts.[61]

The hopes to surprise the *Tirpitz* had been frustrated, but Lucas made a decision that would subsequently be criticized. It was customary to attack large warships from several directions, and in this case it would have been preferable to split the 12 machines into four sections—each consisting of three aircraft—and attack within short intervals from different directions. Such a procedure would make it difficult for the enemy warship to evade the torpedoes from the first section without getting in the way for subsequent torpedo salvos. But now Lucas was concerned that the Albacore aircraft would accumulate ice on their wings, which could lead to a serious loss of lift. In the prevailing weather conditions, the risk was very real, and Lucas did not want to delay the attack.[62]

Lucas still hoped that the Germans had not observed his squadrons. If the Albacores managed to reach the positions from which a coordinated attack could be initiated, they would almost inevitably have been seen from the *Tirpitz*, thus forfeiting the element of surprise. Convinced that it was preferable to attack unexpectedly from the stern, rather than carry out the revealing and time-consuming flight to attack from the bow, he decided to take action immediately. A few moments later, the other pilots heard him on their headsets, ordering them to make individual attacks. Lucas' own section initiated the first dive from the port quarter, while the other three sections approached from the starboard. Suddenly the battleship opened fire, virtually all her guns blazing. As the air between the Albacores and the *Tirpitz* was filled with tracer rounds and brown smoke clouds, Lucas realized that surprise was no longer attainable; at this stage it was too late to change the plan. His attack had already begun.

Topp saw the three aircraft level away just above the surface and release their torpedoes. However the distance was far too great, and he realized that the airmen must have misjudged the range—an understandable mistake considering the size of the *Tirpitz*. Soon the hydrophone operators confirmed the observation. Aided by excellent water conditions, the hydrophone operators could continuously report the range and course of the approaching torpedoes, despite the battleship's high speed. The information from the hydrophones indicated that the first salvo was harmless, and soon the torpedoes could be seen passing about 150 meters behind the stern.[63]

While the German anti-aircraft fire concentrated on Lucas' section, another section of three aircraft from his squadron approached, shifting to attack from the port side rather than starboard. Soon three Albacores attacked from the same angle as Lucas' section, but at slightly closer range. When the British aircraft dove to the surface and straightened and released their torpedoes, Topp ordered a sharp turn to port, but at this stage Vice Admiral Ciliax almost made a grave mistake.

"No!" he shouted. "Steer hard-a-starboard."

The helmsman—who was well aware that Topp, not Ciliax, should give such orders—hesitated and stared at Topp.

"I command this ship, Admiral—not you!" Topp shouted to make himself heard above the noise from the anti-aircraft guns. "Helmsman, hard-a-port."

The helmsman obeyed, and the *Tirpitz* veered to port so sharply that she listed to starboard. Ciliax felt rebuked and moved slightly to the side. Probably he had intended to reduce the area exposed to the torpedoes, but such a maneuver would have exposed the ship's broadside to the remaining two sections, which now approached on the starboard quarter. As the battleship turned to port, according to Topp's orders, these two sections ended up astern. Ciliax realized that he had exceeded his authority and that a starboard turn would have been a mistake.[64]

Neither of the aircraft in the second section scored a hit. However two sections remained, and as the German battleship was momentarily on a northerly course, Sugden hoped he could position himself between the *Tirpitz* and Narvik. This could possibly enable a coordinated attack on the battleship's bow, but Topp outwitted him and returned to an easterly course. As a result of the maneuvering, the Albacores had closed in on the battleship. Thus they could release the torpedoes at very short range, and in some cases the oblong gadget splashed into the water about 200 meters from the battleship. After releasing the torpedoes, the aircraft sprayed machinegun fire as they passed the battleship. It is easier to understand how daring the attack was if we contrast the range to the fact that the battleship was over 250 meters from bow to stern. One of the aircraft was hit by Flak and caught fire after releasing its torpedo. It appeared to stagger in the air, as if the pilot were drunk. Then, for a moment, he regained his composure and landed his Albacore on the water. One man struggled out of the cockpit and climbed onto the fuselage. The *Tirpitz* passed the burning but still floating wreck at such short distance, that Bidlingmaier could see the terror-stricken face of the British airman, who realized that nobody would be able to save him from drowning in the icy water. Lieutenant Räder also recalled the sight of this aviator, who sat on the wing root and awaited his destiny.[65]

Another Albacore aircraft was shot down. On the *Tirpitz*, three men were lightly wounded by the fire, but otherwise the battleship and its crew were unhurt. Aided by the work of the hydrophone operators and the watchfulness of the lookouts, Topp could make the decisions required to avoid the torpedoes, although one of them passed a mere ten meters from the battleship's hull.[66]

As the remaining ten aircraft disappeared, Admiral Ciliax returned to the bridge. He was impressed by Topp's maneuvers, and was probably slightly ashamed of his impulse ten minutes earlier. Loudly, he praised the captain before all present at the bridge. "You maneuvered meritoriously, Topp," he said. "Lucky ship!"[67]

All the efforts and sacrifice of the British airmen were in vain. The *Tirpitz* could continue east at high speed, while the British had to accept the loss of the two Albacore aircraft and crew. Also, no further British aircraft were on their way to attack the battleship. It would take about two hours to have another go at her.[68]

Exultation and relief were earnestly felt on board the *Tirpitz*, but none of her men and officers knew how Tovey had disposed the Home Fleet's resources. The crew remained on tenterhooks, and Topp informed his fire control that he expected an attack from British dive-bombers soon. Merely two minutes later, an air-raid alert sent the crew to full attention. The aircraft remained outside the range of anti-aircraft guns, however, and the Germans concluded that it was only shadowing the *Tirpitz*.[69]

The ensuing hour remained uneventful to the crews on board the German ships. Those on deck could see the clouds covering the sky, but visibility at sea level was excellent, in stark contrast to the days vainly spent searching for convoys. Low-flying aircraft could easily find the German ships. Soon after 11.30 an aircraft indeed appeared, but this time it was a German Heinkel 115. It was a relief, but the German aviators soon sent a message: they had seen a submarine and warned of the impending danger. A minute later, the hydrophone operators detected submarine noise and warned accordingly. Topp wasted no time. He gave the helmsman orders to turn to port to avoid the menace.[70]

The Germans detected a torpedo shot, but again they remained unscathed. With their superior speed, the two German ships soon left the lurking danger behind. At noon, the westernmost islands of the Lofoten could be seen by the lookouts, whereupon the *Tirpitz* and *Friedrich Ihn* entered the Vestfjord. At 13.00 the bridge was informed that the Arado aircraft had safely reached Bodø.[71]

Topp still had to take the submarine threat seriously, but when two Messerschmitt Bf-109 fighters were sighted at 13.15, the German sailors understood that the enemy carrier was less of a menace. In fact, the fighters ought to have appeared earlier, but a communications failure on land delayed the *Tirpitz's* request for fighter cover. Belatedly the fighters appeared, but at this stage, the British had given up their efforts to attack the *Tirpitz*. Undamaged, she entered the Ofotfjord, and a pilot embarked at 16.00. Two hours later, the battleship anchored in the Bogen Bay north of Narvik.[72]

After the failed torpedo attack, Tovey awaited the returning aircraft. When they had landed on the *Victorious*, he set a westerly course. He was keenly aware that German aircraft operating from bases in Norway could attack his ships if they remained close to the coast. Somewhat later, a German reconnaissance aircraft did appear, which strengthened Tovey's resolve. The Home Fleet sailed toward Scapa Flow. However, this was not the last British effort to sink or damage the *Tirpitz*. Destroyers and submarines were dispatched to attack the German battleship, as she was expected to put to sea soon.[73]

The temporary pause was used by the Germans to repair the

Tirpitz's machinery. After 48 hours of hard work, she was again capable of exceeding 30 knots. The respite was also used to transfer 300 cubic meters of fuel from the battleship to the *Friedrich Ihn*. [74]

Ciliax had no intention to remain in Narvik longer than necessary. On 12 March he issued orders to return to Trondheim. Anchor would be weighed at midnight. Tovey's suspicion that the *Tirpitz* would soon put to sea again thus proved correct, but the destroyers he sent did not arrive until 13 March, when the *Tirpitz* had already reached far south. Neither did the British submarines along the Norwegian coast sight the German battleship, which was escorted by destroyers as well as torpedo boats, minesweepers, and aircraft. Except for a few drifting mines, the Germans saw no signs of the enemy. They reached the Trondheimsfjord soon after 17.00.

The *Tirpitz* could once again anchor in the Fættenfjord, where she wouldn't be found by the British until five days later.[75]

The War at Sea—The Initial Years

On the eve of war in 1939, the British as well as the German Navy had formed a clear list of priorities. The British first and foremost had to ensure that sufficient imports of raw materials and other products reached the British Isles, primarily by shipping over the Atlantic. In this respect, the situation was almost identical to 1914, but this time the British could capitalize on their experience from the Great War. They knew that submarines posed a serious threat, but also that the convoy system had proved instrumental in staving off disaster.

Clearly, there were also important differences between the two wars. In particular, the German Navy was provided far less major warships in 1939 compared to 1914, when the Imperial German Navy possessed an impressive battle fleet. The development of active sonar, the ASDIC, was a major advantage according to the British Navy. The system could detect submerged vessels, and British decision makers had great confidence in it, as it promised to diminish the threat to shipping posed by submarines.

Evidently, a much weaker German Navy was a major advantage to Great Britain; but on the other hand, a former ally—Japan—had turned into a menace to British possessions in Asia. Hence, the British armed forces, including the Navy, would probably have to commit resources to the Far East. Nevertheless, in 1939 the British Navy was in a much stronger position than its German counterpart.

In 1939, the German Navy was far from ready for a major war. With only a few submarines on hand, it was impossible to seriously threaten British shipping, and the surface fleet was even less capable of challenging

British dominance at sea. With her weak Navy, Germany had to resort to a mode of operations called "cruiser warfare." Grand Admiral Erich Raeder was the main proponent of the concept, which meant that German surface ships would pass the line from the Faroe Islands, via Iceland, to Greenland undetected. Thus they would reach waters where British convoys were not escorted by large naval vessels, allowing the German raiders to attack merchant ships almost with impunity.

During the initial years of the war, the German concept met with only marginal success. For various reasons the warships spent little time on the Atlantic, and consequently only modest results were achieved.[76] Despite the German problems, the Royal Navy nevertheless had to maintain constant vigilance, and numerous forays were made to intercept presumed German attempts to reach the Atlantic. This meant a constant strain on the ships and crews of the Home Fleet. Still, there was a more significant threat to British shipping: a resurgence of the German submarines, which began to appear in greater numbers, scoring notable successes during the second half of 1940.

During the first half of 1941, the battle on the Atlantic intensified. As the threat of a German invasion of Britain faded, which was evident already in the autumn of 1940, the British Navy could strengthen its convoy escorts. Thus the German submarines found their task more difficult and dangerous. On the other hand, the German surface fleet was poised to make its presence felt on the oceans.

To begin with, the cruisers *Admiral Scheer* and *Admiral Hipper* put to sea from German ports at the end of October and the beginning of December 1940, respectively. They operated as single ships and could only attack shipping not protected by heavy escort, or else they might not be able to sustain operations over a long period. A more ambitious enterprise was initiated in January 1941, as the two battleships *Scharnhorst* and *Gneisenau* began Operation Berlin. Expectations were high, but despite operating on the Atlantic for almost two months, the number of merchant ships sunk wasn't that impressive, even though better results were achieved compared to previous efforts.

During Operation Berlin, the weak main armament of the two participating German battleships forced them to avoid action against older British battleships, which escorted some of the convoys. However, in the spring 1941, the brand new battleship *Bismarck* was fully prepared for operations on the Atlantic. Her armament and protection was deemed to be powerful enough to accept greater risks, but still caution remained an important constraint to the German decision makers, as a new sortie was being prepared.

Operation Rheinübung, in which the battleship *Bismarck* and the heavy cruiser *Prinz Eugen* took part, was initiated in mid-May 1941, but it was soon known to the British that the German squadron had sailed. Their first attempt to force the *Bismarck* to battle ended disastrously. After a very brief exchange of fire, a shell from the *Bismarck* ignited a magazine on the battle cruiser *Hood*, which blew up, leaving only three survivors. Subsequently, the two German ships managed to shake off the shadowing British ships. By a series of lucky events, the British found, damaged, and finally sank the *Bismarck*. The cruiser *Prinz Eugen* managed to sneak into the French port of Brest, where she would remain for several months and, together with the battleships *Gneisenau* and *Scharnhorst*, be subjected to numerous attacks by the Royal Air Force.

The loss of the *Bismarck* was a major setback for the Germans, and soon most of the supply ships they had stationed on the Atlantic to bunker their warships were lost too. Without them, the Germans could not mount operations of the kind hitherto conducted. Furthermore, in contrast to previous assumptions, Operation Rheinübung had shown that British radar technology was not lagging behind. Further advances in radar would have significant implications for the German prospects of successfully reaching the Atlantic. The entire concept of cruiser warfare was clearly questionable.

At the same time, a major shift in German priorities occurred which had significant implications for the conduct of naval operations. Since the fall of France in June 1940, Britain had been the sole German enemy, which made Raeder's arguments for a consistent naval strategy plausible. He was, however, well aware of the intentions to attack the Soviet Union, and when this invasion was launched on 22 June 1941, the Atlantic became a backwater.

To Raeder's comfort, it was expected that the campaign in Russia would be over in a few months. When the Soviet Union collapsed, the German war effort would again be focused in the direction Raeder preferred. In fact, already on 27 June 1941—a mere five days after crossing the border of the Soviet Union—a directive for the reduction of the Army was issued, which would enable more resources to be allocated to the war against Great Britain.[77] With the comfort of hindsight, such a directive appeared remarkable indeed, but Hitler and the men around him—like decision makers in many other countries— did not believe that the Soviet Union could withstand the onslaught. As the elimination of the Red Army would mean that no major land powers remained in Europe to challenge Germany, it would no longer be necessary for the Germans to maintain a large army.

In the meantime, Raeder could not conduct a naval war according to his preferences during the summer of 1941. Two of his three battleships remained in Brest for repairs. British air attacks on the port caused damage to the ships almost at the same pace as previous damage was repaired. The *Tirpitz* was still conducting trials and training exercises in the Baltic and was not ready for action. Also, warships of the German Navy supported the ground forces that advanced in the Baltic States. Finally, the fate that befell the *Bismarck* discouraged new endeavours on the Atlantic. Hitler regarded losses of major naval vessels as a severe blow to his prestige.

At a conference on 25 July, Raeder again defended the concept of cruiser warfare. According to the Grand Admiral, the mere threat of German incursions into the Atlantic tied up considerable British resources. Nevertheless, he emphasized that active commitment of the Luftwaffe was essential to success and demanded better coordination. In particular, he stressed the need for air reconnaissance, which had low priority in the Luftwaffe. Hitler promised that decorations would be awarded not only for successful combat sorties, but for meritorious reconnaissance missions as well.[78] To what extent Hitler's promise was realized, or had any impact, is unclear, but undoubtedly Raeder had been pointing to something important when he demanded a more substantial and coordinated effort from the Luftwaffe.

During the pre-war years, most of the funding had been assigned to the army and air force. Considering its geographical position, Germany could probably not have pursued any other alternative. Furthermore, the Luftwaffe was mainly designed to cooperate with the German Army, not the Navy. In the early part of the war, when Germany crushed many of her neighbors one by one, the situation altered fundamentally. During the summer of 1940, Raeder could forcefully argue that Britain was the main enemy, and could only be subdued by the kind of strategy he envisaged, one which included the use of airpower.

However, even if he had rallied the support of Luftwaffe chief Hermann Göring, a certain amount of time would have been necessary. The Luftwaffe had hitherto acquired aircraft and experience of another kind of war than that demanded by a maritime strategy. Admittedly, more could have been done in the short-term perspective, but a major reorientation was something completely different.

During the autumn of 1941, several events occurred which affected the German maritime strategy. Most importantly, contrary to predictions, the Soviet Union did not swiftly collapse as Hitler had hoped. Optimism still prevailed in September and early October, but the prospect of a war dragging into the following year was ominous. With the onset of autumn rains—about a week into October—chances of ending the war before the summer of 1942 were slim.

It wasn't only the Germans who were surprised by the tenacity of Soviet resistance. It gradually dawned on the British that the Soviet Union might come to play a significant part in the defeat of Hitler. Initially, they had been sceptical about the Soviets' chances to resist the German assault. Granted, the German offensive in the east was a relief to the hard-pressed British military forces, but it appeared to be a temporary one. Furthermore, there was very little the British could do to assist Stalin. As the military resources of Britain were already strained, it was hardly possible to send combat units to the Eastern Front—at least not to an extent that would have any influence on the course of events.

One way to assist the Soviet Union, however, was to send weapons and other products essential to its war effort. Important Soviet factory equipment had been transported east to avoid the German panzer formations plunging forward. This caused a temporary drop in production, making virtually any British deliveries valuable. Great Britain did, however, remain hesitant. It had already lost a good deal of equipment when evacuating its troops from Norway, France, and Greece, and also across North Africa when Rommel's forces advanced rapidly. As the Soviet Union might well succumb to the German attackers, any equipment sent to the Russians might end up in German hands—a result the British had had enough of. Furthermore, the British had no cornucopia of equipment themselves, although their war production had increased substantially, and in fact exceeded German output. Unfortunately, the British were not aware that their industry at this stage of the war outperformed Germany's. They were, however, well aware of the difficulties involved in transporting various products to Russia. Geography only permitted two alternatives: the first was to haul weapons and other equipment through Persia, and the second was to send merchant ships across the Polar Sea. Both alternatives were arduous, dangerous, and of limited capacity.[79]

On 1 August, the British mine cruiser *Adventure* sailed into the port of Arkhangelsk. She carried various items of equipment, which were to be transported south on the railway running from Arkhangelsk to central Russia. The quantities delivered were miniscule compared to the huge conflict that raged on the main front, but at least it was a symbolic gesture. The visit made by the British ship could not mark the beginning of regular deliveries, however, as the sea outside Arkhangelsk froze during the winter. At best, convoys could only reach that port during the warm months of the year.[80]

There existed an alternative: the port of Murmansk, which had been built during World War I, partly with British aid. The intention had been to provide the Csar's forces with equipment from France and Britain. After Turkey entered the war on Germany's side, British and French forces had tried to break through the Dardanelles, an attempt that ended disastrously. This left the Western powers with only one alternative in order to bring weapons and other equipment to Russia: the northern route. Unfortunately, no existing port on the northern shore of Russia remained ice-free during the winter. Such a port simply had to be created, and the place chosen was called "the end of the world" in the language spoken by the local population. Also, a railway to bring the commodities to central Russia was built. Thus equipment could be brought from the industrialized states in the west to the Russian armies, which suffered from shortages of ammunition as well as heavy weapons. Eventually, Murmansk would have a similar role in World War II, but on a greater scale. The main disadvantage with Murmansk was its proximity to German airbases in Norway. Also, the railway running south from the port was exposed to German attacks. But except for the summer and autumn—when Arkhangelsk could be used—no alternatives existed.[81]

Against this background, the Admiralty sent Rear Admirals Philip Vian and Geoffrey Miles to the main base of the Soviet northern fleet at Polyarnoje to investigate the possibility of sending convoys to the

Soviet Union. Many circumstances had to be considered. The port had to have sufficient capacity to unload the ships and at least temporarily store the goods before they were sent south on the railway. The merchant ships, as well as their escorting warships, had to be provided with fuel oil and provisions before returning to Britain. Defense against German air attacks was vital, and the British officers saw plenty of evidence of German air raids, which had inflicted substantial damage.[82]

After forming an impression of Murmansk, Miles continued south to Moscow, while Vian returned to London where he presented his views. He painted a gloomy picture: the largest crane in Murmansk was unable to handle tanks, the air defense was weak, and port facilities were sparse. Furthermore, Murmansk is situated at the end of a long inlet, forcing the merchant ships to anchor in poorly protected positions, with little or no room for maneuver before berthing the quay and discharging their cargo.[83]

At the same time, Harry Hopkins, envoy of President Roosevelt, visited London and Winston Churchill to discuss the war. Although the United States was not yet a belligerent, President Roosevelt was firmly committed to supporting the nations at war with the Axis powers. Thus American weapons and other equipment, as Hopkins told Churchill, might well be sent to the Soviet Union shortly. Despite Admiral Vian's concerns, substantial efforts would soon be made to establish continuous convoy traffic to Murmansk.[84]

At the end of September 1941, a number of ships assembled at Hvalfjord, a large bay just north of Reykjavik on Iceland. Eleven merchant ships massed together with their escorting warships, the latter including the cruiser *Suffolk*. The cargo included 20 tanks and 193 fighter aircraft intended for the Soviet armed forces. The convoy was destined for Murmansk and weighed anchor on 28 September. Sailing under the designation PQ1, it passed through the Denmark Strait and reached the Soviet port unscathed. Simultaneously, a convoy called QP1 sailed from Murmansk in the opposite direction. Obviously, ships had to sail in both directions, or else they would amass in the Soviet ports. Usually the ships returned without cargo, but in this case they did bring something unusual. During the German attack on Poland in 1939, some of the Polish soldiers had escaped east, only to fall into Soviet captivity when the Red Army invaded Poland on 17 September 1939. Many would die in Soviet captivity, but at this stage of the war Stalin allowed some of the prisoners to be sent to Britain, where Polish units would be formed.[85]

Thus the first Arctic convoy met with success. However, the cargo brought on the 11 ships was miniscule compared to the vast needs of the Eastern Front. The 20 tanks delivered can be compared to the fact that the average Soviet monthly output would soon amount to 2,000 tanks. The 193 fighters constituted only a slightly more substantial contribution, but even this quantity only equalled a few percent of the Soviets' monthly production.[86]

However, at this time, British and German decision makers had scant knowledge of the magnitude of Soviet war production. Experts in both countries seriously underestimated the output of Soviet factories, as well as the Soviets' ability to reconstitute facilities that had been hastily transferred east. Consequently, the importance of the convoys appeared greater, and PQ1 was to be followed by many more. Furthermore, the size of the convoys and the quantities shipped would increase substantially.

Initially, the Germans paid little attention to the incipient convoy traffic in the Arctic. Admiral Raeder was far more concerned with the American attitude, which appeared increasingly menacing to him. So far, experience suggested that the German raiders were less vulnerable if they operated far from the British Isles. The western Atlantic was regarded as a safer area. Nonetheless, if America entered the war, it would be much more difficult for the Germans to conduct operations on the Atlantic. For the time being, though, such concerns were secondary, as no heavy German warships would be ready for action until early 1942.[87]

Nevertheless, Raeder had not shelved his plans for resuming cruiser warfare on the Atlantic; at least this seems to have been his position in September 1941. Hitler, on the other hand, had begun to consider transferring the heavy German warships to Norway. Perhaps Hitler's thoughts should not be regarded as too foresighted, as there were many possible reasons that might lead to the idea of transferring the ships to Norway. In particular, the British air attacks on Brest were clearly a major problem for the German naval units there. The short distance to British air bases limited the time available for the German fighters to intercept the bombers attacking the *Scharnhorst*, *Gneisenau*, and *Prinz*

Eugen. Hitler had hoped to obtain permission from Franco to use the Spanish port at el Ferrol. It was located a comfortable distance from British air bases and allowed even better access to British convoy routes on the Atlantic. Franco did not, however, accede to Hitler's proposals.

Bases in Germany also had serious shortcomings. Although the harbors on the North Sea coast were farther away from British airfields than Brest, they were still well within reach of British bombers. In the Baltic, Germany possessed ports that were not particularly exposed, but when leaving the German ships would have to pass narrow straits. Sailing through these narrow waters meant that the warships might be observed. In contrast, bases in Norway had few of these disadvantages. Quite possibly, such considerations may have been the background that spurred Hitler to transfer the warships to Norway. Bases in Norway offered several options, and one of them was to initiate operations on the Atlantic, especially during the ensuing period of long, dark nights. Since the British had reinforced their patrolling of the waters around Iceland, such visibility conditions were of particular importance.

It was evident that developments had rendered German cruiser warfare on the Atlantic more difficult, but Raeder still clung to his notions. However, in the autumn something happened that could not be disregarded: the stocks of fuel oil dwindled. Sufficient quantities were an indispensable prerequisite to his plans. In November 1941, he intended to send the *Tirpitz* to Norway with the intention to initiate operations on the Atlantic as soon as she was fully operational, but the shortage of fuel forced him to shelve these plans.[88]

The lack of fuel also constrained the use of other warships. At a conference with Hitler at his field headquarters, the Wolf's Lair, on 13 November, Raeder described his intentions for the *Scharnhorst* and *Gneisenau*. He estimated that they would be fully ready for operations in February 1942, and he considered short-term operations on the Atlantic difficult but feasible. He preferred not to keep the ships in Brest, and hinted at a possible shifting of the German naval forces to Norway. Still, the final decision was not made until January 1942, as the strategic situation changed continuously. In particular, if the Germans achieved further success in Russia, Raeder and Hitler still hoped for a more cooperative Spanish attitude. Also, a Japanese entry into the war was expected, which would force Britain to send forces to the Far East.[89]

Raeder and Hitler were correctly assuming that the war would take new turns. However, the ensuing developments were not, as seen from their position, favorable. First of all, the German offensive toward Moscow finally came to a halt early in December. On 5 December the Red Army initiated a counteroffensive that finally showed that the German attempt to swiftly defeat the Soviet Union had failed. Thus, German hopes that success in the east would render Franco more cooperative were frustrated.

This was just the beginning of a series of reverses for Hitler and his officers. It came as no surprise when Japan entered the war, but her attack on Pearl Harbor was unexpected. Though the British war effort would be further stretched, now America had joined, and its president had the conviction of "Germany first" if his public's initial outrage against Japan would allow it. Hitler vacillated a few days and then declared war on the United States, a decision that has been a riddle to posterity. Obviously, these events profoundly impinged on German naval strategy. The only favorable consequence was the added strain on British military resources, as the Japanese followed up their surprise attack on Pearl Harbor with an offensive directed against British Far East possessions.

The altered situation called for new decisions, and on 29 December Hitler and Raeder again discussed naval strategy. The *Tirpitz* was one of the items on the agenda. It was intended to transfer her to Norway in two weeks, and there were many motives for the decision—one being that Hitler wanted to strengthen the defenses there. Also, the mere presence of the battleship would tie up considerable British naval forces which might otherwise be used in the Mediterranean, Indian Ocean, or the Pacific. Furthermore, the *Tirpitz* could attack the convoys to Murmansk, which the Germans by now were well aware of.[90]

It was still not decided to transfer the *Scharnhorst* and *Gneisenau* to Norway. Both ships, as well as the heavy cruiser *Prinz Eugen*, would technically be ready for action, but the proficiency of the crews had deteriorated, as the long period in Brest had not permitted much training. Thus, at best, they would not be fit for operations on the Atlantic until March 1942. As the nights would soon be shorter, it was not advisable to launch an operation at such a late date. If the ships in Brest were committed on the Atlantic, the main target would be British convoys on the route between Africa and the British Isles.[91]

Hitler had become more and more convinced that Norway was seriously threatened by an imminent British attack, and preferred to send most of the German Navy to protect it. Exercises conducted in Brest and its vicinity would merely arouse British suspicions. A daring dash through the English Channel was, according to Hitler, the only possible alternative. If it could not be accomplished, he preferred to disarm the heavy ships and use their artillery and crews to reinforce the defenses of Norway.[92]

Obviously, this latter intention of Hitler's was particularly indigestible to Raeder and the other high-ranking naval officers. They claimed that the mere existence of the squadron in Brest forced the British to commit substantial resources, despite the fact that the German ships were still being repaired. Furthermore, it was argued that Germany's most important Allies—Japan and Italy—would be upset if Germany disarmed her heavy warships. Hitler emphasized his resolve to strengthen the defenses in Norway, but no decision was made.[93]

Soon Hitler's will prevailed over Raeder's misgivings. On 12 January the commander of the German Navy presented a plan for the *Scharnhorst, Gneisenau,* and *Prinz Eugen* to sail through the English Channel. Hitler's intention to assemble the heavy German warships in Norway appeared soon to be realized. His conviction that Norway was seriously threatened had by now become firmly rooted. On 22 January, he claimed that British and American forces would attack northern Norway somewhere between Trondheim and Kirkenes. He was convinced that the Allies would be supported by Sweden, which would receive Narvik and ore deposits near Petsamo as reward for its assistance. Finland would have her independence guaranteed within her old borders. Hitler claimed that he had proof of Sweden's willingness to cooperate with the Allies.[94]

Such a course of events would ultimately be very disadvantageous to Germany, and Hitler claimed that he would reveal the alleged British and American scheme—as well as Sweden's attitude—to the world press. Also, he intended to appoint Field Marshal Kesselring as commander of the armed forces in Norway. It all came to nothing. Quite possibly, Kesselring might have accomplished a coordinated inter-service defense of Norway, but he never received the mission. Rather, he was tasked to attain similar results in the Mediterranean.[95]

The British also pondered the enemy's intentions. Admittedly, the

Royal Navy possessed far more warships than the German Navy, but it also had to make its presence felt in many other parts of the world. Thus, it was necessary to muster in advance the resources needed to counter the German plans. Early in 1942, it was clear that the *Tirpitz* would be fully operational at any moment. Also, the heavy cruisers *Admiral Scheer* and *Admiral Hipper*, which had been refitting, would soon be ready for action. Furthermore, the squadron in Brest could be sent into action almost at any moment, prompting intensified air attacks on them. The efforts of the British Royal Air Force, however, were futile, and considerable thought was devoted to the alternatives open to the German warships in Brest.[96]

While the two combatants considered the same situation, there were also some important differences in how they perceived it. First of all, Hitler's grave concern over Norway did not correspond to British intentions. Second, the dire German fuel oil situation could not be capitalized upon by the British. Although the top-secret codebreaking coup the British had achieved, Ultra, may have provided information on the German shortages, it would be rash to discount the possibility of a German incursion into the Atlantic. On the other hand, the British Admiralty's deep concern for the convoys to Murmansk made Norway an important area to them, but for other reasons than Hitler believed.

Several circumstances conspired to attract attention to Norway and the Arctic Ocean at the beginning of 1942. When the Admiralty received information on 17 January that the *Tirpitz* had put to sea, tension rose. Tovey acted cautiously. PQ9, which was just about to sail, received orders to remain in port. Surveillance of the waters around Iceland and Norway was intensified, and he positioned forces closer to Iceland. Nevertheless, all these efforts were in vain, as the German battleship was not at sea when Tovey received the information. In fact, the *Tirpitz* had left Wilhelmshaven at 02.00 on 15 January and sailed straight to Trondheim, where she berthed on 16 January, one day before Tovey received the information. The British remained uninformed of the whereabouts of the German battleship for a week. Not until 23 January did they learn that the *Tirpitz* was moored at the Trondheimsfjord.[97]

A few days later Churchill wrote in a letter to General Ismay, Chief of the Imperial General Staff, stating, "The destruction or even crippling of this ship is the greatest event at sea at the present time. No other target is comparable to it." He continued to claim that "the whole strategy of the war turns at this period on this ship."[98]

Undoubtedly Churchill exaggerated, but the British ambition to cripple or destroy the German battleship was firm. Several air attacks were made in the ensuing weeks. We will come back to them in the following chapter, but can already mention that they met with no success. The German battleship remained undamaged.[99]

Soon thereafter, at dusk on 11 February, the *Scharnhorst, Gneisenau,* and *Prinz Eugen* weighed anchor in Brest and sailed through much of the western part of the English Channel before British countermeasures were initiated. All British attacks on the German squadron were repelled, but the *Scharnhorst* was damaged by two mines and did not reach Wilhelmshaven until 13 February. The *Gneisenau* also hit a mine, although she reached port before the *Scharnhorst*. Hitler's plans to transfer the battleships to Norway would thus have to be shelved for the time being.

Two weeks later, the *Gneisenau's* bow was seriously damaged during a British air attack on Kiel. The Germans decided to decommission the *Gneisenau* and move her to Gdynia for reconstruction. The *Scharnhorst* would also be delayed, and as the *Prinz Eugen* had received a torpedo hit outside Trondheim, all three German heavy ships stationed at Brest had been damaged before reaching Norway. Hitler's hopes were dashed.[100]

As Hitler's plans for these ships resulted in nothing, the convoys to Murmansk were not as subjected to as grave a danger as the British had feared. After postponing PQ9, the convoy traffic was again resumed with PQ10, which was soon followed by PQ11 in mid-February. Neither of these were sighted by the Germans. However the following convoy, PQ12, was found by the Germans as we have already seen.[101]

Despite the meager results of Operation Nordmeer—one merchant ship sunk—it prompted several decisions. The Germans had initially emphasized the importance of carriers, yet on 29 April 1940, according to a proposition by Raeder, they decided to discontinue all work on the carrier *Graf Zeppelin*, as well as some other warships. It seemed to be the most sensible thing to do at the time, as it was believed that the war would be over before she could be completed. In March 1942, after Operation Nordmeer, the German decision makers were no longer convinced of the wisdom of this choice. The previous decision was rescinded and work on the carrier resumed.[102]

However, much work remained before the carrier could be regarded as completed. At least a year would be required before the Navy could accept her, and in the meantime other measures had to be taken to improve air defenses for the German warships in Norway. Raeder demanded better cooperation between the Navy and the Luftwaffe, and also wished strong air units to be based in Norway. Hitler concurred and wanted to create a strong naval force, consisting of the *Tirpitz*, *Scharnhorst*, *Graf Zeppelin*, two heavy cruisers, and 12 to 14 destroyers.[103]

Such a force would have constituted a serious threat to the British, but much had to happen before Hitler's plans became reality. In particular, the German fuel oil situation had to improve. In the meantime, it was thus more likely that the Germans could attack the Murmansk convoys with air power, submarines, and light surface forces.[104]

As the spring was approaching, conditions for attacking the convoys improved from day to day.

New Weapons, Indirect Strategies

The British commanders also learned from experiences gained during the German Operation Nordmeer. Tovey considered the decision to employ the Home Fleet for convoy protection unwise, as he preferred to concentrate on bringing the main enemy force to battle. Preferring to take the offensive rather than wait for German initiative, he regarded the destruction of the *Tirpitz* much more important than the safety of any single convoy. The threat posed by the *Tirpitz* burdened not only Tovey, but many other British officers as well. Churchill was also disturbed that the mere threat of the German battleship tied up four British and two American battleships, assets that were sorely needed in other theatres. The *Tirpitz* had hardly arrived in the Trondheimsfjord before the British initiated preparations to attack her.[105]

The first attempt began soon after midnight on 30 January when 16 bombers—seven Stirlings and nine Halifaxes—took off for the Fættenfjord. Due to poor weather and visibility the attack hardly had any chance of success, and it proved a futile effort. On board the *Tirpitz*, not a single bomb was observed. After this disappointing attempt, the weather became so poor that no attack could be mounted for several days. Also, British intelligence suggested that German air defenses in Norway had been strengthened.[106]

The British remained determined to attack the *Tirpitz*, however, while it was still in port, not out at sea. An alternative was to use Beaufort aircraft, which could attack at a lower altitude. However, their range was insufficient to fly back to bases in Scotland. If such missions were to be initiated, the crews would have to find some way of

59

surviving, for example by landing in Sweden and being interned. The project resembled suicide missions, but preparations continued until mid-March, when this operation was finally shelved.[107]

Meanwhile other approaches were considered. A major problem was the lack of weapons suitable for attacking the heavily-armored battleship. Torpedoes could not be used where she was berthed, as torpedo nets protected her, and the steeply-sloping mountains surrounding the fjord made it almost impossible to attack at the proper altitude and range. The bombs in use were too light and lacked fuses with sufficient delay. An alternative was to modify sea mines and drop them from bombers. With some luck they might, together with conventional bombs, disable the *Tirpitz*. Planning was initiated and it was decided to attack on 30 March.[108]

While the plans to attack the *Tirpitz* from the air proceeded, a weapon that could attack her from the sea—despite being protected in port—was being developed. Since 1940, work had been conducted on the development of a midget submarine, which could enter narrow fjords and get through submarine nets. The idea of a small craft carrying a powerful explosive device had been conceived many years earlier. In 1909, Commander Godfrey Herbert demonstrated blueprints on a "manned torpedo" to the Admiralty. Submerged, it could carry two divers with a considerable explosive charge to an enemy ship in port. He called the weapon "Devastator."

Herbert tried for several years to sell his project to the Royal Navy, but they showed no interest—even after World War I had broken out. Interestingly, Winston Churchill, who was First Sea Lord at the time, regarded Herbert's proposal worth considering. The objections mainly concerned the risks imposed on the crews, and also the feeling that the entire concept appeared to be "a weaker nation's weapon," and thus unworthy of the world's leading sea power.[109]

In 1915, Herbert presented another project, a midget submarine with a crew of three. It had a "Wet-and-Dry chamber" (hereafter referred to as Wet-and-Dry) which allowed the divers a way in and out of the vessel while submerged. The Wet-and-Dry was a pressure chamber, which could be closed and flooded. When the proper pressure had been achieved a hatch could be opened, allowing a man with a breathing apparatus to enter or exit. The latter was patented by Robert Davis of Sebe Gorman & Co, and would henceforth be known as the

"Davis Submarine Escape Compartment." The Admiralty was still not interested, and the First World War ended before any further progress was made. Six years later, one of the foremost British submarine commanders, Max Horton, submitted a number of proposals on midget submarines. One of them, a craft called "C," was almost accepted, as it allowed the crew to return to the submarine after accomplishing the mission. Previous designs had not provided that capability. The dangers to the crew still remained unacceptably grave, plus the craft had to be transported close to its target by some other vessel.[110]

When World War II broke out, matters took a new turn. Retired Commander Cromwell Varley presented a new design. It was 16 meters long, had a crew of three, and also included Herbert's Wet-and-Dry chamber. Varley had been removed from the Royal Navy lists after World War I, and he offered his experience in engineering and construction to civilian companies. As the British position deteriorated gravely in 1940, "a weaker nation's weapon" didn't seem so repugnant an alternative after all. Varley's proposal was accepted by the Admiralty, in no small degree due to Varley's friendship with Max Horton, who at the time was chief of the British submarines.[111]

The midget submarine was far from operational in the spring of 1942. The first prototype, X-3, had just been completed. Not until mid-1943 would the weapon be ready for operational employment. But the British were also considering other methods of attacking the *Tirpitz* below the surface of the sea. The manned torpedo, called "Chariot" by the British, had reached relatively far in its development.[112]

In December 1941, six Italian divers had sneaked through the defenses of the port of Alexandria and seriously damaged the British battleships *Valiant* and *Queen Elizabeth*. They had transported the explosive charges by small crafts that resembled torpedoes. The divers had been sitting on the crafts, almost as if riding a tandem bicycle. When they had reached the warships, the divers dragged the charges beneath the battleships. Little remained of the crafts after the explosions, but the British had captured two of them in conjunction with a failed Italian attack on Malta. Agitated by the attack on Alexandria, Churchill asked the Chief of Staff Committee why the British weren't capable of doing the same thing as just demonstrated by the Italians. In fact, he thought the Royal Navy should be in the lead.

As the midget submarine project would require time, it was decided that a manned torpedo, akin to the type used by the Italians, would be developed and a training program for frogmen initiated.[113]

The British did not, however, only contemplate attacking the *Tirpitz* directly. A battleship requires a significant infrastructure to conduct operations. Without wharves, harbors, and repair facilities, a warship like *Tirpitz* would soon be rendered useless. Battle damage as well as defects of other kinds would have to be repaired, or else the ship would be unfit for operations. For example, very few dry docks on the Continent were large enough to accommodate a ship as large as the *Tirpitz*. Outside Germany, only one port could be used if the *Tirpitz* had to be repaired after sustaining damage on the Atlantic. If such capabilities were denied the enemy, her freedom of action would be seriously curtailed.

It was impossible to prevent the *Tirpitz* from sallying forth to the North Sea or the Arctic Ocean from Trondheim. However, it was not impossible to discourage the Germans from sending her out on the Atlantic, as had they had done with the *Bismarck* in 1941. If no port on the coast of Western Europe could accommodate her for anything more than superficial repairs, the Germans might be reluctant to send the *Tirpitz* to the Atlantic. The only port in the area with a dry dock large enough was St. Nazaire. If this dock was destroyed, the Germans could only direct the *Tirpitz* to Germany for major repairs. Thus, the destruction of the repair facilities in St. Nazaire might well deter the Germans from further forays in the Atlantic.

The dry dock in St. Nazaire was the largest in the world. It had been created to accommodate the passenger liner *Normandie*, which had been launched in 1932 with a displacement of 80,000 tons. She required a dry dock of huge dimensions. The one in St. Nazaire was 350 meters long, 50 meters wide, and no less than 60 meters deep. The locks, one pair at the end of the dock near the Loire River and one pair facing the northern harbor basin, were enormous. The locks could be hoisted into a chamber on the western side of the dock, where the station that pumped water into and out of the dock was located. If they were destroyed, the dock would be rendered useless.

But how could it be accomplished? The target could not be destroyed from the air; at the time, the precision achieved by Bomber Command was insufficient. Nor was massive bombing, with the hope that at least one bomb would find the mark, feasible. Such an attack was bound to result in innumerable civilian victims, and there were strong political arguments against substantial bloodshed among French civilians. The French resistance was deemed incapable of mounting a sabotage operation on the proper scale, and the logistical difficulties involved appeared insurmountable.[114]

Finally, it was decided that the target would be destroyed by an Allied warship ramming the lock of the southern dock. The responsibility for planning the mission was given to Charles Forbes, who had formerly commanded the Home Fleet and now was in command of the Plymouth sector. [115]

The operation was given the name "Chariot."

Operation Chariot

The destruction of the huge caissons, used as locks to regulate the water level in the *Normandie* dock, was not easily accomplished. Undoubtedly they would be seriously damaged if a large ship ran into them, but to move such a ship to St. Nazaire undetected was far more challenging. Also, the damage inflicted must be severe enough to prevent the Germans from quickly repairing the locks. Probably the latter difficulty was among the easiest to overcome. The chosen ship would simply be packed with explosives set to detonate a few hours after the ship had been rammed into the dock. It was also decided to include numerous commandos on the ship. Immediately after contact, they would disembark and blow up the machinery that opened the caissons and controlled the water level. After such extensive damage, much time would be required to make the *Normandie* dock serviceable again.[116]

It was decided to employ an old destroyer, the ex-American *Campbeltown*, for the destruction of the southern caisson. She had been one of the 50 destroyers given to Britain almost two years earlier in return for bases in the western Atlantic and the Caribbean. She would be accompanied by motor launches and torpedo boats carrying further commandos. Also, two other destroyers would provide escort up to the Loire estuary. Commander Stephen Beattie was given command of the operation. The key issue was to approach St. Nazaire without being observed by the Germans, or else they might destroy the British force by air attacks or fire from coastal batteries.

Undoubtedly, the most important prerequisites for success were

64

secrecy and surprise. The first part of the journey was the most straight-forward. The attack force would leave Falmouth at dusk, follow a shallow half-circle at a safe distance from the French coast during the night and the ensuing day, and then assume an east-northeasterly course to approach the Loire estuary at dusk. The attack would be carried out in darkness.

Inevitably, a significant part of the voyage would have to be made in full daylight, with the attendant risk of being observed by German aircraft or E-boats. No option was available however, though a few measures were taken to at least reduce the inherent risks. By removing two funnels from the *Campbeltown*, her appearance would resemble a German *Möwe*-class torpedo boat. Perhaps the Germans might be confused by the ruse. Also, all ships would hoist the German Navy flag until fire was opened. During the crossing, a wide formation would be employed, as if the formation was searching for submarines. If the Germans observed it, it was hoped that they might believe it was an anti-submarine patrol.[117]

After passing the Loire estuary, matters were more complicated. Off St. Nazaire, shoals and mud flats limited the freedom of movement. Large ships were essentially confined to a narrow deep-water channel near the western riverbank where the city and its port were situated. Outside this channel, the water was only about five meters deep.[118]

Aside from the navigational difficulties, the threat from German artillery was considerable. In all, there were 28 guns with calibers ranging from 7.5cm to 24cm, such as the railway guns at La Baule. Also, there were 43 anti-aircraft guns, which might also be used against naval targets. The German garrison at St. Nazaire included a number of guard companies that were lightly armed, but included machine guns. The Germans probably regarded the submarine installations the most likely target if the area were to come under a British attack. In the southern harbor basin, there already was a concrete complex designed to protect submarines. Altogether, there were approximately 5,000 men in the area.[119]

It was unthinkable to conduct complicated navigation in the narrow channel below the German guns. Hence, the attack had to be made over the shallow water. This posed no problem to the smaller ships, especially if the attack was made at high tide, but the *Campbeltown* had to be stripped of all her armament, except one gun

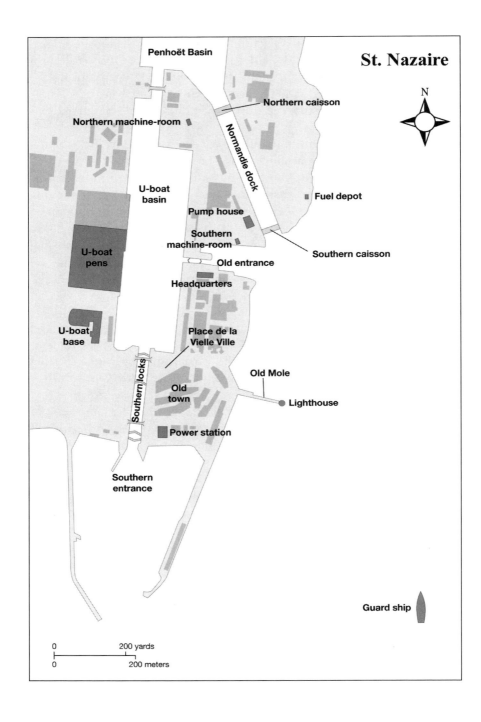

Penhoët Basin

Northern caisson

Northern machine-room

Normandie dock

U-boat
basin

Fuel depot

Pump house

Southern
machine-room

Southern caisson

Old entrance

U-boat
pens

Headquarters

U-boat
base

Place de la
Vielle Ville

Southern locks

Old Mole

Old
town

Lighthouse

Power station

St. Nazaire

N

Southern
entrance

Guard ship

0   200 yards

0   200 meters

and eight small Oerlikons. Also, much of her equipment was removed, which was superfluous in what was presumed to be her last mission. These measures reduced her draft sufficiently.

Thus, a satisfactory solution had been found to the navigation problems, but the German coastal defenses remained. It was decided to pretend that the attack force was actually a German naval unit by utilizing their signals, as it might fool the enemy for awhile. Also, a mock attack was to be made by Bomber Command to attract German attention to the skies rather than the sea just before the naval force approached. First, bombs would be dropped on the harbor, but as the raiding force closed in, the bombers would shift to targets in or around the city. Hopefully, any noise from fighting between the raiding force and German defenders would be either drowned out, or misinterpreted by the explosions caused by the bombing and German anti-aircraft fire. Furthermore, four of the motor launches were fitted with torpedoes to attack German warships that might be present in the harbor. The motor launches would also fire on ground targets to prevent the Germans from concentrating their fire on the *Campbeltown*. A fifth motor launch would also closely monitor the destroyer to see if it rammed the southern caisson properly. If not, it would fire torpedoes to cause at least some damage to it.[120]

During the attack the MGB-314, a gunboat of the Fairmile C-class, would be in the lead. The commander of the naval force, Commander Robert Ryder, as well as the leader of the commando force, Lieutenant Colonel Charles Newman, were both present on board the MGB-314. The gunboat had been fitted with a sonic depth finder to locate any rocks or reefs that might endanger the *Campbeltown*.

MGB-314 would be followed by two launches designated to support the attack by firing upon German gun emplacements and anti-aircraft gun positions. They were to be followed by the *Campbeltown*, which in addition to her load of explosives carried 67 commandos. These elite troops, consisting partly of demolition parties and partly of support and assault groups, would disembark and attack the underground fuel store east of the dock, destroying the pumps which regulated the water level and the machines that opened and closed the caissons. They were also supposed to destroy the northern dock caisson, and be prepared to blow up the southern cassion if the *Campbeltown's* ramming attempt failed.[121]

Behind the *Campbeltown*, 12 launches in two columns would send their commandos—164 men in all—ashore, both at the old entrance near the St. Nazaire basin and at the old mole. Like the commandos on board the *Campbeltown*, they were divided into demolition, support, and assault groups. The left column, known as Group 1, was allotted the task to destroy defense and anti-aircraft positions around the quays, the power station south of the old town, the movable bridges, and the locks at the southern entrance to the submarine basin. They would also secure the old mole. Group 2 would eliminate a number of defense positions and anti-aircraft towers, repel counterattacks from the area around the submarine bunkers, prepare the locks and bridge at the old entrance to the submarine basin for demolition, and establish head-quarters south of the latter. Two motor torpedo boats made up the rearguard. When the mission was accomplished, the commandos would assemble at the old mole to be taken aboard the launches.[122]

Late in the afternoon on 26 March 1942, the British force left Falmouth. The evening and night went by without any notable event occurring. On the morning of 27 March, it had reached a point southwest of Bretagne and the German Navy flag was hoisted. Apart from a few scattered clouds, the sky was clear, a circumstance Commander Ryder found discomforting. The force reduced speed and altered to a southeasterly course. Ryder's main worry, that German air reconnaissance would find his ships, did not materialize. Soon after the course was altered, the lookouts on the destroyer *Tynedale* saw an object on the surface of the ocean at a distance of about ten kilometers. It was soon identified as a stationary submarine. It was the U-593, commanded by Lieutenant Gerd Kelbling.

As the *Tynedale* closed the range, Kelbling started his diesel engines and turned away from the destroyer. He could observe the German naval flag, but there was something ominous about the ship.

When eight kilometers separated the two warships, Kelbling fired five silverwhite flares as identification. The destroyer did not reply, but steadily closed the range to the submarine. Kelbling repeated his iden-tification, and this time he received a reply from the destroyer's signal lamp. By a stroke of good luck, Commander Tweedie, who was on board the *Tynedale*, had sent the correct German signal that he was unable to reply with flares. Thus the destroyer gained the time needed to get within firing range. When she had reached close enough, the

Tynedale opened fire. The U-593 immediately submerged. Again the *Tynedale* fired, but no hit was scored. The destroyer swept the area and rolled depth charges.[123]

Ryder was deeply concerned that the submarine had made a report before submerging, but he found it unlikely. In any case, the submarine commander could hardly have observed his smaller vessels. A glance at the sky revealed that the clouds were gathering, and he decided to proceed with the operation.

As the two destroyers temporarily departed from the main force and set a different course in case the German submarine commander followed them in his periscope, the Chariot force approached St. Nazaire. The lookouts watched for German aircraft in a sky that was increasingly concealed by clouds. The British had been lucky. Not only did the weather change favorably, Kelbling's report did not cause the Germans to take proper countermeasures. When he again resurfaced, about half past two, he reported the sighting of three destroyers and ten torpedo boats heading west. The Germans concluded—mainly because of the erroneous course reported by Kelbling—that the observed ships were on a mine-laying mission.[124]

Later, Ryder received a message from Plymouth telling him that air reconnaissance had found five German destroyers in St. Nazaire that had not been previously observed. They had probably entered the port to bunker fuel oil. Thus, the Chariot force might encounter them as it approached the target. However, again luck helped the British. Kelbling's report led the Germans to send the five destroyers out to search for the force he had reported on a westerly course. Consequently, the German destroyers searched the wrong area. Ironically, had not Kelbling encountered Ryder's ships, the German destroyers would probably have been in St. Nazaire and opposed the attack.[125]

The Chariot force suffered another mishap before reaching St. Nazaire. One of the two engines in one of the launches suffered a breakdown. The launch could not continue, but one other had been designated as a backup if a problem of this kind developed. The 12 commandos were transferred from the stricken launch to the properly functioning one.[126]

When the darkness of night fell over the sea off St. Nazaire, and thick clouds covered the area, the raiding force approached the French coast with the escorting destroyers covering both sides of the formation. The motor launches and other ships formed into two columns to be employed during the attack. Two hours later, Ryder's force reached the Loire estuary, where the submarine *Sturgeon* waited. She directed the attack force with light signals at a stage when the operation could be easily upset. Fog had formed and visibility did not exceed three kilometers. Had the submarine made a navigation error, the entire operation might be jeopardized. However, Ryder's navigation officer, Lieutenant A. Green, was not unduly worried. He was convinced that the formation was sailing on the proper course. He was correct. Suddenly a signal light gleamed in the night, exactly where Green had expected it.[127]

The gauntlet could begin!

At midnight, the crews and commandos of the raiding force could hear the bombers approaching St. Nazaire. German anti-aircraft batteries opened fire and the flashes could be seen far away on the horizon. Two hours earlier, after passing the *Sturgeon*, the escorting destroyers had reduced speed while the raiding force continued. The destroyers would not participate in the actual attack; rather, they waited for the other ships to return and were then supposed to cover the withdrawal to Britain.[128]

Thus far the operation had proceeded according to plan, but now the first serious misfortune occurred. The cloud cover that had protected the naval force also concealed the city and the harbor from the air. As the Allies were reluctant to put French lives at undue risk, the bombers did not drop their lethal load. Rather, they circled above the city and dropped a few flares while waiting for the clouds to clear. Soon, unwanted consequences would follow.[129]

While the men on board the *Campbeltown* and the smaller vessels could hear the distant noise from the German Flak fire and saw the searchlights lighting up the clouds, they proceeded through the estuary. The soldiers almost whispered, which was quite unnecessary given the engine noise of the ships. It was still pitch dark, but it was nevertheless possible to discern the ghost-like wreck of the British liner *Lancastria*. She had been sunk almost two years earlier when British forces were evacuated from France in June 1940. The loss of the liner, her crew, and all the British soldiers on board was, in human cost, the worst naval catastrophe in British history. Now, the faint shadow of the wreck reminded the men on the ships about the misfortunes suffered by

Britain. Would the Germans repeat their success, this time against the *Campbeltown*?

The raiding force passed a known radar station and several heavy batteries without anything happening. The commandos were sitting or lying on the decks with arms and explosive charges nearby, ready to storm ashore at the proper moment. Sub-Lieutenant Nigel Tibbits, who was responsible for the massive charge in the bow of the *Campbeltown*, had already primed the detonators. Then the detonators and the explosives were sealed to prevent the Germans from disarming it. Tibbits could not know exactly when it would go off; he only knew that it would explode between 05.00 and 09.00.[130]

An hour after midnight, the Flak fire diminished and then ceased altogether. Soon after, the searchlights were switched off. The humming noise from the British bombers could still be heard, although it was weaker than before. This lead to uneasiness on board the MGB-134 and *Campbeltown*. Why did the German fire cease?

Ashore, the German commanders were puzzled by the strange behaviour of the British aircraft. When no bombs had been dropped, they seemed to return to Britain. Captain Karl-Konrad Mecke realized that the British bombers must be part of a ruse. Mecke commanded the Flak defenses in the area, and he issued a series of orders. To help the enemy locate their target appeared unwise, and he saw to it that the searchlights were switched off and the guns ceased firing. The remarkable action displayed by the Bomber Command made Mecke very suspicious, and he ordered the gun crews to remain at their stations, ready to open fire immediately. He believed a British invasion might be imminent, and that maybe the aircraft had dropped parachutists. He instructed his men not only to investigate if an air landing had been made, but also keep a watchful eye on the sea.[131]

His initiative was soon rewarded. From one of the cliffs at St. Marc, 400 meters south of St. Nazaire, an observant lookout found the British ships in his night binoculars. He reported to the harbor master that 17 ships were approaching. However, his report was initially regarded with scepticism, as a force of that size was not expected. Perhaps it was assumed that some of the destroyers that had been searching for the British anti-submarine patrol had returned.[132]

When Mecke was informed of the sighting, however, he ordered all his units to full alert for fear of an imminent invasion. All guns that could lower their barrels sufficiently to fire on naval targets would prepare to repel a seaborne attack. As a result of Mecke's orders, Ryder's ships were steering into the jaws of a prepared German defense.[133]

By now the time was 01.20, and only a quarter of an hour remained until the *Campbeltown* was to ram the dock, when a lone searchlight was switched on. The light beam swept across the water. It missed the destroyer, but found the launches in the van. Then it suddenly went out. The British held their breath. Had they been discovered?[134]

Two minutes passed while the dark shadows of the harbor grew larger before the approaching British. Suddenly innumerable searchlights were lit and the sea was flushed with light. The beams blinded the British and made it difficult for them to discern the contours of the land.

The Germans had reacted; all that remained for the British was to trick the Germans into not opening fire. On board the MGB-134, Ryder and Leading Signalman Pike prepared to play some tricks. Pike was what the British called a headache rating, a signal man who spoke German and could confuse the enemy by using their codes and signals, as far as the British knew them. Pike began with an unknown call sign, and then continued in plain German: "Proceeding into the harbor according to instructions."

Soon a German request for identification flashed.[135]

"Two damaged ships in company," Pike replied.

Several searchlights were switched off, and another demand for identification followed. At the same time muzzles flashed as a Flak battery opened fire; the cracks appeared abnormally loud. The British held their fire. Instead, Pike sent a brief message to the effect that the batteries were firing on friendly ships.[136]

The guns fell silent, and valuable time was gained. The Germans carefully studied the ships with the German flags, while the British force got closer to the harbor. The seamen squinted their eyes in the bright light, while the commandos remained hidden behind metal shields fitted to the destroyer and motor launches. Ryder's hand clasped the butt of his flare gun, which was loaded with the German reply pyrotechnics for the present three-hour period. Pike remained next to him, prepared to reply to any further calls from the harbor.[137]

The bluff could not work forever. At 01.28, when the bow of the *Campbeltown* was 800 meters from the caisson, muzzle flashes punctured the darkness between the searchlights. The thunder from heavier guns blended with the sharper cracks from the rapid-firing guns. Seemingly slow green and red tracer trajectories came pouring toward the ships in Ryder's force. He raised his signal pistol, but instead of darting toward the sky, the projectile just plopped out from the weapon and disappeared into the river. Unknown to him, the projectile was intended for use from aircraft and thus had no propellant. There was nothing he could do about it.[138]

A few seconds elapsed before the British responded to the intensive fire, since they were still sailing under false flag and could not fire. On board the *Campbeltown*, sailors and commandos could see the German Navy flag lowered and replaced by the White Ensign. A moment later, the destroyer opened fire with her guns. The British mainly targeted the searchlights. Many of them were switched off, making the British gunners believe they had been hit, but it was only a ruse from the Germans. When the lights were out the target disappeared in the night. Soon the searchlight was switched on again, until tracer rounds howled around the British crews. Thus, the searchlights were switched off and on. The frustrating game causing the British to waste energy and ammunition.

At first, the Germans concentrated their fire on the *Campbeltown*, whose size made her stand out among the smaller craft, but after awhile, the German fire was more coordinated and the batteries fired at different targets. Soon some of the motor launches caught fire, or veered off uncontrollably when their steering system had been hit.

On board the *Campbeltown*, Beattie followed on the heels of Ryder's gunboat. The bridge had been abandoned for the better protected wheel house. Twice Beattie felt the keel scraping the sand reefs below, but the destroyer's speed was sufficient to bring her across the obstacles. At 18 knots, she passed the guard ship anchored across the path of the raiding force. A brief salvo was fired from this ship, but then ceased immediately when the British returned fire.[139]

Ryder's forces quickly passed the guard ship, which was fired upon by each motor launch. It banged and rang on board the *Campbeltown* as German projectiles of various calibres hit the metal. Fortunately the already abandoned bridge, as well as the funnels, seemed to receive most of the hits. However some rounds even penetrated into the engine room, where everybody—except key personnel—took cover between turbines and condensers.[140]

On *Campbeltown's* bridge, helmsman Wellsted got hit and fell to the floor, blood rushing out from a gaping wound. The radio officer replaced him, but he was also wounded, though less seriously. He fell on his knees and steered the ship from the floor by using the emergency steering system.[141]

Briefly, Beattie glimpsed the lighthouse at the old pier ahead. He had just given the signal to prepare for ramming, when he saw the lighthouse again and realized it had moved to the right. He understood that the ship had veered off course and ordered the helm to be turned to starboard. The *Campbeltown* turned in time to avoid a menacing breakwater. As the German searchlights blinded them, Beattie and the other men in the wheelhouse lost sight of the lighthouse. All they could see was the wake of the MGB-134. Someone made his voice heard above the noise of battle and informed the crew that Wellsted was dead. Beattie gave orders that someone should take over the helm and that medics should attend the wounded radio officer.[142]

Sub-Lieutenant Tibbits, who no longer had a specific task after priming the detonators, took the helm to allow the wounded to move away. At this moment the beam from one of the German searchlights fell on the lighthouse, which helped Beattie to calculate a new course, allowing the destroyer to head straight toward the dock. He saw the MGB-134 turn to starboard, allowing the *Campbeltown* unobstructed access to the target. The illuminated breakwater—where two bunkers with bursting machine guns were positioned—could clearly be seen as the *Campbeltown* passed it. The caisson appeared in the darkness. Beattie shouted, "Course 350!" to Tibbits.[143]

A German shell hit the bow and tore a large hole in the port side and above deck. However, the *Campbeltown* was so close to the dock that she could no longer be stopped. A shock went through the destroyer as she rammed the torpedo net protecting the caisson. Her speed hardly diminished, and the men at the forward gun had already moved to safety when the *Campbeltown* cleared the final meters to the locks.[144]

Suddenly a loud metallic squeak could be heard above the shooting. The destroyer came to a halt with such force that men were thrown to the deck and parts from the superstructure fell down on the foreship. From their position on the MGB-134, Ryder and Newman could see how the destroyer rose above the dock gate and partially cut through it, coming to rest with its bow above the dock. A thick white cloud belched out from the point of collision.[145]

In the wheelhouse, Beattie, Tibbits, and the other men regained their composure after the ramming. Momentarily it appeared that the German fire was directed against other targets, as the *Campbeltown* was no longer a threat. Rather, the Germans seemed to apprehend the situation that was unfolding elsewhere. Ardent yells could be heard from the commandos outside the wheelhouse as the officers urged their men forward. Beattie glanced at the crumpled-up bow and the upper part of the caisson, where the metal fence had been pushed down and the timber on the walking path had been splintered.

"OK, we seem to be there," he said, without revealing any particular emotion. He briefly looked at his watch. "Four minutes late, I believe."

The *Campbeltown* had completed her task. Now it was up to the commandos.

Until the *Campbeltown's* bow rammed into the dock the commandos had been passengers, but in a brief second it all changed.

Major Bill Copland—the highest ranking army officer on board the *Campbeltown* and responsible for establishing Newman's headquarters

HMS *Campbeltown* at the St. Nazaire drydock in France shortly before she explodes.

and preparing the evacuation—hastened through the smoke to see how the destroyer had hit the dock. In the beams from the German search-lights, he could, with relief, see that it would be possible to get down on the caisson. Beattie's first lieutenant, Lieutenant Commander Gough, was already there and shouted to his sailors to bring forward the ladders intended for that purpose. Copland took notice of the two tankers inside the dock.[146]

The destroyer's weapons still fired against searchlights and Flak positions, and as German shells tore into the *Campbeltown*, it became evident that the Germans were aware that she had not been neutralised by the collision. On the river behind the destroyer, intense firing raged as the motor launches approached their intended targets at the old entrance and the old mole. In one place, the water was on fire. Painful cries were heard from the men who tried to swim away from the flames. Copland did not have time to pay attention to the screaming men. Rather, he returned aft, where he shouted to his two assault groups to disembark. "Roderick!" he roared. "Roy! Go! Go!"[147]

Many wounded men blocked the narrow doors and gangways, and he curtly pulled them aside to allow the heavily laden demolition groups free passage. "Sorry to hurt you mate, but my men must get through here."

Lieutenant Roderick led his men forward to the ladder lowered beside the hull. According to the plan, he would have 13 men to roll up the German nests on the eastern side of the dock, but enemy fire had already decimated his group.

Private Bill Holland was just about to move to the bow when one of his dying comrades asked not to be left behind. "Don't worry," Holland lied. "They are coming for you." Then he rushed to follow his commander.[148]

When he reached the quay, Roderick and three men dashed toward the nearest Flak position. One of the British soldiers was hit and staggered back to the destroyer, bleeding from his wounds. The remaining three reached the German position. While Roderick and another man fired brief bursts with their submachine guns, private Woodiwiss dashed forward and lobbed a few hand grenades. After they exploded, Woodiwiss threw himself to the opening and completed the deed by killing the survivors with his submachine gun. He attached his explosive charge to the anti-aircraft gun, dashed away, and a few seconds later the explosion shattered the gun.[149]

Roderick's group grew as a few men joined it. They continued to the next position, which was neutralized with hand grenades and fire from submachine guns. When they reached the third Flak gun, they found it had already been destroyed during the fire fight when the ships approached their targets. Roderick, however, was unable to set the underground fuel store ablaze. The British soldiers could not enter it, and therefore tried to ignite the fuel by throwing hand grenades into the ventilation shafts. It was ineffective. Roderick had to contend with silencing the Flak guns east of the *Normandie* dock.[150]

Captain Roy's Scotsmen, the assault group allotted the task of neutralizing the two Flak positions on the roof of the pump house, stormed up the quay west of the dry dock. Unlike the other commandos, Roy's men wore checkered kilts, but this was not the only way the group differed. One of the men carried a strange bamboo ladder, which was to be used to climb up the roof. As they dashed forward they were met by German fire. The men who had disembarked the destroyer remained unscathed, but to their consternation, they soon found that the ladder had been hit and damaged to such an extent that it could not be used.[151]

In an attempt to find another way up to the roof, they snuck around the building. However, the defenders on top of it had seen the commandos. They realized that these men were not survivors of an unhappy collision, but rather some kind of elite soldiers. The Germans abandoned their guns and fled down the stairs on the rear side of the building. Soon some of Roy's Scotsmen had ascended to the roof and blew up the guns. Once there, Sergeant Donald Randall was struck by an eerie thought: the roof was probably one of the safest places in St. Nazaire. He was aloof from the noise and yelling below. Over the river, tracer trajectories darted across the water, and motor launches could occasionally be seen when beams from the searchlights happened to spot them. Randall could see that some of the ships were ablaze, one of them rather close to *Campbeltown's* stern. Fires raged on the water around the destroyer, and terrible screams could be heard from the flames. For a moment, Randall was riveted by the drama, until he realized that the pump house would soon be a very dangerous place. The demolition group tasked to destroy it was probably already finding its way down the cellar. [152]

Five demolition groups had been on board the *Campbeltown*. They were commanded by Lieutenant Chant, who would destroy the pump house; Lieutenant Smalley, who was allotted the task of destroying the machine room operating the southern caisson; Lieutenants Brett and Purdon, who would blow up the northern dock gate and the northern machine room; and finally Lieutenant Burtinshaw, who would blow up the southern gate of the *Normandie* dock if the ramming failed.[153]

Chant's group was the first to leave the *Campbeltown*. He and his four men climbed down the ladder and hastened to the pump house a few minutes after Roy and his Scotsmen. Chant had been wounded in the leg, and with the 30 kilogram charge as a burden, he found that the loss of blood dangerously weakened him. Also, Sergeant Chamberlain had been hit by a shell splinter in his shoulder. He was in such serious condition that he believed himself unable to climb the 16 meters down the stairs to the pump room, which was the same level as the bottom of the dock. He was left at the entrance as a guard.[154]

The lock on the door to the building was blown up. As Chant's stamina dwindled, he and the other men descended the stairs to the large pumps that regulated the water level in the dock. As the huge charge in *Campbeltown's* bow might not detonate, it was vital to destroy the pumps. The British believed it would take at least a year to repair them.[155]

The building was very dark inside, and the men had to feel themselves forward cautiously. However, during their training, Chant's men had practiced the kind of situation in which they now found themselves. Soon they could perform their work almost instinctively. The watertight covers were removed from the charges, which were placed directly on the pumps to maximize the damage. The detonators were connected to set off all the charges simultaneously.[156]

When the work was finished, Chant sent two of his men to help Chamberlain get away from the building before the demolition charges went off. Suddenly, a slight vibration in the floor was felt and a dull rumble told Chant that Smalley's group had blown up the southern machine room, located about 100 meters from the pump house.

Chant could feel how the loss of blood depleted his strength, but he was well aware of his responsibility. When he heard that everything was ready he set the detonators to 90 seconds and, with the help of Sergeant Dockerill, managed to climb upstairs and get out of the building before it was too late. They had barely got out before they heard the deafening noise of the explosion, followed by the crash of part of the building's structure collapsing. Chant and his men returned to inspect the results of their efforts. A brief examination showed that no more charges were needed. The floor, with the electric motors that propelled the pumps, had caved in and two of the motors had fallen down in the pump house. The remaining two had been torn from their mounting brackets and could not be used.[157]

As these actions took place, other groups had attacked the northern end of the dock. While they moved in darkness along the 300-meter-long western quay, the three groups—which had been reinforced by Lieutenant Burtinshaw's men, as they were no longer needed to blow up the southern caisson—came under fire from a German trench. Some of the commandos provided fire support, while others threw hand grenades into the trench and killed the defenders. However, the action attracted fire from other positions, including the two tankers inside the dock. At the northern end of the dock, German resistance stiffened. Fire from concealed machine guns swept the area, which was illuminated by the searchlights. Simultaneously, small groups of German soldiers approached.[158]

The commandos mined the northern machine room, which would be blown up as soon as the northern caisson had been destroyed. However, when the commandos tried to place the charges, major difficulties occurred. It was intended that some of the charges should be placed on the Penhoët basin side of the caisson, while others should be placed inside the hollow walls of the caisson itself. When trying to accomplish the latter, they couldn't open the door leading into the chamber. At the same time, accurate German fire hit the British. Lieutenant Burtinshaw was killed, as were five other men. Many others were wounded. The British had to contend with detonating the charges lowered down in the water next to the caisson. Thus the water level would be raised, and the explosive charge on the *Campbeltown* would be enhanced. Several explosions were followed by cascades of water, and soon it flushed from the Penhoët basin into the dock. The commandos also destroyed the machine room before withdrawing toward the headquarters Copland should have established south of the bridge over the old inlet. [159]

The damage already inflicted on the *Normandie* dock was sufficient to prevent the *Tirpitz* from utilizing it, at least for some time. If the charges on board the *Campbeltown* went off as planned, considerable destruction would be wreaked. So far, Operation Chariot had been a spectacular success.[160]

However, elsewhere the operation's progress was far less encouraging. Let's go back in time, to see what happened to the motor launches and the men on board. When the two columns passed the eastern jetty of the new breakwater, they were subjected to intense fire from Flak guns on the quays, as well as machine gun positions on the old mole. The right column—which carried the commandos of Group 2—was aided by the fact that the German guns concentrated on the left column. Nevertheless, it still suffered terrible casualties. The first launch was damaged so badly that it could no longer be controlled. It hit the quay at the eastern jetty, where it was abandoned. The men had to swim ashore. The second and third launch missed the intended landing point and had to turn around and make a new attempt. The fourth launch caught fire and exploded. The fifth was subjected to such intense fire that its commander decided to break off the attack. Only the sixth reached the quay according to plan. Warrant officer Haines and his assault group disembarked on the southern side of the old entrance.

One of the two launches that had turned around to make another attempt was badly hit, caught fire, and drifted into the central part of the river. However, the other launch did manage to put Lieutenant Woodcock and his demolition team ashore on the northern side of the old entrance. At this moment, shouts were heard and Lieutenant Smalley's team, which had just blown up the southern machine room, asked to come aboard. The launch picked them up and proceeded on the river, only to be found by a German searchlight beam, which was immediately followed by accurate fire. Several on board, including Lieutenant Smalley, were killed. At the same time, the German blocking ship woke up and spewed fire on the launch. Thus the British were caught in a crossfire.[161]

The left column was even less successful. Four of it's vessels were subjected to such violent fire that they had to withdraw after sustaining heavy casualties. A fifth launch reached the old mole, where it would put Captain Birney's assault group on shore. However, due to the German fire it missed the stairs where the soldiers would jump ashore. The commander tried again, but when the boat was hit by a heavy shell it immediately caught fire, and the few survivors tried to save themselves by jumping into the water.[162]

Only one launch from the left column managed to put its commandos ashore before withdrawing. Ironically it was Captain Bill Pritchard—the officer responsible for checking that the demolition task given to Group 2 had been properly carried out—who alone managed to reach any of the targets. He and four men had disembarked, together with Walton's demolition team, to destroy the railway bridge and the inner gate of the southern locks. They had been put ashore at the stairs next to the old mole. The instructions issued to the soldiers of Group 1 emphasized that control over the mole was more important than the destruction of the targets allotted. Hence, every assault or demolition group should ensure that this position was in British hands before proceeding toward the designated targets. The mole was necessary for the evacuation of the commandos. After seeing German soldiers abandon the breakwater with their hands above their heads, Pritchard, like other British officers, got the impression that the breakwater had already been secured. They continued toward their designated targets without ensuring that the breakwater was defended by British troops. Soon the Germans again took up their positions on the mole.[163]

Pritchard's group reached Place de la Vieille-Ville, near the railway bridge, when it was realized that contact with Walton's group was lost. They halted to wait for Walton and his men, but nobody showed up. Pritchard decided to blow up two tugs, anchored next to each other close to the quay. His men went aboard and positioned an explosive charge between the two vessels, to blow a hole in both hulls. Thereafter Pritchard decided that he and Corporal Maclagan would move to the southern lock gate and the power station, to see if any of the other groups had made it there. Meanwhile, the remaining three men would blow up the railway bridge, without waiting for Walton.[164]

While the sound from the exploding charge between the tugs echoed over the submarine basin, Pritchard and Maclagan moved in the darkness, running along the southern locks. When they reached the outer lock gate, they found no British soldiers. They continued to the power station, but again found no British soldiers, nor any German defenders. Pritchard realized that something had gone awry and decided to return to Place de la Vieille-Ville, this time across the narrow streets of the old town. Suddenly, as Pritchard and Maclagan turned a corner, they faced a German soldier, who instinctively thrust his bayonet into Pritchard. In the seconds that followed, the German soldier was thrown to the street and hit by a burst from Maclagans submachine gun. Pritchard was mortally wounded, and urged Maclagan to continue to Place de la Vieille-Ville and leave him behind. When Maclagan finally reached it, he only found the dead body of Lieutenant Walton. He then decided to try to reach the place where Newman's headquarters would be established.[165]

When the *Campbeltown* rammed the gates to the *Normandie* dock, Newman, together with Ryder, was still on board the MGB-134. While the result of the ramming was observed, the small ship made a tack on the river and her weapons fired on German searchlights and Flak positions. When the German guard ship opened fire, an exchange of views took place on board the MGB134, whose radio had malfunctioned. Ryder wanted to move alongside one of the torpedo boats and order it to attack the guard ship. Newman, on the other hand, wanted to establish his headquarters ashore as soon as possible. In the end, the latter's will prevailed and the MGB-134 closed in on the old entrance, where Newman shook hands with Ryder before he and his group jumped ashore.[166]

Newman and his seven men moved along the quay to the large building near the old lock bridge, which had been designated as headquarters. They presumed that it had already been occupied by sergeant Moss and his group, but the latter had been on board one of the launches set ablaze. When Newman's group had almost reached the entrance, they encountered a German soldier who immediately threw down his rifle and eagerly gesticulated that he surrendered. Newman called for Captain Terry, who spoke German.

"Are there more of you inside?" Terry asked, pointing toward the building.

The German soldier nodded. "Yes, yes," he replied anxiously.

"Well, go in there and tell them to come out with their hands high."

The enemy soldier did as he was told, but the British never learned if the Germans were willing to surrender.

Suddenly a small ship, only 70 meters away, opened fire. Almost immediately, anti-aircraft weapons on the submarine bunker roofs joined in. The British hastily withdrew.[167]

Sergeant Moss had been given the task of destroying targets around the submarine basin, but his men never got ashore. Fortunately, Warrant Officer Haines and his men appeared. He had discovered that the targets he was allotted did not exist. Thus, he decided to proceed to Newman's headquarters, and emerged just in time to help Newman respond to the German fire. With his mortar, Haines scored hits on the submarine bunker roofs, which silenced the guns.

The British snuck back to the headquarters and threw hand grenades through the windows. Subsequently, Newman established his command post and waited for the commandos that had been on board the *Campbeltown*. Also, a radio was set up, but it proved as unable to communicate as the one on board MGB-134.[168]

On the Loire, the motor launches were sunk one by one by the murderous German fire. Many of the commanders decided to pull out. Sub-Lieutenant Wynn, on board the MTB-74, who was to fire time-fused torpedoes on the *Normandie* dock caisson in case the Campbeltown did not succeed, saw that this task was unnecessary. He turned his boat toward its secondary target—the gates at the old entrance—and fired the torpedoes. Their time delay was considerable, and they did not detonate until two days later. In the heat of battle, the Germans did not notice what happened and the torpedoes hit the intended target, where they came to rest on the bottom. With his mission fulfilled, Wynn steered toward the Loire estuary. His ship could make 40 knots and he stood a good chance of escaping, but this would not happen. Suddenly, he saw two British on a Carley raft. In stark contrast to standing orders, Wynn halted to pick them up. The Germans saw what happened and released a hail of shells against the MTB-74. Only three men survived, among them Wynn. His gallant deed cost him his boat, his men, and one of his eyes.[169]

On board the *Campbeltown*, Beattie had ensured that the scuttling charges were properly primed, and was preparing to move the wounded from the bow down to the dock caisson, when he realized it would be easier to bring them onto one of the launches directly from the destroyer's stern. Ryder had reached the same conclusion, and maneuvered the MGB-134 next to one of the yet unharmed launches. He ordered the commander to bring his boat next to the *Campbeltown*, and soon many of the wounded had been transferred to the ML-177. With Beattie, Tibbits, Gough, and about 30 men on board, the launch left the destroyer to its fate. The MGB-134 also took a few men from the *Campbeltown* on board.[170]

The ML-177 managed to withdraw from the harbor area, but when she reached the water outside, she ran out of luck. A heavy German shell hit the engine room, causing her to stop. Thus crippled, she was an easy target. Repeatedly hit, she sank quickly. Many of the wounded drowned, while other men died in the cold water. Beattie would survive, but Gough and Tibbits were both hit as German gunfire blasted the area.[171]

On board the MGB-134, Ryder understood that withdrawal was urgent. He could see several launches burning outside the harbor, and fire directed at his own ship intensified. It was also clear that the Germans held the old mole. Another 30 minutes remained until the commandos were to embark from this place—provided they managed to capture it—and Ryder doubted that his ship would survive that long. He employed a smoke-float to cover MGB-134 while he talked briefly with his officers. It was decided to depart with the wounded and those already taken aboard.[172]

Ashore, Newman had converged with Copland at the headquarters, which was again under heavy fire from the German bunkers on the other side of the submarine basin. The initial reports had been very optimistic, but subsequently bad news dominated. It became apparent that most of the launches had been lost on the river, and many commandos had lost their lives. The old mole was in German hands, and an attempt to recapture it had scant chance of success. It was probably pointless to try to assault it. Even if it could be retaken, few or no ships would be able to take the soldiers back on board. Belatedly, Maclagan appeared and reported that no targets south of the old entrance had been destroyed, save for two French tugs.[173]

There were only two alternatives left to Newman: to surrender, or to try to break out into the open country beyond the city, and from there attempt to reach Spain and Gibraltar. "Shall we call it a day?" he asked Copland.

"Certainly not, Sir," Copland replied. "We'll fight our way out."

Leaving dead and wounded behind, Newman and his men tried to break out from St. Nazaire. They stormed the bridge between the old and new town, but got no farther; regular German troops had arrived and sealed off the city. Only five of the men who tried to break out succeeded and eventually managed to reach Gibraltar. At sea, the remaining launch and MGB-134 reached the two rearguard destroyers. They sunk one damaged boat and proceeded to Britain. All other soldiers and seamen still alive went into German captivity. The Germans collected the remnants of the force that had attacked St. Nazaire, while the *Campbeltown* remained silent, her crumpled bow still above the dock gate. The most likely hour for her explosives to go off had passed, and soon the far end of the time interval for the detonation had passed as well. Had the detonators been damaged in the collision after all?

German naval personnel had already made a brief investigation of the *Campbeltown* and concluded that such a ship was not a serious loss to the British Navy. Thus, the ramming of the dock caisson must have been deliberate. Apparently, the Germans did not suspect that the destroyer might be mined, since the naval experts were soon followed by other German officers, including mistresses, as well as representatives of the city and harbor authorities, and French collaborators. An impressive crowd gathered around the *Campbeltown*.[174]

Lieutenant Commander Beattie, together with several other survivors, had been hauled up from the Loire river by a German trawler. At about 11.00 the trawler berthed at the quay, and Beattie was brought to an office in the harbor area where he was interrogated. The German officer conducting the interrogation had hardly finished explaining to Beattie that he found it unbelievable that the Admiralty thought a dock gate of such dimensions could be destroyed by a small ship like a destroyer, when a huge explosion shattered the windows. The *Campbeltown* was torn apart, the dock caisson collapsed, and the inrushing water swept the remains of the destroyer and the gate into the dock. Debris rained down over the surrounding area. Many British soldiers had ceased to hope that Tibbit's charge would go off, but suddenly they felt a bitter satisfaction. At least the terrible casualties had not been in vain.[175]

The Arctic Convoys

Apparently, the British attack on St. Nazaire was a surprise to Hitler, as well as the senior naval commanders. Attacks on the German-occupied Atlantic Coast were expected—and Operation Chariot was not the first example—but there were many possible targets. It was very difficult to predict which one the British would choose.

Could Operation Chariot be regarded as a tactical success? In the sense that the destruction of the *Normandie* dock was accomplished, the answer is yes, although many of the secondary targets were not captured or destroyed. Out of 611 men that participated, no less than 169 were killed, and 215 taken prisoner. Only four of the motor launches returned to Falmouth, but the *Normandie* dock was rendered unusable for a long time, even if the Germans put a major effort into repairing it.

On the other hand, if the operation is viewed from a strategic perspective, it was not a success. The Germans mainly intended to use St. Nazaire as a base for submarines. At the time they had no plans to send the *Tirpitz* into the Atlantic, and in fact they would not repair the dock before the end of the war. In a sense, the British had struck a powerful blow into empty air, but as they did not know the intentions of the Germans, the operation appeared successful. To them it was one part of their effort to neutralize the *Tirpitz,* and the sacrifices justified the results perceived.[176]

Obviously, the destruction of the dock at St. Nazaire imposed no restrictions on the German attacks on the Arctic convoys. Rather, as longer days and better weather would come with the spring, chances of success against the convoys improved. The long winter nights and ferocious weather —with storms, snow, and fog—had made it difficult to find the convoys. Due to these adverse conditions in the north, few German submarines had been positioned there. In November 1941, only two had been detailed to attack the Arctic convoys, and only a modest reinforcement was planned.[177] This would soon change completely.

With spring approaching, the longer days and better weather would facilitate not only submarine operations against the convoys but the further use of air power. Thus, German air units stationed in northern Norway could expect considerable success. However, there were still difficulties associated with air operations. Many of the Luftwaffe units in northern Scandinavia were seriously worn after the winter. Several of them would have to return to Germany for rest and refit. Thus, reinforcements were required merely to keep numbers up. To actually increase the number of aircraft would require considerable reinforcements.[178]

Another problem for the Luftwaffe was a lack of units trained for anti-shipping operations. In the Mediterranean, the Germans had the X Air Corps, which had gained considerable expertise in this field, but the units in northern Scandinavia had mostly been used for supporting the German Army units participating in Operation Barbarossa. Furthermore, much of the success against shipping scored by the Luftwaffe had been achieved by the dive-bomber, the Junkers Ju-87 Stuka, but its range was insufficient to attack the Arctic convoys. As the temperatures rose, the pack ice would retreat north, allowing the convoys to travel farther from the air bases in northern Norway. An alternative was level-bombing, but it was not as accurate as divebombing. Also, torpedoes could be launched from aircraft, but as yet, the Luftwaffe had not spent much effort on creating torpedo units.[179]

Thus far in the war, mainly carrier aircraft had used torpedoes to attack enemy ships, but there existed examples of land-based aircraft able to torpedo ships, one being the Italian Savoia-Marchetti Sm-79. Compared to her brother-in-arms, the Luftwaffe languished behind in this respect. However in 1941, the Germans began to work seriously to create air units capable of attacking ships with torpedoes. One of the first units converted to the torpedo bomber role was I./Kampfgeschwader 26, which arrived in northern Norway during the spring of 1942. Also, Kampfgeschwader 30 was sent to northern Norway. It was a level-bombing unit that had been operating over the Atlantic from bases in France, and thus had gained considerable experience.[180]

Air power was valuable not only for its ability to attack enemy ships. Equally important was the reconnaissance role, which could provide invaluable information to surface ships and submarines. In the dark winter nights, the reconnaissance units were greatly hampered, but in the spring and summer, the convoys would find it hard to escape the prying eyes of Luftwaffe aviators. During the summer the sun would not set below the horizon at all, and with 24 hours of daylight, the Luftwaffe air crews could not be more fortunate.

The Luftwaffe had further alternatives. Aircraft could drop mines, but the vast sea areas would require a prohibitive number of them. However, the Murmansk inlet was a tempting target. It was also easy to find, as it formed a bay perpendicular to the coastline of the Kola Peninsula.[181]

The majority of the German air units in northern Scandinavia were subordinated to Luftflotte 5. The most important air bases were Bardufoss and Banak. Already during the spring it was evident that the Luftwaffe would have to carry a significant burden of the operations against the Murmansk convoys, and not only due to the change of season. A major impediment to the German naval units was the shortage of fuel. On 7 March 1942, Marinegruppe Nord reported that stocks in Norway included 27,372 cubic meters of fuel, of which slightly more than 10,000 cubic meters were located in Trondheim.[182]

The stocks in Norway thus remained low, despite the fact that a few weeks earlier Raeder had claimed that the situation was improving. Considering that the *Tirpitz* could hold about 9,000 cubic meters of oil, it is clear that sustained operations on a significant scale would soon exhaust stocks of fuel. Prospects of an improved oil situation were marginal, as much of the German fuel had actually been delivered by the Soviet Union as part of the Molotov-Ribbentrop agreement in 1939. When Germany attacked the Soviet Union on 22 June 1941, obviously such deliveries came to an end. Simultaneously, the Germans had to provide fuel for the Italian Navy, which lacked resources of its own, for its continuing operations in the Mediterranean. Thus, less oil could be transferred to the Norwegian ports. Strict rationing was enforced and when the ships were moored, they were only allowed to provide heating and electricity from coal-fired generators, either on board or on auxiliary vessels.[183]

The British also had their share of troubles. An air attack on the *Tirpitz* planned for the night of 30–31 March miscarried. During the afternoon of 30 March, a Mosquito plane flew over Trondheim to photograph the *Tirpitz*, but it was observed by the Germans, who scrambled fighters. The Mosquito hurriedly retreated, and although it was not shot down, the British commanders feared that the Germans had been alerted. The implications of the incident were uncertain. The Germans were probably on high alert anyway, and several hours elapsed between the reconnaissance flight and the actual bombing.[184]

Despite everything, the attack was launched in the evening, and at 23.04 the air-raid warning sounded on the *Tirpitz*. The Flak defenses opened fire as the British airmen strived hard to hit the target, but the results were indeed meagre. Only the remains of a flare actually hit the battleship. British losses were far from negligible. Four Halifax bomber planes were shot down by the German Flak, and two more crashed into the sea as they tried to return. It was a disappointment, but the decision makers in London realized that the *Tirpitz* was a difficult target. Their resolve remained strong and further attacks would follow.[185]

While the Chariot drama took place at St. Nazaire, the convoys to Murmansk continued their arduous voyages. On 20 March PQ13, consisting of 21 merchant ships, sailed from Reykjavik. Tovey still wanted to synchronize the convoys, but QP9 was delayed following reports of German submarines off Murmansk. On 21 March the convoy finally departed and the delay probably had little impact. A more serious threat appeared in the shape of the German heavy cruiser, *Admiral Hipper*, which sailed into Trondheim on 21 March. Tovey did not know what plans the Germans had for her.[186]

There were further threats to the convoys, and two days later the rage of nature hit QP9. A violent storm forced the sailors to fight for their very survival. They also struggled to keep the convoy together, as the merchant ships would be much easier prey for submarines and aircraft if they no longer sailed together. The storm raged the entire day before finally abating in the evening 24 March. Thus far, heavy snowfall had concealed the convoy, but as the storm continued west, the snowfall ceased and at this moment, a German submarine was sighted by the crew on board the mine sweeper *Sharpshooter*. The commander, Lieutenant Commander Lampen, immediately gave orders to ram the submarine. By the time the lookouts on the U-655 saw the mine sweeper, it was too late. The *Sharpshooter* rammed the submarine, and Lieutenant Adolf Dumrese and his 44 crew members died in the icy water. The collision also damaged the *Sharpshooter,* and Lampen could no longer lead. He handed over command to Lieutenant Commander Ewing on the destroyer *Offa*.[187]

Initially PQ13, which traveled in the opposite direction, was more fortunate. The easterly wind helped the ships, and a German submarine group could be avoided thanks to Ultra information. The maneuver brought the convoy closer to the German airfield at Bardufoss, but a worse menace was waiting for PQ13. The storm that had tormented QP9 hasted west, and on 25 March it hit the PQ13.[188]

The already heavily-laden ships were washed by huge waves. The water that did not immediately pour off the ships froze on the decks and superstructures. Machines broke down. Cargo fastened to the decks broke loose, and sailors trying to prevent it from falling into the sea were injured or washed overboard. Lookouts, with ice forming in their eyebrows and beards, tried to keep an eye on what was happening around the ships. It was a vital task, given that the ships could not be allowed to sail so close that they might collide, but not be allowed to widen too much either, as the convoy might break up. It was a delicate balance, not made easier by the seasickness felt by many crewmen. An order was issued that the convoy would reassemble south of Bear Island. This meant a considerable risk of encountering drift ice, but on the other hand it was necessary to remain as far as possible from the German airfields, especially after the storm abated.[189]

On 27 March the sea became much calmer, but visibility remained poor. The scattered ships of PQ13 could not expect to find each other by optical means. Radio messages had to be avoided, as the Germans might locate any transmitting ship. However at 12.00, the ether came alive as the whaler *Sumba*, located at a position northeast of Bear Island, reported that she had almost no fuel left. Fear that the Germans might have intercepted the message spread, but the British appear to have been lucky. The German war diaries do not mention anything on the incident. The British could search for the *Sumba* without any

German interference, and at 16.00 they found her. Refueling was hazardous in the difficult weather, but no other option remained. While oil flowed through the hoses, the lookouts searched for German submarines and aircraft. The visibility was still poor—which made their task difficult—but it was comforting to know that the Germans would also find it difficult to see anything.[190]

The ships of both convoys remained undetected by the Germans on 27 March, but on the following day the weather cleared. Predictably, the Germans did find one of the convoys. At 09.37 Lieutenant Heinrich Brodda, commander of the U-209, reported that he had sighted two merchant ships and two escort ships heading east. Correctly, the Germans assumed that they were part of PQ13, and the information was also sent to Luftflotte 5. U-209 followed the ships for a few hours, but then lost contact. However, at that time, reconnaissance aircraft from Luftflotte 5 had already started and found the other ships of the convoy.[191]

The scattered ships of PQ13 now faced the prospect of running a gauntlet. Luftflotte 5 sent bombers to attack the merchant ships, and submarines were directed to the area. Also, the 8th Destroyer flotilla—consisting of the destroyers Z24, Z25, and Z26 stationed at Kirkenes—put to sea to attack the merchant ships. The *Tirpitz* and the other ships in Trondheim were too far from the scene to intervene and so remained at their moorings.[192]

During the afternoon the bombers attacked the ships that had been located. The German airmen claimed to have found at least 12 merchant ships, one cruiser, and an unspecified number of destroyers. The cruiser was unsuccessfully attacked, but before dusk made any further air attacks impossible, the Luftwaffe claimed to have hit four merchant ships and one of the destroyers. Except for one Ju-88 belly-landing, all bombers returned safely. In actuality, two merchant ships had been sunk, but no other ships seem to have sustained any damage.[193]

As the German destroyers had left Kirkenes rather late, they did not find any Allied ships before dusk. Soon after midnight though, they did find the Panama-registered freighter *Bateau*, whose crew was called upon to surrender. The sailors accepted and the Germans took them on board before they sunk the freighter. By interrogating the crew, the Germans obtained information on where they could find the convoy, but no trace of it was seen before dawn.[194]

However at dawn, the Germans did encounter three enemy ships: the cruiser *Trinidad* and two destroyers, which were part of the convoy escort. In the ensuing battle, the Z26 was severely damaged. Also, the *Trinidad* was hit in the stern by a torpedo. The destroyer *Eclipse* received two hits in her stern as well, but neither ship was sunk. Soon the remaining German destroyers were busy rescuing the crew from the sinking Z26, while the British were fully occupied trying to take the crippled *Trinidad* and the damaged *Eclipse* to Murmansk. At last, the British cruiser reached Murmansk, where an inspection of the damage suggested that she had been hit by a British torpedo whose steering gear had probably malfunctioned in the severe cold. The *Eclipse* also made it to Murmansk, despite the attention she received from a German submarine.[195]

While the warships battled and limped back to port, the remaining merchant ships endeavored to reach Murmansk. Most of them made it, but two were sent to the bottom of the ocean by German submarines. Altogether, PQ13 lost five merchant ships, about a quarter of all that had left Reykjavik. It was the worst fate yet suffered by a convoy bound for Murmansk.[196]

Tovey made no illusions about the dangers to the forthcoming Murmansk convoys. Also, available intelligence suggested that the Germans were bringing reinforcements to the northern theatre. He wanted to reduce the number of convoys during the light summer months, but this did not happen. Rather, political and strategic circumstances led the Allies to intensify the convoys. Although the Red Army had pushed the Germans back outside Moscow, their success might well prove temporary.[197]

President Roosevelt was convinced that Germany, not Japan, was the most dangerous enemy. However, so far, few American units had fought against any German forces. Thus, one of the main U.S. contributions was the delivery of weapons and other important goods to the Soviet Union, which bore the brunt of the fighting. Had the U.S. not sent war materials to the Soviet Union, it would have been tantamount to sitting with arms folded and letting the other powers do the fighting. The convoys would continue, and the next—PQ14 with 24 merchant ships—would be larger than any before.[198]

Despite sailing in the spring, PQ14 would experience many dangers imposed by nature. The convoy sailed on 8 April from Reykjavik, but by 11 April it already encountered small drifting icebergs. To make matters worse, visibility fell sharply as fog covered the area. Only eight of the ships continued to Murmansk, while the remaining turned back to Iceland.[199]

During the days that followed, the eight ships proceeded on course. Nothing particular occurred, but the Germans were aware of the convoy and strived to position submarines in its path. The surface ships remained in port, however, due to lack of fuel. The destroyers in northern Norway would not put to sea until the convoy's position had been established with sufficient certainty, and if the circumstances were deemed favorable enough. During the first few days, air reconnaissance was fruitless, but on 11 April the Germans found an explanation. Their radio intercepting service noted that PQ14 had only passed the northern tip of Iceland on 9 April. Thus, it was still farther west than had previously been assumed.[200]

The new information made it clear that the German dispositions had to be altered, and more was to follow. Before 12.00, German air reconnaissance found QP10 still fairly close to Murmansk. Luftflotte 5 dispatched 32 Ju-88 bombers to attack it, but 14 of them never found the target, as the visibility was poor. The remaining aircraft, however, did press the attack home and claimed to have sunk one ship and damaged another so badly that it would sink. One Ju-88 never returned, and another belly-landed at Vadsø. The commander of the formation was injured in the latter incident. British records show that the freighter *Empire Cowper* was sunk in the German air attack.[201]

The following day QP10 was almost spared further German air attacks, but at 21.35, the Luftwaffe again found the convoy. As the hour was late only a half-hearted attack was made, which proved inconsequential. The German submarines posed a greater menace during the day. Despite strenuous efforts by the escort to fend him off, Lieutenant Siegfried Strelow maneuvered the U-435 into a position from which he hit and sunk two merchant ships.[202]

The QP10 continued its gauntlet the following day, when Luftflotte 5 sent out 41 bombers. The German aviators claimed to have sunk one ship and seriously damaged two more. Actually, only one ship had been damaged—the *Harpalion*, whose rudder was blown off. The escort deemed her damaged beyond salvation and sunk her after taking the crew on board. No other ships were lost, as fog put a blanket over the QP10 and the wind increased to a gale. The bad weather not only protected the convoy, it was also a serious danger to the German aircraft as they returned to their bases. They had been flying as far as their range allowed, and with the strong headwind, fuel consumption rose. In two of the bombers, the crew saw the fuel gauges indicate that the tanks were empty before any land could be seen. Also, one plane had been shot down by the convoy escort, while two developed engine troubles that prevented them from reaching the airfields. Thus five aircraft were lost to Luftflotte 5.[203]

As the weather protected QP10, it could continue without suffering any further losses. As we have seen, PQ14 had been shattered, and the ships that proceeded east soon encountered QP10. That meant that the Germans would shift their attention to the eastbound convoy. The weather remained favorable to the convoys and only one ship was sunk from the PQ14. The *Empire Howard*, carrying a cargo of ammunition, was hit by two torpedoes from U-403, commanded by Lieutenant Heinz-Ehlert Clausen. When the ammunition it carried on board exploded, the freighter was cut in half. Out of her crew of 55, about 40 men jumped into the water, where they hoped to be saved. Unfortunately, one of the escort ships rolled depth charges at the same moment, and when the shock wave from the detonations reached the men floating in their life vests their bones were broken and inner organs crushed. Some men were lucky enough to only suffer unconsciousness, while others were killed instantly. Nine of the 18 bodies rescued were already dead when they were hauled on board.[204]

The fickle weather saved PQ14 from further losses. Over the ocean and German air bases thick clouds created a lid that prevented air operations, except for sporadic efforts. As it was very difficult to locate the convoy, the German surface forces had little information to base decisions on. Nevertheless, the destroyers at Kirkenes made an attempt, but it only resulted in the consumption of precious fuel.[205]

To both the British and Germans, the results from the actions associated with convoys QP10 and PQ14 appeared indecisive. The paramount importance of weather and light conditions was evident. The German submarine commanders preferred to attack during the night, as they were less vulnerable to the escorts in darkness. As the nights rapidly became shorter, their task would be more difficult. The

German submarines would become more dependent on air reconnaissance, as precise information on the convoys would allow them to take up good positions in advance to make best use of the few dark hours.

On the other hand, the Luftwaffe clearly benefited from the longer days. The reconnaissance aircraft had more time to search for the convoys, and the bombers could take off soon after the sightings had been reported. Also, the short nights meant that the convoys had little chance to shake off pursuers during darkness.[206]

Likewise, the German prospects of successfully using their surface ships was affected by the weather and season, but the location of their bases was also of paramount importance. Ships based at Trondheim required early warning, should they be able to intercept a convoy. Thus bases in northern Norway were preferable, but most of the oil remained in Trondheim, as did most of the anti-aircraft batteries, artillery, and other important equipment. No railways—and hardly any roads—connected northern Norway with Trondheim. Inevitably, such assets would have to be brought north on freighters. Hence, there were good reasons to continue using Trondheim as a naval base. With the long days to come, early information was likely.

Clearly, air power would be the most important component in the

Tirpitz anchored at Bogen near Narvik in 1942. The heavy cruiser *Admiral Hipper* can be seen in the background to the left.

German efforts to halt the convoys during the spring and summer. Thus Luftwaffe reinforcements were highly desirable, but the poor infrastructure in northern Norway prevented a rapid build-up. Nevertheless the transfer of Kampfgeschwader 30 continued, and soon elements of Kampfgeschwader 26, which had trained in the torpedo bomber role, would arrive and operate from bases near Kirkenes.[207]

In addition to the reinforcement of Luftwaffe units in northern Norway, naval reinforcements were also discussed. For example, it was suggested that the *Admiral Scheer* be moved to the Bogen bay, about 20 kilometers west of Narvik, with the hope that she could soon be transferred to the Altafjord. She would then be positioned as close as possible to the Allied convoy routes. It was also intended that her sister ship, the *Lützow*, would join her, creating a significant concentration of naval forces.[208]

The British were aware of German efforts to bolster their forces in the north, and possibly even overstated the German build-up. The First Sealord, Dudley Pound, as well as Tovey regarded the threat against the Murmansk convoys unacceptable. They urged that no further convoys be sent until the autumn. Their warnings remained ineffective. By mid-April 1942, it was evident that the Germans had contained the Soviet winter offensive and would soon regain the initiative on the Eastern Front. Stalin's troops would need all the equipment possible, and the risks to the convoys would have to be accepted.

PQ15 and PQ16

Soviet historiography has often downplayed the role of the Lend-Lease, emphasizing that the number of tanks and aircraft delivered was small compared to Soviet production, which is correct. Also, the quality of the tanks delivered has been described in unfavorable terms. However such comparisons were often made with the T-34 as a yardstick, but this is somewhat misleading. Admittedly, many of the tanks sent by the British were indeed inferior to the T-34, but light tanks made up a considerable part of Soviet tank production, and they were hardly any better than the British vehicles. Later, the U.S. Sherman tank would be shipped in significant numbers and it was approximately equal to the T-34.[209]

The importance of the supplies from the Western powers, however, cannot only be gauged from the number of tanks, aircraft, and guns that reached the Soviet Union. Western Allied help to the Soviet Union consisted of much more than heavy weapons. For example, more than half the trucks received by the Red Army were of U.S. production, and they were technically superior to the models produced by Soviet factories. Without these motor vehicles, Soviet mobility would have suffered considerably.[210]

In certain key areas, the Western contribution was even more important. Aviation fuel is a good example. The fuel received from the Western Allies had a much higher octane rating, therefore it was mixed with Soviet aviation fuel to improve the quality of the latter. This allowed increased power output from Soviet aircraft engines.[211]

The Allies' contribution was even more striking in other fields, like equipment for the railways. Soviet production of engines and railway cars was virtually halted during the war, as the factories were switched to produce heavy weapons. Production of rails was also curtailed during the war. In 1942–45, only 92 engines were produced in the Soviet Union, compared to almost 2,000 received from the Western powers. Also, more than 11,000 railway cars were handed over, which is more than ten times the number produced by Soviet factories.[212]

Evidently, Lend-Lease contributed significantly to the Red Army's mobility and to its capacity to bring ammunition, fuel and other supplies to the front. Given the immensity of the Eastern theatre, this was very important, especially when the Soviets conducted offensive operations. But not only must the ammunition be transported from the factories to the troops, it must first be produced, and again the Western Allies made a vital contribution, as one third of all explosives used by the Soviet forces during the war came from the Western powers.[213]

Another important contribution was advanced tools for industry, like lathes shipped to Soviet factories. In addition, important raw materials like aluminium and copper were shipped in great quantities, as was food, tires, and other goods where deliveries from the West made up a significant share of Soviet consumption.[214]

It can be claimed that most of the help sent from the Western powers arrived during the second half of the war, when the fortunes had already turned in Stalin's favor. A study of when deliveries occurred confirms this. Thus it can be said that the assistance from the Western powers mainly helped the Red Army to conduct its offensives in 1943–45. On the other hand, in the spring of 1942 it was unknown what would happen in the years ahead. Indeed, to the decision makers in London and Washington, it was not evident that the Soviet Union would be able to contain the German summer offensive that was expected. In fact, the latter uncertainty could be construed both as an argument suggesting further convoys as well as an argument against them. On the one hand there was a risk that equipment delivered would fall into Hitler's hands; on the other hand the equipment delivered might be precisely what was needed to keep the Soviet Union in the war. The latter argument won the day, and it was decided that more convoys would be dispatched.

The Admiralty's views on the situation in Norway and the Arctic remained unaltered. The menace from German submarines, surface ships, and air units was growing stronger, and the long days would improve their chances of attacking the convoys. Obviously, the situation would improve if the German military assets in Norway were destroyed or damaged. Thus the efforts to attack the *Tirpitz* continued. She was regarded as the worst threat to the convoys, and while she remained in Trondheim she was still within reach of British air power.

The failed attack at the end of March had not weakened British resolve to eliminate the German battleship. Neither did intelligence reports on German efforts to reinforce the air defenses in the Trondheim area. The British planned to attack the *Tirpitz* with Halifax and Lancaster bombers on 25 April or soon thereafter, using several types of ordnance. Each Lancaster would carry a two-ton bomb and four lighter bombs. The Halifax bombers would drop mines. It was hoped that the latter would roll down the mountain slopes near the battleship's mooring and hopefully detonate under her keel, causing severe damage to the rudders and propeller shafts.[215]

On 25–26 April, dense fog covered the Scottish airfields, but on 27 April, conditions were favorable. Reconnaissance showed that the heavy German ships remained at their moorings, and in the evening the British bombers took off and set course for Trondheim. Like the Lancasters, some of the Halifax carried two-ton bombs, which should be released at an altitude of about 2,000 meters.[216]

Altogether, 44 bombers took off, but three of them had to abort the mission before they reached the Norwegian coast. Considering what lay ahead, it was probably no loss to the British. At 23.08, reports from radar stations were received on the *Tirpitz*, giving ample warning of the impending British attack. Quickly the Flak batteries assumed full alert. When the British bombers arrived over the target area they were met by a hail of fire, and soon the *Tirpitz* was also concealed beneath thick smoke. None of the bombers could release their loads accurately, although 32 crews claimed to have attacked the battleship. The remainder attacked secondary targets, but no hits were scored. The only consequence of the attack noted by the sailors on board the *Tirpitz* were dead fish jolting on the water, having been killed by the British mines. Five bombers were lost in the attack.[217]

The following morning, British air reconnaissance confirmed the disappointing result. To the bomber crews, it meant that they would have to make yet another dangerous effort as soon as possible. The night before 29 April offered good visibility and once again the bombers started, but this time only 23 took off, of which two were forced to return over the North Sea. Again the Germans were warned by their radar, and the event resembled the one that had taken place two nights earlier. The *Tirpitz* was only hit by stone splinters from bombs exploding on the mountain slopes next to the Fættenfjord, while two British bombers were lost.[218]

The disappointing results of the two air attacks did not deter the Allies from sending further convoys to Murmansk. Actually, on 26 April, the PQ15 had already sailed from Reykjavik. At this stage, hopes that the *Tirpitz* had been damaged may still have been nurtured. However, despite the lack of any information suggesting that the German battleship had been hit, the convoy proceeded east. Possibly it was hoped that the mines had caused damage to the *Tirpitz*, but as such damage would be confined to the lower parts of her hull, it would not be discernible on aerial photographs. It was dangerously close to wishful thinking, but as the overall situation called for more convoys, the PQ15 continued.

Twenty-five merchant ships made up PQ15, and its escort was stronger than on previous convoys. In particular it had stronger anti-aircraft defense than prior escorts, such as the *HMS Ulster Queen*, a liner that had been converted to an anti-aircraft cruiser. Another innovation was the so-called CAM ship. CAM was an acronym for "Catapult Aircraft Merchantman," and was an old Hurricane fighter plane positioned on a catapult and fitted to the bow of a merchant ship. If a German reconnaissance aircraft were observed, the Hurricane would be launched to shoot down the enemy, but the plane could not be landed after the attack. The only option available to the pilot was to parachute from the aircraft and hope that some of the escort ships would pick him up.[219]

At this time of year the sun no longer set at northern latitudes, allowing German reconnaissance aircraft to follow a convoy 24 hours a day and continuously report its position and course. Probably the CAM ships were mainly motivated by the fact that nights would no longer allow a respite from German air reconnaissance. If the enemy aircraft were shot down or chased away, the convoy could more easily evade attacks. The best protection for the convoy was to avoid detection.

As was customary, a convoy called the QP11 also left Murmansk to head back west. As usual, Tovey would cover PQ15 until it met the QP11, and then begin to focus on protecting the latter. To accomplish his mission, Tovey had received reinforcements from the U.S. Navy: the battleship *Washington*, the cruisers *Wichita* and *Tuscaloosa*, and four destroyers. He also had several warships from the Royal Navy: the battleship *King George V*, the carrier *Victorious*, the cruiser *Kenya*, and six destroyers. Thus, Tovey had an impressive array of warships at his disposal. Not only was the U.S. contribution of warships significant, no less then 15 of the 25 merchant ships were American as well. Roosevelt was not just pushing the British to send convoys, he also ensured that his own nation contributed with ample resources.[220]

Meanwhile, the Germans made further efforts to strike against the convoys. As always information was paramount, and Luftflotte 5 conducted reconnaissance over the Arctic Ocean. On 26 April, the cloudy weather prevented effective air reconnaissance and nothing was found. Instead, the Germans launched air attacks on Murmansk. The following day the weather remained poor and no air strikes were made.[221]

On 28 April, hopes were sparked at Luftflotte 5 headquarters when a reconnaissance aircraft found QP11, but soon the plane developed engine troubles forcing it to turn back to the airbase before any other aircraft could replace it. Thus contact with the convoy was lost, and although it was found again on the following day, the poor weather prevented any further action. On 30 April, the same reason again forced Luftflotte 5 to remain on the ground.[222]

Despite the fact that bad weather prevented the Luftwaffe from attacking the QP11, it was absolutely clear to the Germans that the merchant ships were continuing west. Also, a German long-range reconnaissance aircraft, not subordinated to Luftflotte 5, had found PQ15 soon after its departure from Reykjavik. The convoy was again sighted one day later and also on 28 April. From these observations, Marinegruppe Nord calculated that PQ15 would reach the area around Bear Island on 5 May, where it could easily be attacked by German air power.[223]

Clearly, German air reconnaissance had provided good information on the convoys. Also, the B-Dienst had worked to break encoded radio messages that were intercepted. As a result of these efforts, the Germans knew about the U.S. warships that had reinforced the Home Fleet. Soon German air reconnaissance confirmed the presence of the American warships at Scapa Flow.[224]

While the ships in the two convoys ploughed the ocean, the Germans deliberated on how they would deploy their warships in Norway. The British air attacks on Trondheim had been ineffective, which the Germans attributed to their equipment for creating artificial fog over the area. Nevertheless, to remain within range of enemy bombers was risky. It was considered to move the ships to Narvik, which would also reduce the distance to the convoy routes. Nevertheless, the Germans retained the warships at Trondheim where, as noted previously, air defenses, underwater protection, and equipment to create artificial fog afforded good cover and defenses.[225]

The weather had shielded QP11 from Luftwaffe attacks, but dangers also lurked beneath the waves. On 30 April, Lieutenant Max-Martin Teichert maneuvered his U-456 into firing position and released a salvo against the British cruiser *Edinburgh*, which was hit by two torpedoes. Her cargo included four and a half tons of gold, payment for the British aid to the Soviet Union. Also, the cruiser carried the flag of Rear Admiral Bonham-Carter, who commanded the QP11 escort. To his horror, he learned that the ship's stern had been blown off. As the rudders were unusable, the only remaining alternative was to bring the crippled cruiser back to Murmansk, a distance of almost 500 kilometers through waters infested with enemy submarines, surface ships, and aircraft.[226]

The *Edinburgh* received no further damage on 30 April, as an attack by German torpedo planes was rendered too difficult by the weather. However on 1 May, three German destroyers found QP11, but the escort fought gallantly and only one merchant ship was sunk. The German destroyers abandoned their efforts to attack the convoy, but instead found the *Edinburgh* and a confused melee ensued. As she was damaged, the cruiser could neither turn nor sail quickly, but her guns were still fully operational. She hit the German destroyer *Hermann Schoemann*, which was put out of action. [227]

The fortunes then swung in favor of the Germans, as the *Edinburgh* was hit by a torpedo. Also, the British destroyer *Forester* was badly hit.

Shortly afterwards a third destroyer, *Foresight*, was struck by a torpedo as well. Fortunately for the British, the two remaining German destroyers were busy taking on board survivors from the sinking *Hermann Schoemann*. The *Edinburgh* was also doomed, and a minesweeper saved most of her crew before the cruiser disappeared. The two damaged British destroyers limped back to Murmansk.[228]

Allied losses were not confined to the actions fought around QP11. Mishaps also occurred farther west, when a serious incident came about in front of the bridge on the *King George V*. As usual, the Home Fleet provided distant escort to the convoys. When the ships entered an area where the threat from enemy submarines was considered grave, the ships began zigzagging. Suddenly, fog surrounded the ships and Tovey ordered them to cease zigzagging. However, the destroyer *Punjabi* did not receive the instruction and veered across the bow of the flagship, which hit the *Punjabi* amidship and cut through her. Fortunately most of her crew could be saved, but not only was the *Punjabi* lost, the *King George V* was badly damaged as the destroyer's depth charges went off. The *King George V* had to return to Scapa Flow, and the *Duke of York*—one of her sister ships—arrived to assume the role of flagship.[229]

The loss of the *Punjabi* was not the extent of the misfortunes. On 2 May, some of the warships escorting the PQ15 found a submarine on their ASDIC systems. They immediately attacked and sank the submarine. Unfortunately their victim was a friendly ship, the Polish submarine *Jastrzab*, built in the U.S. and manned by Polish sailors who had escaped when Germany invaded Poland in September 1939. Thus two Allied ships had been sunk and one damaged purely due to mistakes.[230]

All these adversities had befallen the Allies before PQ15 reached the most dangerous area. When the two convoys met on 2 May, the men on board the ships sailing for Murmansk realized that the worst was yet to come. However, they were fortunate to be helped by the weather. During 1–2 May, no German air attacks could be initiated, but on the night before 3 May, German torpedo aircraft appeared and came back later during the day, sinking three merchant ships. The low clouds remained and covered the convoy on its subsequent voyage to Murmansk, which the ships reached without suffering any further losses.[231]

At last the merchant ships in PQ15 and QP11 reached their respective destinations. Helped by the weather, which prevented the Germans from launching but a few air strikes, most of them made it. To the British, the loss of escort ships was alarming, and the arrival of the merchant ships at their destinations did not put an end to the losses of warships. The *Trinidad*, which had been damaged in March and struggled back to Murmansk, was sent to Britain after temporary repairs. However on 14 May, when en route to Britain, she was attacked by German aircraft. One of the German bombers struck near the previous damage and started uncontrollable fires. After a few hours, it was evident that the cruiser could not be saved, and the British decided to sink her.[232]

The Royal Navy had not been enthusiastic before, and the heavy losses of warships reinforced the misgivings. Neither were any attacks on the *Tirpitz* scheduled in the imminent future. Despite all concerns, the next pair of convoys—PQ16 and QP12—were to sail soon. With 35 merchant ships, PQ16 would be the largest convoy sent to Murmansk so far.[233]

At first glance, it may appear strange to send such a large convoy at a time of year when little protection could be expected from the weather or darkness. However, operations analysis showed that large convoys suffered fewer losses than many smaller ones. If more merchant ships were concentrated into less frequent convoys, the escorts could more effectively protect them, particularly against submarines. To search for convoys, the German submarines had to spread over vast areas, making it difficult to concentrate for the attack. Thus, fewer large convoys made the escort stronger compared to the attacking submarines.

However, during the summer months in the Arctic, the main threat to the convoys was not the German U-boats. They preferred to attack on the surface at night, but as the sun never set during the summer, the escort ships could more easily locate the submarines. Also, radar technology had developed to the point that some escort ships had been fitted with sets allowing them to locate submarines on the surface. Thus dark nights and poor weather could no longer be relied upon by the German submarines.

On the other hand, German airpower was a very serious threat in the Arctic summer. Furthermore, German surface ships would more easily find the convoys in the prevailing conditions. The advantages associated with large convoys still held against these threats.

Both PQ16 and QP12 sailed on 21 May 1942. It was a perilous voyage, but the QP12 fared surprisingly well. Except for a Russian ship that had to return to Murmansk, all 15 reached Reykjavik. Convoy PQ16 was less fortunate, although German surface ships never appeared. Eight of its 35 merchant ships were sunk, as was one destroyer. Except for one merchant ship, all losses were caused by German air attacks.[234]

Luftflotte 5 had indeed made an impressive effort. PQ16 had been sighted early, and the German aircraft could attack when it reached a point of suitable distance from the German airfields. In particular, Luftflotte 5 made a strong effort on 27 May, when no less than 101 Ju-88 and seven He-111 bombers took off to attack PQ16. On the following day, bad weather prevented the Germans from launching further air attacks, but in the evening they were resumed. Before PQ16 reached Murmansk, the German airmen claimed to have sunk half the convoy. Undoubtedly, the claim was exaggerated, but losing eight out of 35 merchant ships was serious.[235]

Apparently the Luftwaffe was the most dangerous threat to the convoys, and subsequently the Allies had to place air defense as one of their top proirties. Furthermore, British intelligence suggested that the German surface ships would pose a greater threat in the future. The reports said that the *Admiral Scheer*, as well as the *Lützow*, had been transferred to northern Norway. The *Tirpitz* remained at Trondheim, but she might join the other ships at any moment.[236]

The fact that the convoys were threatened by three different kinds of weapons systems placed the British in a dilemma. To protect the convoy from submarines, several light ships were required. On the other hand, they were vulnerable to German heavy surface ships. To provide protection against German heavy warships, in particular the *Tirpitz*, battleships and carriers were needed, but it was not advisable to put these valuable vessels at risk in areas dominated by the Luftwaffe. The Admiralty tried hard to find an acceptable balance between the risks imposed and the need to protect the convoys.

Despite the efforts, no obvious solutions were found.

Prelude to Operation Rösselsprung

Although few warships had been lost during the actions fought when PQ16 and QP12 sailed on the Arctic Ocean, disquietingly many merchant ships had been sunk. In particular, PQ16 was hit hard, resulting in the loss of much of its cargo. Out of 201 aircraft being carried aboard the ships, 77 were now located on the bottom of the ocean. Also many tanks had been lost, no less than 147 of the 468 loaded on the ships before they sailed. Such losses were serious and if they continued to mount, the wisdom of the convoy traffic could be called into question. For the time being, however, the convoys were not suspended.[237]

During most of June the Arctic convoys had to wait, as the Home Fleet sent strong forces to the Mediterranean, where other important convoys were underway. Thus Tovey was unable to provide an escort, and the convoys to Murmansk and Archangelsk had to wait until the warships returned from the Mediterranean. Both sides used the respite to ponder future operations in the Arctic.[238]

Until now, the Germans had largely improvised their efforts against the Murmansk convoys. Luftflotte 5 had originally been organized to support operations in Finland and the Murmansk area, including the railroad running south from the port, and to provide air defense in northern Scandinavia. Warships had gradually been transferred to Norwegian ports, but no explicit plans had been established on how to use the naval assets. Before the next pair of Allied convoys—PQ17 and

QP13—set out, a more elaborate plan was created and given the codename "Rösselsprung."

The period also saw a change to the German command structure. Previously, Vice Admiral Otto Ciliax had held the position "Befehlshaber der Schlachtschiffe" (Commander of the battleships) and been allocated the heavy warships in Norway. In June the position was abolished. Instead, the position "Befehlshaber der Kreuzer" (Commander of the cruisers) was created and Vice Admiral Oskar Kummetz was appointed to the position.[239]

The Vice Admiral, who was in his early 50s, had previously gained combat experience in Norway, but not of the kind he had hoped for. In 1940 he commanded the naval force tasked with the capture of Oslo during Operation Weserübung, the German invasion of Norway and Denmark. The attempt ended in catastrophe, as Kummetz's flagship, the heavy cruiser *Blücher*, was hit by artillery fire, as well as torpedoes from the Norwegian fortress Oscarsborg. The cruiser went down with a heavy loss of life. Despite the debacle, Kummetz's career advanced. Oslo was captured by elite German troops landing on the airfield at Fornebu, close to the Norwegian capital, and Kummetz was awarded the Knight's Cross. For awhile, he held the position of torpedo inspector before being promoted to Vice Admiral, and appointed Befehlshaber der Kreuzer by Hitler.[240]

Part of the Befehlshaber der Schlachtschiffe staff was transferred to the *Lützow* on 2 June, where Kummetz would hoist his flag. He would command a force consisting of the *Lützow*, *Admiral Scheer*, and six destroyers, which were transferred to Narvik. Somewhat later, on 12 June, Admiral Otto Schniewind arrived on board the *Tirpitz*. He was "Flottenchef," i.e., the highest position held by any German naval officer at sea. He brought his own staff and also incorporated parts of the former Befehlshaber der Schlachtschiffe staff. According to the plans, he would command a force consisting of the *Tirpitz*, *Admiral Hipper*, and six destroyers during Operation Rösselsprung.[241]

Schniewind and Kummetz would command the naval forces in Operation Rösselsprung, but they were certainly not allowed to make all the decisions. In fact, Raeder and Hitler had the final word. As the German dictator feared the British carriers, he conditioned the use of the heavy ships. Not until the enemy carriers had been found and neutralized would the surface ships be allowed to attack. Hitler did not delegate the authority to decide whether the heavy ships would put to sea or remain in port. He did, however, allow Raeder to decide whether to move them to the bases in northern Norway.[242]

As Hitler's reluctance to put the heavy warships at risk was growing stronger—the air attack against the *Tirpitz* on 9 March did not alleviate his fear—it was unlikely that the *Tirpitz* and the other heavy warships would engage an enemy. On the other hand, Tovey was very reluctant to send his heavy ships within range of the Luftwaffe. Thus a kind of deadlock ensued, as Tovey would remain outside the range of land-based German aircraft unless he had solid evidence that the German heavy ships had put to sea. Hence, the Luftwaffe would hardly find any opportunity to attack the British carriers, which in turn meant that Hitler's willingness to take any risks would be virtually nil.

Planning for the coming operation had been initiated by Ciliax in May, in fact while PQ16 was still at sea. It resulted in a draft entitled, "Operational use of naval forces in the north." Here Ciliax outlined the essentials of what would subsequently be known as Operation Rösselsprung. He relied to a fair degree on experiences from the efforts against previous convoys, which seems to have been wise, as Rösselsprung would mainly be conducted according to Ciliax's draft.[243]

The German planners capitalized on a number of favorable circumstances. First of all, the pack ice still reached far to the south. Thus the convoys could not avoid German air attacks by sailing far to the north. When a convoy reached a point about 150 nautical miles west of Bear Island, it would enter an area dominated by the Luftwaffe. Also, favorable weather was expected. Storms, like the ones experienced earlier during 1942, were rare in the summer, as was fog. German reconnaissance could be expected to find the convoys early.[244]

The German fuel shortages, in general as well as in the harbors in Norway, still limited the alternatives available to the German Navy. As a result it was considered to use only the *Admiral Scheer* and *Lützow*, as these ships had diesel engines, plus the destroyers whose fuel consumption was low. However, such a force probably was not strong enough to defeat the convoy escort. An effort of this kind would most likely result in fuel being consumed with no positive results. For these reasons, it was decided to include the *Tirpitz* and *Admiral Hipper* in the operation. It would result in increased fuel consumption, but the chances of accomplishing a major success would improve considerably.

Tirpitz in the Faettenfjord, near Trondheim, one of its three main anchorages in Norway during the war.

It was preferred to consume more fuel on something that promised success rather than spending less fuel on something that would be fruitless. This time the officers were determined to act, despite the problematic fuel situation, but they were well aware that Hitler would have the final word.[245]

With the forces available and the favorable weather and season, the Germans hoped to inflict a shattering defeat on the forthcoming convoy, perhaps even annihilate it. The most important prerequisite was early detection of the convoy, but it was not something that could be taken for granted. The Germans had several sources of information, but none of them was comprehensive or flawless. Thus they were forced to combine information from several less than secure sources. One example was the air reconnaissance conducted northeast of Iceland. At 08.00 on 22 June, a Ju-88 found four or five trails of oil patches in the water, about 50 kilometers south of Jan Mayen. Each was somewhat less than a kilometre long, and were found at intervals of three to four kilometers. It certainly resembled traces from a convoy that had recently passed. Fifteen minutes later, the aircraft was hit by tracer ammunition, which damaged one of its radiators. The crew could not establish the source of the fire, as the clouds made observation difficult. Clearly, the event suggested that a convoy had departed from Iceland and already reached a point far east. However, Marinegruppe Nord suspected that the aircraft had simply made a navigation error and received fire from Jan Mayen. A similar incident had occurred a month earlier.[246]

Nonetheless, the Germans had good reasons to be concerned. Had the convoy already reached a position far to the east—and was also fortunate to enjoy the benefits of bad weather—it might prove impossible to launch a powerful attack. For the moment, the Germans had little else to do except intensify their reconnaissance efforts. Meanwhile the incident was examined more carefully and more information was obtained. First of all, the crew had not—as was previously believed—observed tracer. It turned out to have been a misunderstanding. Second, a technical investigation of the aircraft showed that the radiator had been damaged by a bolt that had come loose from the propeller.[247]

Difficulties of this sort surrounded many types of intelligence. The event described is just one example of unreliable reports. The officers had to examine each piece of information carefully and compare several reports with each other. Thus a fairly reliable picture of the enemy's whereabouts could be obtained, but it might take time, and in the interim the situation could change.

There was, however, a source that might provide timely and accurate information. If encrypted enemy radio messages were intercepted and decoded, highly valuable information could be obtained. This, of course, required that the enemy use radio, and that the codes could be broken quickly. There were many periods during the war when the German B-Dienst successfully read British encrypted messages, and the summer of 1942 was one of them.[248]

The British were able to intercept and decode encrypted enemy messages as well. On 4 June, Marinegruppe Nord issued a directive for Operation Rösselsprung. Ten days later, the Admiralty received a copy of it—informed by Captain Henry Denham, the British attaché in Stockholm—and its content worried the decision makers in London. Particularly distressing was the German intention to commit the *Tirpitz*. The worst British fears seemed to come true.[249]

Tovey had long been skeptic about the Arctic convoys in summertime. He could not chase the *Tirpitz* without endangering his own ships to German air attacks. Such an attempt might well prove disastrous. His deliberations on the dilemma resulted in a proposal: PQ17 would turn west if indications of an impending attack from the German battleship were received. He hoped the convoy would then perform the role of bait, luring the Germans into a position where he could attack them.[250]

To improve the chances that the Germans put to sea at an early stage, the British would "leak" the information that two invasion forces were assembled, one on Iceland and one at Scapa Flow, each intending to attack Norway. The deception operation was given the code name "Tarantula."[251]

The realism of the plans were called into question, and Pound turned Tovey's proposal down. Instead, the First Sea Lord suggested that the convoy would scatter if attacked by German surface ships, something Tovey regarded as "pure murder." Tarantula was still viable, but it required that the existence of PQ17 was revealed to the enemy. It was a risk, but a slight one. In good weather the Germans would probably find the convoy anyway; in bad weather they would have problems locating the ships, whether they knew about them or not. It was hoped that the Germans would be bluffed and direct their search efforts south of the convoy route. Perhaps then an opportunity to fight the *Tirpitz* would present itself.[252]

No matter how the British looked at the facts, the major problem remained: the Luftwaffe dominated the skies above the Arctic Ocean and the Barents Sea. Already during the actions off Norway in 1940, the German air force had proved a serious menace to the Royal Navy. Later that same year, most British naval actions took place in the Mediterranean, where the Italian Navy was the primary opponent. However, soon another threat loomed greater than Italian warships. In the winter of 1940–41, the Germans sent X Fliegerkorps—which could be regarded as the Luftwaffe's specialists in maritime warfare—to bases on Sicily. At this stage, the Royal Navy was committed to transporting supplies to Malta, and the carrier *Illustrious* formed part of the escort. She was subjected to a series of heavy attacks on 10 January 1941, when the X Fliegerkorps scored seven bomb hits on her. With luck the British were able to salvage her and bring the carrier to the U.S. where she was repaired, though the damage was so severe that she could not serve again until 1942.[253]

This incident, as well as several others, led the British to avoid waters where the Luftwaffe might attack when weather or darkness did not provide cover. During the battle of Crete—when the Royal Navy evacuated significant British ground forces—the ships again had to operate within range of the Luftwaffe in daylight. The cost was very high. Two cruisers and six destroyers were sunk, and further ships damaged. About 20,000 soldiers were evacuated, but the British Mediterranean Fleet was badly drained.[254]

Against this background, escorting a convoy to Murmansk or Archangelsk seemed perilous, especially when there was no cover of darkness. Of course to send the convoy without escort was not a realistic solution, and to postpone the convoys until autumn was impossible for political reasons, as the German Army prepared to launch a summer offensive on the Eastern Front. Despite endlessly pondering the alternatives, the British found that each of them had one or several grave disadvantages.

During the summer, Murmansk was not the only major harbor on the Russian Arctic coast. Archangelsk could also be used, and as it was located farther east, German air power could not attack the harbor and the railroad as easily as at Murmansk. Accordingly, some of the ships of QP13 had assembled in Archangelsk, while others assembled in Murmansk. As the ships berthed in the former had a longer voyage, they put to sea on 26 June, one day before the ships in Murmansk weighed anchor. Altogether, 35 merchant ships were included in QP13.[255]

The westbound convoys were in greatest danger during the first part of their voyage. As the two convoys met, the Germans usually shifted their attention to the eastbound convoy. QP13 was fortunate, as bad weather prevented the Germans from launching air strikes on 27 June–2 July. To be sure, QP13 was found by German air reconnaissance on 27 June, but the day was cloudy and the German aircraft lost contact. When the weather improved on 3 July, QP13 had already got so far west that Luftflotte 5 did not make any more efforts to find the convoy.[256]

Despite the fact that no German air attacks had developed, the seamen on QP13 could not relax. On 3 July, three of the escorting destroyers were detached to search for the *Tirpitz*, as the British had found that she no longer remained at her moorings. However, the destroyers did not find the German battleship, and the only consequence of the detachment of these ships was the weakening of the QP13 escort. The following day, the Admiralty ordered QP13 to split into two parts. The first, consisting of 19 ships, set course for Loch Ewe in Scotland and reached its destination without loss. The remaining 16 ships headed for Hvalfjord on Iceland.[257]

Initially, the Hvalfjord group proceeded according to plan, but the cloudy weather made it impossible to measure the altitude of the sun or observe the stars. Dead reckoning was used, but when a storm hit the convoy, calculations were upset and the position could no longer be established with sufficient precision.

The storm abated in the evening, when the ships had reached a point north of Iceland. For a while, it was believed that land had been sighted, but it turned out to be a large iceberg. Nevertheless, a change of course had been ordered, which would prove to have fatal consequences. As the convoy split, vital information was no longer available to the Hvalfjord group. The commander of the group, Captain Hiss, was not properly informed about the British minefields north of

Iceland. At 21.05, a sharp detonation was heard when the minesweeper *Niger* detonated a mine and went down with heavy loss of life. Also, five merchant ships sank after hitting mines as well.[258]

Perhaps the British had feared an even worse outcome when QP13 sailed west. If so, the loss of 5 out of 35 merchant ships might be regarded as some sort of success, but the fact that all the losses had been caused by their own mistakes was scoffing. Still, regardless of the bad luck suffered during the final part of its journey, the QP 13 was more than compensated by the favorable weather enjoyed as the ships sailed through the area where the threat from German air power was immediate. Without being prevented by weather, Luftflotte 5 could have wrought havoc in the convoy. Also, as the air reconnaissance was almost ineffective, it was difficult for the German surface ships and submarines to attack the convoy.

PQ17—The Tragedy

While QP13 left Archangelsk and Murmansk, PQ17 completed its preparations to depart from Iceland. The latter convoy encompassed 36 merchant ships, which was more than any previous convoy destined for the Soviet ports. The cargo included 297 aircraft, 694 tanks, 4,246 vehicles, and more than 150,000 tons of other goods. The size of the convoy meant that some ships would have to sail to Murmansk and some to Archangelsk, as the former's port capacity was limited. Most of PQ17 would sail for Archangelsk.[259]

The task to protect the convoy was, as the British officers were well aware, very difficult. Essentially, they intended to use the same concept that had been previously used. Rear Admiral Hamilton commanded the close cover, which consisted of two British cruisers, the flagship *London* and the *Norfolk*, as well as two American cruisers, the *Tuscaloosa* and *Wichita*. Also, Hamilton had three destroyers: the British *Somali* and the American *Wainwright* and *Rowan*. Hamilton's ships would follow PQ17 to Bear Island. As usual, Tovey commanded the distant cover, consisting of the battleships *Duke of York* and *Washington*, the cruisers *Nigeria* and *Cumberland*, the carrier *Victorious*, and 14 destroyers.[260]

The terms close and distant cover can be somewhat confusing. To call Tovey's force distant cover hardly causes any ambiguity. He was not expected to bring his ships close to the convoys. It might be more confusing to call Hamilton's force close cover, as the term might invoke the impression of a force remaining within sight of the merchant ships. This, however, was not the intention. Admittedly, Hamilton would keep closer to the convoy than Tovey, but not necessarily within eyesight.

Hamilton was supposed to shield the merchant ships from German surface forces, a task that could be accomplished at some distance from the convoy. The threat from German submarines and aircraft, however, could only be averted by warships in close physical proximity to the merchant ships. Thus, Commander Jack Broome's six destroyers and four corvettes sailed with the convoy and made up the so-called escort.

On paper, the Allies mustered an impressive array of naval resources. It was much stronger than the available German naval forces, but against German dominance in the air the few planes on board the Victorious were insufficient. This was also the reason that Tovey did not expect to send his ships far east of Jan Mayen, unless something extraordinary took place.

The British assembled a smaller convoy, consisting of empty ships, with the purpose of simulating an invasion force heading for Norway. It was part of the watered-down Operation Tarantula. The phantom force left Scapa Flow at the same time as Tovey's main force. Thus the British battle force served dual purposes. On the one hand the phantom threat against Norway was magnified, and there was hope that this could bring a German reaction force to battle. On the other, Tovey's ships had to put to sea to fulfill the role of distant cover for PQ17 in any case. If the Germans would find the decoy force as well as PQ17, they might interpret the observations as an imminent invasion of Norway. As Hitler feared an Allied invasion of Norway, chances were good that he would swallow the bait. If this didn't happen, Tovey would still be present to cover PQ17. However, the Germans never found the decoy invasion force.[261]

Thus far, the British could not know that Tarantula had produced nothing worthwhile. They continued according to plan. On 27 June, PQ17 left Hvalfjord and proceeded into the Denmark Strait. The planned route would bring the convoy past Jan Mayen, Bear Island, and hopefully to Archangelsk or Murmansk. Neither Broome's nor Hamilton's ships had yet joined the convoy, but several other ships followed the merchant ships. For example, submarine chasers, minesweepers, air defense ships, rescue ships, and tankers were included in the convoy.[262]

It soon became evident that all of these ships would not reach their destination. Very early, the American Liberty ship *Richard Bland* ran aground and had to be left behind, thus reducing the convoy to 35 merchant ships. Soon thereafter, another mishap occurred. Drifting ice was encountered in the Denmark Strait and the tanker *Gray Ranger*, as well as the freighter *Exford*, were damaged. The *Exford* sent a distress signal, which could have revealed the convoy to the Germans, but the Allies seem to have been lucky. The German war diaries give no indications that the signal was intercepted. The damage to the *Exford* made it imperative for her to return to Hvalfjord. Also, the *Gray Ranger* had to return after distributing her fuel to other ships.[263]

On 30 June, Broome's close escort joined the convoy. In addition to the previously mentioned destroyers and corvettes, Broome brought minesweepers, smaller submarine chasers, and two submarines. These ships were intended to protect against submarines, mines, aircraft, and surface ships of modest size. Nevertheless, Broome had pondered on how to act if the *Tirpitz* appeared. None of his ships was actually designed to confront such an adversary. Despite this, the destroyers' torpedoes could perhaps damage or deter the battleship.[264]

Early on 1 July, Hamilton's four cruisers and three destroyers put to sea from Seidisfjord on Iceland. Their superior speed, compared to the 8 knots made by the convoy, ensured that they would soon catch up. If this part was easy, the mission in itself produced some problems for Hamilton. His primary task was clear enough: to ensure that PQ17 reached Soviet ports. However, he had also been given a secondary task. If a favorable situation developed, an attempt should be made to bring Tovey's forces into battle with heavy German warships. Hamilton did not intend to engage the *Tirpitz*, but lighter forces could be attacked.[265]

To what extent Hamilton's designs would be realized was, of course, largely up to the Germans. They prepared to find and attack PQ17. Their submarines had an important role. A group of six, called "Eiswolf," had been positioned northeast of Iceland. One of the submarines, U-334 commanded by Lieutenant Hilmar Sienom, reported that dense drift ice stretched farther south than expected, prompting a shift of the Eiswolf group about 60 nautical miles south. However, this meant that the group would encounter the convoy at a later moment than previously presumed.[266]

In the afternoon on 27 June, the commander of Marinegruppe Nord, Admiral Rolf Carls, judged that the "Eiswolf" group was positioned so badly that it might miss PQ17 altogether. One of the fundamental problems was establishing the southern limit of the polar ice, and several efforts were made to gain knowledge. On 26 June, for example, the U-376 was dispatched to investigate the ice situation in the Jan Mayen area. Four days later, the submarine reported that PQ17 would not pass north of the rugged island, as the ice conditions were too severe.[267]

Such pieces of information were evaluated by the German staffs at the end of June, because as yet no trace of PQ17 had been found. However, on 28 June, a Focke-Wulf 200 had reported a battleship and three destroyers at the north-eastern corner of Iceland. A few hours later, the report was corrected, stating that the alleged battleship was actually a *Fiji*-class cruiser. Soon another Fw-200 confirmed the correction.[268]

The following day, the commander of the German coast defenses in northern Norway ordered high alert in the Narvik-Tromsø-Hammerfest area. He feared an Allied invasion. Admiral Carls, however, remained skeptic. He did not find the threat more credible than previous rumors of an imminent Allied invasion. It turned out that Carls was correct. The rumor was yet another example of false information the commanders had to separate from the correct information. In such a quagmire of false, misleading, incorrect, and

Aerial photo of convoy PQ17.

then sometimes correct information, the officers should make decisions.[269]

The most important piece of information, however, was the sighting of a convoy in the Barents Sea. Admiral Schniewind concluded that it was the QP13 going for Iceland, and that PQ17 must thus already be on its way in the opposite direction. Carls agreed, and as we have seen, the German estimate was correct.[270]

On the morning of 1 July, PQ17 reached the area near Jan Mayen where Broome's destroyers received fuel from the tankers. After completing bunkering, the destroyers returned to the task of protecting the convoy, a task which was soon to become urgently needed. At noon, German submarines were sighted and the observation was reported on radio. This turned out to be a serious mistake. The message was intercepted by the Germans, and within a few hours the B-Dienst had broken the cipher and could read the entire message. It contained the exact position of the convoy.[271]

The information obtained by the B-Dienst was most important. The submarines had submerged in order to escape the Allied escorts and could not report until later. Furthermore, the submarine commanders' estimates of their own whereabouts were not wholly accurate, as was shown by the fact that they did not report identical positions. Thus Marinegruppe Nord mainly relied on the information provided by the B-Dienst. The Germans now had the information needed to set their plans in motion.[272]

On board the *Tirpitz*, Schniewind decided to raise the readiness level on the evening of 1 July. By then, German reconnaissance aircraft had confirmed the report broken by the B-Dienst. For the time being, the German battleship remained in the Fættenfjord, but Topp assumed that his ship would put to sea next day. Luftflotte 5 remained rather inactive on 1 July too, mainly because of adverse weather conditions. Nevertheless, the air units were ready to launch air strikes as soon as weather permitted.[273]

The men on the ships that made up PQ17 had no illusions about the perils they were facing. Often they were reminded by the sight of one or more German reconnaissance aircraft. When one of the aircraft made a radio transmission, the Admiralty in London intercepted the message and interpreted it as a signal to submarines to guide them toward the convoy. Somewhat later, when the convoy's lookouts observed silhouettes of some unidentified warships, suspense rose. A trawler was sent on the thankless task of revealing if the ships were hostile, but fortunately it turned out to be Tovey's force. With confidence again instilled, the convoy proceeded east. The men on the convoy did not know that they would never see Tovey's warships again.[274]

On the night before 2 July, PQ17 headed east. The weather was pleasant. Although it was slightly cool, the sea was calm and the wind almost negligible. A few bands of fog reduced the otherwise excellent visibility. In such conditions, the QP13 could easily be found. It was sighted on 2 July, at a point almost 400 kilometers northeast of Jan Mayen. On the PQ17 it was observed, with relief, that the westbound convoy had made it without losses so far. Less reassuring was sightings of wreckage from other convoys, such as partly water-filled lifeboats, rafts, and other remnants jolting in an otherwise empty sea. Nothing visual remained to suggest that men had clung to these objects before they succumbed, and that these men had disappeared in a way the seamen would rather not have thought about. But easy as it was to imagine, it was just as impossible to brush off one's mind.[275]

The German reconnaissance aircraft that remained within sight were even more ominous. Thick clouds and heavy mist were high on the wish lists, but suddenly something happened that attracted attention: a U-boat alert. The entire convoy veered off, to avoid torpedoes probably fired by Teichert in the U-456. The submarine chasers hasted to harass the disturber. No ship was hit, but it was a somber reminder of what lay ahead.[276]

In the evening another German attack was launched, this time by Heinkel 115 seaplanes armed with torpedoes. The air attack was repelled by the ship's anti-aircraft guns and one German aircraft was damaged. It landed on the sea. The crew was unhurt and luckily for them, another He-115 landed next to the stricken aircraft and took them on board. Up to this point even the convoy had been lucky, but far away from the PQ17, wheels that would have a profound impact on the future of the merchant ships were already set in motion. [277]

At Trondheim, the weather resembled what could be expected in autumn, rather than the summer day suggested by the calendar showing

2 July. The thermometer hardly reached ten degrees Celsius and one squall followed after another. At 13.40, Admiral Schniewind ordered "Exercise directive 404" to be effective from 15.00. Few knew the meaning of the order. The wording was chosen to convey the impression that the *Tirpitz* and the other ships commanded by Schniewind were about to conduct exercises, but Topp knew better. The target was PQ17.[278]

As the readiness level had been raised on the previous day, no particular preparations were required before the ships could weigh anchor. A pair of Arado aircraft was taken aboard, thus giving the battleship a total of four aircraft. In the prevailing weather, the chances to actually use them were much better than they had been during "Nordmeer" in March.[279]

At 17.20 the *Tirpitz* left her moorings, slightly later than scheduled, as the tug had been delayed when taking the *Admiral Hipper* from her berth. However, the delay was insignificant and the battleship passed the protective nets at Aasenfjord and proceeded into the Trondheimsfjord. She was followed by the *Admiral Hipper*, the destroyers *Karl Galster* and *Theodor Riedel*, and two torpedo boats. The destroyers *Friedrich Ihn* and *Hans Lody* also followed, but as they suffered from engine troubles, they sailed separately.[280]

Again the German shortage of precious fuel oil was notable. To conserve it, some of the boilers were not used on the battleship, thus reducing her maximum speed to 24 knots. However, in the narrow waters where she now travelled, the disadvantage was marginal. Schniewind's squadron sailed close to the Norwegian shore, sometimes with large islands on the port side. The lookouts on the German ships could enjoy the spectacular scenery, as nothing of importance transpired until 22.00 when the lookouts saw a German plane crash into the sea. Nevertheless, the warships did not alter course, since a Blohm & Voss BV-138 seaplane saved the pilot.[281]

Just before midnight, Schniewind's force reached the latitude of Kaura lighthouse. At this stage, the threat from enemy submarines and mines was deemed serious enough to use all boilers on the battleship, although the steam pressure was limited to 40 atmospheres. The squadron still sailed at less than 24 knots. It would turn out that the speed was more than sufficient, since the British were not yet aware that the German ships had left Trondheim.[282]

Weather forecasts were one of the most important pieces of information on which commanders based their decisions. One hour after midnight, Schniewind received a forecast telling him to expect a cloud base of 300 meters, occasional rain squalls, and some bands of fog north of the 67th latitude. Visibility on the sea would vary between 10 and 25 nautical miles. Schniewind found the forecast promising. The cloud base was high enough to allow the German reconnaissance aircraft to follow the already detected convoy, while British aircraft would be hard put to find his warships. But it still remained to be seen whether the favorable weather would persist until Hitler agreed to begin Operation Rösselsprung.[283]

During the night before 3 July, the *Tirpitz*, *Hipper*, and the other warships remained close to the Norwegian coast. At 01.40 the squadron entered the narrow strait Nærøysundet, near Rørvik, north-northeast of Namsos. It was a difficult channel, where the battleship was offered the assistance of the tug *Atlantik*, but by travelling at speeds of only 9 to 12 knots, Schniewind's ships made it without help.[284]

No problems occurred in the strait, and once past it Schniewind ordered the ships to increase speed. Soon, however, troubles of a different kind arose. The clock had just passed 04.00 when an important message arrived. Air reconnaissance had observed an enemy naval task force consisting of one battleship, one carrier, and two cruisers about 600 kilometers west of Harstad. Given Hitler's insistence on the elimination of the enemy carriers before allowing Operation Rösselsprung, Schniewind clearly understood that his freedom of action might be seriously curtailed.[285]

Ten minutes later, another message with bad news arrived. As we have seen, Vice Admiral Kummetz had brought the heavy cruisers *Admiral Scheer* and *Lützow* to Narvik in early June. According to the intentions in the directive for Rösselsprung, Kummetz had left Narvik in the evening on 2 July. His ships should be transferred to Altafjord, which was a base better located for striking at PQ17. Kummetz chose to sail through the narrow strait Tjeldsund, between Narvik and Harstad. When navigating through the difficult fairway, fog suddenly surrounded the German warships and the *Lützow* ran aground. Her damage precluded any participation in Rösselsprung. Kummetz and his staff had to transfer to the *Admiral Scheer* and continue north, while the *Lützow* had to return to the Bogen Bay outside Narvik for temporary repairs. She would subsequently transfer to Germany for more exhaustive repairs. The number of heavy German ships had been reduced by one quarter.[286]

Little more than 20 minutes later, another air reconnaissance report was received on board the *Tirpitz*. Again, it concerned an enemy naval task force that included a carrier. The position differed somewhat from the previous report, but most likely both reports described the same enemy task force. Although clouds had prevented a clear view of the ships, the aircrew estimated that they roughly included one carrier, two battleships, and three cruisers. It was hoped that further reconnaissance would bring clarity.[287]

Schniewind, however, would be disappointed. The reconnaissance aircraft lost contact with the enemy warships, and soon thereafter it was reported that contact with PQ17 had also been lost. The German Admiral was well aware of the vital importance of accurate information, in particular on the whereabouts of the enemy carriers. If Hitler did not know where they were, he would not allow Operation Rösselsprung to continue. Still, there remained a glimmer of hope. If the British still believed that the *Tirpitz* remained in the Trondheimsfjord, Tovey would perhaps keep his heavy ships far to the west.[288]

It must be remembered that so far Schniewind was merely moving his ships from one base to another. The actual operation had not yet begun. For the time being, the primary task was to move the ships to Altafjord without being noticed by the enemy. Schniewind's battle group continued along the Norwegian coast.

On 3 July, the promised air cover did not appear. Schniewind decided to send a very short radio message asking, "Question: fighter cover?" An hour later, the lookouts on the battleship could discern two German fighters following the squadron.[289]

Thus protected, the German warships continued to Gimsøstraumen, a strait between two islands in the Lofoten archipelago, where they would bunker. The *Tirpitz* would not receive any oil, but the smaller ships had to be replenished. The procedure was begun at about 14.00 and consumed most of the afternoon, but not before another accident happened. Three of the German destroyers— *Karl Galster*, *Hans Lody*, and *Theodor Riedel*—ran aground at the mouth of Gimsøstraumen. Like the *Lützow*, they could no longer participate in the planned operation.[290]

While Schniewind swallowed his annoyance and supervised the bunkering, the British were even more nervous. At the same time the *Tirpitz* and *Admiral Hipper* reached the Lofoten archipelago, the British discovered that the Germans ships were no longer to be found in the Trondheim area. They had no information on what course they might have set after reaching the open sea, but as the British could rely on Denham's report, it was not difficult to surmise what general direction Schniewind had chosen.

The most important uncertainty was how far the German squadron might have sailed. As long as the convoy was well assembled, the escort and close cover could offer fairly good protection against submarines and air attacks. However, it could not be expected to protect against an adversary of the caliber represented by the *Tirpitz*. In such a scenario, a closely gathered convoy was a suitable target for a German squadron. In other words, the British found themselves in a difficult dilemma. Soon, it would force some kind of decision.[291]

While Schniewind rearranged his forces, PQ17 had continued toward the most dangerous area. At 07.00 on 3 July, the convoy had reached a point about 300 kilometers west of Bear Island. It altered course from northeast to east. Fog shrouded the ships and prevented German air units from shadowing the convoy, which now sailed straight toward Bear Island. However, as the summer warmth had pushed the pack ice limit north, it was possible to go north of the barren island. Thus the distance to the German airfields in northern Norway could be extended, and possibly result in fewer opportunities for the Germans to launch air strikes.[292]

The limit of the pack ice had been established by recent reconnaissance, which had been made available to the Admiralty which in turn passed it on to Hamilton and Tovey. Hamilton instructed Broome to advise the convoy's Commodore to choose a more northerly route, but Broome preferred to turn only a few degrees to the north, as he wanted to reach as far east as possible before the fog lifted.[293]

Hamilton still pondered on how he could best use his assets. He suspected the Germans might send one of their forces, including the *Tirpitz* and *Admiral Hipper*, against QP13, while the other, with the *Scheer* and *Lützow*, attacked PQ17. In such a scenario, he could engage the latter. His four cruisers would be sufficient for the task. If everything worked out favorably, Tovey might also engage the *Tirpitz* and *Admiral Hipper*.[294]

Before 12.00 on 3 July, the fog lifted. Broome's ships were immediately concerned with the threat from German submarines. They rolled depth charges, probably aimed at U-88, commanded by Lieutenant Heino Bohmann, but no damage seems to have been inflicted. On the other hand, the German submarine did not score a hit on the ships in the convoy either. Bohmann had to be content with shadowing it and reporting its position and course. This was very valuable to the Germans, as contact with the convoy had been lost in the fog.[295]

To the men on board the ships in the convoy, the detonating depth charges were a somber reminder of the dangers that awaited them. The physician Wilkins, on the rescue ship *Rathlin*, recalled that the mood on board was tense but expectant, which was amplified by the lack of sleep and the knowledge that the most dangerous part of the voyage still remained. Unlike the submarines, which could hide under the vast expanses of water, or aircraft that could disappear in the air whenever they saw fit, the merchant ships were confined to the boundary between these two elements. Once the Germans had located the convoy, it was at their mercy. The ships could alter course and try to avoid the U-boats, but if such maneuvers were to be successful, knowledge of the submarines' positions was required. It was impossible to evade the German air attacks. When PQ17 headed east, and the smoke from the coal-fired ships was visible from far away, the sailors knew that poor weather would provide the only chance to reach Archangelsk or Murmansk unharmed—save the unlikely possibility that the escort ships could stave off all attacks from submarines and aircraft. Perhaps Wilkins would have been more alarmed if he had known that beneath the waves several German submarines had—thanks to their hydrophones—detected the depth charges. The submarine commanders had no problem guessing what these sounds indicated.[296]

During the afternoon, Commander Broome and Rear Admiral Hamilton received a message from the Admiralty, informing them that the *Tirpitz, Hipper, Karl Galster, Hans Lody, Friedrich Ihn, Theodor Riedel*, and two torpedo boats had sailed from Trondheim. As adverse weather had prevented air reconnaissance during the preceding days, it was unclear how far north the German ships could have sailed. As the German battleship could cover the distance from Trondheim to the convoy's present position in a day, the message was indeed stressful.[297]

As we have seen, Schniewind's warships were actually bunkering at Lofoten, thus they had only covered half the distance from Trondheim to the convoy. Schniewind had also lost a significant part of his ships due to grounding, which reduced his chances of attaining a significant success. However, Schniewind's gravest worry was the lack of information on enemy carriers. No more observations had been made since the morning of 3 July. Therefore, the conditions demanded by Hitler did not exist.[298]

By asking the Navy High Command, Admiral Carls tried to probe Hitler's views on Rösselsprung, but he did not receive a clear answer. At least he could instruct Schniewind to proceed to Altafjord, where Kummetz had anchored. Perhaps the heavy ships could be committed so far east that the enemy would not dare risk his carriers too close to the German air fields at Bardufoss and Banak.[299]

In fact, Schniewind had already weighed anchor when he received Carls' instruction. Carefully, the German ships maneuvered through the difficult Gimsøstraumen. The previous groundings certainly suggested this caution. While measuring the depth, the German ships made it through the strait, only to set course for another narrow lane, Sortlandsundet. Here the Germans decided to use a lead to measure the depth. On one occasion it was only 13 meters, sufficient for the *Tirpitz*, but not by a wide margin. Regardless, Schniewind's squadron could continue along the Norwegian coast without further mishaps.[300]

During the night before 4 July, several messages were received. To Schniewind's consternation, none of the reports contained any information on the British carrier. Furthermore, a British reconnaissance aircraft had been observed over the moorings at Trondheim. Thus, it had to be assumed that the British knew Schniewind's squadron had put to sea. At least it was some consolation to learn that contact with the convoy was maintained.[301]

Hitler's strict demands meant that Schniewind could not capitalize on his knowledge of the convoy. The only option was to proceed to Altafjord, and at 20.00 his ships reached the mouth of the fjord. After some maneuvering in the narrow waters, the German warships could anchor and maintain two hours readiness. The smaller ships again received fuel.[302]

There was still no information on the enemy carrier available, but

German air reconnaissance had located Hamilton's force, and it was assumed that the carrier was not far away. Heino Bohmann in the U-88 maintained contact with the convoy, but Schniewind could not do anything before he received permission from Hitler to initiate Rösselsprung.

One can imagine how Schniewind's fingers were itching. Although the groundings had robbed him of a significant part of his resources, he still commanded a strong naval force. About 600 kilometers to the north, PQ17 headed east. He could cover that distance in 12 hours. He also knew the convoy was not escorted by strong forces in its vicinity. The only uncertainty was the distant cover, but if the Allies chose to send the carrier so far east that its aircraft could attack his warships, the enemy would also move within range of the Luftwaffe. Given this background, it is understandable if Schniewind was frustrated. However, he did not know that his sneaking along the Norwegian coast would soon promote dramatic effects in London.

The fact that the German warships lay idle in Altafjord did not mean the danger to PQ17 was over. Rather, it had reached so far east that Luftflotte 5 could launch powerful air strikes. Early on 4 July, He-115 torpedo planes took off to attack the convoy, but the low cloud base and the anti-aircraft fire from the ships prevented the German aircraft from even aiming their torpedoes, despite trying for an hour.

A group of torpedo-armed He-111's was more successful. Visibility remained poor, but one of the aircraft took advantage of it. The pilot dived through the clouds and thus achieved surprise. The Allied ships tried to shoot the Heinkel down, but it released its torpedo and disappeared so quickly that the fire proved ineffective. The torpedo went straight for the anti-aircraft ship *Palomares*, which turned to avoid it. The maneuver was successful, but the torpedo continued and hit the Liberty ship *Christopher Newport* in its engine room.[303]

The men on board this American ship had probably hoped for a more peaceful celebration of their national day. Fate was not on their side, but at least no ships in the convoy collided with the stricken freighter, and the rescue ship *Zamalek* saved 47 survivors. *Zamalek's* commander, Captain Owen Morris, a Welshman short in stature but strong-willed, was surprised by the cheerfulness displayed by the men from the *Christopher Newport* when they were hauled on board. To Morris' dismay, the men brought small arms and baggage, which he insisted was improper. The space on board the *Zamalek* was limited and would soon be needed for other purposes.[304]

Surprisingly, the *Christopher Newport* remained afloat. The commander of another ship, the *Aldersdale*, offered to tow the damaged Liberty ship. It might have succeeded, but it was very dangerous for *Aldersdale* to stop engines while making arrangements for the towing. German submarines were likely to use this opportunity to attack if they were near. Broome decided that the British submarine P-614 should sink the *Christopher Newport*. The attempt failed, and so did the resort to depth charges. PQ17 left the deserted *Christopher Newport* behind, still afloat. A few hours later, it was found by the German submarine U-457, which finally sunk the Liberty ship.[305]

Meanwhile, Hamilton continued east, not far from PQ17. When the German air attacks began, the anti-aircraft gun crews were on full alert. They could see the German aircraft attack the convoy, but Hamilton's ships did not attract any attention from the enemy, except for a Blohm & Voss seaplane, which circled around them. One of the destroyers is said to have used a signal lamp to ask the pilot on the German plane if he could not "circulate in the other direction for a while, as we become giddy." Soon the German plane replied, "Whatever it takes to please an Englishman," and turned around and continued to keep an eye on Hamilton's ships from the other direction.

If this story is accurate, it was not the only episode that differed from the normal routines. During the afternoon on 4 July, British lookouts suddenly saw something very surprising. The American ships lowered their Stars and Stripes. It caused some uneasiness before an explanation became evident. The American ships had simply lowered the worn flags and replaced them with new ones, which had been taken on board before departure, but had not been previously used to honor the national day.[306]

Later in the afternoon, the German air attacks intensified. Torpedo planes of the types He-111 and He-115, as well as Ju-88 bombers, were used. The low cloud base made the German efforts problematic, but nevertheless they scored hits. Flying Officer Hennemann aimed for one of the merchant ships and released his torpedo. A moment later his Heinkel was hit and struck the sea, but the torpedo found its prey, the merchant ship *Navarino*. Another torpedo, from Squadron Leader Bernot Eicke, hit the American freighter *William Hopper*. Both ships went down.

One of the German pilots who tried to attack a merchant ship made a mistake as he was blinded by the sun reflected in the sea. Flying Officer Georg Kanmayr flew his Heinkel just above the water and headed straight toward a merchant ship, when he suddenly realized that it was a warship, the destroyer *Ledbury*. All its guns blazed. The perspex canopy was shattered into hundreds of small splinters. Kanmayr and his observer were wounded, but he managed to ditch his plane and the crew was picked up by the ship they had intended to sink.[307]

According to the estimates made by the German airmen, four merchant ships had been sunk, while four or five had been damaged. It was—as usual—an exaggeration, as only two merchant ships had been sunk and one tanker had been damaged.[308]

When the rescue ships had saved the survivors from the sunken freighters, and it had been decided that the damaged tanker *Azerbaijan* could sail at nine knots, PQ17 continued east. No air attacks were noted during the following hours, but the menace from German submarines remained. However, the midnight sun helped the convoy, as the submarines were easier to find when not protected by dark nights. The German submarine commanders preferred to attack on the surface in darkness. Their crafts were hard to see in such conditions, and the British ASDIC system was not suited to find vessels on the surface. Furthermore, from the low submarines, it was usually much easier to see the high silhouettes of the merchant ships against the night sky.

Such advantages were lost to the submarine commanders during the light summer nights in the north. Partly aided by radar and partly by the light, the convoy escort could stave off the submarines. Broome, as well as Hamilton, felt confident, as they had already passed Bear Island and gradually increased the distance from the German airfields at Bardufoss and Banak.

When Broome turned his destroyer *Keppel* around and sailed along the rows of merchant ships, with the glimmering midnight sun reflected in their metal surfaces, he was lulled into a very false sense of security. Before he lay down in his bunk to get some rest, he noted in his diary: "My impression on seeing the resolution displayed by the convoy and its escort was that, provided that the ammunition lasted, PQ17 could get anywhere."[309]

The commanders of PQ17 may have been fairly confident, but at the Admiralty anxiety reigned. As we have seen, many senior British officers were deeply concerned about the PQ17 before it departed from Iceland. In particular, the *Tirpitz* made them anxious. The British were well aware that PQ12 and QP8 had been saved by fortuitous circumstances such as the poor visibility. However, the midnight sun and the weather expected did not suggest that PQ17 would enjoy the same luck, especially as it was known that German submarines and reconnaissance aircraft were following the convoy and continuously reporting its position and course. If the Germans wanted to attack with the *Tirpitz*, they could do it almost at any time, unless the Allied warships could prevent her. However, as Tovey's heavy ships were still about 500 kilometers west of PQ17 on the evening on 4 July, they could hardly appear in time.

In London, the Admiralty worked feverishly to make some very difficult decisions. The hub of all the decision making was the First Sea Lord, Admiral Dudley Pound, who may already have been affected by the brain tumour that would end his life in 1943. When a particularly important convoy was at sea, he visited the OIC (Operational Intelligence Centre) several times a day, and 4 July was no exception. Commander Norman Denning, chief intelligence officer for German surface units, explained that the Germans had recently switched code keys for their Enigma machines. The Ultra worked hard to break the new codes, but as yet without any success. Pound studied the large plotting map, which indicated the position of the convoy as well as all friendly forces, and the presumed positions of the enemy units. He asked Denning how far the *Tirpitz* could have reached, and if she had moved directly from Trondheim to attack the convoy. A few quick calculations were made, which showed that she would already be within striking distance of PQ17. Denning remarked that it was hardly realistic to assume that the German battleship had followed a straight route. Rather, she would have used the Norwegian coast as protection. Also, the Germans would probably enter Narvik or Tromsø to refuel the destroyers.[310]

Pound decided that Hamilton would remain close to the convoy unless further information prompted a new decision. It was hoped that Ultra would report soon. In the evening, just after 19.00, two intercepted messages were decrypted by Ultra. One of them was a Luftwaffe air reconnaissance report, stating that an enemy force of three cruisers and one battleship had been sighted. Evidently, the report referred to Hamilton's ships. The second was a signal from Raeder to Kummetz, notifying the latter that the *Tirpitz* would arrive at Altafjord at 09.00 and instructing the Vice Admiral to arrange moorings for the battleship, as well as prepare to refuel the destroyers immediately upon arrival. The second report confirmed Denning's assumption that the *Tirpitz* had not headed directly toward the convoy.[311]

Did this mean that the gravest threat to PQ17 would soon materialize? As there was a delay in the Ultra decoding, the German ships might already have left the northern Norwegian fjord. Even if they had not, they were most likely ready to depart at any moment. Thus the major question was: did the *Tirpitz* remain in Altafjord on the evening on 4 July, or was she already heading toward PQ17?

As the darkness of night set over London, Pound called for a meeting to discuss PQ17. Before the meeting he again consulted Denning, who reiterated that he did not believe the *Tirpitz* had put to sea, and presented further arguments supporting his thesis. Signals from German submarines showed that they still shadowed the convoy, but nothing suggested that Marinegruppe Nord had warned them that German surface ships might be operating in the area. Neither did any increase in the number of radio transmissions suggest that German surface ships were at sea. Before Pound went from the OIC to the meeting, he asked Denning a very specific question.

"Can you assure me," he said, "that *Tirpitz* is still at anchor in Altafjord?"

It was impossible to guarantee. Although Denning was convinced that *Tirpitz* was still at Altafjord, he could not ensure it.[312]

Rear Admiral Clayton, the head of the OIC, was one of the officers participating in the meeting. On his way there he was stopped by Denning, who had received a third Ultra message since Pound left. It had been sent from Marinegruppe Nord to all German submarines positioned to attack PQ17. The message contained no information on German surface forces operating in the area. Rather, all warships would constitute legitimate targets. As the countermanding order could not be issued and received instantly—the submarines could not receive messages when submerged—Denning concluded that the German battleship had not put to sea. Clayton agreed and brought the message to the meeting.[313]

The meeting was held in the U-boat tracking room. Before PQ17 departed from Iceland, the option to scatter if the *Tirpitz* was about to attack had been discussed. Tovey was also informed. It seems that Pound considered the alternative and asked for the opinion of the other participants. A prolonged discussion took place where, despite Clayton showing the latest Ultra message, it was more or less presumed that the German battleship had already put to sea. According to the post-war statement of Pound's deputy, Admiral Henry Moore, the First Sea Lord remained silent, listening to the opinions of the other participants. It was quite typical for Pound, but it was a habit that sometimes gave the impression that he was asleep during important meetings. He did not enter the discussion; rather he quietly listened, pondered, and tried to put himself into the position of the enemy. The task was obviously difficult, but finally he grasped a pen, wrote down a few words on a form, and showed it to the other participants.[314]

While the meeting was still in session, another Ultra message arrived. It was a German air reconnaissance report, saying that a battleship, a carrier, and two cruisers had been found. The process of breaking this signal had taken a long time, but it was interpreted as an indication that the Germans believed a carrier was included in Hamilton's close cover. Denning was convinced that the latter, unless other intelligence suggested otherwise, would persuade the Germans not to accept the risk of sending the *Tirpitz* against PQ17. He wrote a draft message intended for Tovey and Hamilton, where he presented his conclusions. However, he did not intend to send it until the meeting in the U-boat tracking room had ended.

When Clayton returned from the meeting, he revealed that Pound had already made his decision. Denning showed Clayton the fourth message and the latter once again talked to Pound, hoping that the new information would make him change his mind. However, Clayton soon returned, telling Denning that Pound was adamant.[315]

It would prove to be a momentous decision.

"Convoy is to Scatter!"

The first person to receive a message as a direct consequence of Pound's decision was Rear Admiral Hamilton on board the *London*. The signal's brevity left no room for interpretation: "Cruiser force withdraw to westward at high speed."

Hamilton obeyed the order and reported to Broome. The cruisers had been sailing about eight kilometers ahead of the convoy when they received the message. Had it not been for a previous signal sent by Hamilton, Broome would have pondered little on the order. Clearly, the Admiralty had long been reluctant to risk the cruisers near the German airfields, and the threat from German submarines motivated high speed.[316]

However, about an hour earlier, the *Keppel* had received a message from Hamilton's flagship referring to a previous intention to adjust the course to 45 degrees, stating, "Due to proximity, surface forces report when convoy is on 045 degrees."

It was the first time Broome was told about any enemy surface forces in 24 hours and it worried him. He considered the orders he might have to issue to the other escort commanders, and this moment soon arrived. The Admiralty sent a new order, addressing not only Tovey and Hamilton, but Broome as well. The urgent message instructed PQ17 to disperse and proceed to Russian ports.

As Broome was uninformed about the drama involving Tovey, Hamilton, and the Admiralty, he found the order difficult to comprehend. He instructed his commanders to form two groups in preparation for a possible attack by enemy surface forces. The

Admiralty's order to disperse, however, remained puzzling. Such an order was usually given when the destination was not far away, and each ship could proceed to the port it was bound for. However, in this case, only two relevant ports existed—Arkhangelsk and Murmansk—and several days still remained before the ships could berth. It was far too early to disperse. Such a move was not advisable if enemy surface forces attacked either, as the ships would remain quite close to each other regardless.

Broome had little time to muse on the implications before another message from the Admiralty was received. This time it was marked "very urgent."

When Broome read the text it was, as he later described, like receiving an electrical shock.

"Convoy is to scatter."

Broome could not immediately grasp what had happened. First the order to disperse, then the sight of Hamilton's cruisers withdrawing at high speed, and finally—just 13 minutes later—the order to scatter. He could only conclude one thing: the *Tirpitz* could not be far away. Maybe her lookouts had already found the convoy.[317]

Most of the officers on the bridge searched the horizon, while Broome issued the necessary orders: the smaller escort ships should proceed to Archangelsk and Murmansk, the destroyers should join the *Keppel*, and a signal flag to scatter would be hoisted. Leading Signalman Elliot, who hastened to get the proper flag, noted that his commander was restrained, but obviously indignant.

Never before in the history of the Royal Navy had an order to scatter a convoy been issued by an officer who was not on the spot. Usually, such an order would only be issued as a last resort to save a convoy from imminent danger when all other alternatives had failed. Detailed instructions had been worked out in case the situation should arise. The merchant ships would maneuver according to a pattern that would allow them to increase the distance to each other quickly, thus forcing the enemy to choose among several distant targets. Thereby at least some of the merchant ships might escape.[318]

While Broome prepared to protect the convoy from the presumed imminent attack, Elliot hoisted the white flag with a red St. George's cross half way up the yardarm. The flag was seen by the signalmen on the other ships in the convoy, including the tanker *River Afton*, where

Commodore Dowding received the news. To instill urgency, Broome used the signal lamp to inform Dowding, and also sent the information on the R/T. Dowding hoisted his flag about a quarter up the yardarm, indicating that he had received the message but did not believe it.[319]

Broome maneuvered the *Keppel* near the *River Afton*, and by using a megaphone he yelled to Dowding. The latter was completely uninformed about any possible German surface forces and could not understand what had prompted the order. Broome briefly shouted that the Admiralty must have some information that he was not aware of. Probably the *Tirpitz* was not far away. The *Keppel* and the other destroyers would try to cover the convoy while it scattered. Dowding, who had sailed many convoys together with Broome, showed that he understood, but his face relayed that he was far from convinced.[320]

The distance between the two ships increased as the *Keppel* turned to gather the other destroyers. Broome flashed a final message to Dowding, telling him he was sorry that they had to leave them in this way.

Dowding replied with a farewell and a wish for happy hunting.

When the women and men on the ships in the convoy saw the escorting warships turn west, they must have understood that something serious had either already happened or was about to occur very soon. They had not yet seen any German surface warship. Thus far submarines had threatened the convoy, but the escort had gallantly fended them off. The threat from the Luftwaffe had been graver, but despite the loss of three ships to air attacks, the escort had nevertheless provided protection. When the convoy was ordered to scatter and Broome and Hamilton turned west, the enemy submarines and aircraft at once became a much more serious threat. To make matters even worse, when the convoy scattered, the work of the relatively low number of rescue ships would be far less effective.

Ironically, when PQ17 scattered at 22.30 on 4 July, the German warships still remained in Altafjord. Lingering uncertainty prevented Operation Rösselsprung from being initiated. According to a situation assessment at 17.00 by Admiral Carls, the location of the British carrier was still unclear. Also, precious little time remained if the *Tirpitz* was to intercept PQ17 before it reached too far east. According to Carls, the German warships would have to attack within 24 hours. If they remained at Altafjord on the evening on 5 July, they would be transferred to other ports on the Norwegian coast, except possibly the

Admiral Scheer, which might stay in Altafjord.[321]

It seems that incorrect intelligence confused the Germans. For example, at 01.00 on 4 July, Hamilton's cruiser force was reported as one battleship, three cruisers, and three destroyers, thus suggesting that heavy Allied warships were operating farther east than their true position. The misunderstanding seems to have remained on the morning of 5 July.[322]

Soon the Germans became aware that the convoy had scattered. One hour after midnight on 5 July, aerial reconnaissance reported that the merchant ships were spread out over an area about 25 nautical miles wide. As submarines and air power simultaneously operated against it, Admiral Carls presumed that it was the German attacks that caused the convoy to scatter. Consequently, heavy Allied warships might still be in the vicinity. Had the Germans known that the convoy scattered following an order from the Admiralty, their conclusions would perhaps have been different. To scatter while heavy friendly warships remained close made little sense.[323]

On board the *Tirpitz*, the ether had been monitored and on the morning of 5 July, the events that took place hundreds of kilometers farther north were well known. At 07.45, Topp noted that the convoy had scattered and had suffered substantial losses. Also, it was finally understood that the presumed British battleship was actually a cruiser. A second enemy formation, including a carrier, was estimated at a position about 300 kilometers west of Bear Island, which coincided well with Tovey's true position.[324]

Topp complained that an excellent opportunity had been wasted due to incomplete information, as well as an overestimation of the enemy's capabilities. With every passing hour, Topp's hopes dwindled as the scattered ships of the convoy traveled farther east. However, a gleam of hope appeared as an order for 30 minutes readiness was issued at 09.00. An hour later, he received an instruction to be ready to sail at 11.00.[325]

At 10.55, the *Tirpitz* weighed anchor and began to wriggle her way past the nets, barriers, and other obstacles in the fjord. Perhaps she would attack PQ17 after all, as the mighty battleship was soon accompanied by the *Admiral Hipper*, *Admiral Scheer*, and seven destroyers. Two groups were formed: *Tirpitz*, *Admiral Hipper*, and four destroyers, commanded by Schniewind, and the *Scheer*, and three destroyers under Kummetz. However, the narrow Altafjord could not be negotiated swiftly, and an hour later the German warships had neither reached open sea nor received any instructions. Would they return to Narvik or Trondheim? Or would they intercept PQ17?[326]

At 12.00 an answer was received. The German force was instructed to attack PQ17. The decision could hardly have been postponed any further. Not until 15.00 had the warships left the fjords, islands, and rocks behind.

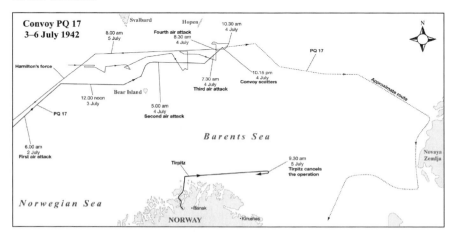

The Tirpitz set a north-northeasterly course and increased speed to 24 knots, as did the other ships, while maintaining a distance of about 2,000 meters. Perhaps they would be able to score a notable success.[327]

Allied submarines had been positioned off the coast of northern Norway, mainly to report information on any German warship that sailed, but with some luck the German warships might be torpedoed too. The Soviet submarine K-21 was patrolling off Altafjord, and soon after the *Tirpitz* left the estuary, she was seen through the periscope. The commander of the submarine, Ranga Lunin, decided to attack and fired four torpedoes.[328]

Nobody on the German warships observed either the submarine or the torpedoes. Schniewind's vessels sailed at 24 knots and soon left Lunin's submarine far behind. Probably he had fired the torpedoes at too great a range, but at least the Germans had been revealed. It remained to see if Allied forces could capitalize on the information.[329]

Unaware of what had transpired beneath the waves, Schniewind continued toward PQ17, but it was unclear what remained of it. The B-Dienst intercepted several messages from merchant ships belonging to PQ17 that described attacks by submarines and aircraft. As the convoy was evidently suffering disastrously, the need for an attack by surface forces diminished. A tightly assembled convoy could defend against aircraft and submarines, but hardly against the *Tirpitz*. A scattered convoy, however, was easy prey for air power and submarines, but attacking individual merchant ships with a large battleship was not optimal. For the time being Schniewind continued, but at 20.33, a message from Marinegruppe Nord arrived. An enemy submarine had reported one battleship and eight destroyers near Nordkapp.[330]

The ominous message was soon followed by a final order. An hour later, Schniewind was ordered to break off the operation. Lieutenant Edmund Kuhnen was on duty on the bridge when he saw a signal flag hoisted from the Admiral's bridge above.

"Red flag," the signal officer commented, meaning the battleship should turn 180 degrees. Kuhnen called for Topp, who immediately went to the Admiral's bridge. He soon returned, unable to hide his feelings. "We're going back," he said with disappointment etched on his face. "Berlin has cancelled the operation."[331]

Once again, the *Tirpitz's* gunners had to abstain from firing heavy shells against the enemy. Schniewind's ships turned, and on the morning of 6 July they berthed in Altafjord. In the evening, the *Tirpitz* and *Admiral Hipper* again weighed anchor and set course for Narvik, arriving early on 8 July after an uneventful voyage.[332]

Once more the sailors on the *Tirpitz* had only seen German ships. No worthy target had appeared within range of her heavy guns. Clearly, many realized that she had just pointlessly burned fuel, as nothing had been achieved. Such sentiments on board the German battleship were understandable, but the men on the merchant ships belonging to PQ17 begged to differ. The mere presence of the *Tirpitz* in the area had provoked Pound's decision, and on 5 July the Allied sailors were exposed to devastating attacks from submarines and air power.

Although the weather was fickle, Luftflotte 5 launched several attacks. As a consequence of a series of air sorties by Kampfgeschwaders 26 and 30, a fair number of Allied merchant ships went down. The American freighter *Peter Kerri* was the first victim. She was subjected to a dive-bombing attack from Flying Officer Clausener in a Ju-88. Three additional American ships were lost: the *Washingon*, *Pan Kraft*, and *Fairfield City*. Also, three British ships were sunk by German aircraft—the merchant ship *Bolton Castle*, the tanker *Aldersdale*, and the rescue ship *Zaafaran*. The final victim to the Luftwaffe was the Dutch *Paulus Potter*, which was dive-bombed repeatedly while trying to escape by sailing close to the pack ice. She was finally abandoned but remained afloat for a week, when Lieutenant Reinhart Reche in the U-255 torpedoed her.[333]

German bombers as well as torpedo planes had attacked during the day, and the aircrews claimed to have hit 14 ships, of which seven were sunk. In fact, the claim was unusually accurate. If the *Paulus Potter* is included, no less than eight ships from PQ17 had been lost to air attacks on 5 July.[334]

Also, submarines inflicted further losses. Sienom in U-334 and Teichert in U-456 sank one ship each, while Bohmann in U-88 and Biefeld in U-703 sank two each. The latter torpedoed and sunk the *River Afton*, Commodore Dowding's ship.

The loss of 14 ships in a single day was a disaster and the gauntlet was still not over. No help was to be expected from Hamilton or Broome, as they were sailing west according to the Admiralty's orders. The only realistic alternative that remained was to seek cover in fog banks and pray for favorable weather. Some ships sailed close to the pack ice, where the combination of humidity and cold might result in fog. An even more remarkable gambit was used by the three merchant ships *Ironclad*, *Silver Sword*, and *Troubadour*, which together with the trawler *Ayrshire* sailed straight into the ice area, deliberately getting stuck. The crews painted their ships white and waited for two days, and then sailed for the Matochkin strait at Novaya Zemlya where they waited for a week. Finally, they continued to Archangelsk on 20 July.[335]

Other ships were not as fortunate. During the days leading up to 10 July, the Germans sank another seven ships. The lighter warships sailing with the convoy, which Broome had ordered to continue east on their own, gathered around the anti-aircraft ship *Pozarica*. After many emergency transmissions were received, the corvette *Lotus* turned west to search for survivors. Eighty-five were found, among them Dowding. The survivors, who had expected an almost certain death on the icy ocean, felt an immense relief at the sight of the stem of a British Flower-class corvette. However, the general attitude toward the escort ships was mixed after having seen Broome's destroyers turn away, leaving the merchant ships to be massacred. When the corvette *Poppy* passed along the American ship *Bellingham*, the commander of the warship asked if the merchant ship wanted to be escorted. He received the reply: "Go to hell!"

When *Poppy's* signalman handed the reply to the commander, the latter commented: "I can't blame him."[336]

Most of PQ17, including her cargo, was lost. Of 594 tanks, 430 were lost, as were 210 out of 297 aircraft. No less than 4,246 motor vehicles had been loaded before the departure from Iceland, but only 896 reached Soviet ports. Of the remaining cargo, which amounted to 156,492 tons, 99,316 tons ended up at the bottom of the Barents Sea.[337]

Luftflotte 5 had made a major effort. Altogether, 130 Ju-88's, 43 He-111's, and 29 He-115's had attacked the convoy. Two He-111's and one He-115 were lost, as were two reconnaissance aircraft.

This was a low price for the success achieved. Not only did air attacks account for more than half the ships sunk, it was mainly the threat from the Luftwaffe which prevented the heavy Allied warships from operating in the Barents Sea. Had it not been for the German dominance in the air, Tovey might have sent his warships farther east, perhaps positioning them between the *Tirpitz* and the convoy. In that case, the convoy would hardly have been ordered to scatter, but the menace from the air deterred the Allies from sending battleships and carriers farther east.[338]

The disaster that befell PQ17 provoked a fierce debate in London. An explanation was sought and the debate mainly centred around Pound's order to scatter. With hindsight, it appears to have been an incorrect decision. Before it scattered PQ17 had fended off enemy attacks quite successfully, but after the order was received, disastrous losses occurred. We also know that Hitler's reluctance effectively meant that the *Tirpitz* would not come close to the convoy. It seems likely that PQ17 could have reached Archangelsk with much fewer losses had it proceeded according to the original plan.

Such a line of thought appears convincing, but it must not be forgotten that it is problematic to judge historical decisions by using information not available to the decision makers. One example is the weather. As we have seen, QP13 was protected by favorable weather, which saved it from German air attacks. PQ17, on the other hand, did not enjoy such weather conditions, which was a fact largely unknown to the decision makers. If low clouds had covered the sky on 5–6 July, the threat from German warships would have been more important than the threat from the air. To what extent such considerations affected Pound's decision remains unclear. It is just one of the many examples of uncertainty the decision makers had to cope with, as they did not enjoy the benefits of hindsight.

Also, it should not be forgotten that there were previous occasions when scattering had saved convoys. For example, on 5 November 1940, HX84 had scattered when attacked by *Admiral Scheer*, and on 12 February 1941, SL64 had scattered when attacked by *Admiral Hipper*. Furthermore, it could not be taken for granted that PQ17 could have repelled the heavy Luftwaffe attacks on 5 July. It seems that Pound had only had bad alternatives to choose among. Possibly he chose the worst of them.

It is clear, however, that Tovey as well as Pound had grave misgivings even before PQ17 sailed from Iceland. The main problem was German air power in northern Norway. The Allies had no solution to the problem nor an effective countermeasure. No matter what Pound may have decided on 4 July, the Arctic convoys were dangerously exposed in the summer 1942. Pound and Tovey had advised against sending convoys prior to the autumn. The catastrophe that befell PQ17 ensured that no more convoys would be sent to the Soviet northern ports until dark nights and harsh weather could restrain German air power.

Operation Title—The Human Torpedos

The PQ17 disaster spurred the British to finally put the *Tirpitz* out of action. The midget submarines were still in development and could not be used soon, but it was hoped that divers could attack the German battleship before the end of 1942. The vessels to be used were not yet ready, but training could be initiated.

Commanders "Tiny" Fell and Geoffrey Sladen were appointed to recruit the necessary personnel. The former was an amiable man originating from New Zealand. He had previously commanded a submarine flotilla, and had also organized raids on French ports where the Germans had assembled shipping for their stillborn attempt to invade Britain—Operation Seelöwe (Sealion). In addition to this, Sladen had participated in the Vaagsø raid in December 1941, as commander of the landing ship *Prince Charles*.

In March 1942, Fell entered the building in London where submarine operations were directed. His purpose was to find information on former colleagues, but he was summoned to Max Horton. The latter had already intended to contact Fell and now seized the opportunity. Horton informed Fell on the success achieved by Italian divers in the harbor of Alexandria.

"Would you like to do something similar?" Horton asked the surprised Fell.

"Of course sir," the latter replied after regaining composure.

"Well then …" Horton regarded the matter as settled. "I want you to join Sladen and the madmen he has gathered. You will form and train a group of underwater commandos."[339]

142

Soon the two officers had initiated the project. Aside from their background in the submarine arm, they were almost inconceivably different. Fell was calm, charming, and sympathetic; Sladen was more like greased lightning. His unlimited energy knew no boundaries, neither physically nor mentally. He tackled all problems with the kind of determination he had displayed in his four international rugby matches. His list of qualifications included several missions off the Norwegian coast and a few visits to Murmansk. Sladen had commanded the *Trident* when it torpedoed the cruiser *Prinz Eugen.*[340]

An event during one of Sladen's visits to Murmansk eventually became told so often in British mess rooms that it acquired the status of a folktale. Due to the *Trident* needing repairs, Sladen and his crew spent some time at the harbor, and one evening he dined with a Russian admiral. They discussed the climate in Britain and on the Kola peninsula. Sladen told the Russian officer that his wife hated the winters, as it was arduous to pull the stroller up the steep slopes where they lived. The admiral immediately came up with a solution. "What you need is a reindeer to pull the carriage," he suggested with a grin.

When the *Trident* was about to depart, a sack from the admiral was handed over as a surprise gift to Sladen. He presumed that it contained some extra food, took it into the submarine and weighed anchor. When at sea, the sack was opened and the astonished seamen found a tightly-lashed reindeer calf. The small animal was christened "Polyanna," and accompanied the *Trident's* crew the following month. Her smell was not always appreciated by the crew, but perhaps Polyanna was less than pleased by the odor from 56 poorly washed men as well. When the submarine finally arrived in Britian, Polyanna had grown too large to fit through the hatch. Only by lashing her tightly again could she be brought out in the fresh air. She was handed over to a British zoo, where she lived until 1946.[341]

Sladen and Fell made a perfect team. While Fell developed a suitable craft, to be dubbed a "Chariot," Sladen worked to create useable diving equipment. Also, in April 1942 they gathered the first group of volunteers. The men—hereafter referred to as "Charioteers"—only knew they had applied for some kind of dangerous service involving diving. Their motives differed, from discontent with previous assignments to a desire for excitement. However, they would only learn what they had enlisted for once the training program started. After awhile, Fell supplied a mock-up of a Chariot that was about seven and a half meters long, complete with rudders. It was propelled by compressed air and the divers christened it "Cassidy."[342]

While the men waited for a real Chariot, they were thoroughly taught every aspect of diving by a plump petty officer named Chadwick. He knew all about the Royal Navy and could drink any youngster under the table. The responsibility for the training on Cassidy rested on two men. One of them was Tom Otway, who would later be remembered for asking, "Do you feel comfortable?" before the trainees were sent into the water. The other was Jack Passy, who strained the pupils to the utmost. If one of the trainees emerged too early, Passy pushed their head down with a heavy boot. Nevertheless, the divers probably found their existence more tolerable than most enlisted men in the armed forces. The training was tough, but the summer days in Portsmouth were pleasant. In June, 24 Navy officers, 2 Army officers, and 31 privates were in training.[343]

The rosy existence ended abruptly when the first casualty occurred. Despite almost perfect conditions, one of the Navy officers drowned

A Chariot (sometimes called a "human torpedo") with crew.

during an exercise. The tragedy had a sobering effect on the young men. In action, courage and youthful enthusiasm would not suffice; skill, experience, and mastery of the equipment were indispensable. The lesson was not forgotten when the depot-ship *Titania* brought the charioteers to Loch Erisort on the Hebrides, where they would continue to prepare for the future mission.[344]

The training increasingly became more challenging. The memory of the tragic accident lingered, but all the men devoted their energy to the task. Bob Aitken, who could not foresee the horrendous incident he would encounter in a Norwegian fjord little more than a year later, recalled that the period at Loch Erisort was among the best he had experienced in his 19-year life. Of course he had to do as he was told, but after years in school he did not find it peculiar. The summer on the Scottish west coast was wonderful, and his days consisted of three components: training, physical exercises, and sleep. What else was needed? When not training on Cassidy he was fishing or catching crabs—taking life easy.[345]

While the training program continued at Loch Erisort, the first manned torpedo was delivered to Sladen and a few divers who remained at Portsmouth. As the training had so far been made with mock-ups, the torpedo was simply called "The Real One." It was as large as a normal torpedo and had a 300 kg charge in the fore section, which could be disconnected. The Chariot was battery powered and had an endurance of about five to six hours when going at a speed of three knots.

Like Cassidy, The Real One was a two-seater and had a simple joystick to operate the rudder and hydroplanes. At the front seat, from where the torpedo was controlled by the commanding diver (Number One), there was an instrument panel—not unlike that of a car—with a compass and other luminous dials. The main ballast tank was located between the two operators, and the second diver (Number Two) had a box at his back containing wire-cutters, ropes, magnetos, and other tools needed to force a submarine net. Sladen tested the torpedo and found to his delight that everything worked as it was supposed to do.

Soon Sladen and The Real One joined the men at Loch Erisort. Until then, training had focused on learning every aspect of diving, but from now on they concentrated on learning how to operate the human torpedo. Gradually, more equipment arrived and a very intensive

training scheme was adhered to by the men. To create realistic circumstances, Boom Defense Department provided Sladen and Fell with
torpedo nets for the divers to penetrate. When not in the water, the
Charioteers discussed recent experiences on board the *Titania*, and
suggested alterations to the equipment and tactics. No field manuals
had been written on the operation of the Chariot; everything was new
and had to be tested. The officers and enlisted men worked closely
together, thus gradually breaking many barriers associated with the
ranks. They were one big team with one common goal: to perfect the
efficiency of their weapon.[346]

Few alterations to the equipment were needed. The diving mask
originally had two separate openings for the eyes, but subsequently it
was changed to a model with one large vision opening. The oxygen
tubes were made by steel, which interfered with the compasses.
Unfortunately, the British did not have any aluminium oxygen tubes,
but inaccurate compasses could not be accepted. Eventually, it was
learned that aluminium oxygen tubes had been found in shot-down
German aircraft. After minor alterations, these could be used by the
Charioteers. Orders were issued to search all German aircraft wrecks in
southern Britain for tubes, and a sufficient number was found to
proceed with the Chariot project.[347]

Soon the base at Loch Erisort was found insufficient by Sladen and
Fell. The team moved to Loch Cairnbawn in mainland Scotland, where
the battleship *Howe* anchored to allow the Charioteers to conduct
realistic exercises. It was surrounded by several layers of torpedo nets,
which had also been fitted with hydrophones. Furthermore, whalers
patrolled the area outside the nets.[348]

Despite the fact that the crewmen on board the *Howe* were well
aware of the exercises, the Charioteers were very successful. Several
techniques were tested out. Some groups simply cut their way through
the nets, while others tried to find a way around them. Only one
Chariot was observed by the whalers, and even then only after the
dummy charge had been fastened to the battleship. Four out of seven
teams successfully placed their charges while three had to abort—two
of them due to encountering problems with the equipment. The seventh
Chariot was lost as it entered a fresh-water area. The lower density of
fresh water caused the Chariot to sink and hit the bottom. The divers
managed to escape, but their ears were injured in the process.[349]

Another "attack" was launched on the following night. Four pairs of divers penetrated the defense and secured the dummy charges. Two pairs were observed when they retired, but again the *Howe* would have been sunk or severely damaged if real charges had been used. In subsequent daylight, the Chariots were maneuvered back and forth along the nets to evaluate the noise they produced. The tests showed that very little noise could be heard from a Chariot, even when it passed close to the listening device. The only significant exception was when one of the divers tauntingly hit one of the hydrophones with a spanner, not realizing the danger he caused to the hydrophone operator's ears.[350]

On the third night, disaster again befell the Charioteers. Lieutenant Jack Grogan suddenly became unconscious when he was about to place a mine below the *Howe's* bow. His Number Two managed to maneuver the Chariot with one hand while holding Grogan with his other. Unfortunately, it was too late to save Grogan's life. His death was attributed to oxygen poisoning. It was yet another reminder of the dangers inherent in the task, even when the enemy did not react.[351]

Despite the accident, the Charioteers were keen to prove their mettle against the real enemy. The training gradually turned into routine, which in turn lead to gloominess. Restlessness and irritation followed, and some new occurrence was needed. However, there was actually no need for concern. While the Charioteers trained and perfected their tactics, the planning for an attack on the *Tirpitz* proceeded swiftly. The decision to use the Chariots had been taken in June and the operation was given the code name "Title." The most important problem to solve was how to cross the sea between Scotland and Norway without arousing the Germans. It was decided to use a fishing boat or small freighter. It could sail into the Trondheimsfjord under false pretext, and launch the Chariots when the German battleship was close enough.

Toward the end of summer, plans for Operation Title were more or less complete. Only one major obstacle remained: the *Tirpitz* had berthed near Narvik after Operation Rösselsprung, and had still not sailed for Trondheim. Unless she moved fairly soon to the more southerly port, the cold autumn weather might jeopardize Operation Title.

Wunderland

During the summer of 1941, the Germans accomplished in the Arctic Ocean what they had vainly tried to achieve in the Atlantic: halt the Allied convoys. Why did the Germans succeed in the north and not on the Atlantic? Obviously many factors contributed, and one of the most important was the location of the German bases. In the Atlantic, German warships had to sneak past British air and naval bases to reach the oceanic convoys. In the north, the roles were reversed. The convoys and the Allied warships had to sail close to German bases. Furthermore, in the northern theater, German air and sea power could more effectively cooperate. Admittedly, German long-range reconnaissance aircraft could reach much of the northern Atlantic, but the Luftwaffe could not launch attacks of the magnitude displayed against PQ17. Also, the 24-hour daylight in the north, as well as relatively favorable weather, exposed the convoys to air attacks.

These circumstances forced the Allies to deal with three simultaneous threats: the air, surface forces, and submarines. Thus they faced a dilemma for which there seemed to be no solution. PQ17 had been dispatched to Archangelsk and Murmansk despite grave misgivings, and clearly the disaster meant that another convoy would not be sent soon. In fact, it was rather unlikely that major operations would again be conducted in the Arctic Ocean before the autumn.

While the German goal was to halt the Arctic convoys, the attainment of the goal was not without disadvantages. The performance of the naval units depended on more than just the technical characteristics of the warships. Crew proficiency was also very important, and long periods of inactivity reduced training standards. As the Germans were short of fuel, and Allied submarines patrolled the area off Norway, the former were reluctant to send the ships on exercises.

The Germans preferred to train in the Baltic where the narrow, shallow sounds between Jutland and Sweden prevented British warships from entering. Also, the Germans had created a mine barrier in the Gulf of Finland, which held Soviet naval forces at bay in Leningrad. However, safe as it was, a voyage from northern Norway to the Baltic still carried risks and depleted scarce fuel stocks. It was a realistic option only for longer periods of training. Finally, some seasoning could be conducted while the ships were moored, but it was no substitute for exercises at sea.

Considering the above situation, real operations were important to retain the proficiency of the crews, but the heavy German ships conducted very few of these. Even Rösselsprung was limited, and as it was prematurely aborted, many German Navy officers felt morale could suffer. As the top commanders appeared pusillanimous, the seamen might conclude that in a real combat situation, the chances of success were slim while the dangers were grave.

Undoubtedly the German naval forces in northern Scandinavia had to do something, but without undue dangers, as any risky plans might be vetoed by Berlin. The *Tirpitz* remained in Narvik, but on board the *Admiral Scheer*, plans for an unusual operation were prepared. She had probably sailed longer on the oceans than most other German warships.[352] In the autumn of 1940, she left Germany to operate on the Atlantic. Then she continued south and passed the Cape of Good Hope and proceeded into the Indian Ocean, where few German warships had sailed. The *Admiral Scheer* was about to enter yet another area seldom seen by German seamen.[353]

Already before PQ17 was attacked, Marinegruppe Nord had evaluated the possibilities of attacking Soviet shipping in the Kara Sea, i.e., the area east of Novaya Zemlya. German merchant ships had previously sailed these waters as recently as August 1940. They had reported on Soviet shipping, which suggested that worthwhile targets might be found, although they were not in any way decisive.[354]

The ice conditions were of paramount importance in the Kara Sea. The warm water of the Gulf Stream kept the Barents Sea free from ice during the summer, but the Kara Sea was different. Novaya Zemlya, two islands separated by the narrow Matochkin Strait, formed a barrier between the Kara Sea and the Barents Sea, making it difficult for the warm water to reach the former. Thus, much more difficult ice conditions were expected east of Novaya Zemlya. Furthermore, the Germans noted that conditions had varied considerably and unpredictably from year to year. To facilitate planning, two specially equipped fishing vessels were sent to investigate the ice. They would sail from a Norwegian port and take advantage of the frequent fog in late July and early August.[355]

The mission given to *Admiral Scheer*—called Operation Wunderland—would result in traveling very long distances. As the crow flies, the distance from Altafjord to the eastern Kara Sea is about 2,000 kilometers, almost identical to the distance from Altafjord to Iceland. Furthermore, the ice and the Novaya Zemlya would force the Germans to make detours. Destroyers could not accompany the mission, due to insufficient fuel capacity. Thus the original plan only included the *Admiral Scheer* and the *Lützow*, but as the latter went aground, it was decided to send the *Admiral Scheer* alone.[356]

In mid-August, the conditions were suitable for launching Operation Wunderland. On 10 August, a reconnaissance aircraft reported that ice conditions near Novaya Zemlya were favorable. During the following days, further aerial reconnaissance confirmed the initial report. Also, submarines were sent to the area. On 15 August, U-251 and U-456 left Harstad and Kirkenes to take up positions at the Kara Gate and in the Jugor Strait.[357]

On 7 August, the final plan for Wunderland was issued. The *Admiral Scheer* would sail with three destroyers, which would escort the heavy cruiser, but return to port before the squadron reached Novaya Zemlya. It was intended to sail north of the islands and proceed into the Kara Sea, where the *Admiral Scheer* would search for Soviet shipping. Thus the responsibility for Operation Wunderland mainly fell on the commander of *Admiral Scheer*, Captain Wilhelm Meendsen-Bohlken. As surprise was vital, radio silence would be enforced. Thus the commanders ashore would have very little information on which to base decisions. Only the commander on the spot would know the situation well enough to make tactical and operational decisions.[358]

When the *Admiral Scheer* and the three destroyers departed from Narvik on 16 August, the commanders ashore could no longer expect to control the course of events. Such a situation was not unusual, and they could only wait and see if some messages prompted a decision. When the destroyers returned two days later, their commanders could report that the first phase of the operation had proceeded according to plan. However, nothing would be heard from the *Admiral Scheer* for about a week.[359]

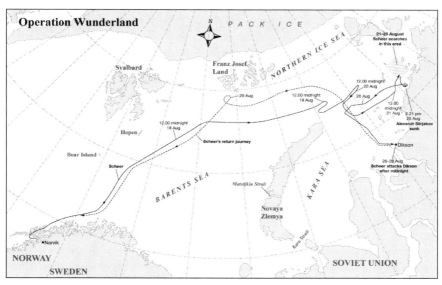

While the commanders waited ashore, the *Admiral Scheer* entered the Kara Sea. With every meridian she passed, the ice became more difficult. Not only did she encounter icebergs, the surface of the sea was sometimes frozen. Her seaplane was used to reconnoiter the ice, as well as search for enemy ships. In addition to the ice, dense fog presented difficulties. The sturdy construction of the ship proved valuable, but great caution had to be observed to avoid damage to the propellers. On one occasion the *Admiral Scheer* got stuck in the ice, but she reversed herself out of the precarious situation.[360]

On 25 August, the struggle against the ice was interrupted as another ship was sighted. It was the Soviet ice-breaker *Alexander Sibirjakov*, which defied the German call to stop her engines. The

warning shot fired by the *Admiral Scheer* was returned. Meendsen-
Bohlken decided to sink *Alexander Sibirjakov* immediately, but before
she went down, a radio signal was transmitted by the Soviet ship. Thus,
Meendsen-Bohlken feared that the operation had been disclosed. He
decided to attack the port of Dikson on the Tajmyr peninsula.[361]

Two days after the sinking of the Soviet ice-breaker, Dikson could
be discerned from *Admiral Scheer's* bridge. Meendsen-Bohlken allowed
his ship to close in on the port before opening fire. The port was
subjected to an intensive bombardment. Some Soviet batteries managed
to reply in earnest, although without damaging the German cruiser.
Two Soviet ships in the port were damaged before Meendsen-Bohlken
decided to break off the action. The German commander had
considered sending parties ashore, but due to the resistance from the
Soviet batteries, such plans were relinquished.[362]

After bombarding Dikson, Meendsen-Bohlken decided to set course
for Narvik. The *Admiral Scheer* initially sailed in a north-northwesterly direction, bringing her between Novaya Zemlya and Franz Josef
Land, before heading straight toward Narvik. On 30 August, she put in
at Narvik, thus ending the operation. She could not boast of any
significant success, but unlike the *Tirpitz's* crew, the men on the
Admiral Scheer had at least maintained their navigation skills and fired
their guns in anger.[363]

PQ18—The Battling Convoy

The lull that followed the PQ17 disaster gave the Germans time to conduct operations like Wunderland. However, at the beginning of September the tranquil period would soon come to an end. The British were again resolved to send convoys to the Soviet Union.

Undoubtedly, Luftflotte 5 contributed greatly to the German success against PQ17, but as the autumnal equinox drew near, air power would not be able to assert its dominance to the same extent. Obviously, the longer nights would hamper air operations, but unfavorable weather conditions for air power could be expected as well. This was a very significant change, but the Luftwaffe still remained a very serious threat to Allied warships and merchant vessels alike. To attain a reasonable chance of success, the Allies had to come up with some means to challenge German air superiority. It was decided to include the escort carrier *Avenger* in PQ18 and, in addition to this, British air units were deployed on the Kola Peninsula.[364]

Not only did the planning for PQ18 include strengthened air power, the surface forces would be used in a new way as well. The fundamental principle was to provide very strong defenses in the immediate vicinity of the 39 merchant ships that made up PQ18, which were accompanied by one rescue ship, three tankers, and three minesweepers. The close escort included two destroyers, two anti-aircraft ships, four corvettes, three minesweepers, four trawlers, and two submarines. Also there was a force called "Fighting Destroyer Escort," consisting of the cruiser *Scylla* and 16 destroyers. The aforementioned carrier *Avenger* had been

153

allotted two destroyers as protection. All these ships were presumed to keep close to each other. As had been the case with PQ17, there was a close cover force consisting of three heavy cruisers, and a distant cover force made up of the battleships *Anson* and *Duke of York*, as well as the cruiser *Jamaica* and five destroyers. Tovey had decided to stay at Scapa Flow on board the *King George V*. His second in command, Vice Admiral Fraser, exercised command over the distant cover force from the *Anson*.[365]

Previously, the east and westbound convoys had departed almost simultaneously and met between Jan Mayen and Bear Island, with the consequence that neither convoy was well protected in the Barents Sea. This time, QP14 would wait until PQ18 had almost reached Soviet ports. Thus the escort would follow the eastbound convoy almost to its destination, and then cover the westbound convoy. The scene was set for violent battles between the convoy and attacking German forces.

Of course the Germans monitored the British preparations, and aerial reconnaissance was an important source of information. On 6 September an aircraft reported many warships in Seidisfjord on the east coast of Iceland, including carriers, battleships, cruisers, and destroyers. Admiral Carls was of the opinion that the crew had seen a naval force assembled to cover a convoy bound for Murmansk or Archangelsk. His estimate was hardly controversial. On the following day another recon-naissance aircraft confirmed the observation.[366]

At this moment, the B-Dienst intercepted and decoded an important message. It revealed vital information on the PQ18, including its intended course. Thus the Germans could quite accurately estimate where the convoy would be at a given time. Also, the message allowed the Germans to conclude when QP14 would put to sea. This was useful information that helped the Germans plan for countermeasures. However, it also told them that these countermeasures would not be easy to implement, as the Allied plans and strong preparations would make it difficult for the Germans to attack with their surface ships. Already at this stage, Admiral Carls realized that air power and submarines would mainly conduct the German attacks.[367]

The recent information did not prompt Luftflotte 5 to make extensive preparations, as the air units could attack from their present bases. The submarines, on the other hand, needed time to take up suitable positions. Of the 15 U-boats available to the Germans, 10 were already at sea. The other five could, aided by the excellent intelligence mentioned above, put to sea in time to reach the designated positions.[368]

Late on 8 September, a Focke-Wulf 200 flew over the Denmark Strait in yet another of the innumerable reconnaissance flights conducted by the air forces in World War II. Usually they resulted in nothing, but this time the crew found a large number of ships, including a cruiser and four destroyers. The Germans could hesitate no longer. PQ18 had departed. From the available information, the Germans concluded that the convoy would reach Jan Mayen on 10 September.[369]

Despite their knowledge, the Germans would not score the first hit. On 12 September, as the convoy was not far from the southern tip of the Svalbard, the destroyer *Faulknor* located and sunk the German submarine U-88. However, on the following day the German U-boats avenged their loss by sinking two merchant ships: the Soviet *Stalingrad* and the American *Oliver Ellsworth*. Until then, fog, rain, and even snow squalls had prevented air attacks, but during 13 September the weather gradually cleared.[370]

Squadron Leader Werner Klümper commanded the I Gruppe of Kampfgeschwader 26, which was equipped with the torpedo version of the Heinkel 111. The unit had no commander when Klümper arrived in August 1942. Thus far the senior Staffel commander, Flight Lieutenant Eicke, had led the unit. On 13 September, PQ18 had reached sufficiently far east to be within proper range of German bomb and torpedo units. In the same way as the naval forces felt the lack of fuel, the air units were mostly grounded due to oil shortages. This had curtailed training as well. There was no doubt, however, that PQ18 would be attacked by air forces during the afternoon.[371]

Klümper's aircraft took off from Bardufoss and headed north.[372] The reconnaissance aircraft had provided good information on the speed and course of the convoy. Also, they had sent a homing signal at fixed intervals to enable Klümper's unit to easily find the convoy. However, for some reason, the signals were not received on the torpedo planes. Later, Klümper would learn that the plane shadowing the convoy had suffered technical problems, forcing it to turn home before a replacement could arrive. The torpedo planes were approaching at the very moment when no reconnaissance aircraft followed the convoy.[373]

The weather was far from ideal. Visibility was about ten kilometers, but a drizzle made it difficult to see. Plus, thick clouds as low as 800 meters made it problematic to find the convoy. Klümper led his unit on a course that would result in him passing behind the convoy without finding it. After a while, Klümper realized that his aircraft had flown too far north. He asked the radio operator if any homing signal could be heard, but the latter shrugged his shoulders and replied, "No signals."

Finally Klümper had to turn first south, then east. Suddenly a crewman yelled that he had seen a submarine. Klümper realized that the convoy could not be far away and soon it could be seen by the naked eye.[374]

Klümper wasted no time. He formed his unit for the attack, in two waves of 14 aircraft each. They would go in almost at a right angle to the convoy from starboard. When the German formation had completed its turn, it was met by a hail of fire from heavy anti-aircraft guns and medium artillery. Klümper's unit was flying almost at sea level, but the cascades from shells hitting the surface of the water forced his aircraft to climb to an altitude of 40–50 meters. Suddenly he became aware of aircraft behind him at an oblique angle. To his relief, the aircraft were German and belonged to the III Gruppe of Kampfgeschwader 26. They were also armed with torpedoes, but had taken off from Banak. Flight Lieutenant Klaus Nocken commanded the formation.[375]

As the reconnaissance had revealed the presence of a carrier in the convoy, Klümper issued a short but vigorous order: "All-out attack on the convoy, concentrate on the carrier."

The order was not as easy to implement as Klümper had hoped, since the Germans did not know where in the convoy the carrier was positioned. Neither could they spend much time searching for it, as the enemy would be allowed to prepare against the attack, for example by launching aircraft from the carrier. Thus the attack fell on the merchant ships and they suffered accordingly.[376]

On board the convoy, the lookouts observed the German aircraft with a combination of horror and admiration as they approached through the anti-aircraft fire on the starboard bow. The Allied ships had already survived several dive-bombing attacks, but it was clearly too early to rejoice. The commander of the convoy ordered a turn to starboard, hoping that the ships would thus present a smaller target area to the torpedoes. Unfortunately, only the ships in the left columns followed the order. The starboard wing continued on its original course when the German aircraft released their torpedoes at very short range. One German pilot flew so close that he must have misjudged his speed and range. Nevertheless, the ship he had chosen as a target was unlucky. Whether the German crew released the torpedo in panic or cold-blooded calculation will probably never be known. It left its mountings and entered a hatch on the American *Wacosta* without ever touching the water, exploding inside the ship. Though she sank quickly, several more explosions were heard. When the German torpedo aircraft turned away from the convoy, eight ships had been hit and damaged so badly they would eventually sink.[377]

Soon after the attack, Klümper's formation received an order to land at Banak rather than Bardufoss. All crews did not apprehend the order in time and Klümper's command became separated at two different air bases, but it was not a serious disadvantage. He lacked time to launch another attack on 13 September, and any problems could probably be solved before the following day.[378]

Further air attacks had been conducted on 13 September, but PQ18 fended them off without suffering further losses. The fighters launched from the *Avenger* played an import role. However, early on 14 September the tanker *Atheltemplar* was badly damaged by a torpedo fired from U-457, and eventually the British had to sink the stricken ship.[379]

Again the Admiralty suspected that the *Tirpitz* had put to sea. Reconnaissance flights had revealed that she was absent from her moorings at Narvik. Further reconnaissance showed that the cruisers *Admiral Scheer*, *Admiral Hipper*, and *Köln* were anchored, but no trace of the battleship was found.[380]

In fact, British fears were exaggerated. The *Tirpitz* was not operational during the first weeks of September, as her electrical power supply needed an overhaul. Thus, she had been undergoing repairs in Bogen Bay, but on 14 September she sailed for a short exercise to test the electrical system. Actually, the battleship needed more extensive maintenance, and she had been scheduled for a yard period during the winter of 1942–43, but in September Hitler decided that she would remain in Norway with repairs conducted there.[381]

The German surface ships did not threaten PQ18. Not only was the *Tirpitz*'s readiness limited, Hitler's unwillingness to risk the heavy ships remained. Rather, the main danger to PQ18 came from the air. As expected, Werner Klümper again led his unit in an attack on 14 September, and this time the emphasis on the carrier was even more pronounced. Other ships in the convoy would be regarded as secondary targets.

Klümper's Gruppe had 22 operational aircraft, slightly fewer than the previous day but still a considerable force. On 14 September, Klümper had to reckon with clear weather. Thus it would be easy to find the convoy, but on the other hand Allied lookouts could also see the German aircraft at long range and allow fighters to take off from the carrier. As the torpedo planes had to attack from very low altitude, the fighters did not have to spend time to climb.[382]

When Klümper's Gruppe had attained the desired formation after taking off from Bardufoss and Banak, the torpedo bombers steered toward PQ18. This time the homing signals worked properly. As the reconnaissance aircraft flew higher, Klümper's Gruppe could fly at sea level, making them hard to find on the radar. Soon Klümper could see smoke funneling out from the merchant ships. A few moments later, he saw a particularly large ship that sailed in the center of the convoy. He presumed it was the carrier and ordered his unit to conduct a pincer attack.[383]

The German aircraft formed two groups and maneuvered into position for attacking. The masts quickly grew taller while the pilots flew their aircraft a few meters above the sea, taking care to have the sun behind them.

Suddenly a shout was heard on the radio: "Attention! Enemy fighters twelve o'clock!"

Klümper presumed that the homing signal had been noted on the carrier, prompting the British to start fighters. Otherwise they would not have taken to the air in time. In any case, the British fighters appeared at a moment when Klümper's aircraft were very vulnerable. The formation adopted could result in numerous individual air combats, where the torpedo planes would be at a disadvantage. Hence, Klümper ordered his pilots to fly closely in groups of two or three aircraft, allowing them to support each other with fire.[384]

Suddenly Klümper made another disquieting discovery. The ship he had aimed for was not the carrier, but an unusually large freighter. Actually, the *Avenger* sailed farther back in the convoy, causing

Klümper to re-evaluate the situation. The planned massive attack was no longer feasible. He could choose to break off the attack and resume once the fighters were short of fuel, but his own aircraft were operating at the limit of their range. Also, more fighters might be launched from the carrier. Klümper decided to press home the attack despite the adverse situation. He instructed his crews on the change of target.[385]

Meanwhile, the *Avenger* had made a turn to port, while more Hurricane fighters dashed along the flight deck and took off into the clear air. Alongside the carrier, the destroyers *Wheatland* and *Wilton* opened up with all their guns against the approaching torpedo bombers. When the *Avenger* had sent ten Hurricanes into the air, she turned to position herself behind the convoy.[386]

The German attack was no longer coordinated, and Klümper would soon receive too much attention from the enemy to be able to command his unit. One of the fighters attacked his Heinkel, forcing the pilot to make an evasive turn. Another Hurricane joined the fight, and soon Klümper was separated from the other torpedo planes. His situation got even worse as he approached a destroyer while a third Hurricane closed in. Klümper remained cool, and ordered his pilot to turn alongside the destroyer at a distance of about 500 meters. The warship fired violently, but the Heinkel continued through the hail of fire. Bangs were heard as shrapnel hit the fuselage, but no vital parts of the aircraft were damaged. The British fighter pilots did not follow the Heinkel through the anti-aircraft fire from the destroyer.[387]

When the enemy fighters had been shaken off, Klümper directed his Heinkel toward the carrier, but the strong anti-aircraft fire forced him to release the torpedo at a range of one and a half kilometers at a dis-advantageous angle. After releasing the torpedo Klümper's Heinkel turned away, but to his disappointment the carrier, which could maneuver freely after temporarily leaving the convoy, evaded the torpedo. He subsequently learned that only one other Heinkel had actually attacked the carrier, also without scoring a hit. The other torpedo bombers attacked the merchant ships.[388]

The German airmen only scored one success. With an ear-splitting thunder, the freighter *Mary Luckenbach* blew up. Her cargo included over 1,000 tons of TNT, which disappeared in a gigantic explosion. An enormous flame shot up toward the sky, followed by thick, black smoke. The resulting pressure wave was violent enough to make the commander of an adjacent ship, the *Nathaniel Greene*, believe that his ship had been hit. As sailors were thrown onto the deck, hatches blown from their hinges, and debris, including anti-aircraft cartridges from the stricken ship, fell onto the Liberty ship. When another Liberty ship, the *William Moultrie*, which had sailed astern of the *Mary Luckenbach*, passed the area of the explosion, nothing remained. "No rafts, no wreckage—not even a ripple on the water."[389]

Klümper's attack had been costly. One aircraft in his unit was shot down and the crew killed, plus several more were damaged. Three Heinkels landed on the water at a safe distance from the convoy and the crews entered their rafts to be saved later. Two crews were indeed found by a German rescue aircraft, but the third was less fortunate. It was saved by a German submarine, which was sunk soon after. The airmen as well as the crew of the U-boat were killed. Finally, one Heinkel had only a single engine in working order after being hit, but it managed to almost reach the Norwegian coast. It landed on the sea, and the crew bailed out into a raft and were subsequently saved.[390]

Two days of fighting had taken a heavy toll on the German air units. Klümper's Gruppe (I./KG 26) had lost 12 machines, and Flight Lieutenant Nocken's Gruppe (III./KG 26) had lost eight. The British claimed to have shot down 28 torpedo planes, which was an exaggeration, especially considering that the German losses included aircraft that went down beyond British sight. However the Germans exaggerated too. Klümper reported that his unit had sunk three ships during 14 September, and other air units added four. In fact only one ship was lost—the unfortunate *Mary Luckenbach*—but the margin had been slight for many other freighters. Three Hurricanes had been shot down, all of them after receiving hits from the convoy's anti-aircraft guns.[391]

The following day, the men on PQ18 did not have to endure such fierce attacks as they had experienced the previous days. The German aircraft did indeed take off to attack the convoy, but when they reached it, thick clouds concealed most of the Allied ships. The Germans did attack, but in the adverse conditions they could inflict no losses. Attacking German submarines failed to score any hits either.[392]

In the evening on 15 September, the convoy had reached halfway between Svalbard and Novaya Zemlya. Thus it would gradually increase the distance to German airfields. In fact, PQ18 had reached so far east that the escort shifted to QP14 on the following day. With its 15 merchant ships, the latter had departed from Archangelsk on 13 September. For PQ18 the dangers were almost over. Only one other merchant ship was lost to a German air attack before the convoy reached its destination.

Like many previous westbound convoys, QP14 enjoyed favorable weather. During the critical days, very poor visibility prevented the German air units from attacking.[393] Thus the convoy only lost ships to German submarines, which sank three merchantmen, and on 20 September scored a hit on the destroyer *Somali*. She was badly damaged but remained floating. Her sister ship *Ashanti* towed the damaged vessel, but later on the same day a violent storm hit. The damaged destroyer was broken into two parts and sunk. Also, the U-boats sunk a tanker and one minesweeper.[394]

Undoubtedly such losses—together with the 13 ships lost by PQ18—were severe. This meant that almost one-third of the merchant ships in PQ18, along with one-fifth in QP14, were sunk. As the ships had to travel both to Archangelsk or Murmansk and back, an outcome like the one suffered by both convoys meant that the probability of a merchant ship surviving one voyage back and forth was little more than 50%. Considering that the escort put up stronger resistance than ever before, such facts were ominous.

This time, however, the German losses had also been heavy, and while PQ18 had suffered gravely, it had not been dealt such a crushing blow as PQ17. Furthermore as the dark winter was rapidly approaching, although the U-boats would find better conditions to operate, the German trump card—the Luftwaffe forces in northern Norway—would no longer be able to assert such a dominating influence. Other means would have to be used.

Therefore, only one additional card remained in the German deck: the heavy warships.

Shetlands-Larsen
and the Fishing Boat

The suspension of Arctic convoys during the summer did not adversely influence the preparations for Operation Title. On the day before PQ17 departed on its ill-fated journey, the Admiralty decided that the human

The fishing boat *Arthur* with her crew that was used in Operation Title.

torpedoes would be used to attack the *Tirpitz*. The proposal to bring the divers to the Norwegian coast by British warships had been turned down. Instead, it was intended to smuggle the sabotage group to the target on a fishing boat or freighter. Such a mission could only be entrusted to a very reliable person, as the Germans must be made to believe that the ship was genuinely Norwegian. After careful consideration, a man named Leif Larsen was chosen. He was a Norwegian patriot who had previously served the British, having brought agents to Norway from the Shetlands and delivered munitions to the resistance while reconnoitring the coast. He had already distinguished himself, and was asked if he would accept the mission to bring a new weapon to Norway. He was told that it was intended to attack the *Tirpitz*. Larsen—or Shetlands-Larsen as he was usually called—immediately accepted and was informed about the Chariot project. He was allowed to choose his crew, and by September 1942 he was fully involved in the detailed planning for Operation Title.

Initially, Larsen had to concentrate on finding reliable men who would accompany him on the mission. Among those chosen was Palmer Bjørnøy. He was a mechanic who had participated in several missions with Larsen, for example off Stadtlandet, when their ship was lost during mine laying. They had been forced to move by land a few days before reaching the small village of Gamlen, where Bjørnøy's parents hid them. They stole a smack, which had just arrived in the little harbour, and sailed back to the Shetland Islands. In addition to Bjørnøy, Larsen chose two reliable friends as seamen: Johannes Kalve and Roald Strand. The latter was not only an experienced seafarer but also a skilled radio operator.[395]

For the mission, the smack stolen by Larsen and Bjørnøy would be used. The small ship was called "Arthur." It was rebuilt to create a hidden nook between the engine room and the cargo compartment, where the British divers could hide. A door that could be locked from inside was concealed behind the electrical instrument panel. Other modifications included more powerful davits to handle the torpedoes. Also, a looped bolt was mounted under the keel, and two steel wires were attached to it to allow the torpedoes to be towed under the surface. At first, it was intended to tow the torpedoes all the way from the Shetlands, but the idea was abandoned. Rather, the warheads and the torpedoes would initially be stowed on the deck and in the cargo compartment. Off the Norwegian coast, the warheads would be fitted and then the complete torpedoes would be lowered into the sea and towed, almost invisible to prying observers on land. Hopefully, the water would be calm enough in the fjords. Finally, the divers would take over and maneuver the torpedoes during the final phase.[396]

Larsen and his men soon became acquainted with the Charioteers: the Scottish Lieutenant Percy Brewster, Sergeant "Shorty" Craig, and Corporals Robert Evans, Billy Tebb, "Slim" Brown, and Malcolm Causer. Brewster and Evans were Number Ones on the two torpedoes, with Tebb and Craig as Number Twos. Brown and Causer were included as mechanics and back-ups if something unforeseen occured.[397]

Before leaving the Shetlands, a large-scale exercise was conducted. The battleship *Rodney* assumed the role as target at Loch Broom, a river estuary on the Scottish west coast. In many ways the area resembled a Norwegian fjord. The exercise was conducted with the team chosen for the real mission. Fell supervised as if he had been a father caring for his child. The exercise proved a success. Off Ru Coigach, Larsen anchored *Arthur* in a small bay near Summer Isles. The warheads were fitted and the torpedoes lowered into the cold October water, where Brewster and Evans ensured that the Chariots were connected to the steel wires. For an observer standing on *Arthur's* deck or close to the small ship, the weapons could be discerned as nothing more than two grey shapes in the water. With this phase completed, Larsen weighed anchor and steered west toward the bay where the *Rodney* waited. [398]

At midnight, *Arthur's* anchor again broke the surface. Brewster, Evans, Tebb, and Craig put on their diving gear, which was tedious—even painful—with the diving suits used in those days. After completing the procedure, the four men moving clumsily on the deck resembled a combination of frogs and grotesque monsters. Fell gave them some final advice and then they went into the water. Soon they were no longer visible.[399]

From this moment, Larsen and his crew could only wait. The night was silent. Fell, the four Norwegians, and the two back-up divers knew that Brewster and the three others were under the keel, but it was impossible to hear them work. Only a few gleams in the water suggested that something was going on down there. Had the breathing apparatus emitted bubbles, the divers would have been much easier to discover. However, the equipment did not emit used air during a dive, despite the fact that the divers could be submerged for more than six hours.[400]

A ripple was seen on the surface a slight distance from *Arthur* as Evans and Craig mounted their Chariot, soon followed by Brewster and Tebb doing likewise. The two crews started the motors and appeared alongside *Arthur*. Brewster gave a thumbs up before the two teams disappeared into the darkness.[401]

As Larsen and the others on board the *Arthur* could no longer make any worthwhile contribution, they proceeded to Loch Broom, where the *Rodney* was moored and protected by three layers of nets. After the *Arthur* had anchored, Fell envisaged the two teams encountering the first torpedo net. The divers felt a kind relief when they reached the nets, as the unpleasant feeling of hanging weightless in the water, with perhaps 50 or 60 meters of darkness beneath, was replaced by a false sense of security when clasping the net. However, the divers knew they had to act quickly. With their special wire cutter they would force a passage through the nets and continue toward the target. During previous exercises, it had proved difficult to find the proper depth for placing the warhead on the hull. It had been attempted to approach close to the surface and then follow the hull down to the right depth, but that was time-consuming. The frogmen had also tried to close in on the target at great depth and then move upwards toward the keel, but such a procedure was dangerous. Finally, it was decided to approach at the same depth as the ship's draught until the Charioteers saw the shadow of the ship above.[402]

Several hours would elapse before the exercise ended, thus Fell, Larsen, and the others went to bed. While they slept, Brewster, Evans, and their assistants cut through all torpedo nets and attached the warheads to the *Rodney's* hull with magnets. The commander of the battleship had been informed of the exercise and positioned 17 extra lookouts, but none of them saw the Charioteers, neither before nor after the charges had been attached to the hull. Had it not been an exercise, the *Rodney* would probably have been sunk or severely damaged.[403]

The exercises with the *Rodney* continued for some time. Only once, when the clouds broke at the very moment one of the Chariot teams surfaced to take a bearing, did the lookouts observe the underwater attackers. In the second half of October, Fell considered the teams to be well prepared for the task. They were transferred to the Shetlands together with all their equipment. The final preparations were made on this group of islands. They concerned underwater navigation, the fabrication of false identity papers, and other documents needed to get *Arthur* through the German checkpoints. She would sail disguised as a fishing boat temporarily used to transport peat to Trondheim. The only major German checkpoint to pass was located at Agdenes at the entrance to the Trondheimsfjord, but German patrol boats might also endanger the operation. All documents were meticulously checked to ensure that no errors would arouse German suspicions, as were the details concerning escape after the mission was completed. *Arthur* would be sunk, as she could hardly be expected to go back the same route used to enter the Trondheimsfjord. Larsen and the others would have to contact the resistance and try to escape to Sweden.[404]

Only one major problem remained unsolved: the German battleship had not returned to Trondheim. At the end of October, however, she left Narvik and sailed south. Soon after midnight on 24 October, she moored again in the Fættenfjord, where she would be overhauled.

Operation Title could thus begin—and there was no time to lose.

After receiving the latest information on the *Tirpitz* from agents, air reconnaissance, and Ultra, Larsen and his crew weighed anchor on the morning of 26 October. Fell, on board the depot ship *Alecto*, greeted Larsen and his men as the *Arthur* sailed by. They barely heard him as the surging wind and the smack's thumping engine almost drowned Fell's words. The Charioteers, except Brewster who was in the wheelhouse, waved farewell. Some of them kept *Alecto* within sight, until the man who was one of the creators of the Chariot project was no more than a small dot against the pale superstructure behind him, reminding them of a vanishing period of education, training, and exercises.

Now this was all over.

Ahead of them lay Norway, the Trondheimsfjord, and the *Tirpitz*.[405]

"Have you any use for peats?"

Poor weather on the Norwegian Sea made the voyage more difficult than expected. To make matters even worse, the *Arthur*'s engine broke down and a sail had to be set while it was repaired. Plus most of those on board, even some of the Norwegians, suffered from seasickness. In short: none enjoyed the passage.

Late on 28 October, two days after leaving the Shetlands, the wind abated and the sea became dead calm. A few hours before this happened, distant land had been sighted. Larsen presumed that they were approaching a mountainous area near the small village of Bud, south of Kristiansund. The moon was not visible, and after enduring the harsh weather, the dark, silent night appeared unreal—almost uncanny. The dawn exposed a rocky coastline in the east, partly covered in white snow. This scenery attracted a very special interest from Causer. He was born in Brazil and had seen nothing like it before. The distant, shimmering summits absorbed him for a long time.[406]

Finally they reached a bay among a few smaller islands west of Edøy, where the torpedoes would be lowered into the sea and attached to the keel. Despite the fact that there were no significant sea lanes in the vicinity, Larsen ordered Kalve to keep a vigilant eye on the surroundings. As the procedure had been rehearsed repeatedly before the operation started, everyone knew what to do. The peat sacks were removed from the cargo compartment and the warheads brought forward. However, suddenly Kalve warned: "Aircraft!"

"Cover the torpedoes with the nets!" Larsen shouted. "Close the hatches to the cargo compartment!"

While the aircraft approached, the Norwegians quickly made *Arthur* look innocent again. Larsen and Bjørnøy pretended to work with the nets, while Kalve unzipped his pants and emptied his bladder into the sea. The British Charioteers were hidden below the deck. For awhile, it seemed that the German pilot had not observed *Arthur*, but then he banked and closed in. The four Norwegians remained unperturbed, but one of the frogmen, Billy Tebb, reacted. Believing that the enemy aircraft was about to attack, he dashed to the stern where a machine gun was hidden.

"What the hell!" Larsen burst out. "Stop, damned idiot!"

Larsen was not a man who raised his voice unnecessarily. Tebb froze in the middle of his movement and looked around sheepishly. The enemy aircraft, which was identified as a Messerschmitt Bf-109, passed ahead at an altitude of about 20 meters. The pilot seemed not to observe anything suspicious, but neither did he disappear from the scene. He began to conduct a serious of maneuvers, as if he wanted to impress the men on board the *Arthur*.

"Nobody moves," Larsen said, with his normal voice. "Behave as usual."

The German fighter lingered over the area for a long time. The men on board *Arthur* grew increasingly frustrated. The warheads could be prepared, but as long as the Messerschmitt remained above, no other work could be done. The men on board *Arthur* did their best to appear relaxed without looking indifferent. If they had ignored the German pilot completely, they might have aroused his suspicions. Hence, Larsen and the other men occasionally interrupted their apparent work and gazed at the aircraft, which dived, rolled, and banked. A few times the fighter seemed to fly away, but again the small aircraft appeared. When it finally disappeared, another German aircraft approached. However it passed ahead, seemingly on its way to a patrol area, and only took a brief look at the smack.[407]

When the sound of the last German aircraft had died down, it was already past 12.00 and the wind had increased. Worse, the sea became too rough for the men to lower the torpedoes into the water. Larsen decided to find shelter, and when they ventured farther into the bay, they found that the sea was calmer. Unfortunately, the anchor failed to get stuck and the boat drifted away. Finally, Larsen brought the anchor ashore and secured it in a cleft. By now, it was too late to initiate an attack. It was decided to try to get past the German checkpoint at Agdenes in the morning. To postpone further would jeopardize the mission, as the forged documents would be invalidated by a certain date.[408]

"We remain here for the night," Larsen decided. "You Britons have to sleep well. All your strength will be needed tomorrow."

At dawn another attempt to attach the torpedoes to the loop bolt was made. The warheads were fitted and the first Chariot was lowered, while Brewster and Evans jumped into the cold water. They checked the instruments and the electrical motor. Subsequently the second Chariot was attached to the davit and winched into the water. When both had been checked properly, the two divers attached the torpedoes to the loop under the keel.[409]

After the Chariots had been properly secured under the fishing boat, and the two divers had climbed aboard, the men felt they deserved a short break. However, Brewster and Evans had not yet got out of their diving suits when Bjørnøy warned: "Careful, a boat is approaching."

A rowboat with a man in it was indeed approaching, and undoubtedly heading for *Arthur*. Larsen hurried the British under deck. Soon the boat had reached *Arthur*. A grey-bearded old man sat in it, his clothes appearing to have experienced much wind and salt.

"Any luck, fishing?" Larsen asked when the rowboat thumped against *Arthur's* hull. The old man stood up and let his arms rest over the boat's gunwale.

He did not reply to Larsen's question. "Why have you anchored here?" he asked instead.

"We are fishermen," Larsen said. "We suffered engine problems and decided to anchor here for the night."

"And those are your nets?" The old man scrutinized the heap of nets, which had previously concealed the two torpedoes.

"Of course."

"What do you fish?"

Larsen gave some evasive answer, but the old man didn't seem to listen. Obviously, he was very curious and garrulous; nothing suggested he intended to leave soon. His eyes swept the fishing boat in search of something to comment on or ask about. Suddenly his eyes set on one of the ropes that ran across the gunwale and down into the water. "But what on earth …?"

While the old man grasped the rail and pulled his rowboat toward the stern, Larsen glanced at Bjørnøy. What were they to do? If the old man found the torpedoes, could they let him go? It would be far too risky. Even if he did not contact the Germans, he seemed to be the kind of person who used information as hard currency. How long would it take before the enemy became aware that something was going on? But to retain the old man on board *Arthur* was hardly a realistic alternative, especially since the German checkpoint at Agdenes remained to be passed. All the Norwegians carried a gun beneath their jerseys. Should they shoot a civilian to prevent him from revealing the mission?

The old man had reached the spot where the wire disappeared into the water. He pried to see if something peculiar could be found. He finally saw one of the steel wires that held the torpedoes in position and his eyes widened.

"Try to convince him that we work for the Germans," Bjørnøy hissed in Larsen's ear.

The old man raised his head and looked at them. "What are these used for?" he asked, and pointed to the water beneath the fishing boat.

Larsen decided to follow Bjørnøy's advice. "We use them for minesweeping," he said, and stepped closer to the old man.

"I see." He looked at them with an impenetrable look. "So you work for the Germans," he concluded.

"Yes," Larsen replied. He realized that the next few seconds would be decisive. It was impossible to guess with whose side the old man sympathized. Was he a patriot, pro-German, or simply a bored old man who wanted to chat? Under no circumstances could he be allowed to get on board *Arthur*. But how could they get rid of him?

They are not on board now?" the old man said, after once more gazing at the fishing boat. "I mean the Germans."

"Yes, they are asleep below," Bjørnøy replied. "They don't want us to wake them up."

The old man nodded. It seemed perfectly reasonable that the Germans slept, as it was still rather early. But with the latter statement, Bjørnøy had brought the discussion to a point of no return. If the old man insisted on talking to any alleged German, Larsen and Bjørnøy would have to take drastic action. However, something unexpected happened. "There is very little butter these days," the old man said. It was said in passing, but Larsen and Bjørnøy noted that the man carefully watched their reaction. Was this the reason the old man remained here and talked? To beg for butter?

"As you are with the Germans," he continued, "you do perhaps have some?"

"Yes, of course." Larsen turned to Bjørnøy. "Go and get some butter."

Bjørnøy disappeared below deck, while Larsen began to ask the old man about his family and where he lived. It turned out that he lived alone, but his daughter was married and lived in a nearby cottage. Larsen had hardly begun to ask questions before a torrent of information flowed from the grey-bearded man. Bjørnøy came back with a packet of butter. The old man thanked them repeatedly while his eyes were riveted on the packet. He continued to talk about his life, but suddenly Larsen interrupted: "Now I want you to stop this chatter!" he said. "You have told us enough for us to find you, if your mouth would ever betray what you have seen here."

As if struck by something, the old man's face turned white. "I won't utter a word," he assured.

"Now, if you do," Larsen continued, "the German police will arrest you and your daughter within a few hours. You'll both be shot! Is that clear?"

The old man nodded.

"So get away and remember what I have said!"[410]

The old man rowed away far more energetically than he had approached. Hopefully he would not immediately tell anybody what he had seen, and if he believed that Larsen and his men worked for the Germans, he would hardly go to them first. In any case, Operation Title would be completed—or failed—before any talk from the old man could jeopardize it.

When the old man had finally disappeared, *Arthur* was carefully checked to remove anything suggesting she had come from Britain. All evidence on where she had been was put in a bag and thrown into the water. Even the radio was thrown overboard. The machine gun was removed from its mountings and stowed in the secret compartment, along with the diving suits, rucksacks, and provisions for the subsequent escape to Sweden.[411]

At 14.00 *Arthur* weighed anchor and soon passed south of Smøla, bearing east-northeast toward Trondheimsleia. The wind was slight and the sea calm. On a few occasions they passed other ships, some armed and with the German flag hoisted. The Charioteers stayed in the secret chamber, except for some brief periods at the helm by Brewster. It was already late in the afternoon when Bjørnøy appeared from the engine room with a troubled face. Something was wrong with the engine. At first it had been a barely discernible, discordant sound, but then it began to smoke and run unevenly. Initially Bjørnøy believed some water leak had developed that could be fixed quickly, but soon he realized that it was a serious problem, probably a damaged piston. If the problem were not attended to, the engine would shut down completely. Bjørnøy and Larsen discussed the situation. If they continued toward the Trondheimsfjord, the engine might seize before they reached it. If that happened, a German patrol boat would soon arrive. However, without spare parts, they could not repair the engine. Should they take a chance and hope that the engine did not stop? After all, *Arthur* would not leave the fjord after the attack.[412]

Larsen decided to try to repair the engine. The British had provided him with a number of alternatives in case something like this happened. In the nearby village of Hestvika, Nils Strøm, who ran a general store, had connections to the resistance, in particular a man called Sørli. The harbor was located on the eastern side of Hitra, not far from *Arthur's* present position. Larsen decided to proceed to Hestvika. For a moment he considered shutting down the engine and raising sail, but on second thought he realized that such a measure might attract the Germans' attention.[413]

Smoke belched from the engine when they reached the harbor. Only a few hours remained until midnight, but a surprising number of people were still out in the streets. *Arthur* anchored and Larsen brought Kalve ashore. They were informed that there had been a market in the village and the last visitors were returning home. When they asked how to find Strøm's general store, they were fortunate to chance upon this man's own son. Larsen told him they were in acute need of necessities, and asked the young lad if he thought his father might help. They went to the store, where Strøm was still awake. When they entered, Larsen used the secret password, disguised as an innocent question: "Have you any use for peats?"

It had been agreed that the proper answer was that he had a sufficient amount, but instead Strøm exclaimed happily: "Peats? Of course, I take all you have."

Larsen was speechless for a few seconds. Had they met the wrong person? Were there two general store owners named Strøm in Hestvika? It seemed unlikely. Probably the choice of password was simply inexpedient.

"Well, I have some," he said finally. "But most of my cargo is destined for Sørli, thus you can't get all of it."

By mentioning the name of the resistance contact, Larsen hoped the tradesman would comprehend, but he showed no sign of understanding. He frowned: "Do you mean Andreas Sørli from Orkanger? Why does he need peats?"

"No, I mean *Odd Sørli* from Trondheim."

For a moment Strøm stared at Larsen, then he realized the connection: "Yes, of course," he said and offered his hand. "How stupid of me. You are the man Sørli told us might come here from Britain."

Larsen informed him of their precarious situation. Nils Strøm and his son followed Larsen to *Arthur*, where Bjørnøy had partly disassembled the engine and concluded that a piston was indeed damaged. Strøm suggested that they ask the village smith for help. When they returned to the village, the streets had become empty. All was silent, save the occasional snoring. Finally, they reached the house. No lights showed behind the curtains, so apparently the smith and his family were already asleep. Strøm's son tossed some gravel to rattle one of the windows. After awhile, it was opened and a sleepy face appeared. "Oh, is it you Strøm?" the smith asked. "What's going on?"

The smith needed two hours to repair the damaged piston. Meanwhile the others waited patiently, and Larsen took the opportunity to compare his forged papers with Strøm's, who also owned a boat. It was reassuring. Once back on *Arthur*, Bjørnøy assembled the engine and confirmed that it would at least keep them moving until they reached Trondheim. As *Arthur* would be subsequently sunk, that was sufficient.

After bidding farewell to Strøm and the others, Larsen and his crew sailed toward Agdenes on the Trondheimsleia.[414]

To repair the engine in the midst of an enemy-occupied country was a feat by the Norwegians that deeply impressed the six Charioteers. However, the most dangerous part had yet to come. At Agdenes they would encounter the enemy face to face, and afterwards it would be their turn to act with skill and bravery. To avoid further engine problems, they proceeded at half speed. At one moment a German patrol boat passed, but did not order a halt. As the Germans had mined the sea near Agdenes, Larsen stayed close to the coast. They saw several German pickets, but none paid any attention to the lone fishing boat.[415]

Soon they approached the fort at Agdenes, which controlled the entrance to the Trondheimsfjord. The Germans had positioned a trawler converted to a patrol boat next to the fort. No boat was allowed to pass unless it had berthed near the trawler and all papers had been checked. The Charioteers were already hidden in the secret compartment, where they had also placed the machine gun. Brewster was asleep, as he had not slept for almost 48 hours. Only Larsen, Bjørnøy, Kalve, and Strand remained on deck.

"Warn the British," Larsen told Bjørnøy. "They may not cause any kind of sound. Only if they hear shooting are they allowed to leave the hiding place."

Bjørnøy disappeared. Larsen checked that his pistol was ready to use and tucked it in the shoulder holster under his left arm. The waves told him the wind had abated. Unfortunately, that would make the torpedoes easier to observe. Kalve realized the danger too: "The damned wind is dying," he warned. "Even a blind man can see the torpedoes."

Arthur chugged into a portion of the fjord were the water was calm and clear, as if it were a mirror. Larsen saw how the fishing boat attracted the attention of German seamen. A few of them leaned over the trawler's rail and waited. The Norwegian had to maneuver skillfully. If he reduced speed too suddenly, the torpedoes would continue forward and appear in front of *Arthur*. On the other hand, if he approached too slowly, it might appear suspicious.

"When we slow down, they will protrude," Kalve said, as if he had read Larsen's mind. "And we can not flee or cut the wires."

"We shall not cut any wires," Larsen replied firmly, and gradually backed off on the throttle. "Go to the bow and prepare to throw a hawser."

Bjørnøy returned and took over the helm. Larsen cautioned him against reducing speed too abruptly before bringing the forged papers to the bow, where Kalve waited with a rope. The German trawler's freeboard was slightly higher than that of *Arthur*. Thus, the Germans would look down. A single glance on the water might reveal the Chariots. Fortunately, the Germans seemed more apprehensive about the action on *Arthur's* deck.

"Guten Morgen!" Larsen yelled in an attempt to attract the German's attention. The sailors at the gunwale hardly seemed to care, and the officer on deck talked to some person half-concealed from Larsen. Gradually, the distance between the two boats shrank. Soon, *Arthur* would be alongside the German trawler and the danger would be temporarily over. The German sailors still looked at the Norwegians on the deck, calmly chatting to each other.

All but one.

The young seaman who was to receive Kalve's hawser waited for *Arthur* to come close enough, so he could catch the rope. Daydreaming, his eyes roved absent-mindedly on the surface of the water. Suddenly his eyes became fixed on a point beneath the fishing boat's keel. He strained his eyes, as if he could not make up his mind on what he saw. Then he turned to a comrade nearby, intending to make a comment on something.

At this very moment Kalve threw the rope, which hit the youngster's head and partly fell on his neck. He twitched, as he realized he might be pulled into the water if he did not act, and tore off the hawser. The other Germans began to laugh, but the young lad was not amused. He handed the rope to another seaman and walked away, his pride injured. Larsen and the other Norwegians sighed with relief when he disappeared. They would never know if the youngster had seen the torpedoes, but if he had, the incident with the hawser had saved them.[416]

The gap between the two ships closed. With laughter still in the air, the German officer jumped aboard *Arthur* with a briefcase in his hand. Larsen met him and tried to hand over the documents, but the officer paid no attention to them. Rather, he strolled around and observed carefully. He halted briefly and looked at Bjørnøy in the wheelhouse before continuing astern, asking Larsen to follow him into the cabin abaft. Once inside, he sat down on a bunk and picked up some documents from his briefcase before receiving the identity and registration papers Larsen handed to him.

The German placed the documents on the table and carefully

studied them. He made an occasional note and murmured slightly, almost as if he intended to make the procedure last longer. Seconds turned into minutes, but Larsen did not want to look at his watch. He estimated that the German had studied the documents for about ten minutes. Had he found something strange, some oversight by Larsen or the British intelligence service?[417]

"Do you have your permit for this journey?" the officer asked peremptorily.

Larsen handed him the document. "Here it is."

"Good." The German seemed to relax. "I see that you come from Kristiansund," he said. "You don't happen to know my friend Captain Ormann, the harbor master?"

The question was asked politely, but could it be a trap? Larsen knew that the harbor master's name was Ormann—he had seen as much on the forged documents—but would an affirmative reply lead to more questions? Also, if he waited too long, it might arouse suspicion.

"Yes," he said hesitantly, as if he had to search his memory.

"We were born in the same town and went to school together," the officer said. "And how capricious is not war. We were both inducted into the Navy Reserve and sent to the same area."

Larsen nodded and tried to look as if he found this aspect of the war particularly notable. He did not want to become too amicable, nor did he want to annoy the officer. The German continued to talk about how tragic the war was, yet inevitable as the Germans had to protect Norway from an Allied attack. Meanwhile he picked up a form from his briefcase, made some notes, and finally said: "Here is your permit. Give it to the harbor master at Trondheim when you arrive."

"Thank you."

They strode out on the deck, where the other Norwegians waited nervously. At least 15 minutes had elapsed since Larsen and the German had entered the cabin, and the rest of the crew had feared the worst.

When the officer again felt his men watching him, his overbearing manner returned.

"Your cargo includes peats," he said. "Open one of the bags."

Larsen untied the bag the officer had pointed at and some peats fell out. "Shall we open more?"

The German shook his head. He was no longer interested in the bags, and only took a quick look at the engine room. He did not even set his eyes on the entrance to the secret compartment where the British divers silently listened. After a brief farewell, he jumped onto the trawler and waved to Larsen that he could continue his voyage.[418]

Arthur began to move and it wasn't long before she entered the Trondheimsfjord. Larsen told Kalve that the Charioteers could come out from the hideout, but they should not come on deck as yet. The wind increased once more as they rounded the mountain Rødberget. Larsen sailed near the northern shore to find some shelter. Twilight set in and Brewster walked into the wheelhouse. The Charioteer had slept heavily until only a moment earlier. He did not even wake up at Agdenes when the German officer was on board.

"There is Trondheim," Larsen said and nodded southeast, where more and more lights began to twinkle through the darkness.

"No blackout here," Brewster said. He could even discern the two towers of a church in the city.

"Yes, there is," Larsen said, "but the Germans don't strictly enforce it."[419]

The fishing boat continued in the night on an easterly course. Soon they would be able to see the German battleship with their naked eyes. Brewster told Evans and Craig to put on their diving equipment, and Tebb and Causer came to their assistance. At the same time the sea became rougher and Larsen reduced speed, to prevent the divers from becoming seasick. Brewster became impatient when Evans and Craig did not appear. He and Brown also went to the hideout to prepare.

In the wheelhouse, Larsen grew increasingly concerned when he saw high waves hit the bow and wash over the deck, but to wait another night was unthinkable. The attack had to be made very soon, as it was very risky to wait near Trondheim in daylight. Thus, the Charioteers would have to begin their mission in the night, but could they disconnect the torpedoes in these very difficult conditions?

At this very moment a loud thud was heard. Larsen, as well the men below deck, became petrified. They listened nervously. The sound had to be caused by the torpedoes bouncing against the keel. The boat rose and fell in the sea, and again a thud was heard … and again.

Larsen was first to realize what was happening. When *Arthur* moved upwards in the waves, the wires attached to the torpedoes were stretched. When she fell down again, the wires slackened and the torpedoes collided with the keel, resulting in the thuds. The wires might break at any moment. Larsen's worst fears soon came true. A strange sound, resembling an iron pipe pushed against a rotating saw blade, suddenly vibrated through the fishing boat. The engine sounded as if it were about to die.[420]

Larsen realized that one Chariot had come loose and hit the propeller. He backed off on the throttle and was awarded with a smoother sounding engine. When it ran properly again, he gave it more throttle and then made alternate turns to port and starboard. As he knew how *Arthur* moved in the water with the torpedoes beneath the keel, he could feel that the Chariots were gone.

The door to the wheelhouse flew open and Brewster stormed in, closely followed by the others. A quick glance at Larsen sufficed to confirm their fears. "Possibly one of them still remains below the keel," Larsen said, "but I fear that this is not the case. As soon as we find shelter in a bay, one of the divers will have to go down and check."

To realize that all their efforts—including many months of training, the hazards on the Norwegian Sea, the nocturnal adventure to repair the engine, and the bluff at Agdenes—had been wasted was almost unbearable to the men in the creaking wheelhouse. They stared at each other's blank faces. They didn't even curse—it was pointless. They had made it this far and yet, with only ten kilometers remaining, they had lost. "You will have to go down and see if any of them remain," Brewster said to Evans, who sat on one of the bunks and stared into empty space. "Keep the suit on."[421]

However, there was little hope that the torpedoes remained, and now there was the question of what to do next. According to the plan, four divers would make the actual attack, while the Norwegians and the two remaining divers sank *Arthur* and rowed ashore in the rubber dinghy. They would all gather in a deserted hut near Vikhammar, where members of the Norwegian resistance would help them toward Sweden.[422]

As the torpedoes were lost and the dinghy was too small for ten men, particularly in the rough weather, a new decision had to be made. It was not realistic to make more than one trip with the dinghy. Neither could *Arthur* return on the route it had followed. They had no papers showing that the peats had been delivered in Trondheim.

Finally, Larsen decided that they should proceed to the strait between the island Tautra and the mainland near Frostaland. The water was deep enough to sink *Arthur* so close to the coast that they could make two trips with the dinghy. Of course, no members of the resistance would wait for them there, but it was the best available option.

It turned out that Larsen's judgement was correct. When they reached Tautra, Evans dived below the keel and saw that the steel wires were still there, together with the weights that would prevent the torpedoes from surfacing. As expected, none of the Chariots remained, only the steel rings which attached to the wires. Meanwhile, Kalve rowed ashore with Brewster, Bjørnøy, Strand, Causer, and Brown before returning to *Arthur* with the dinghy. When Evans had emerged from the water and had been helped on board, he was assisted with removing his diving gear. Meanwhile, Shetlands-Larsen steered *Arthur* on her final and very brief voyage.[423]

It was midnight and the wind had abated. The very short gale had, with a kind of cruel irony, decisively helped the Germans to overturn the operation. Neither the enemy's vigilance nor security measures or weapons had done it. Instead, an unforeseeable twist in the weather had ruined the whole enterprise. The *Tirpitz* would still be there, tying up Allied resources much better employed elsewhere.

No German patrol boats could be seen as Larsen turned off the engine in the sound. All equipment not easily portable was left on the boat. He drilled a hole in the bottom with a specially designed drill, opened the valves, and came up on deck, where the three Charioteers waited. They climbed down into the dinghy and Kalve began to row ashore. They watched *Arthur* gradually sink deeper, until she finally disappeared about a kilometer from the coast.[424]

The adventures were far from over for the men who had departed from the Shetlands on board the *Arthur*. They had to find their way to Sweden, an episode largely outside the theme of this book, but one event is worth mentioning. To avoid attracting the Germans, Larsen divided the men into two groups: the first being himself together with Tebb, Craig, Evans, and Kalve, and Brewster and the others in the second. Both groups made it to Sweden, but Larsen's group encountered difficulties when they tried to cross the border near Sandvika on the night before 3 November. It had begun to snow and the men were frozen and wet, in particular Evans, who did not endure the climate as well as the others. When they reached a small village, they decided to find some shelter.

"Halt!"

Two armed men blocked their way. One of them wore a dark uniform and was probably German. The other was dressed as a civilian and talked Norwegian. They had been hidden in the shadow of a building.

"Who are you?" the Norwegian asked—apparently a Quisling, or a native in German service. "Where are you going?"

"Who is asking?" Larsen replied.

"Shut up!" the Norwegian shouted. His voice revealed that the situation made him just as nervous as Larsen and the others. However, the German calmly raised his weapon. Undoubtedly, he would use it if needed.

"I ask the questions here," the Norwegian continued. "Put down your sticks and raise your hands."

Larsen and his companions did as they were told. They had previously provided themselves hiking sticks. Unfortunately, all of them except Tebb had handed over their weapons to a group of Norwegians who had provided assistance. It now proved to be a mistake. If they had all been armed, they had stood a good chance of shooting themselves out of the difficult situation. Now they were at a clear disadvantage. The three British would become prisoners of war, and Larsen and Kalve could only expect a firing squad.

The Norwegian pointed at one of the lanes between the houses. "Forward march!"

They began to walk in the direction indicated with Larsen and Tebb ahead, and Craig, Evans, and Kalve behind. The Norwegian and the German followed a few meters after them, their Luger pistols cocked. As the group neared the corner of the first house, Tebb whispered: "I'll shoot those square-heads. When we round the corner, throw yourself to the ground." It was desperate, but perhaps it was their only chance.

"Good idea," Larsen responded.

A few seconds later they reached the corner of the house, which momentarily concealed Tebb. He fumbled inside his jacket, found the butt, and whirled around to shoot. Larsen, Craig, and Kalve hunkered down or jumped aside. The surprised Evans seemed not to have heard the whispering, as he remained between Tebb and the two enemies when the first shot was fired. In his haste, Tebb missed and the enemies fired two shots. One bullet hit Evans when he instinctively turned away from Tebb's pistol.

A few more shots were heard and people moved in the darkness. The German clasped at his stomach and sank down. Kalve headed for a nearby grove, and the Quisling fled too. He jumped into a ditch next to the road and a few seconds later he was lost in the swirling snow. Larsen and the remaining British had also retired from the scene of the shooting.

"I believe I killed the guy with the uniform," Tebb said, as he saw his victim lying motionless on the road.

"Where is Kalve?" Craig wondered.

"Don't worry about Johannes," Larsen said. "I saw him run into the woods. How is Evans?"

"I am afraid he is dead," Craig replied. "Shall we go back and check?"

Larsen quickly assessed the situation. They did not know where the Quisling was. He was probably far away, but nevertheless he might be lurking nearby. "No, if Evans is wounded he cannot make it across the Swedish border, even with our help," he replied. "Also, the Germans have been alerted now. We have to leave before it is too late. If Evans is still alive, they will take him to a hospital."[425]

Larsen and his men walked east. They made a few subdued calls to see if Kalve heard them, but nothing happened. They went back to the road to Sandvika and tried to reach the border as quickly as possible, despite the risk of being seen from a car. When a small bridge was reached, they believed that the German frontier station was near. Thus they chose to continue on a small road which was rarely used. It ran east and led the exhausted men into Sweden by morning, where they subsequently reunited with Kalve.

They had been wrong about Evans. He had only been wounded, and when the Germans found him he was brought to a hospital where his life was saved. However, his respite turned out to be short. The Gestapo interrogated him until they knew all about the Chariot project and Operation Title. Unfortunately, in early 1943, he was shot on orders from Field Marshal Keitel.[426]

Thus ended the enterprise called Title, yet another operation that failed despite extensive preparations. In all fairness, the ten men who conducted the mission, or those who made it possible, can hardly be blamed for its failure. Had the two Chariot teams been able to maneuver their crafts in the water, they might very well have severely damaged the *Tirpitz*, maybe even sunk her.

Instead, a brief change of weather and a weakness in the mountings of the torpedoes had upset the entire project.

The Shifting Balance

For the people caught up in the turmoil of World War II, the real turning point may not have been so easy to distinguish. However, aided by hindsight, the last quarter of 1942 has often been regarded as a period when the fortunes of war changed, and indeed, after September 1942, the Axis powers experienced diminishing success on all fronts. In the Far East, the Japanese offensive had largely lost momentum after the summer 1942. On the steppes of southern Russia, the Germans had advanced rapidly toward the Volga and Caucasus, but after September 1942 only minor gains were made. Similarly, in North Africa, Erwin Rommel had been promoted to field marshal after capturing Tobruk and dashing into Egypt, but by September 1942 he had firmly been forced onto the defensive. Clearly the German offensives were hampered by a lack of fuel, a problem also suffered by the Kriegsmarine. The German oil shortages had been a major factor behind Hitler's decision to direct his forces toward the Soviet oil fields in the Caucasus area, with the seizure of Stalingrad, for flank protection, an essential component of that plan.

While the German offensives reached their high tide, the Allies prepared their own campaign in the Mediterranean. Despite losses on the Atlantic, the Western Powers had assembled forces large enough to launch main operations, although not as extensive as the Americans had hoped. They had intended to attack the European continent, but instead somewhat less ambitious plans were developed. Rommel's forces in Egypt would be attacked, and the French possessions in northern Africa would be assaulted from the air and sea. According to these plans many warships, as well as merchant ships, would be needed. Thus, PQ18 was not immediately followed by another convoy.

At the end of September, the Germans could not know when the next Arctic convoy would be dispatched. During a conference on 28 September where Hitler discussed naval matters, the experiences from the attacks on PQ18 were not even mentioned. Rather, the U-boat war on the Atlantic received the attention. Of course, Hitler may have discussed the warfare in the Arctic at meetings where minutes were not taken, but nevertheless, it seems the Germans did not consider any significant changes to their efforts to halt the Arctic convoys based on the experiences gained when PQ18 sailed through the Barents Sea.[427]

The notes made by Admiral Carls in the Marinegruppe Nord war diary also support the notion that few changes were introduced by the Germans after the PQ18 episode. He observed that the very strong escort inflicted palpable German losses, but there were no quick fixes to that problem. Strong enemy resistance would inevitably result in higher losses in the naval and air units. However, as the reported losses inflicted were almost always exaggerated, the commanders might have been led to believe that the fighting was more successful than it actually was.[428]

The Germans had clearly noted the strong escort protecting PQ18 and QP14. In a report dated 24 September, it was concluded that the strong escort would make it virtually impossible to attack with surface ships—at least as long as the imposed restrictions remained in force. The latter was a barely-disguised criticism of Hitler's decision not to allow the warships to be used except in very favorable circumstances. A couple of options that remained included attacking lightly-escorted convoys and using mines.[429]

After the actions against PQ18 and QP14, all U-boats were withdrawn from the Arctic Ocean. It was intended to make them ready for simultaneous attacks on a new series of convoys. Possibly, the strong escort had prompted the Germans to make a massive effort, but a prerequisite was good intelligence. Marinegruppe Nord asked for reinforced air reconnaissance in areas deemed to be particularly important.[430]

The German commanders responsible for operations against the Arctic convoys would soon have to contend with diminishing resources. Events in other theaters would enforce changes. Klümper's torpedo bombers would never again attack Arctic convoys, as his unit was transferred to the Mediterranean, where German fortunes were rapidly waning and reinforcements were sorely needed. Furthermore, as the weather and visibility in the northern theater would rapidly deteriorate, such a move is understandable. The only torpedo-armed aircraft to remain in northern Norway were the He-115 seaplanes. Also, about one half of Kampfgeschwader 30 were withdrawn, thereby significantly reducing the number of bombers.[431]

Not only did several air units leave northern Norway, but the deteriorating situation elsewhere would force the Germans to send replacements, spare parts, and new aircraft elsewhere, thus making it more difficult to replace any future losses suffered by the air units of Luftflotte 5. Consequently, other components of the German armed forces would have to assume the main responsibility for halting the Allied convoys to Murmansk and Archangelsk.

The attempts by the German Army to conquer Murmansk or the railway running south of the port had long ago gotten stuck. Due to the very poor roads in the area, it was impossible to send stronger ground forces in a renewed attempt to reach the alluring Kola port. Also, German ground combat units were desperately needed elsewhere. Only one component of the German armed forces remained to be considered: the Kriegsmarine.

The German Navy, however, had its fair share of problems. One of those was numbers. As we have seen, the *Lützow* ran aground during Operation Rösselsprung. She was transferred to Germany for repairs in August, but several months would elapse before she could serve again. Several other large German warships were in shipyards too. The *Prinz Eugen*, which had been hit by a torpedo in February, was among these. Her repairs would be completed in autumn, but the long period of inactivity had reduced the proficiency of her crew. Thus a period of training was required before she would again be fully serviceable. Similarly, the *Scharnhorst* had been repaired after the mine damage she had sustained during the Channel Dash, but she would not be fully operational until early 1943. Even some of the light cruisers were unavailable. *Emden* was undergoing repairs, while the remaining light cruiser, *Nürnberg*, was in the Baltic. The latter would not be transferred to Narvik until December 1943.[432]

Evidently, few ships could be transferred to Norway in the dark autumn period of 1942, so the Germans had to make do with what was already there. The *Admiral Scheer* and *Admiral Hipper* had been in Norway for several months. In July, the light cruiser *Köln* had also been moved there. The *Tirpitz* remained in Narvik, even though the situation changed to some degree during the autumn when the battleship, as well as the *Admiral Hipper*, were both moved to Trondheim during the night of 23–24 October. Of course, from Trondheim the two fast ships could still attack convoys—Operation Nordmeer had been a striking example of that—but during the winter 1942–43, maintenance work would be conducted on the *Tirpitz*, thus reducing her operational readiness.[433] On top of all else, the *Admiral Scheer* would soon be transferred to Kiel for maintenance, thereby further reducing the number of German warships available in the northern theater. In short, the outlook for strong sorties comprised of German heavy ships was not overly promising.

However, as no convoys were sent to Russia, the low number of German heavy ships in Norway mattered little. One convoy consisting of 28 ships, the QP15, was sent from Archangelsk on 17 November. It was hit by a series of storms which scattered the convoy, and the visibility was so poor that even the escorting warships were hard put to find the merchantmen. Thus the Germans could hardly find them either, although two Allied vessels were lost to U-boats.[434]

The Germans couldn't know it at the time, but QP15 was the last of the PQ/QP series of convoys. The next convoy dispatched to Murmansk would be known as JW51. It sailed from Loch Ewe at the end of December, while a convoy called RA51 was sent in the opposite direction. At this stage, the Allied hold on Algeria and other areas in North Africa was solid enough to reduce the need for escorting warships, allowing resources to be used on the Arctic convoys.[435]

During the planning for the next pair of convoys, Tovey insisted upon sending smaller groups. He argued that the threat from the air was much smaller than before, as fewer German air units were based in northern Norway, and the fact that the sun did not rise above the horizon during the winter days also reduced the efficiency of those that remained. As the *Tirpitz* was not fully operational, the threat from German surface ships was reduced as well. Hence, the convoys would mainly contend with U-boats and severe weather. As storms were very common, the convoys risked breaking up. Tovey believed that a small convoy would be easier to keep together than a large one.[436]

These arguments resulted in a decision to split JW51 into two convoys: JW51A and JW51B. When it sailed from Loch Ewe, JW51A consisted of 15 merchant ships, one tanker, seven destroyers, and five smaller vessels. The weather and darkness provided good cover. The war diary of Luftflotte 5 is dominated by comments on weather preventing reconnaissance over the sea. Virtually all air missions were directed at targets on land, in ports, or very close to the coast. JW51A was not found by the Germans and safely reached Murmansk on Christmas Day 1942.[437]

The JW51B was not so fortunate. The weather remained a major hindrance to German reconnaissance when the ships sailed one week after JW51A. On 28 December, however, a storm hit the convoy. Two escort ships and five of the 14 merchant ships were separated from the other vessels. When the storm had abated, the minesweeper *Brumble*, one of the two radar-equipped ships in the convoy, was sent to search for the missing ships. Initially, her efforts produced no results, but she continued to search while the remainder of the convoy continued toward Murmansk.[438]

By now, the Germans had learned that Allied convoys were sailing in the Barents Sea and decided to act. The *Admiral Hipper* and *Köln* had been joined in the Altafjord by the recently repaired *Lützow* and five destroyers. The light cruiser *Nürnberg* and a destroyer were in Narvik, while the *Tirpitz* and three destroyers remained at Trondheim. However, due to the maintenance work, the battleship would not be ready for action until January 1943. Hitler still emphasized the threat of an Allied attack on Norway, which affected his decisions on where the German warships were located. Consequently, hardly any ships except those in the Altafjord would be called upon to attack JW51B.[439]

The fuel shortage still hampered the Germans. Another factor to consider was Raeder's intention to send the *Lützow* into the Atlantic for ocean warfare. Nevertheless when an Arctic convoy was located, despite insufficient intelligence, it was decided to send the *Admiral Hipper*, *Lützow*, and a number of destroyers to attack it. On 30 December, a German U-boat sighted a large collection of ships, prompting Admiral Kummetz to put to sea with the two cruisers and six destroyers.[440]

The operation would be known as "Regenbogen."

In a world where days and nights no longer followed each other, but were replaced by an almost continuous darkness, JW51B headed east. It was bitterly cold, and the low temperature caused ice to accumulate on the 14 merchant ships and six destroyers. In addition to the dangers caused by icing, armament and other vital technical systems might be rendered inoperable due to the weather.

On the decks, where tanks and partly disassembled aircraft struggled for space, cranes and hoists were constantly operated to prevent them from freezing and becoming inoperable by the time the convoy reached Murmansk. Ice was also a problem in the interior of the ships. Condensation resulted in a layer of ice on the bulkheads, which could become as thick as five to ten centimeters. The seamen on the Arctic convoys endured a very harsh life, even when the enemy did not attack.[441]

Initially the convoy had enjoyed close as well as distant cover, but the latter—the battleship *Anson*, one cruiser, and three destroyers commanded by Admiral Fraser—had turned about on 29 December. The close cover was rather weak compared with PQ18. Rear Admiral Burnett commanded the light cruisers *Sheffield* and *Jamaica*, as well as two destroyers. However, the latter were sent back to Britain on 29 December, their stay with Burnett therefore being of short duration. When the destroyers left, Burnett had been close to the convoy, but he increased speed after 12.00 to make a sweep ahead of the merchant ships. On the evening of 30 December, he reached a point about 300 kilometers north of Murmansk before turning northwest. He had to close the distance to JW51B again quickly, as the six destroyers included in the escort could not be expected to ward off heavy German warships. He encountered some difficulties, however, while trying to find the convoy after his sweep eastwards. As he did not know its exact position, he literally stumbled in darkness. He chose to sail on a course that would err to the north. Thus he hoped to get a chance to see the silhouettes against the faint light that might come from the south.[442]

Actually, Burnett would need all the help he could get from the light, as Kummetz's ships approached from the south. The German commander chose to split his force into two groups. He continued on board the *Admiral Hipper*, accompanied by three destroyers, and detached the *Lützow* with three destroyers. Commander Lange on board the *Lützow* commanded the latter group. This measure increased

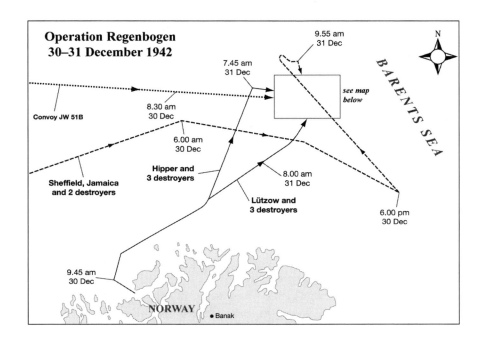

Operation Regenbogen
30–31 December 1942

9.55 am
31 Dec

N

7.45 am
31 Dec

BARENTS SEA

Convoy JW 51B

see map
below

8.30 am
30 Dec

6.00 am
30 Dec

Hipper and
3 destroyers

8.00 am
31 Dec

Sheffield, Jamaica
and 2 destroyers

Lützow and
3 destroyers

6.00 pm
30 Dec

9.45 am
30 Dec

NORWAY

● Banak

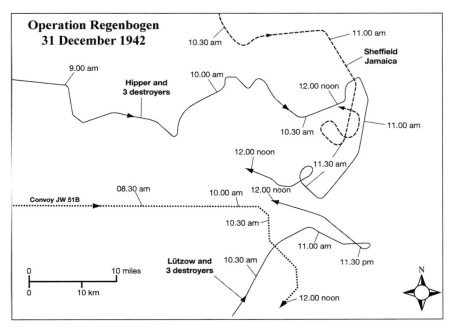

Operation Regenbogen
31 December 1942

10.30 am

11.00 am

Sheffield
Jamaica

9.00 am

10.00 am

Hipper and
3 destroyers

12.00 noon

10.30 am

11.00 am

12.00 noon

11.30 am

12.00 noon

08.30 am

Convoy JW 51B

10.00 am 12.00 noon

10.30 am

11.00 am

11.30 pm

0   10 miles

0   10 km

Lützow and
3 destroyers

10.30 am

10.30 am

12.00 noon

N

the chances of finding the convoy. The *Hipper* was significantly faster than the *Lützow*, which made the two ships an ill-matched couple. Thus, by this decision, the *Hipper* could benefit from its faster speed without being hampered by her slower sister. On the other hand, Kummetz split his forces with the enemy nearby, which could have led to grave consequences. As before, the German ships had to follow instructions to minimize their risks, which curtailed the freedom of action enjoyed by the commanders at sea.[443]

Early on 31 December 1942, when the Germans had reached a point north of North Cape, they split into the groups described. Kummetz's ships continued on their north-northeasterly course, while Lange turned for a more northeasterly course. At the time, most of JW51B was located about 250 kilometers north of North Cape. As a consequence of Kummetz's decision, he would pass behind the convoy, which proceeded on an easterly course. Lange's group would pass ahead of the convoy.[444]

While the two groups of German warships barely missed JW51B, Burnett hasted on a northwesterly course with his two cruisers. He was probably unaware of the urgent need to get between the Germans and the convoy. Soon after Kummetz had passed behind JW51B, he ordered a turn to the east. Thus, the *Hipper* sailed parallel to the convoy at a short distance to the north. Somewhat farther north, Burnett's two cruisers ploughed the ocean. Kummetz had detached the destroyers to search for the convoy, which happened to be located between the German cruiser and the three destroyers. This would result in the first observations.[445]

In the dusky night at about 08.30, the British corvette *Hyderabad* sighted two "mysterious" destroyers. At first, they were believed to be Soviet, but their true nationality would soon be revealed. The British destroyer *Obdurate* also observed these strange ships and was sent to make a closer investigation. At 09.30 the German destroyer *Friedrich Eckholt* opened fire on the *Obdurate*, clearly showing that the mysterious destroyers were hostile. Soon afterwards, lookouts on the *Hipper* found the British destroyer *Achates*. Together with the destroyer *Onslow*, the *Achates* became involved in a confused engagement with the German cruiser. During the first 40 minutes no hits were scored, but then a salvo from the *Hipper* damaged *Obdurate* severely. The destroyer remained afloat, but was no longer battleworthy. Meanwhile,

Burnett's cruisers hastened southeast, as the muzzle flashes had revealed the German cruiser.[446]

Before Burnett engaged, the *Hipper* was found by another British ship, the minesweeper *Brumble*, which was on her own searching for the separated ships from JW51B. The German cruiser was hardly what the men monitoring the radar screens had yearned for. The British minesweeper had also been discovered by the *Hipper*, which promptly opened fire and sunk it. However, Burnett quickly closed the range and obtained radar contact soon after 11.00. He had two cruisers against a single German, but the *Hipper* was more heavily armed and better armored. Also, Kummetz had his three destroyers, although they were currently engaging their British counterparts. Lange's group was still too far south to intervene.[447]

Despite the proximity, the cruisers did not immediately engage, as poor visibility caused by darkness and swirling snow squalls prevented them from firing. Also, as both sides had several ships involved, there was a very real risk of fratricide. Kummetz turned south and found the *Achates*. The German cruiser quickly opened fire and hit the British destroyer, damaging her badly. With the *Achates* still afloat but effectively out of action, the *Hipper* shifted her fire to the *Onslow*, which was also hit.

While shifting her fire between the different targets, the *Hipper* turned and set a westerly course. Thus far, Burnett's cruisers had not opened fire, but at 11.30, the first shells left their gun barrels. For the moment, Kummetz therefore found himself squeezed between the British destroyers and cruisers. Furthermore, the German cruiser was hit at a very unfortunate moment. When she made a starboard turn, she heeled over to port. This was magnified by the high waves and exposed a section of her hull below the armor belt. At this very moment, a shell hit this part and knocked out a boiler. The *Hipper* was certainly not crippled, but Kummetz decided to break off the action and ordered his destroyers to disengage.[448]

As Kummetz's destroyers were located farther east, they were in an unfortunate position, which became evident when the British cruisers opened fire. The *Friedrich Eckholt* sighted a cruiser which was presumed to be the *Hipper*. However, the cruiser opened fire, making the mistake painfully obvious. Soon the *Sheffield* had damaged the

German destroyer so badly that it sunk. No further losses occurred on either side. Kummetz's group sailed west before turning south toward the Altafjord, which was reached without further mishaps.[449]

In contrast to the drama experienced by Kummetz's group, Lange had seen far less of the enemy. His group did catch a glimpse of the convoy and open fire on it—resulting in damage on one merchant ship—but the escort quickly placed a smoke screen that concealed the convoy and no further contact was achieved. The *Lützow*, as well as the three destroyers, returned to the Altafjord.[450]

Thus a confused battle came to an end. In terms of ships sunk and damaged, it was inconclusive. There was perhaps a slight advantage for the Germans, but equally important was the fact that JW51B reached Soviet ports almost unharmed. Similarly, RA51 reached British ports unmolested after sailing from Murmansk on 30 December. The most dramatic repercussions would take place in Berlin.

Hitler became infuriated when he heard the BBC reporting that Kummetz had broken off the engagement. He was subsequently informed by the German Navy High Command, but their side of things did nothing to lessen his anger. Grand Admiral Raeder managed to postpone a meeting with Hitler for a few days to allow the latter to calm down. However, when they met on 6 January 1943, Hitler was very dissatisfied. He began with a 90-minute monologue, wherein he poured out criticism on the role played by the German Navy since 1860. In particular, he focused on its morale and willingness to fight, which he described in disparaging terms. This undoubtedly grieved Raeder.[451]

Perhaps Hitler's anger should be seen in a broader context. During the autumn of 1942, adversities in North Africa loomed ever larger, while even worse misfortunes befell the German forces on the Eastern Front. When the Red Army broke through the Romanian armies protecting the flanks of the German 6th Army at Stalingrad, about 200,000 soldiers became surrounded. Several German officers recommended that the 6th Army should break out, but Hitler vetoed. He gambled that an airlift operation would bring in sufficient supplies and a rescue operation could fight its way to the surrounded force. At the beginning of 1943, it was obvious that Hitler had been wrong, and the 6th Army was literally starving to death.

Possibly, the somewhat lackluster effort in the Barents Sea was the last straw. Instead of a much needed success, the battle had ended in a rather vapid draw. Not even Goebbels could make a triumph out of it.

Evidently, Hitler's anger may not only have been caused by the Kriegsmarine. However, it seems clear that the results achieved by the Navy were not commensurate with the resources allotted to it. When the war began in September 1939, the Navy encompassed 127,523 men. One year later, its strength had doubled to 257,216. In September 1941, no less than 463,088 men served with the Navy and one year later, the personnel strength had risen to no less than 620,601.[452]

In a mere three years, Navy personnel strength had increased by almost 400 percent, while the field army had only expanded by 40 percent. During this period, the Germans had noted tremendous success, which was far more attributable to the Army than the Navy. Perhaps such considerations contributed to Hitler's derision of the ships and their admirals.[453]

Admittedly, Hitler was correct in portraying the Navy as overly cautious, but he conveniently overlooked his own role in this context. Decisions, directives, and instructions from the Führer, clearly illustrated during Operation Rösselsprung, certainly did not promote audacity. Rather he had urged for caution and insisted on having the final word on operational matters. To a significant degree, he himself was the culprit behind the circumstances he vented his wrath upon, but it was Raeder who suffered the blame.

The Grand Admiral hardly got a chance to object. Hitler demanded that Raeder urgently submit a report on the decommissioning of the heavy warships, and how the resources freed could be used elsewhere. From now on, if Hitler's intentions were followed, the German Navy would consist of ships no larger than destroyers. Raeder, who had worked hard for many years to expand the Navy, was of course appalled. Now it was demanded of him to drastically cut down the Navy.[454]

Raeder would not carry out such plans, as he resigned on 30 January, to be replaced by Admiral Karl Dönitz. Most of Hitler's intentions never became reality. The Germans retained their heavy warships, and Hitler's objective to disarm them and use the heavy guns as coastal artillery was only accomplished with ships not in commission. For example, the guns of the incomplete carrier *Graf Zeppelin* were used for coastal defense.

In the Trondheimsfjord, the *Tirpitz* conducted a number of

exercises to check that everything was working properly after the maintenance work. In January, live-fire exercises were also conducted, as she had not yet received an order for the guns to be dismounted. In fact, such an order never came. Rather, Karl Topp, who was promoted to Rear Admiral at the end of January, could focus on raising the proficiency of his crew. It would be his final task on the *Tirpitz*. After commanding Germany's largest warship for almost two years, it was time for him to hand over the responsibility to Captain Hans Meyer, who assumed command on 21 February.[455]

Meyer was a tall and slim person. Shortly after the end of World War I, he had lost an arm while fighting during the Spartacus uprising. He was well versed in naval history, self-disciplined, and a commander used to being obeyed. While Topp had been quite an extrovert, Meyer tended to be more reserved. Considering Hitler's intentions, Meyer could expect to have plenty of time to grow into the role expected of him.

In fact, it could have been fair to question whether he would ever command his ship in actual battle.

The Midget Submarines

Early in 1943, a new British weapon that could be used to attack the Tirpitz came into existence. Although the British midget submarine—known as X-craft—had initially been conceived to lay mines in river estuaries, its potential to be employed against enemy warships soon became apparent. The Admiralty had ordered two prototypes in 1941, which were thoroughly tested in the following year. As the results were very promising, six further craft were ordered, intended for use against enemy warships.[456]

The 12th Submarine Flotilla was formed on 17 April 1943. Captain "Willie" Banks was appointed commander, while Commander Ingram was put in charge of training. Long before the unit was formed, crews for the X-crafts had been training, mainly in Scotland. Many highly qualified officers and men, who could have served with distinction in the regular submarine forces, were transferred to the project. Admittedly, only a few men would actually execute the missions considered, but the highly demanding training would make it possible to select the best. Also, reserve crews would probably be needed.[457]

In January 1943, six midget submarines were delivered to the Royal Navy. They received the designations X-5 to X-10, and it was hoped to use all in a simultaneous attack on the *Scharnhorst*, *Tirpitz*, and *Lützow* only two months after the submarines had been delivered. The urgency was partly motivated by the desire to end the threat posed by the German warships, but darkness was also vital to success, and the nights would rapidly become shorter in northern Norway. However, the nights could not be too dark either. A long night with a full moon was ideal, but after 9 March, such conditions would not occur until the autumn. The ambitious schedule proved too optimistic. The crews had to trim their crafts, and time was needed to evaluate the equipment and ensure that any teething troubles would not jeopardize the operation. The Admiralty decided to postpone the attack—known as Operation Source—until September, when the nights would be sufficiently long again.[458]

During the spring of 1943, most of the components needed for Operation Source were present, but one problem remained: how would the midget submarines move from Scotland to northern Norway? Originally, it had been intended to attack the *Tirpitz* in Trondheim, but as she was transferred to the Kaafjord at the end of March, the distance to be covered by the midget submarines was doubled. One alternative had been for the midget subs to traverse the North Sea on their own accord, but that was fraught with problems. As they were very slow, such a journey was estimated to take two weeks. The crammed spaces in the little craft would strain the endurance of the crews too much. Also, a longer voyage meant increased risk of mechanical problems that, possibly, could not be repaired at sea. Furthermore, it was vital that the midget submarines attack almost simultaneously. A long sea voyage could result in them becoming separated.[459]

Another alternative was to transport the midget submarines to a point off the Norwegian coast on the depot ship *Bonaventure*, but the idea was rejected in February 1943 as it would jeopardize secrecy. Admittedly, it would be a comfortable voyage for the crews, but if the mission was uncovered by the enemy, the actual attack could prove disastrous.[460]

In the end, the Royal Navy settled for an alternative it had not considered earlier. Six conventional submarines would tow the midget submarines to the Norwegian coast. Remarkably, they would mostly be towed while submerged. During the dark hours, the conventional submarine would resurface to charge the batteries, while the midget submarine remained below the surface of the sea. Every third or fourth hour, the midget subs would surface to ventilate for about a quarter of an hour. During the final two days of the voyage the towing submarine, as well as the midget, would proceed submerged. During the final phase—from the Norwegian coast through the fjords and to the targets—the midget submarines would move on their own after disconnecting from the conventional submarines. In order to avoid tiring the crews out, the men who were actually going to conduct the attack remained on board the conventional submarines. During the voyage to the Norwegian coast, the reserve crews would man the midget submarines. Before the attack, the crews were to be switched. It might seem that the reserve crews received the less arduous and also less dangerous task, but in the end their job would prove equally difficult. In all respects, Operation Source would be a very complicated mission.[461]

Let us for a moment put the planning aside and turn to the midget submarines and their crews. The weight of an X-craft was not even one thousandth that of a battleship like the *Tirpitz*. How could a small craft destroy such a large behemoth? At first glance, nothing suggested that it could. An uninformed observer who casually strolled by an X-craft placed on a factory backyard might have mistaken it for some kind of large barrel or container—despite the fact that its length was about 16 meters. The diameter was slightly less than two meters, except at the middle section, which housed the periscope. According to the wartime logic of using what was available, an X-craft was powered by a conventional electric motor when submerged, and a diesel engine of the type used by London buses when the craft sailed on the surface. At six knots on the surface and two knots submerged, the X-craft was very slow.[462]

The midget submarines lacked any kind of conventional armament, like artillery or torpedoes. They were designed to make their way to an enemy warship and place two two-ton amatol charges under its keel. One such charge equalled a salvo of torpedoes fired from a conventional submarine. The amatol charges had been given a shape similar to the hull of the X-craft, in order to reduce drag. Also, they were fitted with floatation chambers to ensure that they were neutral in water. When released from the submarine, a seal was broken and water entered the chamber, thus gradually making the density of the charge greater than the surrounding water. It would slowly sink to the bottom, reducing the risk of any underwater current moving the charge away from the target. The charge was set to detonate by a device resembling an egg timer, allowing up to 36 hours for the midget submarines to disappear. Of course, such a long delay could not be used when attacking the *Tirpitz*. On the one hand, once the charges were released it was important that the X-crafts had time to get away. On the other hand, the *Tirpitz* could not be allowed the same benefit, as that would give her a chance to shift position in the likely event that any of the attackers were sighted. Nevertheless, if the amatol charges were placed properly and detonated as intended, the force of the explosions would tear the hull plates and cause the ship to leak seriously. Furthermore, the explosion would create a huge gas bubble, which would rapidly rise and possibly break the keel of a major ship.[463]

The interior of an X-craft was very crammed. The main battery, which provided light as well as electrical power for the motor, was located in the forward compartment. Also, there was space for one crewman in the forward compartment. By moving the diving gear, he could find a place to sleep if he tucked his legs around the cabinet holding the provisions.

Behind the forward compartment there was the Wet-and-Dry chamber, which could be water-filled to allow a diver to leave the craft while the submarine was still submerged. The diver entered the chamber, connected the oxygen supply, shut the hatch behind him, and filled the chamber with water. Then he could leave the craft—and return—through a hatch above. The chamber also contained another vital component: the lavatory.[464]

After the Wet-and-Dry was the control room, which was the heart of the midget submarine. From there the craft was maneuvered, but the crew also took their meals and snatched an occasional nap there. The engine room was located behind the control room. When the constructors received the specifications for the craft, they were informed that it would carry a crew of four. However, there were almost no requirements for comfort. To make matters worse for the crewmen, they were literally crammed into a machine. There were few surfaces they could lean on without hitting wheels, levers, pipes, gauges, pumps, valves, or motors. If they managed to avoid hurting themselves on such gadgets, they could always stumble on containers or boxes littering the floor, or bump their heads into some protruding object.[465]

Of the four men, the commander obviously carried most responsibility. His position was at the periscope, in the center of the control room. He decided on matters like navigation and tactics, and also monitored all the technical systems. He alone could see anything outside the craft when the other crewmen manned their battle stations. On the back of the craft there was a low extension which contained the periscope, allowing 360° vision. It was very slender, making it almost invisible except at short distance. Most of the vital information needed by the commander to make decisions was obtained through the periscope. However, there were also two portholes, one on each side, which were very important during the last phase of the attack. After taking the final bearing on the target, the periscope had to be lowered or else the enemy might spot the craft. Thus the commander had to maintain the proper course by looking through the portholes. Only the commander could issue orders, and he had to instill confidence in his crew.[466]

The second member of the crew, the first lieutenant, was positioned behind the commander. He was responsible for controlling trim, depth, and speed through changing water conditions. In a larger submarine, a number of men shared these tasks, but in the crammed midget submarine, one person had to do it alone. Furthermore, he had to keep an eye on what the other crewmen did; for example, if any of them moved from the control room to the forward compartment or the Wet-and-Dry chamber. His work would be even more complicated in the Norwegian fjords.[467]

The third member of the crew was the engineer. He controlled the

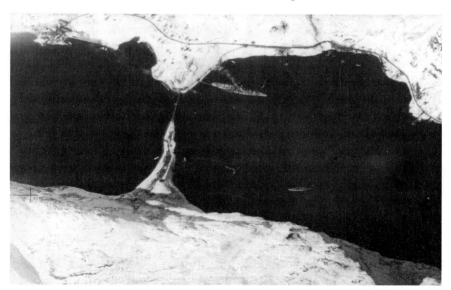

Reconnaissance photo of the *Tirpitz* in the Kaafjord on April 19, 1943.

helm and steered the craft in the direction indicated by the commander. He also had to ensure that all engines and other technical equipment worked properly. He knew how the craft was constructed and could repair many components if they malfunctioned. The humid air inside the craft resulted in condensation, which might short-cut electrical circuits. Technical problems were common, and the engineer could expect to be busy. In the crammed space, it was often difficult to perform repairs—far more difficult than in an ordinary, much larger warship. If he had to work on the engine, he would have to lie on his stomach above it on a narrow girder and work with his hands below and his head just above the hull. If water seeped into the periscope, he had to disassemble it to allow it to dry. Without the engineer, chances of success were slim.

The final crewmember was the diver. Although he was informed on the responsibilities given to the other crewmembers, allowing him to step in and perform some of their jobs if needed, he was mainly expected to carry out tasks within his field of expertise. Through the Wet-and-Dry, he could leave the craft and cut a hole in the nets surrounding warships at anchor with a specially designed cutting tool. Previously, only a crew of three had been envisaged, and one of the other crewmen would double as a diver. However, an accident in May 1943, which resulted in the death of a lieutenant when he cut through nets, led to the decision to include a fourth crewmember. The diver used the same kind of oxygen tube from German aircraft used by the divers involved in Operation Title, thus providing him with sufficient oxygen for six hours. The diver would have to return to the submarine and replace the oxygen tube if the work took longer. As several belts of nets might protect a warship at anchor, the diver might have to leave the craft more than once.[468]

The preparations for Operation Source were dangerous, as the already mentioned fatal accident showed. In another incident, one of the midget submarines foundered, but the crew narrowly escaped. Somewhat later, a crewmember was washed overboard and never found again. At the same time, the Wet-and-Dry was filled with water and separated the two remaining crewmen from each other. Thus the balance of the craft was upset and the nose sank down. The two men remaining inside the craft had to wait several hours before they were saved, when a rescue ship managed to recover the craft. One of the two men was Godfrey Place, who would subsequently play a prominent role in Operation Source. Nevertheless, training progressed, and during the summer many exercises against Royal Navy warships were conducted.[469]

Besides perfecting the weapon and the crews, major efforts were made to gather needed intelligence. However, the long distance to Altafjord from airfields in Scotland severely hampered British reconnaissance flights. As Soviet airbases were much closer to the *Tirpitz's* berth, the British government asked the Soviet authorities if Royal Air Force reconnaissance units could be based in northern Russia. After some time, permission was granted to operate British reconnaissance units from Vaenga, east of Murmansk. It was not much of an airbase, as a stretch of ground was leveled in the forest to serve as a landing strip. However, wooden hangars were erected as well as some other buildings, among them a laboratory to develop the films.[470]

The photographs obtained were valuable, but further intelligence was also needed, such as information on German activities in the Kaafjord. In particular, it was important to know when the battleship left its berth and for what purpose. Also, it was necessary to gather information on small craft patrolling the waters surrounding the berths, how often the nets were checked, if there was some kind of pattern in the German activities, how often depot ships moored next to the battleships, and many other important issues. Torstein Raaby, a member of the Norwegian resistance who had previously worked for British intelligence, was contracted to gather information. He had been forced to flee to England, as the Gestapo was searching for him. Now he was asked to return to Norway and establish a network of agents in the Alta area, with the intention to gather as much information on the *Tirpitz* as possible. The Norwegian accepted and concluded a four month, agent-training program. After the training was completed, he was sent to Norway in a submarine furnished with maps, code books, forged identity papers, a list of persons he could contact, $50,000 in Norwegian cash, and no less than nine radio transmitters. Raaby assumed the role of a road construction worker in the small village of Alta. He made long tours to the Kaafjord and Langfjord, where he observed the German warship's positions and the routines employed. Raaby lived next to a German officer's dwelling. By clandestinely connecting his radio transmitter to the officer's antenna, Raaby sent daily messages to Britain. He also prepared a detailed map on the net barriers protecting the German warships, which he sent to Britain through Sweden. His work, supplemented by the aerial photographs from Vaenga, would prove invaluable to Operation Source.[471]

Meanwhile, the training of the crews and the preparation of the craft continued at Loch Cairnbawn. As the midget submarines would be towed, reliable hawsers were needed, but several times the models used had broken during testing. They were made from hemp and did not last more than three consecutive days. If they failed during the operation, the towed midget submarines would be seriously endangered. After some deliberation, it was decided to use another type of hawser, made of nylon and intended for towing gliders. They were stronger, despite their smaller diameter. The Royal Navy requisitioned six new hawsers, but only three arrived in time for the operation, as it took time to fit a telephone cable to the hawser, and the air ministry had ordered strict rationing of the material.[472]

As autumn came closer day by day, Operation Source was gradually perfected. The final selection of crews for the voyage to Norway and the actual attack was made. Conventional submarines were detached from their other duties to tow the midget submarines, and numerous minor details were sorted out. Also, the date for the projected operation had to be settled. As poor weather during the autumn might spoil the operation, it could not be delayed too long. A full moon was required, but the night had to be long enough. Such consideration led to the conclusion that the period 20–25 September would provide ideal circumstances. Thus, the midget submarines would disconnect from the conventional submarines to enter the fjords on 20 September. As the voyage from Loch Cairnbawn to the Norwegain coast was estimated to require at least one week, it was decided to depart on 11 September.[473]

As August turned into September, the BBC reported Soviet successes on the Eastern Front, and on 3 September Allied troops assaulted the Italian mainland. At the same time, security measures at Loch Cairnbawn became rigorous. No leaves were allowed, only a few select people were allowed to enter or depart from the area, and all letters were withheld until the attack force had sailed. Ships were not allowed to leave the base, but the six conventional submarines arrived one by one, to avoid attracting attention. The midget submarines were hoisted on board the *Bonaventure*, to fit the amatol charges and were then lowered into the water again. Provisions and fuel were also taken on board.[474]

On 27 August, three disassembled Spitfires had been loaded on two destroyers, which set course toward Murmansk. The three aircraft were high-altitude reconnaissance machines and they were to be used for photographic missions from Vaenga. It was intended to fly above the Kaafjord at least twice a day. The films taken by the Spitfires were developed and flown to Britain by Mosquito aircraft. [475]

Only the final decision to launch Operation Source remained, when one of the Spitfire pilots noted that the German battleships were absent from the Kaafjord. The information was confirmed by Raaby and other members of the resistance.

The *Tirpitz* had weighed anchor.

Sizilien—The One Offensive

On 26 February, Hitler and Dönitz discussed plans for the future. According to Hitler's previous orders, the recently appointed commander-in-chief of the Navy reported that the *Admiral Hipper*, *Köln*, and *Leipzig* had been decommissioned, soon to be followed by the *Schlesien* and *Schleswig-Holstein*.

Thus it could appear that Dönitz acted according to Hitler's intentions. However, the *Schlesien* and *Schleswig-Holstein* were two very old ships with limited combat value. The *Hipper* was damaged after the battle in the Barents Sea and would return to service within a year. In her case, Hitler's order only meant that repairs were not rushed. The heavy cruiser would eventually serve with distinction in the Baltic, after the Red Army had raised the siege of Leningrad. The *Leipzig* had been seriously damaged in 1939 and converted to a training ship. The *Köln*, which had been commanded by Hans Meyer before he was appointed to succeed Karl Topp, was decommissioned, despite being serviceable. However, she too returned to service in 1944. Thus, Hitler's intention to decommission and even scrap the heavy ships was never fulfilled.[476]

Dönitz still considered the Allied convoys to the Soviet Arctic ports a suitable target for the German warships. He suggested that the *Scharnhorst* transfer to Norway. She, together with the *Tirpitz*, *Lützow*, and six destroyers would constitute a respectable force. Hitler instantly objected and claimed that defeat had followed defeat ever since the *Graf Spee* had been sunk in December 1939. He did not want to commit the heavy ships to any further operations. As these naval setbacks were discussed, Dönitz used the opportunity to debate the issue of Hitler's restrictions. The standing order not to endanger the ships had been a major hindrance to commanders at sea, who could not employ their ships as they saw fit. Success was not easy to attain when no risks could be accepted. Astonishingly, Hitler denied that he had ever issued such an order. When contact with the enemy occurred, the ships would enter combat.[477]

Considering Hitler's orders—which had profoundly affected Rösselsprung as well as Regenbogen—his objection is a bit of a mystery. Perhaps it resulted in consequences he had not intended, but in that event he must have used poorly chosen words. In any case, Dönitz managed to obtain permission to send the *Scharnhorst* to Norway. The Allied convoys would remain threatened.[478]

Eventually, neither *Tirpitz* nor *Scharnhorst* would attack a convoy during the first half of 1943. The British decided to send two convoys in quick succession in January and February, to make the most of the dark winter months. Both arrived without encountering any German ships except U-boats, and the losses were slight. Thereafter, no Arctic convoys were sent for several months. The explanation for the lack of activity in the north could be found on the Atlantic. At this stage, the German effort to produce more submarines had finally paid off. Dönitz could send approximately 100 U-boats to attack merchant ships, which was necessary given that the Allied convoys had grown in size as well as number.[479] The battles between U-boats and escorts thus intensified, resulting in mounting losses. In March 1943, the Germans concentrated 43 U-boats against the two convoys called HX229 and SC122. No less than 22 ships were sunk, and it appeared that the Germans were getting the better of the Allies. In fact, the truth was different. In 1939–41, the German U-boats sank about 20 ships for every loss of their own. In 1942, the ratio was somewhat reduced, but only marginally. However, in the first half of 1943, one U-boat was lost for every five Allied ships sunk. That was a drastic decline, which resulted as much from better Allied anti-submarine tactics as from improved radar technology. However, in early 1943 and viewed from the Allied perspective, since losses of merchant ships were seen to rise while it took some time to evaluate the enemy losses, it wasn't yet apparent that the balance had shifted decisively against the U-boats. Thus the British sent virtually all their escort ships to the Atlantic theater, and no resources remained to protect any convoys to Murmansk or Archangelsk.[480]

In March 1943, when the Germans embarked upon the deployment of further heavy ships in northern Norway, they were in the dark about Allied intentions. In the Trondheimsfjord, the *Tirpitz's* crew continued training. As a result, the battleship moved between different parts of the large fjord during the exercises. The intention, after several months of inactivity, was to make the ship and her crew fully battleworthy again. However, during the first weeks of March, there was yet another circumstance motivating the activity. As it was intended to transfer the Tirpitz to Altafjord, the exercises could also serve to conceal her departure.[481]

Early on 11 March, the *Tirpitz* weighed anchor. The morning was stern, with strong winds and rough seas; the sky was concealed by thick clouds and intermittent snow squalls. The temperature was below freezing, and visibility alternated between poor and good. Occasionally it was less than a kilometer, and then suddenly it would be possible to see about 20 kilometers ahead. Such conditions were quite propitious for moving the battleship unnoticed to northern Norway. Escorted by the 6th Destroyer Flotilla, the *Tirpitz* set course for Bogen Bay, near Narvik.[482]

The voyage along the Norwegian coast passed without any notable incidents. The *Tirpitz* sailed at 16 knots to conserve fuel, but the speed was sufficient to let her arrive at Bogen Bay during the night of 12–13 March, thus joining the *Scharnhorst, Lützow*, and *Nürnberg*. At 08.00, the Admiral's flag was hoisted on the *Tirpitz*, as Kummetz and his staff went aboard.[483]

Kummetz's squadron remained at Bogen Bay for more than a week, but at midnight on 22 March it sailed for Altafjord. Aside from a few drifting mines observed from the ships, the voyage proceeded without any kind of drama. Early on 24 March, the *Tirpitz, Scharnhorst*, and *Lützow*, as well as the destroyers *Erich Steinbrink, Karl Galster, Paul Jacobi, Theodor Riedel, Z28, Z29*, and the two torpedo boats T20 and T21, entered the Altafjord. It was an impressive gathering of German ships, one of the largest since the outbreak of the war.[484]

As the Allies did not send any Arctic convoys during the spring of 1943, the German warships spent several uneventful months in northern Norway. On 17 May, there was an exception to this dullness as an exercise was organized. It was brief, though, and the warships returned to their berths in the evening. Nine days later, the *Tirpitz* conducted a firing exercise, but in general the days were quite monotonous for the crews on board the warships.[485]

The German fuel shortage seriously curtailed training, forcing the warships mainly to remain behind their protective nets. To keep the crews in good shape, various activities were conducted. The warships had to be maintained, which required considerable time, even when they were moored. Furthermore, due to the threat from the air, all anti-aircraft systems were continuously manned. Certain functions could undergo training when anchored, and sports activities were good to maintain the physical shape of the crews. For example, while there was still snow on the ground, sailors often practiced skiing.[486]

In June 1943 the daily routines remained the same as in the spring. However, late on 5 July Kummetz's warships sailed for an exercise on the sea north of the Altafjord estuary. Combat exercises were conducted on 6 July before the ships returned to Altafjord in the night. Kummetz's squadron did not leave Altafjord subsequently in July or August 1943.[487]

The maintenance work on the *Tirpitz* conducted in the autumn and winter 1942–43 had been incomplete, and when the autumn of 1943 got closer, the battleship needed a period at dockyard for a more extensive overhaul. She would be temporarily out of commission, but not before she had been involved in fighting.

Accurate weather forecasts were crucial to decision making, but good meteorological data was vital to forecasting. Both sides established weather stations in the Arctic to gather data enabling the meteorologists to forecast weather in the area from the coast of Greenland to the Barents Sea. Weather observation ships were also sent to gather data. Another method employed was to place buoys in the area with instruments and transmitters, allowing them to continuously send information on temperature and air pressure, but they did not last long. Permanent weather stations were established at several places in the Arctic, but they were difficult to supply. In particular, Svalbard attracted the attention of the Germans as well as the Allies, where both sides established stations. However, it was particularly difficult to supply them during the winter, when the ice made it difficult for ships to reach the area. To collect weather data, long-range aircraft and submarines could also be employed.

Svalbard, which was mostly covered by glaciers, was also used for other purposes. For example, British ships had bunkered at the Bell Sound, where some shelter against wind and high seas was allowed. There was also a coal deposit at the Svalbard islands. An American industrialist had initiated mining early in the 20th century, and his name was given to the largest settlement on the Svalbard— Longyearbyen. The second most important village was Barentsburg. The coal dug from the mine was valuable, but certainly not of any strategic importance.

The distance from the Altafjord to Svalbard is almost 1,000 kilometers, a distance that could be covered in less than 24 hours by a ship sailing at 20–25 knots. The distance between Scapa Flow and Altafjord was almost 1,700 kilometers, while the distance from Scapa Flow to Svalbard was about 2,200 kilometers. As the Svalbard was among the most northernmost inhabited areas in the world, it is hardly surprising that the distance to the European mainland was considerable.

During August, the Germans planned an attack on the Allied installations on Svalbard. The *Tirpitz*, *Scharnhorst*, and nine destroyers would sail from the Altafjord and attack Barentsburg and Longyearbyen. The name chosen for the operation—which together with Wunderland was the most northerly conducted by the German Navy—was "Sizilien," the German word for Sicily, which was probably a deliberate irony since during the prior month the Allies had invaded Sicily. On 19 August, the final plan was issued. All that remained to settle was the date.

At 12.00 on 6 September, a message was transmitted by flags and signal lamps between the ships in the Altafjord. It read: "Will not put to sea for unit exercise according to order number 2831. Individual exercises permitted. Report intentions for tomorrow at 22.30."[488]

The rather cryptic message was in fact the order to initiate "Sizilien," yet no particular hurry could be seen on the *Tirpitz*. Almost leisurely, the afternoon was spent preparing the ship. Not until 10.00 was she unmoored, so the battleship could slowly and majestically glide through the Altafjord.[489]

It was, of course, impossible to conceal the 250-meter-long battleship from the local population. Rather, the Germans had to create the impression that something other than a concerted operation, involving almost the entire German squadron in the Altafjord, was about to happen. Hence the rather peculiar message. Despite keeping their preparations as secret as possible, the Germans knew quite well that the British would soon learn that not only the *Tirpitz* but also the *Scharnhorst* and nine destroyers had left their berths.

The German warships assembled in the darkness off the Altafjord. The *Scharnhorst* took up a position behind the *Tirpitz*, while the destroyers *Karl Galster*, *Theodor Riedel*, and *Hans Lody* sailed ahead to provide protection against submarines. The *Erich Steinbrink*, Z27, and Z30 protected the starboard side, while Z29, Z31, and Z33 covered the port side.[490]

Before 23.00, the German squadron sailed through Stjernsundet and the wide open sea lay ahead. Kummetz ordered 19 knots on a north-northwesterly course. At 08.00 on 7 September, Kummetz's force had reached halfway to Bear Island. The sea was still empty around the German squadron. A cloud cover concealed it from above, but the visibility along the sea varied between 10 and 20 kilometers. Such conditions were favorable and the Germans proceeded unhindered toward Svalbard. In the evening, a message reporting that a British reconnaissance aircraft had flown over the berths at the Altafjord was received. Thus the British knew that the Germans had sailed, but what conclusions they might infer from the observation were less clear. The British aircraft had passed at 16.45. At that time, only 400 kilometers remained between the target and the Germans. No British naval forces could intercept them before they reached Svalbard. Even if the Home Fleet put to sea immediately after receiving the reconnaissance information, which they would hardly do on the basis of a single report, they would have to sail at high speed for more than 50 hours to reach Svalbard.[491]

The German plans did not envisage any prolonged activity at Svalbard, as it would have allowed the British to act. Rather, the Germans had different intentions. When they reached the southern parts of Svalbard at 22.00 on 7 September, their plans would soon be revealed. At such a northerly latitude the nights were short and fairly light, even early in September. The men on the German ships were enchanted by the magnificent landscape they could observe from the ships as they entered the Isfjord. The name means the Ice Fjord and it was fitting, as huge glaciers dominated the visual impression.[492]

Farther into the Isfjord on the southern shore, Barentsburg and Longyearbyen were located. The German ships prepared for combat and reduced speed to navigate safely in the fjord. The *Tirpitz* aimed for Barentsburg and the *Scharnhorst* for Longyearbyen. On both battleships, floatplanes were made ready to drop bombs.[493]

Just before the Germans were to open fire, an Allied radio station, called Green Harbor, transmitted a report stating that seven destroyers and three cruisers had been observed. The *Tirpitz* had immediately initiated jamming, but it was unclear if this had prevented an intelligible message from reaching receivers elsewhere. Soon thereafter, a floatplane was catapulted from the *Tirpitz* to reconnoitre, and, if such a situation would arise, attack enemy strongpoints.[494]

At 04.00, a radio message from Reykjavik was intercepted which suggested that the report from Green Harbor had been received. The *Tirpitz's* 15-centimeter guns thundered, and 30 shells were fired at the radio station. No further transmission could be noted.[495]

Thus the German attack was in full swing. The destroyers brought soldiers from an infantry battalion, which were put ashore to destroy various facilities. When Z29, Z31, and Z33 entered the Grønfjord, on whose eastern shore Barentsburg was located, they were met by fire from anti-aircraft guns ashore. The guns opened up at a moment when the Germans were vulnerable, as the destroyers were between the *Tirpitz* and the anti-aircraft guns. To avoid hitting friendly ships, the gunners on the battleship had to cease firing, but the respite did not last long. Soon the destroyers had maneuvered away from the line of fire and the *Tirpitz's* heavy guns spoke. The thunder must have been violent in the fjord—which was about three kilometres wide—when twelve 38cm shells left the muzzles of the German battleship. The effect was instant, as the anti-aircraft guns were silenced.[496]

The *Tirpitz* also fired her heavy guns on the coal mine at Heerodden, where devastation and oily smoke soon resulted. Nevertheless, a message from Z29 spoke of strong resistance. Thus, the battleship maneuvered farther into the Grönfjord and fired another 20 heavy shells, which paralyzed the opposition. At 05.00 the commander of the 4th Destroyer Flotilla reported that the infantry had landed according to plan. So far the operation had proceeded smoothly, but Kummetz was concerned about the radio message that had been transmitted. If the Allied warships remained at Scapa Flow, or some port on Iceland, they would have to sail for two days to reach the area between Svalbard and northern Norway. However if they were already at sea, they might constitute a danger. Kummetz urged his units to hurry and wanted all infantry to have embarked by 11.00.[497]

The force centered on the *Scharnhorst* had proceeded farther into the Isfjord to Longyearbyen. At 05.12 it reported that all opposition at Longyearbyen had ceased. At Barentsburg, too, the Germans were fully in control, and the soldiers could begin to blow up the facilities that had been earmarked for destruction. Soon after 07.00, Colonel Wendte, who was commander of the infantry regiment to which the soldiers belonged, reported that his men would have accomplished their mission by 08.00.[498]

In Barentsburg as well as Longyearbyen, the German operation was almost completed. As Kummetz had urged, the infantry embarked at about 09.00, whereupon the warships began to move out from Svalbard's fjords. The Tirpitz finally fired eight shells on magazines and oil depots outside Barentsburg. Extensive fires ensued and buildings collapsed, which completed the devastation.[499]

Also, the *Scharnhorst* had used her floatplanes when she attacked and destroyed Longyearbyen. When the last one was about to be taken aboard, the combination of wind and waves in different directions caused difficulties. Thus, the *Scharnhorst* could not join the *Tirpitz* until 12.00. Thereafter, Kummetz's force left the Isfjord and sailed into the Arctic Ocean at 19 knots.[500]

Sixteen German seamen had been wounded during the battle. One of them was Petty Officer Schrader, who soon died from his wounds. Thus he became the only fatality during Operation Sizilien. The other 15 wounded appear to have survived and could, together with the infantry, hope for an undramatic voyage to the Altafjord.[501]

As the Germans were convinced that Allied radio stations had received the radio transmission from Green Harbor, strict vigilance was required. The German radio operators monitored all possible frequencies for any indication of enemy activities. Nothing was heard. The German warships continued on their south-southwesterly course at 19 knots.[502]

The speed chosen does not suggest that Kummetz perceived any immediate threat. Rather, the relatively low speed indicates a desire to conserve fuel. The Germans maintained their course and speed during 8 September and early on 9 September. Eventually Bear Island was behind them. In addition to monitoring the radio frequencies, the Germans launched floatplanes and other reconnaissance aircraft to search the vast areas around Kummetz's force. However, nothing was found. The only exception occurred at 11.00 on 9 September, when a submarine alarm aroused the crews, but nothing serious ensued. Kummetz ordered 25 knots, so the German warships could enter the Altafjord unscathed at 15.00. Two hours later, they were safely moored.

Operation Sizilien did not qualify as one of the more grandiose that took place during World War II, and did not cause any significant Allied countermeasures. The Germans were aware that the operation was insignificant as well, despite the fact that it had proceeded according to plan.[503] However, aside from destroying the Allied position at Svalbard, the crews on the warships had been allowed a chance to use their weapons, thus improving their proficiency. Most likely, the men serving with the *Tirpitz* would have to wait awhile before again firing their heavy guns. Within eight to ten weeks, a major overhaul would be initiated. Considering the fact that they had seldom left the Altafjord before Operation Sizilien, it appeared unlikely that they would put to sea before the overhaul. As that was estimated to require four months, the battleship would not again be in service until the spring of 1944—if everything proceeded according to plan.[504]

As we have seen, however, the British had other plans.

Operation Source Begins

On 10 September, a German message was intercepted and broken by Ultra. Thus the British were informed that the *Tirpitz* and *Scharnhorst* had returned to the Kaafjord. One person was particularly relieved by the information: Rear Admiral Claude Barry. As commander of the British submarine arm since November 1942, he was very concerned that something had gone wrong when he had learned that the German battleships were absent from the Altafjord. Innumerable reasons could be conjured. Had the Germans found out about the midget submarines? Had one of the Norwegian agents been caught? Were the Germans preparing some major operation, perhaps even on the Atlantic? Or were they simply moving their ships to Germany? No clues had been provided by Ultra. Neither had the message from Green Harbor been received in London. Not until two days after the German attack on Svalbard did the Admiralty learn what had transpired. The Home Fleet put to sea, but it was far too late. On the other hand, the fact that the German warships had returned to the Kaafjord meant that Operation Source could be initiated.[505]

Soon the Ultra decrypt was followed by photographic evidence from Vaenga, as well as reports from Raaby, which confirmed that the German battleships were moored at the Kaafjord. However, the fact that the battleships had berthed did not mean that they would remain there indefinitely. For example, the Germans might transfer the heavy warships to Narvik or Trondheim. In the event such a scenario became real, Operation Source had been divided into three options: "Funnel," "Empire," and "Forced," which denoted attacks on Kaafjord, Narvik, and Trondheim respectively. The planning thus allowed rapid shifting of the target, but nothing could be done if the German warships put to sea after the submarines began their arduous voyage. Barry hesitated, but the favorable moon decided the issue. If the operation were to be postponed, the teams would have to attack in unfavorable darkness. Furthermore, the enemy was likely to put to sea at a later date. Barry ordered the operation to commence.[506]

At Loch Cairnbawn the crewmen made their final preparations. During what he believed to be one of his last moments off duty before the operation, Lieutenant Donald Cameron scribbled a few sentences in his diary. He intended to give it to his wife, Eve, and their four month old son, Iain. "Darling I'm writing this for your enjoyment, I hope, and also for Ian's, when he is old enough to take interest in such matters …"

He went on to describe a dinner the crews had enjoyed together with Rear Admiral Barry, and how optimistic they all were before the mission. Cameron continued describing his testament and other instructions in case the operation ended disastrously. "I look at the familiar hills and isles," he concluded in the letter, "and wonder when I shall see

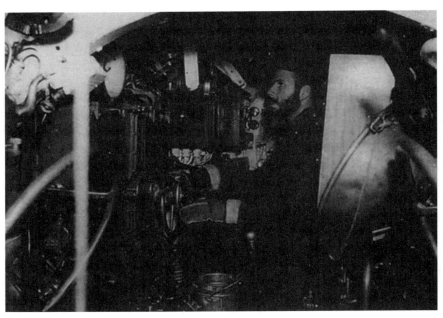

Inside view of an X-Craft.

them again. Say a little prayer for us all, Darling."[507]

In the afternoon on 11 September, five submarines with attached X-crafts left Loch Cairbawn. The first batch included the *Thrasher*, *Truculent*, and *Stubborn*, which towed the X-5, X-6, and X-7 respectively. These X-craft were to be commanded by Lieutenants Henty-Creer, Cameron, and Place. Unless something unforeseen occurred, they would attack the *Tirpitz*. Later in the afternoon *Seanymph* and *Syrtis* sailed, towing X-8 and X-9. The X-8, commanded by Lieutenant McFarlane, would attack the *Lützow* in the Langfjord, while Lieutenant Martin would lead the X-9 in an attack on the *Scharnhorst*. On the following day X-10, towed by *Sceptre*, left Loch Cairnbawn. She would also attack the *Scharnhorst*. Initially the submarines sailed together, but at a level with the Shetlands, they split into groups of two.[508]

The crews of the six submarines and X-craft experienced various problems, hazards, and hardships. All of these can not be described, but let us look briefly at the X-7. During the voyage it was commanded by Lieutenant P.H. Philips, with J. Magennis as first officer and F. Luck as engineer. They soon found life in the crammed midget submarine painful. Their backs ached and the humid air, which made their clothes wet, added to the misery. As the diver would not enter the craft until the final phase, at least two of the three crewmen had to be on duty all the time: one to monitor the depth gauge and one to keep an eye on the inclinometer. Their only contact with the mother submarine was provided by the tiny telephone cable. However, it would prove a tenuous link.[509]

On the second day, X-7 already suffered from an accident. After surfacing to ventilate at 4.30, Philips again submerged. It turned out that the hatch in the Wet-and-Dry had not been properly closed and water seeped into the craft. The designers had only intended that the chamber be used when the submarine lay idle, not when it was towed after a submarine at high speed. If the chamber became water-filled, the balance of the craft would be seriously upset. Magennis reacted quickly and closed the bulkhead between the maneuver room and the chamber, but water could not be removed from the latter. Philips decided to dive to six meters, hoping that the increased pressure from the water would push the hatch into position and prevent further water from entering the chamber. The maneuver succeeded and while the X-7 was submerged, the bulkhead was again opened to allow the water to be evenly distributed in the craft. Subsequently the hatch was again closed, and when X-7 resurfaced the water could be removed.[510]

Soon another problem occurred. Philips and his crew heard a recurring banging sound, but they could not locate the source. As they suspected a loose charge might be the cause of the noise, Philips decided to resurface. It was still dark, but while lying on his stomach and crawling along the hull, he checked the mountings. All seemed normal. He presumed that the sound was caused by the bulkheads and submerged again. A few hours later the sound could no longer be heard.[511]

Later in the evening, the X-7 crew encountered a problem that was not of a technical nature. Philips suddenly became afflicted with seasickness and vomited not only on himself, but also on several of the gauges before he could switch position with another crew member. Considering the crammed space and lack of fresh air, Philips had probably been more popular among his fellows earlier than at the present time.[512]

However, Philips was not alone. Soon Luck also had to vomit, but he managed to reach the engine room in time. To make matters worse, water entered the periscope and the electromagnet log ceased functioning. Such problems had to receive immediate attention. When Philips finally could take a nap, he had a curious dream. Barry tried to have him court-martialed for sailing an X-craft over a dam! To reiterate what we have already mentioned: bringing a submerged midget submarine to the Norwegian coast was no bed of roses.[513]

Despite all the nagging problems and incidents, the voyage proceeded fairly well during the first three days, but on the night before 15 September the weather deteriorated significantly. When the X-7 resurfaced to ventilate in the morning, Philips noted that conditions were worse than ever. The craft rolled and heaved violently, and Philips expected the hawser would snap at any moment. He also suspected that one of the charges had been damaged, but this assumption would eventually prove unfounded.[514]

The weather was harsh on the men on board the larger submarines too. However, they were at least encouraged when a message was received on 15 September telling them that the German warships remained moored and showed no signs of imminent departure. The attack order was thus confirmed.[515]

In the afternoon X-7 suffered further problems. The craft was submerged when Philips and Luck noted how its movements changed. Had the hawser snapped? Philips consulted the instruments, which told him the midget submarine was diving steeply. He injected compressed air in the tanks, which stopped the dive and made the craft return to the surface. Philips opened the hatch and saw the high waves. Cautiously, he proceeded forward on the hull and swore when he realized that the hawser had indeed broken, a danger revealed at Loch Cairnbawn. Only X-5, X-6, and X-10 had received the new nylon hawsers.[516]

Fortunately the towing submarine had realized what had happened and turned back. Soon a dinghy was on its way to the midget submarine. With his eyes dimmed by water from waves that almost washed him into the sea, Philips saw Bob Aitken—the diver from the team that would conduct the attack—in a small boat bringing a new hawser. Philips continued forward on the hull, where his life was endangered by the strong waves, but finally he got hold of the hawser, and together with Aitken managed to secure it. Suddenly a new danger appeared, as the rope between the dinghy and the *Stubborn* broke.

An X-Craft during trials in Scotland.

However by pulling himself and the dinghy by the main hawser, Aitken managed to get back to the submarine. After an hour the voyage resumed.[517]

Not only Philips experienced hawser problems. They also befell X-8, which became detached and drifted loose. Its mother submarine, *Seanymph*, searched vainly for the craft during most of 15 September. The *Seanymph*'s commander, Oakly, reported to the Admiralty, and Barry replied that if damage to the X-8 jeopardized the operation, she could be sunk at sea.[518]

Late in the afternoon, after having been lost for 37 hours, the X-8 was found. However it soon became evident that one of its amatol charges was leaking water, thus upsetting the craft's trim. The charge had to be disconnected. The fuse was set to "safe," but it did not work properly. The charge exploded awhile after release. Luckily, by then it had sunk to a depth of about 900 meters, so the detonation did not damage either of the submarines. Soon, however, it was discovered that the other charge was partly loose. No other option remained but to withdraw the X-8 from the operation. Anyway, as this midget submarine was set to attack the *Lützow*—which was the least important target—the overall damage to Operation Source was limited. When it was decided to release the second amatol charge, the commander of the midget submarine said: "We'll surface, and to hell with the safety delay this time. Set the detonator at two hours."[519]

Despite the fact that the *Seanyph* and X-8 had covered a respectable distance when the charge exploded, the resulting pressure wave seriously damaged X-8. Barry's instructions had to be followed. After the crew had been picked up by a dinghy and brought to the *Seanymph*, the X-8 was sent to the bottom of the ocean. The loss of X-8 was a setback, but at least all crewmen were saved. The X-9 suffered a more unfortunate fate. On 16 September, when the commander on board the *Syrtis*, Lieutenant M.H. Jupp, signalled to the midget submarine to surface, he received no reply. It soon became evident that the hawser had failed. The *Syrtis* turned back to search for X-9, but she was never found. Jupp informed the Admiralty when he had gained sufficient distance from the Norwegian coast. Thus two of the older hawsers had failed. One can't but speculate on what would have happened if all X-crafts had used the older type, or if all had used nylon hawsers.[520]

The three midget submarines X-5, X-6, and X-10 enjoyed fairly uneventful voyages until they reached the Norwegian coast between 17–19 September. The *Stubborn* and X-7 found their way there too. When all the midget subs had arrived, it was time to shift crews. At this stage, an encouraging message arrived from London, stating that technicians on the *Tirpitz* would give their sonar an overhaul on 22 September, thus the risk of detection would be reduced. The information emanated from Ultra, but to conceal the origin it was said to come from Norwegian informants in Alta.[521]

On the evening of 19 September Cameron and his crew prepared to move to X-6, replacing the weary members of the transport crew, who could at last stretch themselves. It was gloaming but not dark, which was a favorable condition—not light enough to make the craft easy for the Germans to see, but still light enough to enable the crews to see the surrounding terrain and large German ships. Cameron and his engineer, Goddard, were the first pair to climb aboard the small dinghy that would bring them to X-6. Strenuously—and with hands ever frozen due to the cold wind and water—they reached the midget submarine by using the towing hawser. Lieutenant Wilson met them as they boarded the X-6. He briefly informed Cameron of the condition of the craft. "Mostly, it has been all right," he said, "but the starboard charge leaks water and we have also observed that one of the ballast tanks has a crack."

Cameron nodded. Despite the increasing darkness, he noted that Wilson had black shadows beneath his eyes and a face that spoke of exhaustion. "I see. Anything else?"

"Yes, the bloody periscope leaks water. Everything else is fine."

"Thanks, Wille. Get some warm toddy and turn in between clean sheets. We can discuss our experiences when we get back."

Wilson briefly stared at Cameron. What were the chances that he and his crew would survive and return? He wanted to say something but could not find the words. He shook Cameron's hand and said, "Good luck, Don."

Wilson and another crewmember entered the dinghy, which was pulled back to the *Truculent*. Goddard had already entered X-6 and Cameron followed him. On board the submarine, Lorimer and Kendall, the first officer and the diver, prepared themselves to be transferred to the midget sub. They walked along the slippery deck toward the dinghy. Suddenly, Lorimer was assailed by doubts. He began to hope that he would trip and break a foot or something else, just to avoid the forthcoming nightmare. When the two men were helped from the dinghy, Lorimer heard a hissing sound.

"It's losing air!" he exclaimed and pointed at the dinghy. "It can't take us to the X-craft."

One of the sailors, who was much older than Lorimer, must have realized what the young man was thinking. "No problem, sir," he said with a paternal voice. "It's just water running out of the holes in the casing."

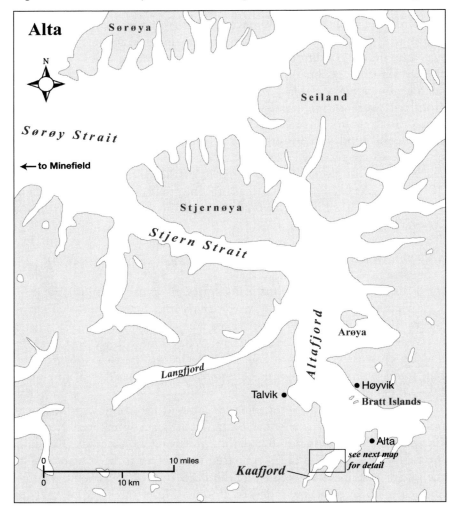

Lorimer was ashamed by his reaction and felt much better when he had entered the dinghy with Kendall. He glanced at the sailors who had helped him. They smiled in the dusk and raised their hands to salute. "Good luck, sir. See you again in two days."[522]

The final phase of Operation Source was about to begin.

Into the Stjernsundet

On Monday, 20 September, all the midget submarines that were to attack the *Tirpitz*—including X-7—separated from the larger submarines behind which they had thus far been towed. The first obstacle was a 25-kilometer-long minefield at the entrance to Sørøysundet. From there, they were supposed to proceed to the mouth of the Stjernsundet, where the Germans were known to have hydrophones and coastal artillery. This part was to be completed under the cover of darkness. During daylight, the midget submarines would continue submerged through Stjernsundet and into the Altafjord, until they reached a cluster of small islands known as Brattholmarna. These were located seven kilometers north of Alta. There, the crews would rest for the last time before breaking into Kaafjord. In the early hours of 22 September, the attack would begin. The first obstacle was a submarine net which covered the entrance to the Kaafjord. Once they had penetrated the net, the craft would continue toward the target—the *Tirpitz*, which was moored at a bay known as Barbrudalen—and force their way through the net cage protecting the battleship. According to a previously established schedule, the charges would be placed under the battleship between 01.00 and 08.00, known as the "attacking period." The charges would be set to detonate between 08.00 and 09.00 to avoid blowing up any other attacking X-craft. If an X-craft did not manage to place its charge before 08.00, it would have to wait until the next attacking period between 09.00 and 12.00, which was followed by another "fire period" from 12.00 to 13.00. The pattern of alternating periods followed until all crews had accomplished their mission. That is, if any of them even made it to the target.[523]

The first daylight could just be seen when yet another incident occurred, one which could potentially have ruined the operation. When the *Stubborn* neared the point where she would disconnect X-7, one of her lookouts observed an object in the water ahead—a drifting mine. It was too late to make an evasive maneuver. The crew on the bridge anxiously saw the mine pass very close to the submarine, but the danger was not over. A powerful wave brought it into contact with the towing hawser, which it followed. The mine "rolled" along the wire and came perilously close to the midget submarine. In fact, it even bounced into the bow of the X-craft. The crew on board the *Stubborn* expected it to explode at any moment. However, none of the horns broke at impact. Rather, the mine's anchor wire became entangled with the towing wire and the mine got stuck at the bow.[524]

Lieutenant Godfrey Place—who had almost lost his life during one of the exercises—noted that something was banging. As he raised his head above the hatch, he saw that the *Stubborn* had reduced speed and men at her bridge were gesticulating wildly. He could not see what had caused the sound, but when he moved forward on the narrow deck, he saw something that would later make him break out in a cold sweat as he recalled the event. As the mine was next to the amatol charges, a detonation would destroy the *Stubborn* as well as the X-7. Place realized that the only chance of survival was to disentangle the frightening object without allowing it to come into contact with the X-7. He first tried to kick it away, but met with no success. Then he tried to push it down with his foot, to see if the mine would come loose. He was prepared to keep it at distance with his foot, but it did not come loose. He soon discovered that one of the contact horns were broken, which was the most likely explanation for why it had not yet exploded—provided that it was not only the detonator in the broken horn that was defective.[525]

Finally, Place laid down to disentangle the wires. He leaned above the black sphere and worked with one hand while holding himself with the other. It took him almost ten minutes, but at last he saw the mine move. He kicked it, and managed to get it sufficiently far away from the X-craft. As the enthusiastic cheers from the *Stubborn's* crew still rang in his ears, he climbed back into the midget submarine, shivering from the cold but deeply relieved.[526]

Later in the evening, Donald Cameron in the X-6 disconnected from the *Truculent* and began his attempt to penetrate the German defenses. When the mother submarine had disappeared, Cameron and his crew were alone. Although the other midget submarines could not be far away, he did not see any of them as he steered toward the minefield. According to information from the Admiralty, the first minefield would not present any danger to ships with very limited draught, like midget submarines.[527]

At the same time, X-5, X-7, and X-10 travelled on parallel courses. Henty-Creer's X-5 and Place's X-7 had no known mechanical defects when they left their mother submarines, and the midget sub crews were confident. Hudspeth's X-10 was plagued by a leaking periscope, and there was also a problem with the pump to the Wet-and-Dry. Nevertheless, Hudspeth believed these problems could be attended to later.[528]

Cameron too suffered from a leaking periscope, and the leaking charge would probably cause difficulties. The latter caused the X-craft to list to starboard, which would make it more difficult to maneuver in the fjords. Cameron had ordered that most of the equipment be stowed on the port side. Also, much of the provisions were dispensed with. Hopefully these measures would suffice.[529]

The night was wonderful; tranquil, with a clear sky and a magnificent aurora borealis. On one occasion, Cameron saw light from a ship, but he estimated that the distance was at least five kilometers, thus any lookouts would hardly see the midget submarines. On the horizon, he could see the dark shades of Sørøya. He reckoned it would take three hours to reach the coast.[530]

Despite the fact that they did not sail far from each other, the crew on board X-6 did not see any other X-craft before the attack. In a sense it was unfortunate, as the sight of any comrades would have been comforting. On the other hand, the fact that the craft could not be seen was reassuring, as the enemy would also find it difficult to observe them.[531]

This notion was encouraging when the X-6 entered the minefield at 00.00. The moon was high on the starry sky. Cameron gazed at the German coastal batteries, which were known to be located to protect the western entrance to the Stjernsundet. However, on this night a light snowfall concealed them. British intelligence had not established the precise location of the minefield, but it seemed likely that the deepest part of the sound was the most densely mined, as a large warship would probably sail in that area. Also, it seemed plausible to assume that the sea next to the shore was mined, to prevent small craft from entering.

Hence, Cameron tried to remain close to the shore, but not too close. He could not know if his decision made any difference, but a few hours later, the X-6 had passed the most dangerous area. Soon the stars paled as the red light of dawn appeared. Simultaneously the sea—which had been dead calm—began to move as the wind increased.[532]

After a final check, Cameron decided to dive to a depth of 20 meters. Two hours later he almost went up to the surface, allowing him to take a look through the periscope, but the glass was misty. He had to dive deeper and disassemble the periscope to dry it. When they again resumed periscope depth, Cameron could see enough to conclude that the entrance to the Stjernsundet was immediately ahead. He also noted that the sun was rising above the horizon. He decided to remain on the northern side, where the mountains cast a shadow on the water, which would render his X-craft more difficult to see from German reconnaissance aircraft.[533]

After plotting the course through the Stjernsundet, Cameron took his periscope down and brought the X-6 to a depth of 20 meters. He and his men were very nervous. Did German hydrophone operators listen carefully enough to hear the whispering sound of the X-6's electrical engine? Would the men in X-6 note anything before the German depth charges exploded? Their manually aimed sonar was used to listen in all directions. Any sound might indicate that they had been found. But nothing was heard.

After having proceeded submerged for a long while, Cameron again took X-6 up to periscope depth. The shadow from the mountains once more proved advantageous. Reflections from the sun might otherwise have blinded him when looking through the periscope. However, except for a few anti-aircraft batteries on the hills, he saw nothing of the Germans. He pulled down the scope and quickly calculated speed and course.

"We continue along the northern shore," he said. "I estimate that we will reach the Altafjord in nine hours."[534]

The X-6 continued through the Stjernsundet in daylight, mostly submerged, but occasionally with the crew checking the course through the periscope. In the afternoon the midget submarine reached the Altafjord and turned south, with Aarøya to port and the mouth of the Langfjord—where the *Lützow* would have been moored—to starboard. At 16.00 Cameron again raised the periscope, only to find that the Altafjord was quiet. No enemy patrol boats could be seen. Dusk was imminent, but several huts could still be observed on the shores. The

Langnesholmen was on starboard quarter and soon the town of Alta appeared to the south. After another two and a half hours submerged, Cameron once more went to periscope depth. After carefully checking the surroundings through the periscope and sonar, it was deemed dark enough to surface. Cameron opened the aft hatch and climbed up on the narrow deck. They were not far from Høyvik, on the eastern shore of the Altafjord. "The coast is clear," he whispered through the opened hatch. "Let's move closer to shore."[535]

Slowly, the midget submarine turned into a small bay and Cameron ordered the engine to be shut down. He inspected the surroundings. To the north, the 500-meter-high Altenesfjællet rose. With the moon behind, it appeared like a huge shadow. Along the shore, snow spots gleamed white. Cold water splashed over the casing and made Cameron's shoes wet. Ahead, he saw the Brattholmarna, which marked the last stage before the attack. Behind them, the lights from Alta could be discerned. In Britain, blackout had been strictly enforced since the first days of war, but at this distant latitude, the Germans felt safe from enemy bombers.

Suddenly Cameron stiffened. A light flashed at him from a distance of less than 30 meters away. It appeared from nowhere and the sight temporarily paralyzed him. At last he realized that there was a building on the shore, and somebody had opened a door. The beam of light fell on the snow, as well as the stones near the shore and on the water itself. A male voice said something in a language Cameron didn't understand. A few heartbeats passed. The voices were neither whispering nor shouting. The two men talked normally, but they did not see the X-6 in the dark water. Cameron did not move, but just stared at the light. Then the door closed and the light disappeared.[536]

Cameron had hardly recovered from the shock when he saw another light. This time it was a small ship approaching. Such dangers were something he was trained for, thus the paralyzation subsided. He dashed through the hatch and immediately gave orders to dive. Submerged, they left the bay, and half an hour later resurfaced. Immediately another ship was seen—this time from the opposite direction—and another crash dive ensued. Cameron had seen a searchlight and presumed it was a patrol boat. He and his crew could hear how the propeller noise intensified. It seemed that the enemy had found X-6 and headed for it. But then the noise reached its peak, changed character, and gradually diminished. They could breath freely again.[537]

"Ships seem to sail during the night in Norwegian waters," Cameron said, thoughtful of thed fact that few ships had been seen in daylight. Now they had almost collided with two ships, one of them probably on patrol. "Thank God they sail with lanterns switched on."[538]

Aided by the sonar, the crew could judge when the last ship was far enough to allow them to resurface. They turned toward Tømmelholm, one of the largest islets in the Brattholmarna. It resembled a submarine and the Germans would perhaps not notice yet another one. Cameron and his crew maneuvered the X-6 into a sheltered position and switched off the engine. Here Cameron, Lorimer, Goddard, and Kendall would wait for the dawn while they charged the batteries.[539]

As Cameron looked at the lights in Alta and along the nets at the entrance to the Kaafjord through his binoculars, he pondered the progress of the other X-craft. Did they, like X-6, wait somewhere in the shadows? Or had they been lost like the X-8 or X-9? In fact, Place as well as Henty-Creer were only a few hundred meters from X-6. Hudspeth would soon arrive. All of them had managed so far, but they had been beset by questions similar to Cameron's. Only one thing was certain: they would do their utmost when the final phase began. The only exception was Hudspeth, as his periscope was almost useless and both his compasses were out of order. It was almost inconceivable to enter the Kaafjord in such circumstances. Most likely, Hudspeth would just risk revealing the operation prematurely if he attempted to carry out his attack. However, he would do his utmost to repair the malfunctioning equipment, unaware that the *Scharnhorst* had already weighed anchor and sailed into the Altafjord. In fact, Place had seen the battleship off Aarøya earlier in the day. The British lieutenant could hardly have known that the *Scharnhorst's* commander, Captain Hüffmeier, had been disappointed with his crew's proficiency during Operation Sizilien and had decided to conduct firing exercises. Place had briefly considered attacking the *Scharnhorst*, but abstained. Unfortunately, he had no means to inform Hudspeth.[540]

The night was peaceful. From the hatch leading down to the control room, Cameron could hear the weak sounds as the crew listened to a BBC broadcast. It was also possible to hear the distant sound from radio bulletins and music from merchant ships outside Alta. At 21.00, several searchlights at the destroyer base at Leiffsbotun were lit, and the Germans also fired flares. At first, Cameron thought one of the other midget submarines had been observed, but soon activity subsided and no destroyer put to sea. It had probably just been a false alarm. Somewhat later, he saw a motor vehicle driving along the shore with headlights lit. It appeared to be a limousine of some kind. Perhaps it was Admiral Kummetz on his way to the *Tirpitz*.

How would the Admiral react if Operation Source proceeded according to plan and his battleship foundered?[541]

Through the Nets

At 04.00 Cameron raised his periscope to check the net blocking the entrance to the Kaafjord, about 800 meters away. Stretching from Auskarneset in the north to Jemeluftneset to the south, it was almost a kilometer long. It had a 400- meter-long turnable net boom in the south, which could be opened to allow ships unhindered passage. According to available intelligence, the net almost reached down to the bottom of the fjord, approximately 50 meters. Only two options remained: to cut a hole in the net or use the gate. The Allies did not know that the Germans had not yet completed the net. Rather, they had placed a number of buoys to dupe agents and air reconnaissance.[542]

Cameron and his crew had left Tømmelholm just before 02.00, dived to a depth of 20 meters, and set course toward the entrance. Kendall had already put on his diving gear and waited in the Wet-and-Dry. When they reached the net, he would leave the craft to cut a hole in it, while the midget submarine put pressure on it. When the net yielded, Kendall would ensure that no parts of the net hooked onto the X-craft. In particular, great caution had to be observed to avoid any rudder or the propeller fastening in the net. Once the submarine had made it though, he would grab the net and manage to re-enter the sluice chamber. Despite all his training, the task was daunting.[543]

During the night the weather had changed and become more favorable—low cloud base, rough sea, and intermittent showers. The waves would render the periscope more difficult to detect and the rain would distract German sentries. However, when the sun rose above the mountains, the weather cleared and the sea became dead calm. Regardless, neither condition improved visibility for Cameron, as all he could see through his periscope was some kind of greenish blur.

"Go down 60 feet," he said. "The periscope has flooded."[544]

Yet again, Cameron disassembled the periscope. Nobody uttered a word, but they all had the same thought: how would they sneak through two nets and position the charges if they constantly had to interrupt the attack and clean the periscope?[545]

When the periscope again had been fitted in its proper position, they continued toward the net. Suddenly they heard a ship approach and pass above them. Cameron ordered periscope depth and glimpsed the stern of a trawler, before water again leaked into the periscope and blurred the ocular. He quickly assessed the situation. If the trawler was entering the Kaafjord, the gate would be open for a short time. This was a piece of luck they had never planned for, but the X-6 could only make two knots submerged, insufficient to make it before the gate closed.

Unless they proceeded on the surface …?

"They're opening the gate to let her in," he said. "Starboard 20 degrees. Come to the surface. Full speed ahead on the diesel."

Lorimer and Godall glanced at Cameron, as if they had not heard him correctly, but then automatically followed the instructions. Soon the midget submarine surfaced and quickly increased its speed in the trawler's wake. Neither the German sentries nor anybody on the trawler seemed to notice the X-craft, or else they presumed it was an object towed by the trawler. No alarm was given and the X-6 entered the Kaaford safely.[546]

After the successful breakthrough, the periscope again required attention. This time they had to disassemble it thoroughly and clean it methodically. However, it became evident that the leak was outside the pressure hull. They could only wipe out the moisture as carefully as possible. The next time they assumed periscope depth, Cameron made his only thorough exploration inside the Kaafjord. He saw several German warships, including five destroyers and several smaller vessels. In all, he counted a dozen warships of destroyer size or smaller. On the starboard, he saw net defenses, but no warship inside. This had been the berth used by the *Scharnhorst*. He considered himself fortunate not to have chosen a course farther to starboard, as he might have got stuck in the net. However, the most important object was seen at Barbrudalen. Below the Lillefjæll, the *Tirpitz* was far larger and more majestic than anything else in the fjord. Between the German battleship and X-6, two destroyers were bunkering from a tanker. Cameron decided to maintain a steady course submerged, and again take the X-6 up to periscope depth after proceeding below the destroyers.[547]

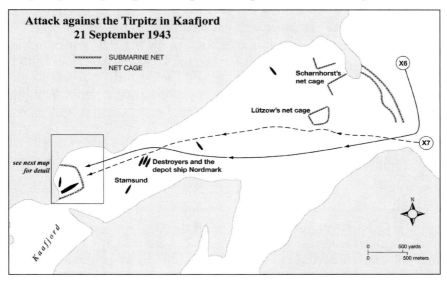

At 20 meters below the surface, Cameron and his crew approached the target. They were virtually blind at that depth, and it was also difficult to maintain trim. The Kaafjord contained a mixture of saltwater from the sea and freshwater from melting snow. As the density differed between salt and fresh water, the submarine either sank or rose as it moved forward. To counter this effect, Lorimer had to pump water in or out of the tanks, causing noise that might be heard by German hydrophone operators.[548]

Minute was added to minute and became an hour until the X-6, which proceeded at a mere two knots, reached the point Cameron had estimated would be located beyond the bunkering destroyers. He raised the periscope and found that he was perilously close to the ships. He immediately dived again, switched off the engine, and silently waited for any signs that X-6 might have been detected, but nothing happened. After waiting a few minutes, they continued toward the final obstacle: the torpedo nets surrounding the battleship.[549]

At the net cage, an unpleasant surprise awaited. According to the intelligence, the nets should not have extended down to the bottom of the fjord, but only to a depth of 20 meters. However, as Cameron looked at them through the porthole, which had been fitted for this purpose, he saw them disappear into the darkness below. Even when Cameron dived to 60 meters and reached the bottom of the fjord, the elusive meshes still prevented any passage.[550]

In fact, what Cameron saw was not a single net. The buoys would never have managed the weight. Rather, the Germans had placed three partly overlapping nets. The first covered the 20 meters closest to the surface, the second prevented any intruder operating a depth between 20 and 40 meters, and the third net covered the remaining section down to the bottom.[551]

Cameron assessed his options. The first was to order Kendall to leave the midget submarine and cut a hole in the net. It was a time-consuming alternative, and additionally undesirable since it was almost 07.00. Little time would remain before the end of the first fire period. Cameron also considered entering below the gate, where the nets perhaps did not extend to the bottom of the fjord.

He again assumed periscope depth to locate the gate. However, he did not know that the Germans had decided to leave the gate open during the day, as the telephone line between the battleship and the authorities on land had been broken due to some technical problem. Through the misty periscope, Cameron could see the blurry spheres he knew held the nets. He also saw a patrol boat on its way into the net cage. He again made a daring decision to surface and go full speed ahead.[552]

The sleek silhouette of X-6 again appeared above the surface, and again she followed in the wake of a German ship. "We have made it," Cameron said. "Dive!"

Incredibly, they were not detected this time either. Through one of the portholes, Cameron believed he saw the Germans close the gate behind them. He informed his crew while the water covered the diving craft and made it invisible in the fjord. The midget submarine followed a west-southwesterly course, about 200 meters from the battleship on her port side. Cameron was in a hurry, as the other X-craft might already have placed charges that could explode within an hour. He decided to position his first charge below the aft turrets, then pass along the keel and place the second charge below the fore turrets. The charges had been designed to explode if another charge exploded. It was hoped that simultaneous explosions at both ends of the ship would lift her and cause the ship to break somewhere in her mid-section. He raised the periscope, but the almost useless lenses only allowed a vague impression of the battleship.[553]

Cameron estimated that a 90-degree turn would bring X-6 right beneath the aft keel, and he was just about to issue the order when the midget submarine hit a sunken rock. The impact threw him on the gyrocompass. Lorimer lost control of the craft and the midget submarine climbed toward the surface. Briefly, the gloom inside the craft suddenly gave wave to rays of daylight entering through the portholes. Lorimer regained composure and managed to dive, and X-6 again disappeared beneath the surface.[554]

However, the harm was already done. On board the *Tirpitz*, a German NCO next to his anti-aircraft gun saw the X-6.[555]

He sounded the alarm.

"Well, then it must have been a porpoise."

Cameron's team was not the only one that managed to penetrate into the Kaafjord. Godfrey Place and X-7 had sailed from the Brattholmarna almost an hour before Cameron. At 04.00, he and his crew penetrated the net blocking the Kaafjord using the open gate, just as Cameron had. In the Kaafjord, he almost collided with a patrol boat and had to dive deep. He lost orientation and got stuck in a net cage where the *Lützow* had previously been berthed. It took him almost an hour to get back on track, and when Place resumed the course bringing him toward the *Tirpitz*, Cameron had overtaken him.[556]

The unfortunate collision with the *Lützow's* net cage had not only caused delay but also damage. The gyrocompass was out of order, as well as a trim-pump. Place was nevertheless determined to continue toward the target. When he arrived at the torpedo nets surrounding the *Tirpitz* an hour later, he too found that the nets reached to the bottom of the fjord. He tried to find a gap in the defenses, but only managed to get stuck. By emptying his trim tanks and using full power to reverse, he managed to get away, but the maneuver caused his craft to briefly surface. Place was fortunate. The Germans did not see X-7 and he could make another attempt, but again he got stuck, despite trying at greater depth. He did not understand that the Germans had positioned three overlapping nets designed to halt torpedoes, not midget submarines. Thus he could have passed the obstacle by first proceeding deep until he reached the net, and then rising along it. Instead, he repeatedly collided with the bottom net and got stuck. Place could imagine how the buoys must have been moving when the X-craft pushed against the net.[557]

On board the *Tirpitz*, normal morning routines were carried out. Several hours had elapsed since the gate had been opened, and the men operating the sonar had turned their equipment off before the scheduled maintenance. Breakfast had been served and many were eating. Those who were off-duty gathered in small groups to chat, play games, or listen to radio broadcasts. The recent attack on Svalbard was discussed, as well as rumors that the *Lützow* would be sent back to Germany for overhaul. The *Tirpitz* would probably be next in line. Maybe they would be home for Christmas. However, several months lay ahead and much work remained. Today, work on the light artillery would be conducted and the guns would be partly disassembled for overhaul, a procedure already initiated. Admiral Kummetz had left the flagship for his daily ride. He had a horse in a stable not far from the berth.[558]

A German NCO was supervising the work at one of the port anti-aircraft guns when he suddenly saw Cameron's X-6 break the surface of the water close to the shore, 200 meters from the battleship. The sight was so unexpected that a few seconds passed before he reacted. When X-6 had disappeared, he shouted to Lieutenant Hellendorn, who was not far away: "Lieutenant! I saw a long, black object over there. It looked like a submarine!"

"Submarine?" Hellendorn turned his head in the direction indicated by the NCO. As the X-6 had already dived, hardly a ripple could be seen. "Where?"

"Over there! At the shore."

Hellendorn inspected the shore incredulously. Then he eyed the NCO. "You are dreaming," he said. "How would a submarine manage to get there?"

However, the NCO remained adamant.

"Well, then it must have been a porpoise," Hellendorn suggested.

"I don't think so, lieutenant. There was a hatch on the back."

"Did it have a tower? A submarine usually has a tower. Did you see any?"

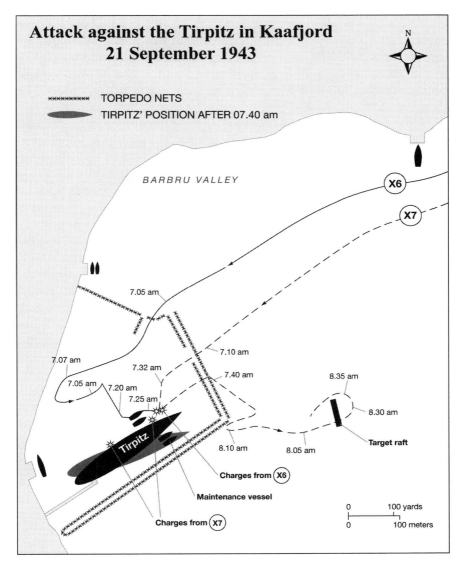

**Attack against the Tirpitz in Kaafjord
21 September 1943**

N

××××××××× TORPEDO NETS

TIRPITZ' POSITION AFTER 07.40 am

BARBRU VALLEY

X6

X7

7.05 am

7.10 am

7.07 am

7.32 am

7.40 am

8.35 am

7.05 am   7.20 am

7.25 am

8.30 am

Tirpitz

8.10 am   8.05 am

Target raft

Charges from X6

Maintenance vessel

Charges from X7

0   100 yards

0   100 meters

"No, it had no tower."

Hellendorn ridiculed the NCO and suggested he book time with the doctor. "A submarine without a tower," he taunted. "You must be crazy. And how do you think the submarine could have made it there? Do you know how shallow it is over there?"

The man who had seen the X-6 became uncertain. Indeed it was shallow near the shore. Could he have seen some kind of animal or something else floating in the water? If he insisted, Hellendorn had to sound the alarm. If nothing were found, the whistleblower would become the laughing-stock of the entire ship. No, it was no good. The matter would rest there.[559]

However, the anti-aircraft soldier was not the only person who had seen something. Coxswain Hans Schmidt had the watch on upper deck when a seaman rushed up to him panting and told him he had seen a submarine in the net cage. Schmidt remained skeptical, but the other stuck to his guns. To appease the excited seaman, Schmidt said he would report the observation. The coxswain found the officer on duty, Lieutenant Wallucks, and reported what the seaman had seen.

Wallucks appeared unconvinced. He had previously caused several false alarms and did not want to stick his neck out once more. "That's just rubbish," he said to Schmidt. "He must have seen a tortoise."[560]

Inside X-6, Cameron and his men listened for anything that might suggest the Germans had observed them. The midget submarine had broken the surface briefly at 07.07, but the minutes were ticking away without anything happening. No patrol boats approached; no depth charges exploded. What was the enemy doing? It seemed inconceivable that nobody had seen X-6. After three minutes, Cameron decided to reconnoiter. However, the impact had destroyed both compasses, thus he could not even know in which direction he was pointed. Cameron decided to start the engine and ordered Lorimer to take X-6 to periscope depth, but the craft proved very difficult to maneuver and again became visible above the surface. The Germans saw it and sounded the alarm.[561]

The battleship's commander, Captain Hans Meyer, was in his cabin. He had been eating when the first officer, Commander Wolf Junge, entered and reported that one of the lookouts had seen what appeared to be a submarine inside the nets. This was the first observation, which had now filtered up through the chain of command. Meyer and Junge temporarily looked at each other. "A small submarine, you say?" Meyer asked thoughtfully.

"Probably yet another false alarm," Junge replied.

Meyer nodded. "At least it is reassuring that the crew is watchful," he said. "However, let us, as a matter of precaution, order action stations. Who is on duty?"

"Wallucks."

"I see. Thank you, Junge."[562]

Godfrey Place had no idea that X-6 had snuck into the net cage; far less did he realize that the Germans had observed Cameron. Also, he had his own problems. At the same time as his X-6 was discovered by the Germans, X-7 had got free from the net closest to the bottom of the fjord, and for a moment it appeared above the surface. Still unaware that there was more than one layer, Place realized that he had nevertheless managed to enter the net cage. The *Tirpitz* loomed large in Place's periscope, less than 100 meters away. He hadn't the faintest idea how they had got inside the nets, but ordered a dive to 20 meters and half speed ahead. Soon he could discern a large shadow in one of the portholes, and soon he felt a thud as the X-craft's stem hit the battleship.[563]

One can only speculate on the men's feelings as they finally reached their target, after years of training and hardship. Place believed they were close to turret Bruno. The first officer let the craft sink toward the bottom and Place set the detonator to explode at 08.10. The midget submarine became lighter as the charge was jettisoned and came to rest in the silt. Thereafter, Place issued an order that would bring X-7 along the keel of the battleship. At this moment, the *Tirpitz* seemed to wake up, as banging sounds were heard from it. Soon propeller noise and explosions were also perceived.

But X-7 had not caused the noise. When X-6 surfaced for the second time, several Germans saw her. The NCO who had initially seen her shouted loudly: "A submarine! A submarine!"[564]

Wallucks heard the shouts and hurried to the port side, where he too witnessed what he had not believed seconds before—a small, underwater craft with a broken periscope surfaced. The casing was only seen briefly before the craft dived again. Many seamen shouted that a submarine had got inside the nets. One of the sentries cocked his rifle. The first shot echoed in the fjord, as he sent a bullet toward the still visible periscope. Wallucks dashed to the telephone and rang Junge.[565]

The slow German reaction on this momentous day was partly the consequence of numerous false alarms. Another explanation was the frequent drills the crew conducted. Meyer's previous second, Heinz Assmann, had tested the crew in all conceivable scenarios, from sabotage to attacking enemy divers. He had been inventive and the exercises had been very realistic. However, there was an unwelcome side effect. The crew became used to "Assmann's tricks." So many alarms had been sounded that the crew was almost dulled.

There is another plausible explanation. While the Germans also developed midget submarines, the efforts were kept secret and few men in the Kriegsmarine knew anything about them. Thus the lookouts knew that an ordinary submarine could hardly get past the nets. They did not expect midget subs. Furthermore, the reaction was hampered by an almost comic event. Wallucks was briefly confused when he sounded the alarm. The normal signal for submarine alert was one long blast followed by five short ones. However in his hurry, he forgot the initial blast and only the five short ones were heard. This was the peacetime signal for the crew to report at the watertight bulkheads, for example in case of running aground. Thus many realized that something had happened but were puzzled, as the battleship remained immobile.[566]

While anti-aircraft gunners hastened to their battle stations and the crews on the light artillery frantically worked to bring their partly dismantled guns back into firing order, many seamen not employed for any specific tasks dashed to the port side where X-6 had been seen. The short distance between the midget submarine and the battleship did not allow the latter's guns to be lowered enough to fire on the target, but small arms could be used, and quick-witted NCOs gave orders to get hand grenades.

Unaware that the battleship was alerted, Cameron proceeded to the position where he estimated the *Tirpitz* was located. He tried to follow the progress through the porthole, but instead X-6 was stopped by something. Cameron at first believed they had run below the battleship and into the torpedo net on her starboard side. In actuality, they were beneath a supply ship and had got entangled in wire that hung into the water. The X-6 tried to get loose by alternating between full power ahead and reverse. Suddenly, the craft came off the wire and burst above the surface before Lorimer could regain control.[567]

When the green, murky water had suddenly disappeared from the portholes, Cameron saw the *Tirpitz* only 20 meters away. At such short distance, the battleship was so huge that he could no longer observe it from bow to stern. Rather, it looked like an endless hull. He clearly saw the faces of German sailors along the gunwale, as clanging and banging was heard inside the midget submarine. Cameron also saw the muzzle flashes from German weapons. It was like facing a firing squad.[568]

Cameron immediately gave orders to dive. Despite the fact that X-6 was disclosed, there might still be a chance to place the charges beneath the battleship. The midget submarine quickly reached the bottom beneath the long keel of the ship. Cameron's watch showed 07.22 and he set the detonator to 08.22—a one-hour delay. Above him, the battleship made tremendous noise.[569]

Place, too, heard the Germans stirred to full activity, as he and his crew reached the aft section of the battleship. When they presumed to be below turrets Caesar and Dora, Place and his crew jettisoned their second mine. Believing that X-7 were the root cause of all the noise, Place decided to hurry for the net cage and get out of the Barbrudalen before the mines exploded.

On board X-6, Cameron decided that it was time to surrender. He realized that even if they made it out of the net cage, the gate at the fjord entrance would be closed. Also, the five German destroyers he had seen would most likely be lying in wait for him.[570]

Cameron looked at his crew; none had any objections. All of them were exhausted as a result of lack of sleep and the tension felt during the previous days. Outside the hull, a few hand grenades exploded. They caused no damage, but the resulting sound inside the crammed craft was terrible.

"Our mission is accomplished," Cameron concluded. "We can't do anything more. Let's surface and scuttle the craft."

Before they reached the surface, secret documents, maps, and sensitive equipment were destroyed. Then Cameron gave his last orders on the X-6.

"Open the seacocks when we reach the surface," he said. "Put the motor going astern with hydroplanes to dive!"

Soon, light again entered the portholes. Rifle bullets clanged at the hull, giving the impression of workers smashing it with sledgehammers. A few hand grenades exploded nearby.

"Who will leave the craft first?" Cameron shouted to make himself heard.

"I will," Goddard replied.

He had just started the engine, which slowly pulled X-6 astern toward the battleship. Water entered the lower parts of the midget submarine, making the crew's feet wet. He opened the forward hatch and the shooting immediately ceased. While greedily inhaling the fresh air, Goddard moved his head above the hatch. His eyes screwed up in the sunshine, but he was nevertheless able to see a motorboat with several German sailors in it. An NCO, holding a grenade in his hand, shouted something in German. Goddard raised his arms above his head and moved on the hull toward the German boat, while the rest of the crew followed behind him.

The Germans made a sign to the British instructing them to jump on board the motorboat, which they could do without wetting their feet. The German NCO had intended to capture X-6, but it reversed ever faster and deeper. A rope thrown to attached the two vessels stretched more and more. The Germans realized that X-6 might pull their boat down and so they cut the rope.[571]

Captain Meyer was still in his cabin when the shooting began. What was it all about? The Norwegian resistance had made several sabotage attempts, for example rolling depth charges down the hill slopes. Had the sentries seen something suspicious? Or was it about the presumed underwater craft again? Meyer had heard Wallucks' erroneous alarm. He assumed, quite correctly, that the officer on duty had made some mistake. Rather it was intended to signal action stations, which Meyer himself had ordered. What he didn't know was that Wallucks had not yet received Meyer's instruction, but sounded the alarm on his own initiative. So from Meyer's perspective, the signal only seemed odd, not alarming. Shooting, however, was something quite different. Admiral Kummetz was ashore, and Meyer hoped that he had not suffered any mishap.

The gunfire ceased just as suddenly as it had begun. Meyer finished his activities and was just about to dress and walk to the bridge when the shooting was resumed. This time he clearly heard hand grenades exploding. He rapidly put on his boots and had just got his coat on when Junge once again knocked on the door.

The slightly panting second entered, telling Meyer that a small submarine indeed *had* managed to get inside the nets. Junge told Meyer that four men had come out of it before the craft disappeared in the water.[572]

Meyer and Junge hurried to the bridge while the proper signal for action stations resounded. Wallucks had finally realized his mistake, but as the blasts once again echoed in the valley, most of the crew had already taken up positions. When Meyer reached the bridge, all around him was calm. The water was like a mirror and nothing could be seen of the enemy. All sections of the ship reported ready for action, a routine that automatically followed after the order to action stations. In the northern part of the fjord, the German destroyers had weighed anchor and now approached the battleship at high speed. Meyer waited for a report on the prisoners, who were being transported to the battleship in the motorboat.[573]

The four British were brought up on the quarterdeck, while German seamen watched them carefully. When Lorimer saw the German naval flag, he turned and asked Cameron, "Shall we salute the flag?"

It was a custom on British ships, and Cameron realized it could appear to their advantage—aside from the irony. "Of course, good idea."

The Germans showed the prisoners where they were to wait. All four British stood at strict attention and saluted the flag. Some of the animosity seen in the German faces appeared to be replaced by curiosity.

One of them asked in German who they were. Cameron replied that they were British Navy officers. The German retorted—in broken English—that they were lying and were actually Russians. How could a small craft of the kind just seen manage the long voyage from Britain to the Kaafjord? The northern Soviet bases, on the other hand, were not far away. The brief exchange of words was followed by a thorough search. The prisoner's possessions were placed in a heap and carefully examined by the Germans, who soon realized that they were indeed British. At this moment, the prisoners heard the signal for action stations and saw German seamen rushing past. The British—who could not know anything about Wallucks' mistake—found the German measures confused. They almost appeared to panic, but at the same time the sentries seemed to triumph.

"Why did you not attack?" one of them asked. "You Englishmen are idiots. You make it so far and then you do not even try to use your torpedoes."[574]

The German assumption was very reasonable, as submarines usually attacked with torpedoes. However, as the minutes passed, a disquieting streak could be seen in the prisoners' demeanor. They did not look like men who had just grossly failed.

Rather, they seemed to be waiting for something—with a mixture of dread and expectation.

Prisoners

On the bridge, Meyer realized that the *Tirpitz* was in obvious danger. He understood that it was impractical to attack with torpedoes inside the net cage. Thus the British must have used mines, either by attaching them to the battleship's hull or positioning them below her keel. Meyer decided that the *Tirpitz* had to leave her cage as quickly as possible. However, no tug was immediately available, and an hour would elapse before the battleship could build up sufficient steam pressure to move on her own. The question was: how much time did they have? Meyer ordered divers to make themselves ready, while other crewmen began to "feel" along the hull sides with long wooden sticks. He also wanted to drag a steel wire along the keel, to see if it got stuck in some object. Meyer had little hope that such measures would produce any useful results, as the sticks did not reach deep enough and only two divers were available. A dozen of the latter would have been more appropriate. However, he had to try something while waiting for the steam pressure to build.[575]

There was one more thing to be done. Several very sturdy hawsers secured the stern, as gales occasionally plagued the northern Norwegian fjords. Efforts to remove the hawsers were already in progress, but half an hour would pass before the work could be completed. However, the bow—which was secured by one chain on the starboard side and one on port—could be moved more easily. Meyer ordered the starboard chain to be retracted, while the port chain was loosened. The maneuver moved the fore sideways, thus no longer right above the three charges placed beneath turret Bruno. It was the most effective of Meyer's countermeasures, but the aft remained above the charge jettisoned by X-7 beneath turrets Caesar and Dora.[576]

Below, on the quarterdeck, the four prisoners waited for the explosion. They could only speculate on what would happen when the charges went off. Perhaps the impact would throw them all onto the deck and provide an opportunity for escape; perhaps the charges would set off the ammunition in the *Tirpitz's* magazines and not even allow them a chance to understand what happened. All they knew was that their watches, now on the deck after the search, were inevitably ticking closer to the preset time.

Such thoughts consumed Cameron and his men, when sudden shouts in German made them look at the water about 60 meters from the battleship. Amazed, they saw a midget submarine attempting to crawl over the row of buoys holding the torpedo net in position. The sight was oddly amusing, but the German reaction lacked all mirthful ingredients. Machine guns rattled, and Hellendorn ordered the 20 and 37 millimeter guns to open fire. The X-7 disappeared below the surface in a forest of white splashes. It had only appeared briefly, but nevertheless Cameron saw that the craft had jettisoned both its charges. Thus, no less than eight tons of amatol were about to explode. Also, it meant that X-6 had not been the only midget submarine to enter the cage. After all the troubles they had had since leaving the mother ship, Cameron found it improbable that yet another craft would have made it. But surely it had, and this meant that an explosion might occur at any moment after 08.00! Cameron's eye fixed upon one of the watches on the deck. It showed 07.40. He, as well as his men and much of the German crew, could be dead in twenty minutes.[577]

Below the surface, not far from the battleship, Place and his men were well aware that a huge explosion might occur soon. After jettisoning their second charge, they had tried to leave the net cage as quickly as possible, but again got stuck in the middle torpedo net. After trying to get loose for 15 very long minutes, X-6 suddenly shot upwards so rapidly and hit the surface at such speed, that it could "run over" the outer section of buoys. They had escaped from the net cage, but both compasses malfunctioned. Also, the compressed air was almost finished up, forcing Place to use the compressor to regulate his depth. Due to the violent maneuvers, Place had lost orientation and effectively made a 180- degree turn, thus running into the upper net once more. They were stuck yet again, this time with the *Tirpitz* and several tons of explosives perilously close. The time was almost 08.00, and they had set their detonator at 08.12.

When the Germans realized that there was more than just one midget submarine inside the net cage, they concluded that a more extensive British operation was being conducted. When X-6 was found and sunk, it appeared to have been just a single attack that had failed. The proof of yet another midget submarine suggested a significant enterprise. If these midget submarines had got so close, perhaps other submarines lurked in the fjord.

As X-7 had been observed, Meyer changed his earlier decision. It appeared safer to remain inside the nets than moving outside of the cage. He was fully aware that the ship had been mined, but he did not know what dangers the Kaafjord presented; perhaps more submarines—only bigger and armed with torpedoes. In that case, it was prudent to remain inside his safe haven, but move the ship from her present position to avoid the mines. Meyer issued a series of orders: an Arado floatplane would be launched to search for submarines; the efforts to move the ship from its present position would be doubled; and the captured British officers would be interrogated more thoroughly.[578]

Cameron had seen X-7 disappear and hoped his comrades would reach the submarine net at the northern part of the fjord. Obviously the Germans would close the gate, but perhaps the midget sub crew could cut their way through the net. Anxiously, he watched the German destroyers, which had already begun to search outside the net cage. His thoughts were interrupted when he and Lorimer were ordered below the deck. Escorted by armed Germans, the two Britons were brought to different cabins. The officer who had talked to them on deck disappeared with Cameron. The officer who was about to question Lorimer was neither an experienced interrogator nor fluent in English. Evidently, he found Lorimer's age important, thus he began the interrogation with the words: "You were born?"[579]

Lorimer confirmed that he had indeed been born, and found no reason not to also inform the German about his age. He thereafter gave the interrogator his rank and name, but refused to answer any other questions. As Lorimer knew that all on board the battleship were in mortal and immediate danger, he did not find the hostile attitude of the German officer offensive. Lorimer's own hands were sweating from fear, and the British lieutenant mobilized all his strength to breathe smoothly. The explosion would occur at any moment.[580]

Kendall and Goddard remained on deck, watching the German destroyers searching for British submarines. Furtively, Kendall glanced at his watch. The minute hand had passed ten minutes past eight.

The thought that less than ten minutes remained before their charges would explode crossed his mind, when suddenly the battleship below him shot up and threw him to the deck as if he were rag doll.[581]

08.12—Explosion!

Many people around the Kaafjord saw the violent explosions, as did many seamen on board the German destroyers and Norwegian merchant ships in the fjord. The *Tirpitz* appeared to rise about two meters from the sea, and men on board fell like leaves. A wave of destruction billowed from stern to bow, buckling bulkheads, bending pipes, and shutting off lights. Automatic fire extinguishers were activated and covered many compartments with foam. All objects not secured were knocked down from shelves, and glass fragments littered many cabins and passages. Below deck, Lorimer had hardly got on his feet again when his guards curtly dragged him to the quarterdeck. Several German sailors were shaking fists toward the British lieutenant. Lorimer heard a distant machine gun firing at an unknown target.[582]

Meyer's decision to use the chains to move the bow sideways saved the battleship from much of the impact. Due to the maneuver, the three mines placed below the forward turrets detonated about sixty meters from the ship. Only the mine jettisoned below the aft turrets by Place exploded where it was intended.[583]

From his submerged position, Godfrey Place too noted the explosion. The pressure waves shook X-7 and the men inside, but also freed the submarine from the net in which it had been stuck. The midget submarine soon appeared on the surface. Place shouted to the first officer and the engineer, telling them to regain control of the craft. Simultaneously, he pushed the plate covering the porthole aside and saw the *Tirpitz* still afloat. Bullets clanged against the hull before X-7 again disappeared below the surface. However, the crew could not control the craft. It resurfaced several times while increasing its distance from the battleship. Soon Place and his crew had reached far enough from the *Tirpitz* to allow her light guns to fire. X-7 received several hits.[584]

On the *Tirpitz's* deck, the prisoners had again been herded together. They saw X-7 appear and dive again. Like the Germans, they believed the craft was headed toward the mouth of the fjord, and thus had managed to put some distance between itself and the German battleship. Helplessly they realized how terrified their comrades must be as shells hit the midget sub. Momentarily the periscope became visible. The German destroyers turned and were soon above X-7. Dark objects fell from them into the water and disappeared, only to be followed by huge cascades of water. The thunder resulting from the depth charges rolled across the valley. Briefly, X-7 had managed to maintain its desired depth, but as it now began to leak water, Place realized it was over. He informed his crew that they would go down to the bottom of the fjord, open the seacocks, wait until the craft was water-filled, and then swim up to the surface 40 meters above by using Davis lungs, a special escape apparatus used in submarines. However, propeller noise as well as detonating depth charges convinced him that another approach had to be used. To swim in the water while depth charges exploded was tantamount to suicide. Place then decided to bring X-7 up to the surface and surrender. Like Cameron, he would open the seacocks to prevent the Germans from capturing the craft.[585]

Navy tradition called for the commander to leave the ship last of all. However, as it was under fire, Place felt bound to go first. He pulled off his white sweater to use it as a flag of capitulation and prepared to open the top hatch. Hardly had the first rays of daylight entered the craft before bullets hit the hull.[586]

The British lieutenant struggled up on deck, waving his sweater. The metal surface of the casing was slippery and he had to support himself on the periscope. The firing ceased, but he realized that they had come so close to a target raft that a collision was inevitable. The impact bounced X-7 out of trim and water flushed down the open hatch. Instinctively, he closed the hatch to prevent his men from drowning. Soon the midget submarine sank and left Place swimming in the cold water. Holding the sweater with his teeth, he swam to the raft and climbed on board it. He had expected the submarine to appear again, but it was nowhere to be found. At this moment he deeply regretted that he had left it before the other men; a decision that would haunt him for the rest of his life.[587]

On board the *Tirpitz*, Cameron, Lorimer, Goddard, and Kendall believed their last moment had arrived. They were lined up against a bulkhead on the quarterdeck and eight Germans armed with submachine guns were eying them intently. "How many?" the officer in command shouted, while menacingly waving his submachine gun. "How many?"

The prisoners did not understand what he referred to—how many submarines or the number of mines? Nevertheless, they had no intention of answering. They silently watched the irritated enemy faces, tried to understand what they said, and waited for the moment when the weapons would be raised against them. The Germans tightened up when a high-ranking officer suddenly appeared. It was Admiral Kummetz, dressed for riding. When he heard the explosions he had gone full tilt back to the battleship. He was on his way to the bridge when the sight of the four prisoners made him halt. In his riding dress, Kummetz appeared out of place. He exchanged a few words with the commander of the guards, who put his gun back in his holster. He had never intended to shoot the prisoners, but they interpreted the sequence of events as if Kummetz had prevented their execution. They breathed more freely. Their task was accomplished and they were still alive. The fact that the German battleship remained afloat was a major disappointment, but clearly she had been damaged.[588]

In the fjord, a motorboat approached the target raft where Place was waiting. He was brought on board the German boat. It turned toward the *Tirpitz* as guns aboard the battleship again opened fire. The prisoners saw another X-craft briefly appear above the surface about 500 meters to the southwest. As Lorimer had seen Place fall from X-7, he concluded that the craft must be Henty-Creer's. The periscope remained visible and once again the craft surfaced, now for the last time. The battleship's guns thundered and the four prisoners thought they saw how X-5 was hit. One German destroyer turned to the area where X-7 had sunk and a few minutes later depth charges exploded.[589] It has never been established how the X-5 was destroyed. It might have been shells from the *Tirpitz* or depth charges from the destroyer. Maybe it was a combination of both. Whatever the cause, the midget submarine X-5 was seen no more.[590]

On the captain's bridge of the *Tirpitz*, Meyer received a succession of damage reports. With every new summary, a gloomier picture emerged. The port propulsion system was knocked out, one generator room was flooded, the electrical power was out in almost the entire ship, radio equipment and hydrophones were inoperable, and the Arado floatplane could not be launched. Also, the ship's fuel was leaking into the fjord.

Twenty minutes after the explosion, 300 tons of water had entered the *Tirpitz*. Despite efforts to pump it out, ten minutes later the amount had increased to 500 tons. The number of wounded rose as the reports arrived, but only one fatal casualty was noted—a seaman who had been thrown into the air was killed when he landed on one of the fore anchor chains. Junge was among the wounded, having suffered a concussion.[591]

In her present condition, the *Tirpitz* was barely capable of defending herself. From the bridge Meyer could see the destroyer Z27, which was searching near the area where X-5 had disappeared. The destroyer took care to avoid getting in the battleship's firing line. Other ships searched with sonar in the outer parts of the fjord. At this stage, the element of surprise was clearly lost and without it further submarines had little chance of success. However, air attacks were a different matter. Wouldn't the Allies be well advised to follow up the midget submarine attack with air attacks—perhaps from carriers off the Norwegian coast? If so, the *Tirpitz* would have limited defensive capability, as many of her guns were inoperable, as was her central fire control system. Furthermore, rangefinders did not work properly. Meyer had to rely on the artificial smoke projectors and anti-aircraft batteries around the Kaafjord. However, the Germans were fortunate: no air attacks had been planned.[592]

Godfrey Place was soon brought to Cameron and the other prisoners. He was glad to reunite with them, but downhearted at the loss of his submarine. Had he known what took place at the bottom of the Kaafjord, not far from the target raft, he would have been even sadder. When Place left the submarine, the other three—wanting to see if the firing would cease—had waited a few fateful seconds too long. X-7 collided with the raft and Aitken realized Place had closed the hatch. The craft sank rapidly, until the impact when it hit the bottom of the fjord told Aitken it would go no deeper. The only way to resurface would be to use the compressor, but its noise would reveal the position to the Germans. As the three men could hear the German destroyers leave, they decided to swim the 40 meters to the surface. A succession of exploding depth charges could be heard through the hull, but clearly these were not close. The three men could not know that the German destroyers were chasing the X-5. Rather, they presumed the Germans were simply searching at the wrong place.[593]

The first officer in the X-7, Lieutenant Whittam—who was of senior rank—assumed command, but the most important person among them was now Aitken, the diver. After they had scuttled the craft, he rehearsed the escape procedure with Whittam and the engineer, Whitley, while the latter two fitted their Davis lungs. Using his diving gear, Aitken was protected from the cold water, but the other two were not dressed for the occasion. They crouched in their seats and pushed the feet against the pressure hull, to remain dry just a little longer.[594]

What had been reminiscent of many previous exercises now suddenly developed into a death trap. The pressure from the surrounding water made the hatches impossible to open until the craft was almost filled with water. Thus they had to wait while the water level rose. However, they did not know that some of the valves had been damaged by the German fire. The icy water filled the submarine at an alarmingly slow pace and the entire procedure would take much longer than anticipated.[595]

An almost ludicrous discovery made their situation even more desperate. Aitken had his diving suit, while the other two had to contend with Davis lungs. They had decided that Whittam should use the stern hatch, as he was too large a man to move into the Wet-and-Dry without difficulty. Thus Whitley would use the forward hatch, and Aitken could use either of the two hatches, depending on which became available first. Unfortunately, with his diving gear on Aitken had become too big, in fact to such a degree that he couldn't pass either of the other two men without taking the gear off. An X-craft simply was too small. Aitken suggested that he should take his chances without the diving suit, but Whitley protested and said that Aitken should use the Wet-and-Dry.[596]

While the water reached their chests, Aitken calmly talked to the other two men. Their Davis lungs would provide air for 45 minutes. Thereafter they had an extra reserve for five minutes. Once this was exhausted, they had two small oxylets attached to their equipment that could provide an extra breath or two in case they needed it when ascending. It was all the air they had.[597]

After remaining on the fjord's bottom for almost two hours, the situation deteriorated further. A hissing sound revealed that the water had reached the batteries. This would soon lead to a chemical reaction, releasing poisonous chlorine gas and making it necessary to start using the Davis lungs at once. "From now on, we have to use the air in our containers," Aitken said as calmly as possible, knowing full well that the margin between life and death had been reduced dramatically.

Those words were their last conversation. They nodded and moved the mouthpieces to their lips. Soon thereafter, the water caused a short circuit and the lights went out, leaving them in pitch black. Each man was left alone with his thoughts, fears, and the struggle to withhold panic. They could feel each other in the darkness, but neither see nor speak. Finally the water level was so high that Aitken decided to open the hatch in the Wet-and-Dry. It remained stuck, despite his frantic efforts. He noted that the air in the tube was almost consumed and switched to the reserve container. The procedure made him reflect on the condition of his comrades. If he—who was rather calm—had consumed the air in the main container, how had the other two fared?[598]

Aitken went back to check Whitley. With grave misgivings, he found the engineer's seat empty. However, he felt something soft against his foot and when he bent down, his hands found the lifeless body of Whitley. His breathing apparatus lay on his chest. Aitken also found the two empty oxylets. Whitley had run out of air and suffocated from the chlorine gases while Aitken struggled with the recalcitrant hatch, only a few meters away.[599]

By now, Aitken had precious little air remaining. Initially he had been confident of getting out of the metal coffin, but now realized that his prospects were very slim. With only the two oxylets left, he made one last attempt to open the hatch.[600]

The minutes that ensued would forever remain obscure in Aitken's memory. He could not recall how he opened the hatch, but he believed that Chadwick—the NCO who had been responsible for escape training at Loch Cairnbawn—would be proud of him as he unfolded his escape apron to avoid ascending too rapidly. The water around him was full of bubbles, and the propeller noise was more clearly audible when he was directly surrounded by water. It became lighter, and the last British sailor to survive the attack on the *Tirpitz* on 22 September 1943 appeared on the surface where a German patrol boat picked him up.[601]

In the Altafjord, Hudspeth and his crew heard the violent detonation in the Kaafjord, and thus knew that the attack on the *Tirpitz* had been accomplished. Despite all their efforts, they had not been able to repair any of their malfunctioning components. Also, they realized that the German defenses were fully alerted by now. Hudspeth had no choice but to break off the operation. At this moment, the Admiralty knew the *Scharnhorst* had left the Kaafjord, but could not communicate the information to X-10.

One might speculate on what would have happened if Hudspeth had found the *Scharnhorst* on 21 September, when he passed Aarøya. Without the protection afforded by the submarine net at Auskarneset and the torpedo net around the ship, Hudspeth could perhaps have successfully attacked the *Scharnhorst* in the darkness. He could have set his detonator at 08.00. However, such an attempt could have revealed him and alerted the Germans, thus ruining the chances for the other X-craft. Perhaps it was better that Hudspeth did not attack. The water was very shallow and navigation in the area was challenging. Neither had any plans been made for such a contingency.

During the six days that followed, Hudspeth would play hide and seek in the Norwegian fjords. The weather gradually deteriorated, until the *Stubborn* was finally found soon after midnight on 28 September. The reserve crew did not replace the utterly exhausted attack team until one day later. By then the weather had become very harsh. At dusk on

Photo taken from the Tirpitz during the X-Craft attack on September 22, 1943. Splashes from gunfire can be seen on the water.

29 September, the commander of the *Stubborn* was permitted to sink the X-10 after communicating with Barry. About two hours later, the last X-craft from Operation Source sank. [602]

Already on 22 September—the very same day as the attack was carried out—Ultra could decode the first of a long series of messages between the Kaafjord and Berlin. Gradually it became clear that the *Tirpitz* had been seriously damaged, a conclusion confirmed by local agents and air reconnaissance, which revealed maintenance ships in the Kaafjord as well as extensive repair efforts. When a report stating that a significant part of the battleship's crew would be sent on leave was decoded, it became clear that the *Tirpitz* would be out of action for several months.[603]

Of the 42 men who sailed from Loch Cairnbawn to participate in Operation Source, 27 returned. Nine had lost their lives, either in the attack or during the voyage across the Norwegian Sea. Another six had become prisoners. Considering the war's insatiable appetite for human lives, this was a very low price for the success attained. German casualties were also small—one dead and 40 wounded—but with the *Tirpitz* momentarily out of action and the *Lützow* on her way to Germany for an overhaul, only the *Scharnhorst* remained a threat to the Arctic convoys.

Cameron, Place, and the others did not remain long on the *Tirpitz*. On the day following the attack they were transferred to a hospital at Tromsø and then to a prisoner-of-war camp in Germany. While still prisoners, Cameron and Place learned that they had been awarded the Victoria Cross.

Considering the affection most commanders develop for their ship, it is laudable that Meyer did not vent any wrath on the prisoners. Rather, he ensured that they did not suffer the fate that befell the unfortunate Evans after Operation Title.

"They will not tell us anything," he said on the same day as these men had seriously damaged his ship. "Further interrogations are pointless. Give them food and then allow them to sleep. They have deserved it."

Ostfront

As we have already mentioned, the Kriegsmarine had intended to conduct a major overhaul of the *Tirpitz* in the autumn of 1943. The midget submarine attack on 22 September made the Germans bring the overhaul forward. But now it had to be more extensive than originally intended. The basic structure of the battleship had withstood the explosion very well, but cracks had ensued and sensitive equipment had been rendered inoperable. Among the latter were vital components like the machinery, range-finders, and some of the bearings supporting the artillery. About 2,000 tons of water had entered the ship, although mainly in less vital compartments. Nevertheless, the damage was severe enough to prevent the *Tirpitz* from sailing to Germany, as the machinery—including the propeller shafts—were out of order. An alternative would have been to tow the battleship, but it was considered too risky.[604]

It remained to repair the *Tirpitz* in Norway. The battleship's crew surely included many technicians, but the extent and character of the damage inflicted by the midget submarine attack called for more extensive repairs than these men could cope with. Equipment, technicians, engineers, and workers from German shipyards were sent to the Altafjord. The personnel was billeted in auxiliary ships, as there was insufficient space inside the battleship. Despite all efforts, it was evident that considerable time would be needed to make the *Tirpitz* battleworthy again. It was unlikely that she would put to sea before the end of March 1944. Meanwhile, the Germans only had one operational battleship left: the *Scharnhorst*.[605]

During the autumn of 1943, no Allied convoys were sent to the Soviet Arctic ports. Thus the damage inflicted on the *Tirpitz* did not affect the convoys, at least not initially. However, in November the situation changed. Bruce Fraser had assumed command of the Home Fleet half a year earlier. Like his predecessor, John Tovey, Fraser opposed convoys across the Arctic Ocean during the summer. When the days became shorter and the nights darker, Fraser regarded convoys feasible. Although he believed the Soviet Union was less dependent on Allied aid at this stage of the war, he nevertheless accepted the task to protect the convoys to Murmansk and Archangelsk.[606]

Accordingly, a convoy called JW54A sailed on 15 November 1943, and enjoyed so propitious weather that the Germans never attacked it. After nine days at sea, part of it reached Murmansk and two days later the remainder entered Archangelsk. On the same day, 26 November, RA54B sailed from Archangelsk and reached Loch Ewe unharmed on 9 December.[607]

The first pair of convoys since the previous winter thus reached their destinations successfully, and other convoys soon followed. JW54B reached its destination undetected by the enemy, but JW55A was observed by a German reconnaissance aircraft, prompting Fraser with elements of the Home Fleet to head for the Barents Sea. He feared that the *Scharnhorst* might put to sea, but the German battleship remained in its fjord. Fraser continued east and four days before the convoy reached its destination, he anchored in the Soviet Union and met Admiral Golovko, who commanded the Soviet naval forces based on the Kola Peninsula. The sojourn was brief, as Fraser soon sailed for Iceland, where he bunkered fuel before the next convoy.[608]

In November 1943 Admiral Kummetz went on leave, although he formally remained Befehlshaber der Kampfgruppe.[609] In his absence, Rear Admiral Bey assumed command. Bey soon became aware that Allied convoys were again sailing for Murmansk, but not until December did the Germans locate a convoy at sea. It was on the basis of that discovery that *Scharnhorst*—which was the only powerful unit available—could put to sea.[610]

Convoy JW55B was sighted by the Germans on 22 December, which prompted three hours of readiness. The most powerful escort ship yet detected was a cruiser, but the *Scharnhorst* remained in the Altafjord awaiting further intelligence. On Christmas Eve a radio message was intercepted by the B-Dienst. It could not be broken, but at least the transmitter's position could be established. It was concluded that it originated from a point about 200 nautical miles from the convoy. Conditions for attacking the convoy appeared favorable, an impression confirmed by a directive from Marinegruppe Nord later on the same day.[611]

The German warships lingered in the Altafjord, while the higher commanders discussed alternatives. As the convoy, plodding ahead far to the west, still had to reach Bear Island, the Germans did not have to make a quick decision. They intercepted another British radio transmission, and the bearings suggested that it originated from a distant cover force between Iceland and Tromsø. The German commanders thus faced a problematic situation, as the *Scharnhorst* could not be expected to attack the convoy without risk.[612]

Early on Christmas Day, a series of teleprinter messages were exchanged between the staffs of Marinegruppe Nord in Kiel and Admiral Nordmeer. The latter was responsible for the operations in the area north of Norway. Both these authorities doubted the wisdom of committing the *Scharnhorst*, but could not make a final decision. Further aerial reconnaissance could not be conducted at the time. In line with the previous guidelines, the situation thus remained sufficiently unclear as whether to motivate sending the *Scharnhorst* against the convoy.[613]

The issue was referred to Admiral Dönitz. As the uncertainties remained, it was not easy for him to decide, but Dönitz acted with his usual promptness. Maybe he still recalled how he had wriggled away from Hitler's intention to decommission the heavy warships, and maybe now he wanted to show what they could accomplish if employed with audacity. Whatever his motives, they resulted in new directives.[614]

"By sending important convoys, the enemy attempts to feed and arm the Russians fighting against our heroic soldiers on the Eastern Front," he began the new order. "We must assist. Convoys shall be attacked by the *Scharnhorst* and destroyers."

He continued by emphasizing that tactical situations should be exploited daringly, and no action should end with only limited success. The main chance of achievement rested, according to Dönitz, upon the *Scharnhorst*'s firepower. Hence, every effort should be made to allow her guns to open upon the enemy. Also, the destroyers should be used similarly. Dönitz left to Bey's discretion whether or when an action should be broken off, but he stated that no withdrawal should be carried out unless strong enemy units interfered. "Crews should be exhorted accordingly," he ended the order. "I have faith in your determination to attack."[615]

Thus, the die was cast. On the evening of Christmas Day, the *Scharnhorst* weighed anchor to commence Operation Ostfront. Rear Admiral Bey and his staff transferred from the *Tirpitz* to the *Scharnhorst*, whereupon the smaller battleship, followed by five destroyers commanded by Commander Rolf Johannesson, began to maneuver in the fjord.

At 20.00 a forecast received on the *Scharnhorst* suggested very harsh weather. Storm winds from the south and rough seas were expected. Rain and snow would make visibility poor. In such conditions, Bey believed the destroyers could not maintain high speed, and it would also be very difficult for them to make torpedo attacks should the need arise. Strangely, he broke radio silence to inform superiors about his conclusions. Admittedly he transmitted while still in the Altafjord, but in doing so he nevertheless took a considerable risk. Perhaps he believed that he would now be given an order to break off the operation, but nothing of the sort was received.[616]

Soon the German force reached the Stjernsundet, from which the X-craft had proceeded three months earlier. However, the weather Bey encountered was very different from what Cameron, Place, and the other seamen involved in Operation Source had experienced. The German squadron was already exposed to strong winds before it left the sound behind. The sea was so rough that breakers washed over the ships, and the howling wind treated the masts and rigging harshly. A few people on land saw the *Scharnhorst* and her escorting destroyers recede from the coast and disappear as dark shadows into the Arctic Ocean on their northwesterly course.[617]

She would never return.

The British were well aware that the *Scharnhorst* was about to leave the Altafjord. Admiral Fraser was commendably informed by Ultra and promptly ordered the refueling of his flagship, the *Duke of York*, as well as the cruiser *Jamaica* and four destroyers. The procedure was finished late on 23 December. He weighed anchor and sailed from

Akureyri in very difficult weather, but nevertheless ordered high speed. He was well aware that a few hours could spell the difference between success and fiasco—the *Scharnhorst* had to cover a much shorter distance in order to reach and attack convoy JW55B.[618]

On Christmas Eve, Fraser realized that another British force, which he called "Force I" while his own was known as "Force II," was located too far east. He decided to break radio silence and ordered Force I, which consisted of three cruisers commanded by Vice Admiral Burnett, to turn west. Probably this was the message intercepted by the Germans that made many high-ranking officers doubt the wisdom of sending the *Scharnhorst* to chase JW55B.[619]

Decisions made almost a decade before had resulted in shortcomings in the *Scharnhorst* as well as the *Duke of York*. With her nine 28cm guns, the German battleship was poorly armed. She had been designed to carry six 38cm guns, but they were not available in time and an existing 28cm gun was used in triple mounts. In 1942, the Germans began to rearm her sister ship, the *Gneisenau*, which was intended to receive six 38cm guns, but the work had been discontinued.

Admiral Bey was not guilty of the *Scharnhorst's* shortcomings. However, his counterpart, Admiral Fraser, had been engaged in the decisions that resulted in the battleships of the *King George V* class. The specifications accepted a top speed of only 28 knots, or four knots less than that of the *Scharnhorst*. It was a serious disadvantage when Fraser was about to give chase to the German battleship. He had to reach the convoy before the Germans and without his force being detected. Considering these circumstances, his decision to break radio silence seems hazardous.[620]

When Bey's German task force reached the open sea, it was hit by the wrath of the storm. The battleship was not unduly perturbed, but the destroyers rolled badly and the cold water often washed over them. They also suffered from icing, which further reduced their seaworthiness. On board the Z29, Johannesson could hardly see his destroyers in the raging weather. The sky was black, without any stars, and sudden snow squalls reduced visibility further. However, he did not intend to inform Bey of the difficulties endured by his destroyers. As the British destroyers escorting the Arctic convoys rode out the same weather, their German counterparts would also hold their own.[621]

The circumstances did not favor Operation Ostfront. Schniewind realized that chances of success were slim and suggested the operation be cancelled. Dönitz, however, said that such an order should not be issued. It was up to Bey to make such decisions. At about the same time, Bey received the delayed instruction from Dönitz which ended, "I have faith in your determination to attack." Such an order clearly called for offensive spirit, which hardly suggested that he should break off the operation.[622]

The German force thus sailed on, with scant hope of finding any convoy in the miserable weather. Bey could only make a calculated guess where the convoy would be located by extrapolating the speed, course, and position according to the latest reconnaissance report. Such a calculation obviously rested on the assumption that course and speed were not altered, but he had no better alternatives. He did not know that Fraser's Force II was approaching from the west and Burnett's Force I from the east. The *Scharnhorst* headed straight into the area between these two enemy forces, but Bey continued north. At 07.30 on 26 December, hoping that the convoy would now be near, he ordered action stations. There was nothing to be seen, however, as the merchant ships were now steaming through the storm about 100 kilometres farther to the northeast.[623]

In the hours that followed, the *Scharnhorst* and the heaving destroyers proceeded even farther north, vainly searching for the convoy. Suddenly a number of star shells exploded, lighting up the sky and then slowly drifting earthwards, also illuminating the violent surface of the ocean. The German lookouts strained their eyes but could not discover the ships that had fired the star shells. In fact it was Burnett's force—the three cruisers *Belfast*, *Sheffield*, and *Norfolk*. Thanks to their radar equipment, they had found the Germans and passed to the north of them. The British commander had seen the *Scharnhorst* on his radar screen, but held his fire until his squadron had sailed past the enemy. He wanted to position himself between the enemy and the convoy before engaging. As it happened, only the *Norfolk* opened fire, since she was inconveniently positioned in the field of fire of the other two cruisers. *Norfolk* fired six salvos, and before long shells began to fall close around the *Scharnhorst*. Two of them hit the battleship. *Scharnhorst* replied wth salvos of her own, but did not score any hits. As soon as his cruisers were out of range, Burnett ordered them to turn and follow the *Scharnhorst*.[624]

One of the two hits sustained by the *Scharnhorst* caused no significant damage, but the other one did. It hit the radar antenna in the fore top. Petty Officer Günter Sträter, who served at one of the aft 15cm guns, was told about the hit through the artillery telephone. He was also told that the ship had placed smoke to avoid further fire. Despite the fact that she had been damaged, Commander Julius Hintze, who commanded the ship, informed the crew that further efforts to find the convoy would be made as soon as the cruisers had been shaken off. Chief Gunner Wibbelhof was ordered to the bridge for a briefing. When he returned, he said that the radar could not be repaired.[625]

It seems that the *Scharnhorst* had sailed with her radar switched off. The Germans presumed the British had receivers that could detect radar waves. Thus a German ship sailing with its radar equipment switched on would be disclosed at long range. Without realizing it, Bey had afforded the British a decisive advantage. The hit on the *Scharnhorst's* antenna ensured they would retain it.[626]

It is puzzling that Bey did not decide to break off the operation when the main radar was knocked out. Clearly, the Germans had had misgivings before the operation was begun. Furthermore, at this stage the British were clearly aware that the Germans had put to sea, and the poor visibility almost ensured that the convoy would not be found, particularly when the radar had been knocked out. Without it, the risk of British warships closing in on the *Scharnhorst* undetected was grave.[627]

Against this background, it would have been prudent to turn south. Admiral Fraser's Force II still remained far to the west and would hardly have caught the *Scharnhorst* if the latter had taken off at high speed. Instead, Bey gave orders to sail north, hoping to attack the convoy from another direction. The *Scharnhorst* proceeded at very high speed and the British cruisers could not follow in the rough sea.[628]

Bey's actions put Burnett in a difficult position. In situations like this, it was more or less stipulated that the cruisers should maintain contact while Fraser's force approached. However, the very high speed of the *Scharnhorst* would soon take her beyond the range of the British radar. Force I had turned and followed the German battleship on an east-southeasterly course, but if the British cruisers maintained this path, the *Scharnhorst* might turn in a direction which could allow her to attack the convoy. The enemy battleship made just that kind of maneuver when she was almost at the maximum range of the British radar sets. With a heavy heart, Burnett decided to turn northwest to converge with Fraser and the convoy.[629]

Since the possible consequences concerned him, Burnett sent a message to Fraser in which he reprorted that he had turned toward the convoy and that the *Scharnhorst* had disappeared on a northerly course. He did not have to wait long for Fraser's reply: "Unless no unit regains contact, I can not find the enemy." However, the following events would play straight into the hands of Burnett.[630]

Aboard the *Scharnhorst*, Bey's efforts to find the convoy were futile. At 12.05 he ordered a turn west, soon followed by a turn south, and finally southeast. Meanwhile, he tried to reconnect with the five destroyers he had dispatched to search for the convoy. Except for a brief exchange of radio messages, by which Bey tried to create a situation in which he attacked the convoy from the north and Johanneson from the south, no contact between the German battleship and the destroyers was established.

Soon, however, Bey would receive contact of a much less pleasant kind. Burnett had moved north toward the convoy and at 11.00, when he found the merchant ships, he had turned northeast and soon the *Scharnhorst* again appeared on his radar screens. Bey's maneuvers had brought his ship within range of the British guns once more. Farther west, Fraser had almost decided to break off the operation, when he received a report from Burnett that the enemy had again been found.[631]

In this second encounter, conditions were slightly different from those in the morning. Although the sun never appeared above the horizon at this time of year, some of its rays were refracted in the atmosphere and shed some light on the Barents Sea. Also, some British warships, among them the *Norfolk*, used a powder that produced discernible muzzle flashes. All of this allowed the men who operated the *Scharnhorst's* range-finders to quickly establish the distance. The German lookouts could see three shadows in the gloom ahead. Again, the British opened fire first. Hardly had the first star shells begun to descend before the cruiser's shells blasted from their muzzles. However, this time the Germans rapidly replied and quickly hit the *Norfolk*. One of her twenty 3cm gun turrets was destroyed. Seven crewmen were killed instantly and five seriously wounded.[632]

At this stage, Bey turned south-southeast at high speed as Burnett's cruisers did everything they could to maintain contact. The second battle had only lasted 20 minutes. Fraser reported that he was doing all in his power to reach the area quickly, but if Burnett again lost contact, Force II could hardly get into firing position.[633]

It seems that Bey finally decided to break off the action. At 12.40 he sent a message informing that he was engaged by one heavy unit. According to instructions, he would break off the operation if such an enemy were encountered. At the same time, the German destroyers were located farther north. They had in fact come very close to the convoy, but had not seen it in the poor weather. Subsequently, the German destroyers would not influence the operation, and they eventually reached their northern Norwegian bases undamaged.[634]

Meanwhile Fraser's force continued east, and if everything worked according to his plans he would intercept the *Scharnhorst* at 17.15. The situation appeared promising. He was continuously informed by Burnett's cruisers, who managed to cling to the wake of the *Scharnhorst* due to their radar equipment. However, as the *Scharnhorst* sailed at very high speed, the cruisers could not afford a single mistake.[635]

It seems that Bey and his staff believed the cruisers had lost contact, as the Germans could not see them without their damaged main radar. Perhaps he was even somewhat optimistic. At 14.30 he informed the crew that the battleship was heading toward Norway, and half an hour later the men were fed at their battle stations. However, the danger was not over. Darkness shrouded all the ships and it was a major disadvantage to lack the main radar. The lookouts were reinforced, but human eyes could not see very far in the darkness.

Fraser suffered from none of these difficulties. He continued east, and at 16.17 his radar operators found an echo at a range of more than 40 kilometers. It was beyond the range of the *Duke of York's* guns, but the distance decreased continuously. Furthermore, informed by Burnett, Fraser knew that the echo originated from the *Scharnhorst* and not from any friendly ship.[636]

Fraser was determined to wait as long as possible before opening fire. The radar operators could see the distance gradually closing on their screens. Captain Guy Russel, the commander of the *Prince of Wales*, wanted to open fire, but Fraser insisted that the optimal distance between him and Bey had yet to be established. As he was puffing on his pipe—well aware of the lower top speed of the British battleship— he said that he would like to open the battle at such short distance that the *Scharnhorst* could not steam beyond the range of the British guns for a considerable time. Finally, the range was down to only 11 kilometers when Fraser—at last—decided to open fire. He ordered a starboard turn, to allow all guns to bear upon the enemy. Then he looked at his watch. It showed 16.50, and as yet nothing suggested that the enemy had discovered the presence of the *Duke of York*.[637]

In fact, the *Scharnhorst's* stern radar, which did not possess as great a range as the main radar, had found the *Duke of York*, but only a moment before the British battleship opened fire. Using the data provided by the fire-control radar, the gunners on board the *Duke of York* had already set all the necessary values for accurate firing. Flares were fired by the British battleship as well as from the *Belfast*, and the British could see the *Scharnhorst* as a huge, silver-grey fish ahead of them. With relief, they noted that the enemy battleship's guns were trained fore and aft. The Germans would not be able to return fire immediately. When the firing bell sounded on the British battleship, it felt as if it took a step sideways when ten 35.6cm shells left their barrels. The first salvos found their mark and the *Scharnhorst's* forward 28cm turret was knocked out.[638]

With one main turret out of action and very limited radar coverage, the *Scharnhorst* was seriously handicapped. And it was not only the *Duke of York* that threatened her. The *Jamaica* and four destroyers, as well as Burnett's cruisers, also joined the battle. The *Scharnhorst* was surrounded by enemies and her only chance to survive was her superior speed. Despite being hit repeatedly by the radar-directed fire from the *Duke of York*, she gradually increased her distance from the enemy. Hintze made a series of turns, which allowed all his guns to fire on the pursuing British, while also putting greater distance between himself and the two Royal Navy forces. As a result of these maneuvers, the German battleship's course became unpredictable to the British gunners. After an hour, the *Scharnhorst* had doubled the distance from her pursuers.[639]

At this stage, Fraser probably cursed the comparatively low speed of the *Duke of York*. If the *Scharnhorst* got away he would be partly guilty, as he had been among those who had decided to accept a lower top speed for this class of battleship. On top of that, the *Scharnhorst's* guns had a greater range. The latter was nevertheless of minor consequence with the current visibility. More importantly, the *Duke of*

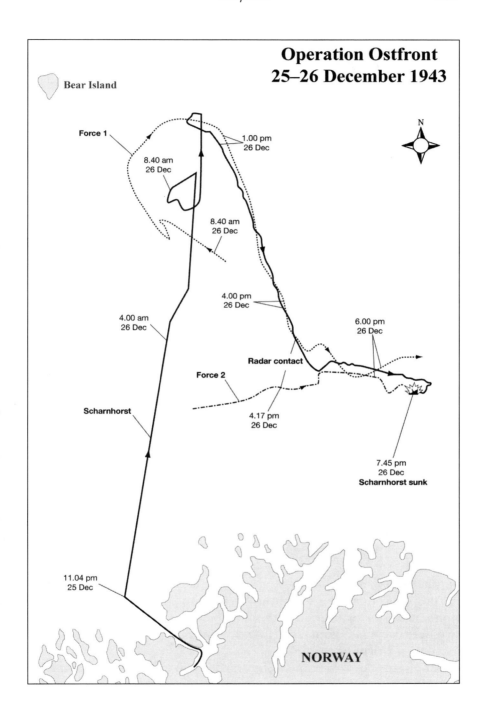

**Operation Ostfront
25–26 December 1943**

Bear Island

N

Force 1

1.00 pm
26 Dec

8.40 am
26 Dec

8.40 am
26 Dec

4.00 pm
26 Dec

6.00 pm
26 Dec

4.00 am
26 Dec

Radar contact

Force 2

Scharnhorst

4.17 pm
26 Dec

7.45 pm
26 Dec
Scharnhorst sunk

11.04 pm
25 Dec

NORWAY

York's fire-control radar broke at 18.24, as a result of the concussions when the heavy guns recoiled. At that moment, the range exceeded 20,000 meters and further firing was pointless.[640]

Just before half past six, a disappointed Fraser gave the order to cease fire. He then ordered his ships to turn to protect JW55B. He sent a message to Burnett, stating that he no longer had any hope of catching the *Scharnhorst* and would rather protect the convoy.[641]

However, soon a report from the chart room told him that the range to the German battleship was no longer increasing. Fraser hardly believed his ears, but said that the order he had just given should not be followed until further notice. Soon other reports showed that the range was actually decreasing.[642]

Fraser had given up too early. One of the *Scharnhorst's* boiler rooms had been damaged, and a feeding pipe for the high-pressure steam had broken. This caused an abrupt loss of speed. The technicians on board worked feverishly and were soon able to increase the steam pressure to sufficiently enable 22 knots, but the British had been given a second chance. Hintze knew what it all meant. At 18.25 he sent a message to Berlin and Hitler: "We will fight to the last shell."[643]

Thus far, Fraser's destroyers had accomplished little, but the *Scharnhorst's* sudden loss of speed provided an opportunity to attack with torpedoes. Soon, the chief gunner on board the German battleship saw dark shadows close in from both sides. The poor visibility made it difficult to estimate the range, and the destroyers got within 8,000 meters before they were fired upon.[644]

When Hintze realized he was exposed to a torpedo attack, he turned south. Consequently, the *Scharnhorst* appeared before two of the destroyers—the British *Scorpion* and the Norwegian *Stord*—which approached head on. The terrified crew on board the *Stord* saw the range close rapidly, but the commander, Lieutenant Commander Skulle Storhet, was not to be hurried. He maintained his course until the range was down to 1,800 meters. *Stord* and *Scorpion* fired one salvo each, but the *Scharnhorst* turned away. Only the latter destroyer scored a hit. At the same time, the destroyers *Savage* and *Saumarez* approached from the opposite direction. The *Saumarez* received several hits, but the two destroyers had gotten so close that the battleship could not lower its guns sufficiently.[645]

In all, the destroyers fired 28 torpedoes on the German battleship, of which three or four appear to have hit. Most ruinous, a boiler room and a propeller shaft were damaged, and the *Scharnhorst's* speed again dropped dramatically.[646]

Fraser soon became aware that the *Scharnhorst* had suffered a grave loss of speed. He ordered all ships to converge on the badly damaged German battleship, which by now was doomed. Günter Sträter recalled that about half an hour after the first torpedo hit, an order to destroy all secret documents was issued. At about the same time, the *Duke of York* again opened fire.[647]

The *Scharnhorst* was subjected to a tremendous shelling. On 26 December the *Duke of York* fired no less than 446 shells from her heavy guns and almost 700 shells from her medium ones. Furthermore, the British cruisers fired more than 1,000 shells. By now, Burnett's cruisers had also come on the scene and, together with the *Jamaica* and *Belfast*, they attacked the *Scharnhorst* with torpedoes. In all, Allied cruisers and destroyers fired 55 torpedoes. How many torpedoes and shells hit the *Scharnhorst* is impossible to tell, but since much of the firing took place at short range, a very large number of hits must have been obtained.[648]

At 19.30, the *Scharnhorst* was clearly sinking. She listed heavily and lay deep in the water. "I bid you farewell," Hintze announced over the speaker system, "and shake hands with you for the last time. I have informed the Führer that we fight to the last shell."[649]

From the bridge, orders to abandon the ship were given. Günter Sträter was among those who could follow them. Many others were less fortunate. Some of them simply could not leave their compartments, as shell damage had blocked them. Others voluntarily remained on the ship. Coxswain Moritz told Sträter that he intended to remain at his battle station, as did Wibbelhof. Subsequently, the latter ordered Sträter and the rest of the crew to leave the gun turret. He lit a cigarette and awaited his fate together with Moritz. The other entered the main deck, where they found many wounded and dead. Those still capable of moving left the *Scharnhorst* and ended up in the ice cold water.[650]

Sträter and many others who had got into the water saw the ship roll and sink. For them, all that remained was to find a raft. The cold was severe and it was not possible to survive long in the Arctic sea. The strength was quickly sapped from the men, who disappeared into the water unless they found something to float on. However, even among those who actually managed to get into a raft, mortality must have been very high. Sträter was one of only 36 saved by British destroyers. The remainder of the almost 2,000 men on the *Scharnhorst* perished.[651]

A survivor recalled seeing Rear Admiral Bey and Captain Hinske shaking hands before preparing to go down with the ship. The two men were subsequently given a tribute by Admiral Fraser, however, who told a group of his officers aboard the Duke of York: "Gentlemen, the battle againt *Scharnhorst* hs ended in victory for us. I hope that if any of you are ever called upon to lead a ship into action againt an opponent many times superior, you will command your ship as gallantly as *Scharnhorst* was commanded today."

After the *Scharnhorst* was destroyed, the Germans no longer had any operational battleship. The *Tirpitz* remained in the Altafjord, where repairs were still conducted. Her crew must have been dismayed when it was informed of the *Scharnhorst's* fate. The two battleships had been moored near each other for almost two months, and the crews had gotten to know each other. They had trained together, played soccer tournaments together, and associated together in other ways.

Now, only half of them remained.

Tungsten

The Allies could hardly escape noting that the *Tirpitz* was gradually being repaired. Admittedly, the reports from air reconnaissance and the resistance were often vague or contradictory, but the German reports intercepted and decrypted by Ultra gave clear and concise information. It was noted that the commanders on the *Tirpitz* criticized Kiel for not delivering requested equipment in time, and that supplies for the divers had been lacking in the latest shipment. A 100-ton crane from Tromsø had been damaged during its sea transport to the Kaafjord, and British intelligence even noted that oil pumps were to be removed from the damaged *Gneisenau*, brought to Norway, and fitted to the *Tirpitz*. The intelligence presented an impression of hard German work to make the battleship combat ready as soon as possible. On 17 March it was reported that the hull, armament, and machinery were in operational condition, but minor repairs remained to be made. Further Allied efforts to destroy or damage the *Tirpitz* were urgently needed.[652]

Another attempt with midget submarines did not appear feasible. German radio messages intercepted and decrypted by Ultra showed that the underwater defenses had been strengthened considerably. Agents in the area reported that German air reconnaissance had become more frequent. The circumstances called for another approach to the problem, and the British chose to rely on air power. However, as the Kaafjord was beyond the range of the British heavy bombers, the task was given to the Fleet Air Arm.[653]

At this stage, the use of carriers was preferred. It was intended to sail them to a point off the Norwegian coast and launch the aircraft. As

265

The aircraft carrier HMS *Victorious* in 1943.

the overall strategic situation appeared favorable, two carriers and four escort carriers were available for the mission. At the end of 1943, the Admiralty began to plan an attack on the Altafjord, not unlike the British attack against Taranto or the Japanese attack on Pearl Harbor. Vice Admiral Henry Moore directed the planning.[654]

The operation was initially called "Thrustful," but later changed to "Tungsten," and it was intended to be launched in mid-March 1944. However, various circumstances caused delays. Ultra reports showed that the *Tirpitz* would soon become operational. She had conducted trials on 15–16 March, and a high-speed trial would be conducted on 1 April. As a large convoy was scheduled to sail at the end of March, such information was disquieting. Further Ultra reports showed that the Germans had postponed the high-speed trial for two days, and the Admiralty decided to proceed with Operation Tungsten.[655]

Carrier-based aircraft had lacked a sufficiently heavy bomb, but a recently developed 725kg bomb had been produced in the USA. It was hoped that these might penetrate the deck armor on the *Tirpitz* and perhaps reach vital components, like the machinery or magazines. Also, 227kg bombs were to be used to penetrate the upper deck. Furthermore, high-explosive bombs were intended to knock out anti-aircraft defenses. The final components were 273kg submarine bombs, which hopefully would damage the hull. It was intended to attack with the high-explosive bombs first, to render at least part of the enemy's air defense ineffective before the main attack. Also, the fighters on board the carriers would attack the anti-aircraft batteries around the Kaafjord, provided German fighters did not interfere.[656]

For the attack on the *Tirpitz*, British Barracuda aircraft would be used. All previous British torpedo aircraft had been biplanes, but not the Barracuda, with its crew of three. Torpedo attacks on the battleship had long been ruled out, but the Barracuda could also be used as a bomber, diving toward its target. Of course, with its 60° maximum dive angle it was not a genuine dive-bomber. Perhaps calling it a glider bomber might be more appropriate.[657]

The development of the Barracuda had proceeded slowly, as most of the Air Ministry's resources were spent on fighters and heavy bombers. Consequently, the Barracuda had to be modified to carry heavier ordnance. Structural reinforcements and a more powerful engine made it considerably heavier and impaired its flying characteristics, also making it more difficult to operate from a carrier. It was regarded as an unusually ugly aircraft, but such sentiments had little relevance when attacking the *Tirpitz*.[658]

On 27 March the convoy JW58 sailed for the long voyage to Murmansk. Three days later, at dawn, the battleships *Duke of York* and *Anson*, the carrier *Victorious*, a light cruiser, and five destroyers sailed from Scapa Flow, commanded by Admiral Fraser. The force would initially serve as distant cover, but elements of it would later participate in Operation Tungsten. Later on the same day, the carrier *Furious*, escort carriers *Searcher*, *Pursuer*, *Emperor*, and *Fencer*, three light cruisers, two tankers, and five destroyers sailed under command of Rear Admiral La Touche Bisset. According to plans, on 3 April *Anson* and *Victorious* would be detached from Fraser's force and converge with Bisset at a point off the Norwegian coast. On the following day, Operation Tungsten would be launched. If the Germans observed any of these forces, they might conclude that it was a distant escort they had seen.[659]

While the two groups approached the Arctic Circle on a northeasterly course, reports received showed that the convoy had only encountered slight opposition, which was easily handled by the close escort. Also, the weather was propitious for air operations. Another report, based on Ultra decrypts, informed that the Germans had delayed the trial of the *Tirpitz* until 3 April. This had two consequences. First, the German battleship would hardly put to sea and attack JW58. Second, with some luck, the battleship might be surprised in a part of the fjord where she was not protected by anti-aircraft batteries and artificial fog. Admiral Fraser decided to launch Operation Tungsten one day ahead of schedule. Favorable weather was not common at these latitudes, and despite any complications that might result from altering the plan, such an opportunity could not be ignored. *Anson* and *Victorious* were detached from the main force and placed under command of Rear Admiral Moore. At the same time, Bisset increased speed as much as his escort carriers could manage. A dangerous incident occurred when the *Pursuer's* steering system malfunctioned at the very moment when a ship ahead altered course in a snow squall. A collision was barely avoided, but at dawn on 3 April all ships had arrived at the predetermined point.[660]

Soon after midnight, the airmen woke up before the final briefing.

Dressed in their flight suits, heavy boots, and life vests, they studied the models of the Kaafjord area. Meanwhile, the aircraft were prepared on the flight deck: their foldable wings were properly secured, and their engines were started and warmed up. On board the *Victorious* a humorous mechanic wrote, "*Tirpitz*, it's yours" on one of the bombs. A war correspondent photographed him for propaganda use.[661]

At 04.15, the first aircraft—ten Vought Corsairs from the *Victorious*—rose into the air. They would constitute a high- altitude escort and soon circled above the task force while other aircraft were made ready. From his bridge, Rear Admiral Bisset watched them take off until the huge formation was complete. He found the sight magnificent. The sun rising above the sea and the droning sound from the aircraft engines added to the impression. It was the largest air operation launched by the Royal Navy thus far. He glanced at his watch; it showed 04.36.[662]

At his controls in the leading Barracuda, the commander of the first wave, Lieutenant Commander Baker-Faulkner, studied his instruments. During the first nine minutes, the formation would follow a 139-degree course. Thereafter, the aircraft would turn to a more easterly course toward the Kaafjord. Until they reached a point about 40 kilometers from the Norwegian coast, the air units should fly low to prevent the German radar from detecting them. Then they would climb to the altitude suitable for attacking, and pass over the coast and a few fjords before they reached the target. The last fjord to pass over was the Langfjord, where the fighters would jettison their drop tanks before turning east. Just before the Kaafjord was reached, the final course was adopted that would allow the aircraft to attack the German battleship along its keel, which had proved to be the best alternative in previous tests.[663]

Baker-Faulkner looked around. The weather was excellent, with only a few clouds at high altitude. Despite flying low, he could see very far. Immediately behind him, he saw the other Barracuda aircraft huddled close together. Not until the air units had almost reached the target would they change formation. If German fighters appeared, such a formation allowed effective firing. However, the fighters ahead and slightly abaft were the most important protection. As their speed was greater than that of the Barracudas, they zigzagged to avoid getting separated from the bombers.[664]

The 12 Barracuda aircraft did not face a simple task. On the mountain slopes surrounding the fjord, the Germans had positioned numerous artificial fog devices, and it was known that such equipment had also been fitted to trawlers positioned in the fjord. If the enemy got ample warning, the target would probably be shrouded in dense fog, which would ruin any hopes of precision bombing. The second layer of defense was the anti-aircraft fire, on board the *Tirpitz* as well as on land. Added together, the lighter guns could deliver more than 140 shells per second, to which the heavier guns of the battleship could be added. Finally, there were Messerschmitt fighter aircraft on bases not far away.[665]

The Norwegian coast appeared before the air armada. Baker-Faulkner identified Loppen Island and knew he was on track. To the left of his rotating propeller he could see the inlet at Sørøya, which was mined. Then he approached the Stjernsundet and Altafjord, but these waters could not be seen from his relatively low altitude. He pulled the control stick and climbed, with the other aircraft following him, to the altitude desired for the attack. Until now, a predetermined course had been followed. The remaining distance to the target would be covered flying according to the map and observations. At this stage German radar found the attack force, but the British were lucky. For some reason the report from the radar station was delayed. The officers on board the *Tirpitz* remained uninformed until they had almost no time to order countermeasures.[666]

The escort flew slightly above the Barracudas. Unaware that radar waves were reflected on every surface of his crooked-winged Corsair fighter plane, Lieutenant Commander Turnbull tried to maintain optical contact with the dozen Barracudas. They were almost invisible against the white snow on the ground far below, but the glinting sun on their wings helped him. Like the Hellcat and Wildcat fighters, the Corsairs had to zigzag. Turnbull's engine was running at full throttle and consumed gas rapidly, but he did not worry. It would soon be time to jettison the external fuel tank and his internal tanks were still full.[667]

When the drop tanks had been jettisoned, Turnbull again searched the surrounding area through the perspex. He had the Langfjord on his left, where his eye caught sight of two destroyers and a tanker. Neither ship opened fire on the approaching aircraft. Soon Turnbull turned to a northerly course. Still no signs of enemy activity could be noted. He pushed the transmission button and said, "Turn off the lights." It was the code words indicating that the Wildcat and Hellcat aircraft should abandon their escort role and instead attack the *Tirpitz* and the anti-aircraft batteries ashore.[668]

While the bombers attacked the battleship, the Corsair unit would make a sweep toward the mouth of the Langfjord and then follow the Altafjord, turn south, and then converge with the Barracuda aircraft as they returned after dropping their bombs. When Turnbull approached the small village of Talvik on the western shore of the Altafjord, he saw the battleship in the Kaafjord and large clouds surging from the mountains surrounding her.

The Germans had finally reacted.[669]

From the *Tirpitz's* bridge, Captain Meyer was silently observing Lieutenant Commander Hugo Heydel, the new navigation officer, making the necessary preparations to bring the battleship out from the protective nets. The morning was clear, with only a few scattered clouds traversing the sky. The water in the fjord was dead calm except for the backwash created by a pair of tugs maneuvering near the battleship. The capstan clattered as the anchor was weighed.

The trial run had been scheduled for 1 April, but was postponed one day and then another as forecasts predicted bad weather, but on 3 April it would finally be conducted. Meyer silently watched as Heydel gave instructions to the men on the bridge; orders that were immediately passed on to other sections of the ship. One of the tugs attached a hawser to the bow and the other positioned itself alongside the battleship. The aft moorings were undone, whereupon the *Tirpitz* slowly began to move in her corral of nets. For the crew, a trial run was a welcome break in the monotony.[670]

At this moment, Meyer became aware of smoke rising from the projectors on the mountain slopes. Hardly had the thought of an imminent air attack crossed his mind when the delayed radar report arrived at the bridge. Lieutenant Hellendorn, anti-aircraft second in command, also received the report. He had doubted the reports on midget submarines inside the net cage in September 1943, but this time there was no hesitation. He immediately pressed the button for the air alarm.[671]

The anti-aircraft guns were ready to fire, but many damage control stations were not fully manned and most of the watertight bulkheads were yet to be closed. Meyer ordered these failings to be rectified immediately, while the noise of anti-aircraft fire resounded in the fjord. It was the batteries ashore that opened fire first. Meyer could see about 30 enemy aircraft approaching over the snow-clad mountain slope to the west. The *Tirpitz's* Flak guns joined the cannonade, but it was clear that the artificial fog would not enshroud the area in time.[672]

Baker-Faulkner's Barracuda bombers still had 15 kilometers to cover before they reached the target area. He ordered the V-formation to be broken, as it now appeared unlikely that any German fighters would be encountered. The bombers assumed a formation for attacking the battleship. Not until only five kilometres remained did they encounter any Flak. As the bombers closed in on the fjord, however, the German fire intensified, although Baker-Faulkner found it badly aimed. He and his bombers remained covered by the summits, while the Wildcat and Hellcat fighters dived to disturb the German gunners.[673]

Beneath the Barracuda units, the commander of 882nd Squadron, Lieutenant Commander Cooper, led his Wildcat fighters in a shallow dive along the mountain slope toward the Kaafjord. Cooper saw the trees not far below him, when he pulled the control stick and levelled out just above the water. The other Wildcats flew alongside toward the bursting anti-aircraft guns on the battleship. Cooper pressed the fire button and felt the vibrations as his machine guns hammered. Feeling the gases of cordite in his nostrils and with adrenalin flowing in his veins, he saw the bullets hit the enormous ship. A few seconds later, he had passed the target and had to climb and turn to avoid the mountain on the other side of the fjord. Something slammed into his fuselage as he saw ski tracks in the snow on the ground. He then completed the turn and flew over the water once again, where he discovered two destroyers anchored. He fired a few brief bursts at them before retiring.[674]

The brief attack by the fighters caused casualties among the flak gunners on the battleship. Extra armor plating for the guns crews had been ordered, but as German industry was hard-pressed to furnish all the units in need of equipment, the delivery had not yet taken place. Seamen at the forward capstan fell like rag dolls when perforated by machine gun bullets, as did many others running toward their battle stations. Also, the main anti-aircraft control center was knocked out, as

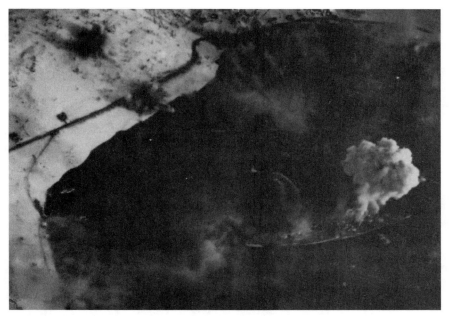

Tirpitz being bombed in Kaafjord by carrier-based aircraft on April 3, 1944.

were several guns.[675]

In his cabin, Lieutenant Kühnen was incredibly lucky. Having no idea the battleship was about to be attacked, he bent to pick up a cigarette on the floor. Above and behind him, a mirror was shattered when a bullet slammed into it after passing through the porthole. Had he not bent down, Kühnen would most likely have been killed.

Meyer and Heydel had remained on the bridge during the attack and seen the tracer rounds dart and disappear in all directions. The air was filled with the loud noise from engines at full throttle, when the Wildcats climbed to avoid crashing into the battleship. It soon became evident that the fire control was out of action, and Meyer shouted at Heydel that he would head to the anti-aircraft directory. A new vibrating sound could be heard as the Barracuda bombers approached right behind the mountains. Anti-aircraft battery commanders shouted to their men to aim their guns at the new danger. However, the enemy aircraft remained behind the mountains and the gunners had to estimate their position from the sound of the engines.[676]

Tirpitz in the Kaafjord. Smoke cover is being generated in an effort to hide the ship.

Baker-Faulkner had aimed the nose of his Barracuda at a mountain peak near the fjord. He had to pull his control stick to avoid crashing into the mountain, but when he had passed it, he saw the *Tirpitz* below. With full dive breaks the British pilot commenced his attack from 1,200 meters. He quickly picked up speed. The battleship grew larger in his sight and at an altitude of 400 meters he released the bomb. Within a minute, 20 Barracudas did the same. Three heavy armor-piercing bombs hit, as did five 227kg bombs and one high-explosive bomb. Another high-explosive bomb splashed into the water close to the battleship and caused a leak not far from the aft boiler room. Kimberley, Baker-Faulkner's aft gunner, could see flames shoot up and huge water fountains fall back into the sea. Dark smoke belched out from the aft sections of the battleship. However, most pilots had released their armor-piercing bombs at too low of an altitude, which meant that they did not develop sufficient speed to pierce the armored deck.[677] The bombing—which had lasted only 60 seconds—nevertheless caused extensive damage above the armored deck.

Aboard the battleship, the morning that had been so tranquil only a few minutes earlier had turned into a nightmare. Men were screaming from pain or agony, orders were shouted, and the anti-aircraft guns still fired, despite the fact that the aircraft were leaving the scene. The faint echo from machine guns rolled between the mountains as the British fighters attacked anti- aircraft positions and other ships in the Altafjord. On the *Tirpitz's* deck lay hundreds of dead and wounded. They lay in their own blood, mixed with the water that had washed over the deck as bombs exploded in the water near the hull. The two tugs had cut the hawsers and disappeared in the artificial fog. The battleship drifted uncontrollably. It suddenly shuddered when the bow hit aground near the western shore. To complete the ghastly scene, bomb damage had made a steam siren become stuck open and it could not be silenced. The sound was heard clearly in the entire valley—as if the battleship was howling out the pain inflicted on her.[678]

Lieutenant Hellendorn lay wounded from splinters in his back. Meyer had also been wounded by splinters soon after leaving the bridge, and he now lay unconscious on the deck. Heydel assumed command and received a report, which showed that the steam pressure was sufficient to move the ship on her own power. He could hardly breathe due to the gases from the explosions. Many communication

This photo shows some of the damage on *Tirpitz* after the attack of April 3, 1944.

systems had been knocked out and he had no clear impression of the situation. Nevertheless, he decided not to wait for the tugs; the *Tirpitz* would have to make it on her own. He gave orders to reverse off the ground and then maneuver back into the net cage.[679]

The second wave of British aircraft started one hour after the first. This time one of the Barracudas crashed into the sea soon after it took off from the *Victorious*. The aircraft immediately sank and took the crew with it. Another Barracuda could not take off due to technical problems, but ten of them safely flew from the *Victorious*. The *Furious* successfully launched nine Barracudas, as did the other escort carriers.[680]

Lieutenant Commander Rance led the second wave. He saw the same beautiful scenario as Baker-Faulkner had observed an hour ago, but there was one important difference. When they approached the target area, he could see dark smoke rising in the chilly air, as well as the artificial fog. This time, too, the defenses were alerted and the anti-aircraft fire more intense. However, the British were lucky. The fog had not yet enshrouded the masts, and the contours of the ship could still be discerned. The target was therefore visible from above, but the fog blinded the ship's anti-aircraft gunners. To make matters worse, the steam siren that had still not been silenced made it impossible for gunners to locate the droning aircraft by their engine noise. Still, the anti-aircraft fire was far from harmless. Rance noted that the flak was arranged in such a way that the aircraft had to fly through what appeared like a wall of explosions. One of the bombers was hit in a wing tank. However, it still carried on with the attack and then gradually climbed, with its nose pointing at one of the mountain slopes. A bundle appeared from the aircraft, as the rear gunner's parachute unfolded. Soon afterwards the Barracuda crashed into the mountain. The remaining bombers left the area while maneuvering to avoid the anti-aircraft fire.[681]

On the *Tirpitz's* bridge, Heydel felt the battleship shake from the new hits, although this time there were fewer. Again the droning engines of the aircraft faded, but the rumbling fires, screams from the wounded, and the hissing sound from escaping steam remained. Commander Junge, the first lieutenant, appeared on the bridge, but after a brief discussion it was decided that Heydel should remain in command. He had got in touch with the chief engineer in the forward conning tower and instructed him how to maneuver the ship. It was reported that enemy torpedo bombers were approaching, and Heydel realized they would have to attack from the northeast. With his face covered in blood and speckles of debris, he turned the ship in such a way that she became positioned along the presumed line of attack. When no more enemy aircraft appeared (it was probably the returning second wave that had been reported), Heydel ordered that the battleship be moved back into the net cage.[682]

Gradually the extent of the damage became clear. None of the 15 bombs that hit the battleship had penetrated the armored deck, and one of the 725kg bombs had hit the bow without exploding, but the damage on the upper deck was extensive. The communications to the bridge had been destroyed, as well as the radio equipment. Many anti-aircraft batteries were damaged. Fires raged in many compartments, such as the wardroom, canteens, and storage rooms. The hangar was also on fire. One of the 725kg bombs had penetrated the upper deck, but not the thick armored deck below. The bomb had exploded above the port engine room, and the resulting pressure wave caused extensive damage and started fires, which were nourished by aviation fuel from a pipe that had been cut. Many crewmen were dead and even more were wounded, among them Meyer, who suffered from broken ribs and was unable to hear. Junge, who was promoted captain and remained in command until November 1944, would replace him.[683]

The returning aircraft from the first wave became visible to the British naval force soon after six and began to land ten minutes later. First came the Barracudas. One of them had had a particularly hazardous flight back. The crew believed they had dropped their 725kg bomb, but one of the other aircraft reported that it still hung below their fuselage. When the carriers were not far away, the crew asked the *Furious* what to do and received the reply: "Fly far away and try to shake off the damned thing." They followed the advice, but the bomb refused to let go. Finally, they made themselves ready to ditch in the sea, when an order from the *Furious* told them to land on the flight deck. When the Barracuda approached the flight deck, many observers waited tensely. The slightest mistake from the pilot could have fatal consequences, but he made a perfect landing. Soon all but one Barracuda had landed. The last one had been lost during the attack. It had been seen flying along the Kaafjord, but it had not been seen crashing.[684]

The second wave returned about an hour after the first. As the *Furious* had a slow lift and the aircraft wings had to be folded, about three minutes passed between every landing. Carrier-based aircraft needed headwind when taking off and landing. Thus the *Furious* had to sail on a course that brought her so close to the coast, that some of the crew joked about going ashore in Norway. Only one accident occurred. A Corsair touched down too late for its arrestor hook to properly catch the wire and crashed on the *Victorious'* deck. Miraculously, the pilot survived. Another fighter—a Hellcat—had to land on the water near the destroyer *Algonquin*, as its hook had been damaged. The whaler was sent to rescue the pilot. Two additional aircraft had had problems dropping their bombs and returned with them still attached. One of the crews managed to shake it off at a safe distance from the task force, but the other landed with the bomb still on board. When the pilot was about to touch down on the flight deck, he could not see a living soul except for the officer who guided him down with his bats. The Barracuda made a perfect landing. Nevertheless, the pilot saw the officer give the sign for shutting down the engine and then disappear quickly behind protective nets under the flight deck. However, Operation Tungsten was over. The losses included one Corsair, three Barracudas, and nine men.[685]

The British aircrews made spectacular claims on the number of hits scored. When adding all claims, the commander of the *Victorious* got a sum of 30 hits, but he reduced it to 17. Nevertheless, he concluded that the *Tirpitz* could no longer be used as a battleship. When Moore sent his report to the Admiralty, he was more cautious: "The *Tirpitz* is badly damaged."[686]

A torpedo attack had been planned for the following day, but as the weather deteriorated during the night it was cancelled. Also, Moore believed that another attack could adversely affect the tired but triumphant crews. If the *Tirpitz* was severely damaged, why expose the crews to another attack, which would certainly not capitalize on surprise. Perhaps German fighters would be encountered. He ordered the task force to return to Scapa Flow.[687]

In England, the attack at the Kaafjord made headlines in the press. The

Times wrote that *Tirpitz* had been crippled in a dawn air attack and added that the German battleship was now useless. King George VI congratulated the aircrews for their "gallant and successful" mission, but there were also skeptical minds. Fraser would have rather seen the *Tirpitz* sunk as opposed to just being damaged. Churchill shared his opinion.

On the basis of available intelligence, the Admiralty estimated the extent of damage inflicted and concluded that the *Tirpitz* would again be serviceable within six months. As Operation Overlord—the Allied assault on Normandy—was scheduled for June 1944, substantial air and naval assets would be involved. Thus the *Tirpitz* could again become the menace she had been for so long. The First Sea Lord, Admiral Cunningham, called Fraser and asked him to prepare another attack on the Kaafjord as soon as possible.[688]

Fraser did not believe that the prospects for a successful attack were bright. First of all, weather conditions as favorable as during Operation Tungsten could not be counted on. Furthermore, German defenses would inevitably be stronger. As the *Tirpitz* had not been attacked since Operation Source, Fraser believed the Germans had become complacent, which was a major factor contributing to the successful outcome of Operation Tungsten. Another attack would face an enemy more alert, with stronger anti-aircraft defenses, thicker artificial fog, and—most likely—German fighters. Finally, no Arctic convoys were scheduled for the time being. Thus it would not be possible to disguise the attack force as a distant cover force. Fraser refused to conduct another operation and hinted that he would resign if it was forced upon him.[689]

Despite the harsh words, Fraser budged and on 21 April, Moore sailed from Scapa Flow. Three days later, the task force, which was almost identical to the task force that conducted Tungsten, had almost reached far enough to launch the aircraft. At that moment, reports of adverse weather in the Alta area were received. The operation—which was called "Planet"—was cancelled. On 15 May, another attempt called "Brawn" was cancelled due to bad weather, after the Barracudas had already started from the carriers. Certainly, the harsh northern weather was turning out to be the *Tirpitz*'s first line of defense. Barely ten days after the second attempt to repeat Tungsten, a third attempt called Operation Tiger Claw was cancelled on 28 May, as clouds covered the target area. Instead, the task force sailed south and attacked Aalesund, where four German merchant ships were sunk.[690] A week later, Allied troops entered Rome and battled ashore in Normandy. The Allies' attention focused on areas far from northern Norway.

Meanwhile, the Germans worked hard to restore the *Tirpitz* to operational readiness. The air attack on 2 April had resulted in 15 hits on the battleship. In a sense, the operation was very successful, as such a high number of hits was unusual. However, the British did not know that not one bomb had penetrated the ship's main armor. Thus, all vital functions remained intact. Outside the thick armor, damage was more extensive, which was also reflected in the number of casualties.

Of the 2,000 strong crew, a substantial portion had their battle stations at the anti-aircraft guns, or at other unprotected positions. The large number of bomb hits, as well as the automatic weapons fire, resulted in 122 killed and 316 wounded.[691]

To judge the damage and lead the repair work, Werner Krux, an engineer from the naval yard at Kiel, was sent to the Altafjord. Together with three other experts, he went aboard the *Tirpitz* on 12 April to be informed on the ship's condition. When his investigation was completed, it was evident that yet another bomb had caused damage, in addition to the known 15 hits. A near miss close to the stern had resulted in leaks, but the rudders and propellers remained unharmed.[692]

The most problematic damage was found at the hull and the funnel. The latter had been damaged when the hangars next to the funnel were hit. Krux estimated that three or four weeks of work were needed, but personnel and equipment would have to be brought to the Kaafjord from Germany. The effort to repair the *Tirpitz* was known as "Paul II" and began at the end of April, when a group of 57 men arrived from the shipyard at Kiel. On 4 May, another 100 men arrived with special equipment so that the work could be accelerated.[693]

The repairs proceeded according to plan. In early June the *Tirpitz* was technically ready for operations, but not fully battleworthy. It had been decided to improve her anti-aircraft defenses, and this work was not yet completed. Also, her crew was in need of exercises after nine months of inactivity, and replacements had to be trained. In any case, she would soon be ready to put to sea again.[694]

In mid-June, Fraser was replaced by Henry Moore. At this time, indications were strong that the *Tirpitz* would soon be capable of conducting offensive operations. The Admiralty decided to attack her once again. Three carriers were earmarked for an operation the following month, and the aircrews began to train for the mission. A month later, on 12 July, air reconnaissance reported that the German battleship appeared fully operational. The information was alarming, as it meant that the Germans had repaired the *Tirpitz* in only half the time estimated by the Admiralty. As a floating platform had been observed near the battleship, it was concluded that divers were still working on the ship. However, photos taken by reconnaissance aircraft suggested that the *Tirpitz*'s armament was in working order. The Admiralty decided to initiate Operation Mascot.[695]

On 17 July, 42 Barracudas again approached the Kaafjord, this time escorted by 18 Corsairs, 12 Fairey Fireflys, and 20 Hellcats. They had started from the carriers *Formidable* and *Indefatigable*, and in this attack all but two bombers carried the heavy 725kg bomb. Fraser's prediction that stronger defenses would be encountered proved correct. Since April, the Germans had improved their radar warning system and communications. They had also increased the number of artificial smoke units in the area. The approaching air armada was detected at a range of 70 kilometers. Soon thick clouds covered the area and concealed everything below an altitude of 300 meters. Clouds reduced visibility further. The German fire control for the anti-aircraft guns had been positioned on land, to allow good visibility despite the artificial fog. Thus the guns could fire effectively while the battleship remained concealed. The British attack failed, as the Barracudas dropped their bombs on an invisible target. No bombs hit the *Tirpitz*, and the task force returned to Scapa Flow.[696]

One month later, the Royal Navy made another attempt to destroy the elusive enemy. The Arctic convoys had been resumed, and another attack, named Operation Goodwood, was about to be launched with convoy JW59 as cover. At 12.00 on 22 August, a large number of aircraft from the carriers *Indefatigable*, *Indomitable*, and *Furious* were launched. This time the escort fighters would not only rake the battleship with automatic weapons, but the crews had also been trained in dive-bombing, and bombs had been attached under their fuselages. There was another novelty. This time the task force would remain off the Norwegian coast and conduct several attacks until the desired result was achieved. Also mines were to be dropped, some around the *Tirpitz* and some in a belt at the entrance to the Kaafjord. The former would be set to detonate at intervals, and it was hoped that the commander of the battleship would be so concerned about the explosions that he would decide to leave the Kaafjord for safer waters, thereby passing over the mines dropped at the fjord's entrance.[697]

Operation Goodwood also failed. Many of the crews participating in Tungsten had been transferred to other units and their replacements were less experienced. All operations after Tungsten had suffered from this reallocation and Goodwood was no exception. Neither was the weather cooperative. First, the operation was postponed one day, to allow the clouds to disperse. When the attack was finally launched, the aircraft carrying the mines were not started, as it was feared they would not find the target and be forced to drop the mines into the sea before landing. As very few mines were available, it was deemed wiser to save them for an attack when the weather was more favorable. The weather also affected the bombers. When the clouds lifted above the task forces, they often remained over the Altafjord and vice versa. To make matters worse for the British, the frigate *Bickertown* and the escort carrier *Nabob* were torpedoed on 22 August. The former sank, and the latter had to limp back to Scapa Flow supported by another escort carrier, *Trumpeter*, a cruiser, and a few destroyers. As the mine-carrying aircraft were based on these carriers, that part of the operation was cancelled.[698]

Four attacks were launched between 22–29 August. Only during the third attack were any hits on the *Tirpitz* achieved. The first struck on turret Bruno. It did not penetrate, but the explosion caused damage to the mechanism that elevated the starboard gun, and a 20mm anti-aircraft gun nearby was knocked out. The second hit was—to the Germans' good fortune—a dud. It found a weak spot in the armor and actually got below the deck, but it failed to explode. It came to rest in one of the switchboard rooms. It might have caused extensive damage had it exploded, but in the end the only 725kg bomb that penetrated below the armored deck was a dud. The 33 Barracudas that had participated in the attack returned to the carriers. The attack had cost the British two Hellcats and four Corsairs, and ultimately was another disappointment.[699]

One week later, on 29 August, the last attack during Operation

Goodwood was launched. Despite using four Corsairs as pathfinders, the artificial fog covered the German battleship so well that no hits were scored. *Tirpitz* remained operational. The task force returned to Scapa Flow after covering convoy RA59A, which sailed from the Soviet Union to Iceland.[700]

Thus ended forever the Royal Navy's attempts to sink the *Tirpitz*.

The Russian Adventure

Even before the final attack wave from the carriers were launched, the Joint Planning Staff in London met to discuss an alternative way to destroy the *Tirpitz*. It was concluded that the Barracudas were too slow to surprise the enemy before the artificial fog covered the target. Furthermore, the aircraft could not carry bombs heavy enough to permanently cripple the German battleship. An alternative considered was to launch Mosquito aircraft from the carriers. They were faster than the Barracudas and could carry heavier bombs. However, few squadrons were available and they were badly needed elsewhere. Also, the Mosquito was difficult to operate from carriers and the probability of obtaining hits at the necessary high altitude was low. Finally, there was a high demand for carriers in the Far East.[701]

The desire to destroy the *Tirpitz*, however, remained strong. Although the German battleship was probably not fully operational, she remained a threat to the Arctic convoys. She might also sail south and attack Allied reinforcements pouring onto the continent. It was also theoretically possible that the Germans would send her into the Atlantic, as they had done with the *Bismarck* in 1941.[702]

The air staff advocated using long-range aircraft. Heavy bombers had attacked the battleship in 1942, but the results had been meager. However, better weapons had since become available, and it was now decided to use four-engine bombers. Eisenhower agreed to release two squadrons from the operations over Western Europe. General Arthur Harris, who commanded Bomber Command, received orders to conduct the attack. He assigned Air Vice Marshal R.A. Cochrane, who

285

commanded the 5th Group, to lead the preparations to attack the *Tirpitz*.[703]

Two squadrons—the 9th and 617th—were chosen to conduct the operation. The latter were the famous "Dambusters," a name acquired after attacking and destroying the German Möhne and Eder dams in 1943. It was a veteran squadron, which had previously fielded well-known names like Guy Gibson and Leonard Cheshire. However the latter had received other assignments, and Gibson had been grounded since he was regarded as too valuable for propaganda purposes to be lost. At the time, 617th Squadron was commanded by Wing Commander J.B. "Willie" Tait. The Dambusters were stationed at Woodhall Spa, while 9th Squadron, commanded by Squadron Leader J.M. Bazin, was based at Bardney, Lincolnshire.[704]

The aircraft to be used was the Lancaster, the best British heavy bomber. It had been developed from the twin-engine Avro Manchester, which was not one of the better designs. The Lancaster, however, was much more successful and required few modifications during its career. It had four Merlin engines, three machine gun turrets, and could carry a greater bombload than any other aircraft operating over Europe. Unlike the American B-17 and B-24, the Lancaster lacked armament against attacks from below, but as Bomber Command mainly operated during the dark hours, it was not a major shortcoming. The British heavy bombers generally had fewer crewmembers than their American counterparts. While the B-17 Flying Fortress had a crew of ten, the Lancaster had only seven. Thus the British bomb aimer also doubled as a nose gunner when needed. Similarly, the radio operator also manned the mid-upper machine guns. With a bombload of six tons, the Lancaster had a range of 2,700 kilometers.[705]

There were four main problems to be mastered to accomplish the destruction of the *Tirpitz*. The first was the weather. Without at least average visibility—which was not common in September—chances to bomb with reasonable precision were slight. However, the weather could not be governed. It only remained to await promising forecasts, while continuously reconnoitring the target area.[706]

The second problem was the long distance from British airfields to the Kaafjord, which exceeded the range of the Lancaster armed with a super heavy bomb. The solution settled for was to fly to a Soviet airfield, where the bombers would be armed and refuelled. From there they would proceed to the Kaafjord and attack the *Tirpitz*, whereupon they would return to the Soviet airfield. There they would again be refuelled and return to Scotland.[707]

After consulting with Soviet authorities, permission to use the airfield at Jagodnik was received. It was located on an island in the river Dvina, south of Archangelsk. The location provided an additional advantage, beyond that of being located within good striking distance to the Kaafjord. A major factor contributing to the many failed attacks was the German tactic of employing artificial fog. The Germans received ample warning from radar surveillance over the sea. The British estimated that ten minutes were sufficient to completely conceal the battleship in fog. However, by flying from the Archangelsk area, the British bombers would approach from another direction, flying over land and thus improving the chances of surprise. If so, the fog would

A Tallboy bomb.

not cover the battleship when the bombs were aimed.[708]

The final problem had been the bombs themselves, which obviously were too light. Heavier bombs, dropped from greater altitude, were needed. The carrier-based aircraft could not carry such ordnance, but the Lancaster bombers could. This time the 5.4-ton Tallboy, a real monster, would be used. It was about six meters long and contained over two tons of explosives. It was designed to penetrate thick surfaces, such as those made of concrete. The Tallboy had first been employed in an attack that destroyed the railway tunnel in Saumur, Normandy in June 1944.[709]

Unlike most bombs, the Tallboy's fins were set at a 5-degree angle, causing the bomb to revolve as it fell through the air, thus conferring stability, which was particularly important at the speed of sound. Although the weapon had not been designed for attacking warships, it was concluded that it probably was the best alternative. Even a near miss might cause considerable damage.[710]

Another weapon to be used was the new JW mine, or "Jonny Walkers," as they were often called. The mine, attached to a parachute, was dropped from an aircraft. It exploded immediately if it hit a solid object, but if it fell into water, the parachute was automatically disconnected and the mine began to sink. When it reached a depth of 20 meters, a mechanism that pumped out water and injected hydrogen gas was activated. This made the mine rise in the water, but at an angle of 30 degrees from vertical. The mine would thus reach the surface at some distance from the position where it fell into the water. If it did not hit anything until it had risen to a depth of 5–6 meters, another mechanism was activated and the sink and rise procedure was repeated until it hit a hull or some other solid object. If a JW mine hit the hull of the *Tirpitz*, the force of the explosion would first push the hull upwards, then it would fall back into the void created in the water. The resulting movement would be violent enough to cause extensive damage, perhaps even breaking the keel. The weapon had a time fuse which caused it to explode after an hour, to prevent the Germans from examining it. A Lancaster could carry a dozen JW mines, and a number of the aircraft detailed for attacking the *Tirpitz* would carry them.[711] The attack from Soviet territory was given the code name Operation Paravane.

The task of transferring two Lancaster squadrons to the Soviet

Union proved difficult, as is well illustrated by the fact that losses during the transfer flights exceeded the number of aircraft lost in the actual attacks. On 11 September, 37 Lancasters from the 9th and 617th Squadrons, one Lancaster from the 463rd Photo Reconnaissance Unit, and two Liberator aircraft took off for the Soviet Union. The PRU aircraft was included to film the attack, whereas the Liberator aircraft carried a maintenance unit with ground staff, a spare engine, and a spare landing gear with an extra wheel. It also brought lots of spare parts for radio and radar equipment and a large amount of tools to maintain the Lancasters in proper order.[712]

The flight across the Norwegian Sea, Norway, Sweden, and Finland proceeded according to plan, although the Lancasters were shot at on some occasions. As neutral Sweden did not enforce a blackout, the lights on the ground aided navigation. Farther east, however, navigation proved more difficult. Poor visibility and monotonous landscape made orientation intricate. The radio beacons were of little help, as they belonged to an unfamiliar system and the codes allotted were incorrect. Many pilots had to descend to an altitude of only 30 meters to actually see the ground. To make matters worse, the aircraft were low on fuel. Several bombers had to make forced landings, but luckily no crewmen were injured. The remainder landed according to plan, but only 23 of the 38 Lancasters—as well as both Liberators—made it to Jagodnik without making a touchdown. Six of the aircraft forced to land were damaged beyond repair and would subsequently be scavenged for spare parts.[713]

One Lancaster, which had been forced to land near the city of Onega, was made ready to fly to Jagodnik. A Soviet C-47 arrived with fuel for the flight and the commander of the Lancaster, Flying Officer H. C. Knilans, and his crew could start again. The Lancaster took off and approached a piece of woodland. Knilans told his flight engineer to retract the landing gear, but the latter misunderstood the order and raised the flaps instead. The aircraft lost height as it was right above the tree tops. Branches hit the fuselage and the pilot dared not pull the control wheel, as he feared the tail might hit the trees and make them crash.

Knilans saw a valley not far ahead and hoped the Lancaster would remain airborne a few more seconds. However, there was a large pine tree at the forest's edge. It was several meters taller than the other trees and Knilans realized it would smash one of the engines, perhaps even the wing. With a presence of mind that would later surprise him, he worked the foot pedals to allow the center section of the aircraft to receive the impact. A second later, the windscreen was shattered. The Lancaster proceeded without its bombsight and bomb doors. Knilans was half blinded, not from perspex splinter, but from the icy wind that swept through the aircraft. It caught the navigator's maps and the radio operator's hat, which disappeared through an opening in the tail gun turret. Knilans managed to maneuver the plane by holding one hand in front of his face and using the other to steer. It was difficult, and the fact that twigs and needles blocked the air intake of the outer right engine made the situation even worse. The engine had to be shut down to prevent it from overheating. A section of the pine tree was resting inside the aircraft, like some sort of involuntary passenger.[714]

Knilans and his crew survived and landed at Jagodnik somewhat later. During the following days, Tait assembled his squadrons and the aircraft were repaired to the best of the ground crew's ability. Finally, 31 operational aircraft were ready, including Knilans's Lancaster, which was repaired one day before the attack. However, as long as the weather above the Kaafjord remained poor, the mission could not be launched. Meantime, the British crews were entertained in various ways. For example, a soccer game was played against a Soviet team, and some parties were arranged where considerable quantities of vodka were consumed. A Canadian radio operator tried to swim back to Jagodnik after a late visit to Archangelsk, but he contracted a bad cold as a result.[715]

Such days far from the harsh realities of the war, however, were bound to come to an end. Early on 15 September, a Mosquito returned from a sweep over northern Norway and reported that the weather in the Kaafjord area was clear. The visibility was excellent.[716]

The report was confirmed by other sources. When the Mosquito landed, the Lancasters were already warming up their engines. During the 30 minutes that followed, they started and set off to the west. On the ground, a Russian band played music.

The time had come for the heavy bombers to attack the *Tirpitz*. Operation Paravane was on!

It took about four hours to fly from Jagodnik to the Kaafjord. To avoid

Photo of a Lancaster above the Kaafjord during the attack against *Tirpitz* on September 15, 1944. Smoke cover tries to hide the ship from the aircraft.

German radar, the 27 Lancaster bombers flew at an altitude of about 300 meters. However, for some unknown reason, one Lancaster pilot flew at 600 meters. Tait considered breaking radio silence and ordering the pilot to get closer to the ground, but concluded that a lone aircraft would probably be less of a risk than breaking radio silence. Above Finland, the Lancasters passed over a German airfield, but no fighters appeared.[717]

Nothing of importance transpired until the Lancaster squadrons approached the target area. When ten minutes remained until the bombs would be dropped, the pilots applied full throttle. This was necessary to reach the altitude needed for the bombs to develop sufficient falling speed. Many factors had to be considered to achieve the success desired. From 4,000 meters, a Tallboy fell for almost half a minute before hitting the ground. As the explosions would throw up huge amounts of water and debris, all aircraft had to drop their bombs prior to the first explosions, lest the pinpoint accuracy of subsequent waves be harder to achieve. To counter this difficulty the aircraft had to fly close together, which meant the risk of collision was far from negligible.[718]

The problem was solved by adopting a formation consisting of five groups, each flying in V-shape, with intervals of 800 meters. Given a flying speed of 370 kilometers per hour, the formation adopted would allow all bombs to be dropped within 22 seconds. Thus all bombs would be released before the first detonated. To reduce the risk of collision, each plane would be separated from the others in the group by 15 meters in altitude. They would also be staggered in such a way that each group flew 300 meters higher than the one ahead. Furthermore, the JW mines had to be released after the Tallboys, or else the mines would be rendered ineffective by the pressure waves from the bombs. They would also be dropped perpendicular to the battleship, to ensure that they fell on both sides of her. The Tallboys would—on the contrary—be dropped along the ship's length, as the lateral accuracy was greater than the longitudinal.[719]

When the British airmen approached the battleship, it became apparent that one of the most important prerequisites was absent. The crews saw fog rising from the Kaafjord and soon the battleship's guns blazed, as did anti-aircraft batteries ashore. The smoke from the firing further obscured the target. Tait's bomb aimer, Flight Lieutenant

Daniel, saw the battleship become enshrouded in haze, but he could still discern masts and muzzle flashes. The Tallboy fell toward the fjord and Tait turned to avoid the flak.

The following aircraft released their bombs without being able to aim properly. In the nose bubble of one of the Lancasters, the bomb aimer thought he saw Tait's Tallboy hit the *Tirpitz*, but he wasn't really sure. Tait himself had turned around to observe how the attack proceeded. He believed that a bomb fell near the battleship—perhaps near enough to damage her—but the thick fog made any observation uncertain.[720]

Some bombers were damaged. Knilans, who had kept a piece of the pine tree as a souvenir, noted that something hit his right wing, and soon the outer right engine began to overheat. However, he waited until he had escaped the anti-aircraft fire before shutting it down. Another Lancaster, commanded by Flying Officer Oram, was hit in the tail, making it impossible to turn. He continued north, but after awhile the aircraft could gradually turn around and head toward Jagodnik. Another two machines were damaged, but neither was shot down.[721]

Two aircraft returned to Jagodnik with their bombs still aboard. They were commanded by Squadron Leader Cockshot and Flight Lieutenant Knights, who hoped to get another chance the following day, but bad weather precluded an attack.[722]

The bombing was filmed by the Lancaster from the 463rd PRU. Once the attack was over, it headed straight for Britain. When landing at Waddington, the crew had been airborne for almost 15 hours. The films were rapidly developed, but did not provide the information sought. Neither could the Mosquito flying with Tait's squadrons provide any proof that the *Tirpitz* had been hit, despite several reconnaissance missions on 15–16 September. The clouds had formed a lid above the Kaafjord and the Germans continued to produce artificial fog.[723]

While the results of the attack were still unknown, the Lancasters started on their return voyage to Britain. On 17 September, the first 16 left Jagodnik, commanded by Tait. As secrecy was no longer vital, a simpler route was chosen, bringing the bombers largely across neutral Sweden, though this was against the rules of war. Tait's Lancasters passed south of Stockhom. Most of the crews had been trained since the beginning of the war, and because of the blackouts in most of Europe, had never seen anything like it. Outbound from Britain they had passed several smaller Swedish towns, but the visibility had been poor, making street lights just a low gleam beneath the cloud cover. Now however, the clear night allowed them to see the Swedish capital with almost all lights burning. It appeared absolutely peaceful, until anti-aircraft shells began to explode. "What the heck, I thought these guys were neutral!" Knilans shouted in his microphone as he made evasive maneuvers.[724]

During the return flight, the squadrons suffered their first fatalities. When Frank Levy's aircraft flew across Norway, it developed some kind of technical problem and hit a mountain slope, killing all on board. The Germans buried them with all the military marks of honor. The accident was a tragic end to Operation Paravane. Had it not occurred, no casualties would have been suffered.[725]

Between 18–21 September, the remaining 12 Lancasters took off from the Soviet airfield. When some of them climbed, a British airman fired two signal flares. Unfortunately they landed in a forest and started an extensive fire. There were strong indications that the Russians did not fully approve of this gesture.[726]

In the Kaafjord, it remained for Junge to assess the effects of the attack. Obviously, the battleship's forebody had been hit by a very heavy bomb. Also, explosions near the bow may have contributed to the damage. About 2,000 tons of water had entered the ship. The damage to the bow was extensive and mainly located below the waterline. It seriously affected the battleship's seaworthiness and made her unable to conduct operations.[727]

At the same time as its freedom of mobility was severely hampered by the bomb damage, military events farther east and south changed in a way that affected the future of the *Tirpitz*. Finland had signed a cease-fire agreement with the Soviet Union, thus forcing German troops to withdraw. At the same time, the Red Army prepared an offensive westwards from the Murmansk area. The impending threat meant that the *Tirpitz* could probably not remain in the Kaafjord for repairs.[728] She had to find shelter elsewhere.

The Allies had no secure information on the damage sustained by the *Tirpitz*. Aerial photographs were examined, but they provided no conclusive information, although it was concluded that four bombs had hit within the enclosure made up of torpedo nets. Soviet aerial photographs suggested that the deck ahead of the forward gun turrets had been damaged, a finding that was also corroborated by British photographs. Reports from Norwegian agents were even more optimistic. Some of them even claimed that the battleship had in fact been sunk, her hull resting on the bottom of the fjord. These observations were obviously ruled out. Nevertheless, the available intelligence at least suggested that the *Tirpitz* had been damaged in the bow, even though the extent of the damage was impossible to assess.[729]

Therefore, to the Allies, the *Tirpitz* still remained a threat.

Operation Obviate

On 15 November, the residents on Tromsøya could see a grey destroyer against the mountains sailing toward them. The sight was not particularly remarkable, as the country had been occupied by the Germans since 1940. The German destroyer caused neither strolling people to halt, nor make men and women interrupt their work. Rather, it was the majestic shape in the wake of the destroyer that had such an impact on the spectators.

Egil Lindberg, a Norwegian agent regularly providing weather reports to the British, immediately realized that the huge warship must be the *Tirpitz*. Lindberg was employed at the meteorological station at Tromsø. Limping and stooping, he hardly fit the conventional perception of an agent, but he had a radio transmitter on the top ceiling at the nearby hospital. Lindberg's physical condition was an excellent pretext for his frequent visits to the hospital, and he never aroused any suspicions. Recently, he had noted that the Germans used a dredger to bring earth and gravel into the water off Kvaløya. He could not make any sense of the work and had refrained from reporting it, but now the implications suddenly became clear. The German battleship was moving to a berth in the Tromsø area, and the dredging was aimed at raising the bottom of the sea near Kvaløya. If damaged by Allied attacks, the battleship would not sink but gently settle on the bottom. He hurried to his radio set and sent a message to London: "The *Tirpitz* arrived at Tromsø in the afternoon."[730]

The Allies did not yet know that the Germans had written off the *Tirpitz* as an operational battleship. The damage inflicted on her bow during Operation Paravane could not be repaired in northern Norway. The Germans estimated that repairs would require nine months and had to be conducted in a shipyard. This gloomy picture was confirmed at a meeting in Germany on 23 September. Soviet forces closed in on the battleship's berth at the Kaafjord and she had to be moved away from the advancing enemy troops. It was decided to make provisional repairs, allowing her to sail south along the Norwegian coast. A new berth had been found for her at Tromsø. It was deemed suitable, as the bottom was solid with a layer of sand above rocks. From this position she could serve as a floating battery, thus supporting the defense line forming in the Lyngenfjord area. However the depth was too great; hence the dredging observed by Lindberg.[731]

The Germans wanted to raise the bottom of the sea beneath the battleship to prevent her from capsizing if she was damaged. By raising the bottom, it was hoped that she would simply settle on it if damaged and water-filled. In many respects the bottom near Tromsø was suitable, but more earth and gravel were needed. Substantial quantities had to be transported to Tromsø. However, the work to raise the seabed was not yet completed when the battleship was again attacked.[732]

It was estimated that the *Tirpitz* would be able to move on 15 October, and the forecast proved correct. Her artillery was still fully functional, but the damage to her bow caused concern. It was difficult to predict what consequences it might have. As a precaution she was accompanied by tugs, but the anxieties were unfounded. The battleship was easier to maneuver than expected, and her speed was gradually increased to ten knots. After an uneventful voyage, she could moor near Tromsø as planned.[733]

The *Tirpitz's* absence from her berth at the Kaafjord was detected by Allied aerial reconnaissance. Soon Lindberg's report was confirmed when a Firefly from the carrier *Implacable* overflew Tromsø and found the battleship. Within Bomber Command, resolve had been strong to attack again when an opportunity occurred. As the distance to Tromsø was shorter, the Lancasters could now fly from airfields in Scotland and return, rather than having to fly from the Soviet Union. Planning for another attack was immediately initiated.[734]

Although Tromsø was nearer to Scotland than the Kaafjord, the distance was still respectable. Several modifications were needed to enable the Lancasters to carry Tallboys to Tromsø. An extra internal fuel tank was installed, and an external drop tank of a type developed for the Mosquito was fitted. The pilot's back armor plate was removed, as was the mid-upper machine gun turret. The weapons and ammunition for the nose turret were removed. Consequently, the defensive capabilities were significantly impaired, as the tail gunner alone would be responsible for defending against enemy fighters. Despite removing armor and armament, the weight still overtaxed the current engines, which were replaced by a more powerful type. In a few days, the technicians changed 120 engines. The attack could then be launched as soon as favorable weather arrived.[735]

The crews selected for Operation Obviate received instructions on the evening of 27 October. They were informed of the route chosen, the radio frequencies to use, and details of the target, as well as a recommendation to fly to Soviet territory in case they could not return to Scotland. Allied intelligence had found a gap in the German radar surveillance between Namsos and Mosjøen. By crossing the Norwegian coast at low altitude through the blind sector, it was hoped that the attacking force could continue into Swedish airspace without being spotted. At a certain waypoint, the Lancasters were then to turn on a more northerly course, still going over Sweden until they reached close to the Narvik area. With a little luck, the defenses at Tromsø could be taken with surprise. On the following morning, the Lancaster aircraft flew north to airfields at Moray Firth.

At midnight between 28–29 October, a Mosquito on a reconnaissance flight over Tromsø reported favorable weather conditions, and an hour later 32 Lancasters took off from Lossiemouth and Milltown. They proceeded at low altitude, passing the Norwegian coast far south of Tromsø. The mountains forced them to climb, but the summits were not as high as the altitude suitable for the attack. However, the bombers did not climb to the desired attack altitude until they were safely over Swedish territory. At this stage, bad luck intervened. The clouds gathered and soon only small patches of clear sky could be seen. Five Lancasters had been detached from the main force to estimate the wind, and they reported their findings to Tait. However, the information was discouraging and he ordered them to make an additional sweep. By now the visibility was so poor that the *Tirpitz* could only occasionally be seen through the clouds.[736]

Tait had no choice but to initiate the attack despite the unfavorable conditions. To penetrate the *Tirpitz*'s armored deck the bombs had to be dropped from high altitude. This would allow gravity to accelerate them to a sufficiently high speed. Thus, the bombers could not descend below the clouds to release the bombs. Also, such a maneuver would expose them to the flak and the risk of crashing into a mountain slope obscured by the clouds.[737]

On the ground, German servicemen and Norwegian civilians saw the bombers approaching the Tromsø area. The air alarm still sounded when the anti-aircraft batteries on the slopes opened fire, soon followed by the battleship's guns. The noise lasted several minutes, while the spectators occasionally glimpsed the bombers between the clouds. Then huge detonations were heard as the Tallboys created enormous fountains of earth and water around the battleship.

But none of them seemed to hit the *Tirpitz*.

From one of the bombers, Flying Officer F.H.A. Watts saw how the clouds concealed the target below him. He had to make repeated runs to allow his bomb aimer to set up the shot. His radio operator reported that the unit commander had ordered the formation to break off the attack, but Watts had no intention of doing so. He told the radio operator to inform the commander that the message had not been properly received, and made yet another run. At that very moment he saw anti-aircraft fire hit a Lancaster. Parts of the aircraft came off and whirled around in the air, but Watts had no time to contemplate the fate of the other bomber, as his own aircraft was shuddering from hits. Light could be seen through the tip of the left wing, and the tail gunner reported that his turret had been perforated by shrapnel. Fortunately, none of the crew were injured. Watts released the bomb and turned toward Scotland, but he did not get far. One of his fuel tanks had been hit, forcing him to land on the Shetlands despite a punctured tire.[738]

No bomber was shot down at Tromsø, but to the crew of the Lancaster observed by Watts, the mission abruptly came to an end. It was flown by Flying Officer Bill Carey and was called "Easy Elsie." Carey had made several runs, but the *Tirpitz* was always concealed by the clouds. During his sixth attempt, the anti-aircraft fire was very intense as few Lancasters remained over the target area, allowing the Germans to concentrate their fire. The bomb aimer caught a brief glimpse of the *Tirpitz* between the clouds and aimed at a point where he believed her to be moored.

Without knowing if he had hit, Carey turned south to return to Scotland. He had hardly completed the turn before they were hit for the first time. The aircraft shook and Les Franks, the flight engineer, reported that the left engine had been hit and fuel leaked from several tanks. Carey shut off the damaged engine, and at the same time realized that the bomb doors could not be closed. The hydraulics had evidently been hit too. He found an inhabited island ahead and steered toward it to allow the navigator a mark to calculate a proper course.[739]

When Easy Elsie flew above Harstad, she was again fired upon. The radio operator, Flight Sergeant Arthur Young, had a narrow escape. He had experienced an ever-growing need to empty his bladder, and finally Carey permitted him to go to the elsan. He was on his way abaft when a nearby German flak battery opened fire. A shell exploded close to the aircraft and shrapnel ripped through the fuselage at the radio operator's seat. At the same time, the outer port engine began to falter.[740]

Carey ordered Franks to check the remaining amount of fuel. Then he told Young to call the destroyers on patrol in the Norwegian Sea, where they waited to pick up any aircrew in distress. Did they still have sufficient fuel to reach the nearest airfield on the Shetlands?

Franks replied almost instantly, "Sorry, boss. Not enough fuel to reach the Shetlands. We have already lost too much."[741]

Neither did the destroyers appear to be a realistic alternative. Young reported that the radio was destroyed. If they landed in the sea, they would probably freeze to death before any help arrived.

"Where the hell is the bleedin' Navy!" exclaimed Witherick, the tail gunner who had a sibling in the Royal Navy. "I shall have to talk to my brother about this."

This was a typical example of jargon resorted to in order to keep spirits high in the face of danger. It had helped them before and it did so now.

A forced landing in Norway would almost inevitably make them prisoners of war. Carey decided to make an attempt to land in Sweden. He asked the navigator, Pilot Officer McKie, for a suitable course. "We can't ditch and we can't get home," Carey explained, "so it's over the mountains to Sweden."

"No, it will ruin my reputation," Witherick protested.

"What do you mean?" Carey asked while he struggled with the controls to keep Easy Elsie flying a bit longer.

"I always get home," Witherick complained. He was flying his 95th mission. "This can't happen to me."

"Can't it?" Carey replied. "You watch."[742]

McKie gave Carey a course that would bring them to Porjus. It was the most natural choice, as it had been their former assembly point, as it was a village in a vast area dominated by desolated forests. Soon they again passed above the Norwegian coast at very low altitude. The mountains loomed large ahead. Carey had to fly between the peaks, follow valleys, and fly over lakes until he crossed the border between Sweden and Norway.[743]

The pilot found an open field in the forest that appeared large enough for a normal landing. The crew positioned for a forced landing, with their backs against the main spar and hands clasped behind their heads. McKie connected the wires from his flying helmet to the socket and informed the pilot that all men were in their positions. Their sense of humor was suddenly gone. It would be dangerous. Carey and Franks remained in the cockpit, as the latter would be needed to assist the pilot with throttles and flaps. He would also help Carey to manually lower the undercarriage.[744]

Given the circumstances, Carey made an almost perfect landing. However, the ground turned out to be very soft. Easy Elsie had come down on a mire and her wheels sank into the mud. The Lancaster skidded and then got stuck; the nose shattered and mud splashed into the cockpit. For a brief moment the aircraft stood up on its nose, then fell back.[745]

Behind the main spar four airmen looked uneasily at each other. The impact had been violent. A parachute abaft had not been properly fastened and had come crashing through the fuselage, luckily without harming anyone. It took the airmen a few seconds to get used to a new sound, until they realized that it was no sound at all, but the silence when the engines had stopped. They all began to laugh and McKie switched on the intercom to talk to Carey. "Well done Bill," he said. "We're all okay back here."

He was interrupted by Carey's painful voice. "My knee struck the bloody compass," the pilot moaned. "Help me out of here."[746]

McKie and the others hurried to the cockpit to see how the pilot and the flight engineer had fared. Carey's seat belt had snapped from the impact and he grimaced, as he had hurt his knee badly. That wasn't all. The flight engineer was nowhere to be found. There was only a large hole in the windscreen ahead of his seat.

"Les, where are you?" they called out.

Fearing the very worst, they didn't expect any reply, but before they had time to leave the aircraft for a more thorough investigation, a faint voice was heard from outside. "I'm here! I'm down in the bog!"

"Are you hurt?"

"No, I'm okay." His face suddenly showed through the hole where the windscreen perspex had once been. "I landed on my head!"

They sighed with relief. "A bloody good job you did," Witherick pointed out. "Or else you might have got *really* hurt."

The old jargon was back!

Except for Les Franks' head, and one pilot in 9th squadron who had been injured in the face, Bill Carey was the only casualty suffered during Operation Obviate. All Lancasters but Easy Elsie returned to British airfields.

Carey was admitted to a Swedish hospital while his knee healed. He would be unable to move for some time. In fact, the same could be said about the *Tirpitz*. The Lancaster from 463rd Squadron, which had participated in Operation Paravane, also observed the results of Operation Obviate. It had descended to 3,000 meters and the crew had seen the results of the bombing. A few bombs fell close to the torpedo nets surrounding the battleship, but most fell too far from the *Tirpitz*. No conclusive observations could be made, but clearly no direct hit had been scored. However, the British did not know that one near miss had damaged the ship's rudder and one of its propeller shafts.[747]

She would never again move by her own steam, and from now on was inevitably a floating battery.

Catechism

Precious little time remained for Bomber Command to knock out the *Tirpitz* before the dark winter days made precision bombing in the Tromsø area exceedingly difficult. Also, the winter meant that favorable weather conditions would be rare.[748]

On 4 November, 40 Lancasters from the 9th and 467th Squadrons flew north to the Scottish airfields, from which another attempt would be made. However, hardly had they arrived before forecasts indicated storms on the Arctic Sea. The bombers returned to the bases farther south.[749]

Within a few days, indications that better weather could be expected were observed. At his office, Cochrane scrutinized the report. Prospects of favorable weather delighted him, but on the other hand intelligence indicated that German fighters had been moved to the Tromsø area. About two dozen single-engine fighters from III./Jagdgeschwder 5 had recently been stationed at the Bardufoss airfield. If they appeared above the *Tirpitz*, they could inflict serious losses on attacking bombers. Nevertheless, higher command echelons insisted that the *Tirpitz* had to be destroyed. Cochrane wanted to talk to Tait immediately.

"The weather forecast for the Tromsø region is supposed to change for the better," Cochrane said. "We want you to fly over to Lossiemouth and Milltown, that way we can make a new try if the situation improves."

Tait nodded. "Very well, sir. When shall we go?"

"When? Why, now of course!" Cochrane was not a man to show

feelings. He looked at Tait as if the question had very much surprised him. "You see," he went on, "9th Squadron is, as you very well know, at Bardney. It'll go to Lossiemoth and Kinross as soon as ordered to. The weathermen think the conditions will change soon. If so, you will be told at the last moment. Then you make the decision."[750]

The squadrons flew north once more. On 11 November, the weather over Norway still remained poor, with clouds and atmospheric conditions making the risk of icing considerable. However, in the evening the weather gradually improved, and soon after midnight a Mosquito landed at Lossiemouth and reported better weather. In particular, the visibility had improved.[751]

Tait had to make the final decision. He considered the pros and cons, and the latter appeared to overshadow the former. Although the weather had improved, it certainly was not ideal. The risk of icing remained substantial, not only over mountainous Norway, but all the way from Britain up to the target. In fact, the ground crews at Lossiemouth were working at that very same moment to remove ice from the wings of bombers. Also, Tait had to consider the German fighters at Bardufoss. How many bombers would they shoot down if they intercepted the Lancasters before the latter reached the target?

On the other hand, these difficulties would remain, and nothing suggested better weather later. Tait made his decision. The bombers would make an attempt.

The crews were on alert. Final instructions were usually given right before the mission, when an officer described the impending attack on a map. Courses, waypoints, fuel consumption, known anti-aircraft-batteries, and radar stations—everything that could have the slightest impact on the mission was considered. The night's identification lights were given, and pilots and radio operators were oriented regarding radio frequencies.

After the briefing the navigators were given time to note the waypoints and coordinates on their own maps, and the aft gunners discussed combat-related matters with the armament officers. The radio operators received additional information on frequencies used by the Germans, as well as call signals to radio beacons and IFF stations. As the mission was almost a carbon copy of Obviate, the preparations were swiftly carried out, whereupon the crews were transported to their aircraft.

The night sky above Lossiemouth was clear when the airmen climbed aboard their bombers. The ground crews still worked to remove ice, but when the moment came to take off, it became clear that some of the Lancasters could not participate. When the commander of 9th Squadron was about to start, his aircraft was found to have excessive amounts of ice. The deputy commander was already airborne and was instructed on the radio to assume command. However, the decision to use the radio was not made without consideration, as the secrecy of the mission could be jeopardized. Nevertheless, it was considered unavoidable, as chaos might result otherwise.[752]

One by one, the bombers ascended toward the night sky over Miray Firth. Several crews found that ice had accumulated inside the cockpits, to the extent that visibility was significantly impaired, forcing them to fly according to instruments. All bombers had their navigational lights switched on during the first part of the flight, to enable the pilots to avoid colliding with other aircraft and afford the formation a chance to stay together. Over the Atlantic, however, the visibility got even worse. With the Shetlands behind them, the formation turned from a northerly to a more easterly course. Soon they began to close in on the Norwegian coast at low altitude, but at this time most of the pilots had lost contact with the other aircraft. As during Operation Obviate, it was planned that the attacking force should enter Norwegian airspace between Namsos and Mosjøen, but several pilots had flown too far north, thereby skirting an area within German radar coverage.[753]

Nothing much was said inside the Lancasters, as the crews attended to their tasks in a habitual, mechanical way. They tried not to think too much about what was going to happen over the target. The risk of encountering Luftwaffe fighter units was still slim, yet the tail gunners let their turrets turn from side to side as they searched the dark sky behind the bombers. Since they were looking westwards, their first sight of dawn was just a faint glimmer on the wings and an increased whiteness of the wave crests down below. Other crewmembers could see the mountain ridges of Norway appear in the early morning light. They also discovered other Lancasters, until now hidden by the night.

Squadron Leader Iveson—one of the pilots who had mistakenly landed at Onega two months earlier—realized that he had flown close behind one of the other aircraft during the night. When he got closer to it, he could distinguish Tait's tail gunner doing some mocking gestures with his hands. Iveson followed Tait as the sea was replaced by Norwegian cliffs, fjords, and mountains. Occasional fog or cloud banks drifted at lower altitude, but with just a little luck these would soon disperse. The two Lancasters gained height to avoid crashing into the ever higher mountains. Then the navigator's voice on the intercom told Iveson that they were now inside Swedish airspace, just in the vicinity of Torne träsk, where the Lancasters would assemble. Ground fog was still evident, and the length of Torne träsk was identifiable only by the likewise shaped cloud resting above the lake. Surprisingly for Tait and Iveson, most of the other aircraft were already there.[754]

Tait circled the lake twice, long enough for the as yet missing aircraft to catch up. Then he fired some flares and set off toward the target with the rest of the force falling in behind. The pilots throttled up to gain attacking height. Still screened from the German radar stations by the high Swedish mountains, the two squadrons flew on a northerly course. They were soon to cross into Norway once more, where they could not avoid being discovered by German radar. With less than 200 kilometers to the target, it would nevertheless be late for the enemy to take effective counter-measures.[755]

A report indicating an impending air attack reached the *Tirpitz* at about 07.30, as a message told that British Lancaster bombers had been sighted near Bodø. Captain Robert Weber had succeeded Junge as commander of the *Tirpitz* on 4 November. He did not know whether his ship was the target or if the enemy aimed for the airfield at Bardufoss. It was also conceivable that the British aircraft were on their way to a Soviet airfield, like they had been before the attack on 15 September. He called Lieutenant Commander Fassbender, the *Tirpitz's* gunnery officer, and asked for more detailed information from Bodø. In particular, he wanted to know the course of the approaching enemy aircraft.[756]

Fassbender made a phone call to the air defense center in Tromsø, which was connected to a large network of radar stations, look-out posts, and other towns with air defense arrangements. A direct communication cable had been laid between Tromsø and the battleship, and the former was in radio contact with the airfield at Bardufoss. However, the reports did not provoke much activity in Tromsø. The messages had been received from Bardufoss in the first place. Why bother the air base by sending the reports back again?

Then another report was received on the *Tirpitz*: "Three Lancasters near Mosjøen, bearing east." Fassbender once more contacted the air defense center and spoke to the commander, Lieutenant Härer, but again little activity was initiated. Härer checked the reports and found no need for concern about Bardufoss. Probably the British aircraft were destined for the Soviet Union. Reports on enemy aircraft had been received at the airfield too, but again the observation was not interpreted as a threat to the *Tirpitz*. Fassbender had the impression that the fighters at Bardufoss were warmed up for imminent take off, but in fact nothing was happening there.[757]

A report of the sighting of another four aircraft reached the battleship; then another observation of four aircraft was received. They were all on an easterly course, as if they intended to fly over Sweden, but Weber dared not wait any longer. He ordered action stations and that air warning flags be hoisted. While watertight bulkheads were closed and the crew rushed to battle stations, Fassbender again called the air defense center to ask if the fighters were ready to take off. Finally Härer reacted, probably spurred by an incorrect report of seven single-engine aircraft approaching Tromsø from the northeast. The air alarm resounded over the town and Bardufoss was contacted.[758]

Great uncertainty reigned on the airfield. Fassbender's request to make the fighters ready had not been received. Only Squadron Leader Ehrler's Messerschmitt Bf-109 and a few of his pilots' aircraft were warmed up. They had landed at Bardufoss after abandoning Kirkenes a few days earlier. Recently, a large number of inexperienced pilots had arrived at Bardufoss, together with brand new Focke-Wulf 190 fighters. Ehrler was one of the top-scoring German pilots, with 199 kills on his list. As the green pilots needed training and the older had to get acquainted with their new machines, Ehrler had decided to stay for a few days and help them. He was temporarily given command of the unit and was also informed that the *Tirpitz* had been berthed at Tromsø. Her exact location was not revealed to him. Neither did he know that his unit had been given the task to protect the battleship. He mainly intended to ensure that the green pilots got some training and the unit could test the new fighters. Thereafter he would hand over responsibility to the original commander.[759]

On this day, Ehrler and the pilots in his Staffel were about to fly to Alta, which was the reason for warming up some of the aircraft. When the air defense center in Tromsø called on the radio and asked the air base if the fighters were ready to take off, an affirmative answer was transmitted. However, the staff at the air base believed the question concerned Ehrler's flight to Alta. Somewhat later, Ehrler happened to walk into the operations room, still unaware of what was going on. When informed about the request from Tromsø, he began to suspect mischief. Ehrler asked for the available information, and the staff replied that there were reports on mounting engine noise to the south. Was an enemy bomber force heading toward Bardufoss or was the *Tirpitz* their target? Ehrler ordered an emergency start and ran toward his Bf-109.[760]

Activity was hectic on the *Tirpitz's* bridge. Runners arrived and reported that the anti-aircraft guns were manned and the batteries ashore had been alerted. There were also two anti-aircraft ships nearby. One of the phones rang and Weber heard Sub-Lieutenant Bernstein at the other end of the line. The latter was responsible for the battleship's electrical power. "I have started two diesel generators, Captain," Bernstein said. "They have been connected to switchboard three. All water-tight doors have been closed and bolted."[761]

Hardly had Weber hung up before another message was received. It reported that enemy air units had concentrated above Torne träsk in Sweden. At the time of the observation, they were about 185 kilometers south of Tromsø. Gradually, the situation became clear. It appeared unlikely that the British aircraft were destined for the Soviet Union. Rather, the information suggested an impending major attack. Did the enemy aim for the *Tirpitz* or Bardufoss? All directors and binoculars were pointing toward the white mountains in anticipation of the first glimpse of the enemy. It came soon after 09.00. The air was uncommonly clear and as the first observation reports came in, Weber became certain that his ship was the target. The sun gleamed on the fuselages, making observation difficult, but at least it was clear that the attacking force consisted of more than a single squadron—perhaps as many as 30 aircraft flying at different altitudes. A message arrived stating that the fighters at Bardufoss could not start, as an enemy Lancaster force flew over the airfield.[762]

"Call Bardufoss again," Weber said, "as soon as possible."

The battleship's main guns as well as the anti-aircraft guns were ready to open fire. The forward turrets, Anton and Bruno, were trained with their guns pointing south. They would open fire first. Weber reached out for the microphone to the loudspeakers: "We will soon be subjected to a powerful enemy air attack," he said. "I know that the crew of the *Tirpitz* will do its duty and give these four engine aircraft a hot welcome."[763]

A message arrived, which said that Ehrler was airborne and on his way toward Tromsø, but the other aircraft had not yet taken off. Weber contemplated the air armada. The range had closed to such an extent that he could see the small dots with his naked eye. He lifted his binoculars, but could not see any German fighters. There was little else he could do. The *Tirpitz* had fought her battles against enemy air power before and would have to do so again.[764]

The bombers had now come within range of the battleship's guns. Weber glanced at his watch, which showed 09.38. "Open fire with the forward guns," he said. The order was conveyed to the gunnery officer. Then the commander, his first lieutenant, the signal officer, and the rest of the bridge group went inside the armored coning tower. The range to the enemy armada was about 20 kilometers and its altitude approximately 5,000 meters.[765]

The battleship shook as its guns recoiled from the first salvo.

When the bombers closed in on the target, the Lancasters climbed to the planned altitude. They had already passed Narvik and Harstad when they began the final leg of their inbound route. The navigators had provided the pilots with the course to the target and began an intensive dialogue with the bomb aimers. They fed the data into their bombsights, checked circuits and contacts, and adjusted the glimmering lines in their lenses so that the latter was seen clearly against the ground. Then the Tallboy bombs were armed.[766]

Sitting in his seat in the leading aircraft, Tait let his eyes wander back and forth between the compass and the altimeter. In his headphones he heard the conversation between the navigator and the bomb aimer. He occasionally gazed at the terrain below. His eyes followed the meandering Balsfjord north; the water resembled a metallic surface between cliffs. The bomber armada had left the clouds behind and the sun blazed from a blue sky. The conditions were almost perfect for the kind of mission Tait led. The fjord widened gradually and ahead lay Tromsø, with its islands, bays, and snow- clad mountains.

And there—"like a spider in its web, caught by the surrounding torpedo nets"—he saw the battleship *Tirpitz*.[767]

Up to this moment the bombers had flown widely separated. As the target became visible, they all began to converge on the same point, causing them to fly closer. The navigators, who had accomplished their task, either stood in the astrodome or behind the pilot in the cockpit, where they observed the other bombers. In case a collision loomed, they would immediately report to the pilot.[768]

In one of the leading groups, Flight Lieutenant Knights could hardly take his eyes off the captivating target. He thought the *Tirpitz* looked almost black against the light surroundings. The German efforts to paint the superstructure white were ineffective in this light. Knights had been one of those who had had to turn away without dropping his bomb during Operation Paravane. Now he heard his bomb doors open and knew that he would not turn away without dropping the bomb this time. He forced himself to take his eyes off the battleship and monitor the compass and altimeter.[769]

While the aft gunners watched the sky for German fighters, the bomb aimers were fully occupied up front, laying on their bellies in the nose compartments. They were making small corrections to their sights as they were simultaneously chanting to the pilots. The huge ship appeared almost ridiculously small at the high altitude, but the muzzle flashes were far from ridiculous. Seconds later enormous smoke clouds burst below the bombers. In the morning light they almost looked orange. However, the enemy seemed to have gotten the range wrong, as the shells exploded too low to be effective.[770]

From his cockpit Tait could no longer see the battleship, as the nose of the Lancaster concealed it, but the black puffs ahead were clearly visible. They were far too familiar and indicated that the lighter anti-aircraft guns had opened fire. An instinctive urge to evade almost overwhelmed him, but he noted that the fire did not appear well aimed. Another danger—which had troubled him before the mission—came from the German fighters at Bardufoss, but so far they had not been seen.[771]

Only one enemy pilot was airborne and close enough to attack: Ehrler in his Messerschmitt Bf-109. He had started from Bardufoss and circled above the airfield to climb. However, he almost immediately ran into trouble. When he tried to contact the ground, he found that something was wrong with his radio. Neither could he call the other aircraft in his unit, which he saw idle on the ground. Why did they not start? He quickly found the answer: a Ju 88 came in for a landing and the fighters had to wait before they could use the runway.[772]

Ehrler realized he was wasting valuable time. He assumed the British flew at high altitude when the weather was clear. He had remained over Bardufoss to gain altitude, but now he had to make a decision. Clearly Bardufoss was not threatened, thus the *Tirpitz* had to be the target. He only had vague ideas where to find the battleship—he only knew that she was moored in the Tromsø area—and there was nothing to suggest that any of his pilots were better informed. He cursed the malfunctioning radio.

To wait for the other fighters was pointless. He set course for the Balsfjord, where he turned north and soon passed above Tromsø. If he had turned west at this moment, he would probably have intercepted Tait's bombers before they reached the target. However, Ehrler continued north and thus would not achieve his 200th victory on this day.[773]

Not far away, in the seat of his Lancaster, Tait's concentration was divided between the instruments and the bomb aimer's words in his headphones. It was vital to maintain correct altitude and speed, since even the slightest deviation would upset the bomb aimer's calculations. Tait adjusted his course with the foot pedals as Daniel had instructed him. A passenger would hardly have noticed the small corrections.[774]

In the nose beneath the cockpit, Daniel saw the cross-hair closing on the battleship—an oblong shape partly hidden behind the smoke from her own guns. This was the third time she had appeared in his sights, but clouds or smoke had obscured his vision on previous occasions. This time he could easily see the battleship. Unlike the 9th Squadron, which still employed a conventional sight, 617th Squadron had been equipped with the new SABS—a precision sight for high altitude.[775] With earlier bombsights, the bombardier had to guide the pilot up to the point of actual release. This left no margin for error, especially when it would always take the pilot a couple of seconds to adjust his flight path to his bomb aimer's wishes. Once the bombardier pressed the trigger, it was too late to make any changes, since the bombs were already on their way. With SABS, the bombardier locked on target about two minutes before actual release, and a gyro-device would feed any alterations to the pilot via his instruments. When time was up, the bomb would be dropped automatically.[776]

Not until now was tracer fired from the lighter guns on board the battleship. The rounds came streaming toward Daniel as he watched the target through his perspex bubble. A few of them passed unpleasantly close, but he concentrated on his task.

"Turn right ... steady ... steady ..." The ship was right under the crossing lines in the sight and Daniel pressed the trigger. "Locked on target!"

The SABS took over the bombardier's task. Tait eyed the dials and figures before him. Less than two minutes remained, and only slight corrections were needed. The control wheel trembled in his hands and the four engines were humming in harmonious rhythm. He glanced to the left and saw the nearest Lancasters. They rose and sank slightly as they passed through the dispersing smoke of Flak. The bombers' protruding nose bubbles made them look determined—as if nothing could stop them now.

Tait's eyes returned to the dashboard. He checked the clock; less than a minute remained. The instruments told him that he was on the proper course. Several minutes had passed since he could view the battleship and Tait could not even see Haakøya now, as the island had gone into his blind angle. Farther ahead, however, he could observe a larger island. It had dark verdure along the edge of the water and in the valleys, whereas the mountain peaks in the center were nothing but a dazzling white. To the starboard, snow-clad mountains could be seen as far as visibility permitted. On the port side there was just the ocean. All the important events took place outside his field of vision.

The Lancaster surged higher in the air once its multi-ton load suddenly disappeared. As the Tallboy fell toward the target Daniel reported, "Bomb gone!" Although it undoubtedly was an unnecessary comment.

Tait made a sharp turn to port.

Behind him, aircraft after aircraft dropped their bombs.

When the large formation of bombers approached the waiting men on board the *Tirpitz*, the battleship's heavy guns had already gone silent. Her main guns were intended to defeat targets on the sea. As they produced high muzzle velocity, the guns could reach far without resorting to high elevation. However, when firing at the approaching Lancasters, high elevation was needed. The *Tirpitz's* heavy guns could fire while the bombers were still far away, but when they closed in the maximum elevation of the heavy guns was insufficient.

However the lighter guns were designed to combat aircraft, and they continued to fill the air with black puffs. When the first Lancaster bombers were almost vertically above the battleship, small arms also joined in, although they could hardly affect the bombers. Despite the combined effort of the light anti-aircraft weapons, all the fire was ineffective. The bombers flew through the anti-aircraft fire with an almost carefree attitude. None were hit.

At such high altitude, bombs could usually not be discerned when they left the aircraft, but Tallboys were so big that they could be seen tumbling down, before stabilizing and falling toward the battleship. The Germans on deck found the bombs alarmingly well aimed, but there was nothing they could do. The first bombs were only a few hundred meters above the battleship, and then an infernal sound deafened all spectators.

Many of the men on deck were instantly killed at the first hit. The same immediate death met the few engineers in the port boiler and engine rooms, which were instantly flooded. On the port side—from the bulge keel to the gunwale—a gaping hole, almost 16 meters in diameter, allowed water to pour into the ship.[777] Around the ship huge columns of water and mud appeared. The *Tirpitz* shook from bow to stern.

The impacts were also felt in the armored conning tower where Weber and his staff had gathered. Sub-Lieutenant Schmitz held on to the rack that held the breathing devices. The concussions were so violent, however, that he suddenly found himself with a loose handle in his hand.

It was clear that the battleship was listing. The signal officer ordered that the armored doors be checked to ensure that they could be opened. A few men, among them Schmitz, moved to the starboard door. They found that the ship listed so heavily that the sheer weight of the armored door prevented it from being opened. The attempts to open the port armored door also failed, as the mechanism had been damaged.[778]

"We remain here at least as long as the guns are firing," Weber decided.

As Schmitz had his battle station in the chart room below the conning tower, he was allowed to leave the room through a hatch in the floor. When he climbed down, one of the seamen asked if there was any risk of the ship capsizing.

"No, she can't," Schmitz answered. "It is not that deep."[779]

Within a few minutes, these words would make him a liar.

Most attempts to contact the various sections of the ship failed. In the main switchboard control room, Sub-Lieutenant Bernstein tried to contact other units of the ship. Everything was chaos—generators didn't work, steam pressure fell, most rooms didn't answer calls, and turret Caesar received no electrical power. He tried several times to contact the main engine room, but received no reply, despite also trying on the loudspeakers.

He did, however, contact Reinert, an engineer in one of the additional engine rooms. Reinert asked Bernstein if they should counter-flood, to reduce list. Before Bernstein answered, one of the phones rang. It was a call from the conning tower, which had managed to get through to the engine room. Despite the sound from explosions and cracking metal, Weber was heard in the receiver. "Bernstein, is that you?" the commander asked. "What is the situation down there?"

Bernstein reported his view of the situation, which was bleak. "Main engine room not answering. Main electrical supply from switch-boards two and four are gone, but one and three still serviceable," he reported.

"I see. Ensure that no watertight bulkheads or hatches are opened. It is vital that the switchboards still work."

"Yes, Captain," Bernstein replied almost automatically. Electrical power to the pumps had top priority, but the artillery and the lighting also needed electricity. At the same time, he realized that the order might well sentence the men in these compartments to death. If the ship was sinking it would soon settle on the sea floor, but if the switchboard rooms ended up below the sea level, it would be very difficult to save the men in those compartments.

"Pump out as much water as you can," Weber continued, "and evacuate all personnel below the armored deck ..."

The connection broke. Bernstein realized that he was caught in a dilemma. How could he evacuate all people below the armored deck if the doors to switchboard one and three remained closed? He decided to

The sinking of the Tirpitz, seen to the right, on November 12, 1944.

compromise. As the switchboards would be rendered inoperable if the list exceeded 20 degrees, he decided to keep the bulkheads closed until the list exceeded the critical value, and then open all doors. Although the list increased, he estimated that it had not yet passed 15 degrees. He did not believe the ship would capsize, as the depth amidships was about 17 meters and only 12 meters at the bow and stern.[780]

In the switchboard room where the power to the artillery was allocated, an electrician named Gerlach watched a number of fuses. He and his closest fellows felt a number of shocks transmitted through the ship, when then came one great concussion that in violence clearly exceeded all those preceding it. In the corner of his eye, Gerlach saw that the photo of his fiancée, which he had put on an empty table, suddenly began to move toward the edge. The battleship was listing heavily.[781]

The fuses went out more rapidly. Gerlach frantically tried to replace them, but he could not keep pace, and the fuses he replaced soon went out too. The men had to wear masks to breathe. Gerlach did not realize that most of the men around him had already fled, as they had understood what was soon was to happen. Only when the photo of his fiancée fell to the floor and the glass was broken did he look around

The hull of the *Tirpitz* shortly after the sinking. A rescue team tries to help crew members trapped inside the capsized ship.

and see that only one other man remained in the room, a comrade named Pille Piontek. Gerlach connected the cables to speak with Piontek through the masks. "The ship is capsizing," he said. "We must get out before it is too late."

"Can we do that? Our orders are to stay ..."

"I know, but it seems all communications are gone. We will probably never receive an order. If we don't leave now, we will remain here forever."

Gerlach removed his facemask, as did Piontek. When they left the room, the list was so great that they walked with one foot on the floor and one on the walls. Behind, they heard a loud crash as the fuse box tore loose from the wall and fell.[782]

When Lieutenant Schmitz had made his way down to the chart room, the list increased more rapidly and a huge explosion—more violent than any before—shook the *Tirpitz*. Fires had set off the aft magazines, and the force of the explosion threw turret Caesar high into the air. Undoubtedly the ship was capsizing. Schmitz expected that Weber and the others would come through the hatch from the conning tower, but nothing happened. He decided to escape onto the deck. Once he got out, he saw the masts and turret Bruno lean toward him. He threw himself into the water and swam as fast as he could away from the battleship. Schmitz was the only survivor from the conning tower.[783]

Another seaman in the water was Petty Officer Ackerman. His battle station was in turret Dora. As the electrical power was soon gone and the ammunition lifts thus failed, he was no longer able to do his duty. Consequently, Ackerman was among the first who could jump into the water. He too saw how turret Caesar was thrown into the air, and then splashed into the water not far from him. A huge surge from the turret washed over Ackerman, causing him to swallow a gulp of oily water before he could breathe properly again. Terrified, he saw how the superstructures and decks of the ship—which had been his home for so long—disappeared and were replaced by the naked keel.[784]

The *Tirpitz* had capsized.

The Tirpitz *Sinks*

The Norwegian population in the Tromsø area found the Sunday of 12 November memorable in many ways. No enthusiasm had greeted the German battleship when it arrived. The inhabitants realized that it could result in homes and public buildings being commandeered for German officers and soldiers. Also, most Norwegians understood that the Allies would try to destroy the battleship, which would put the population at risk. The best alternative was if the battleship was quickly sunk, without any civilian lives being lost or any damage to Norwegian property being sustained.

In a lone hut on Haakøya, Gunvor Wibe heard the first explosions and felt the floor shaking when a lone Tallboy hit the beach next to her house. She had not yet opened the windows to prevent them from being shattered. When explosion upon explosion followed, she crunched on the floor while her two children clutched tightly to her skirt. Then silence followed. She stood up, but told the children to remain still. Walking carefully to avoid the glass fragments, she reached the window facing the roadstead. A huge smoke cloud obscured much of the surroundings, but beneath it, she saw the keel of what had once been the fearsome battleship. Despite the great distance, she heard the yells from seamen in the water. Also, many could be seen on top of the keel. A strange mixture of horror and relief overwhelmed her. People had died, but she and her children were safe now. The *Tirpitz* was gone and the British would not come back.[785]

From another position on the mainland, the head of the local Red Cross had watched the attack together with two friends. They had been

318

bicycling from farm to farm to gather provisions when they heard the air raid warning. From a hill, they had seen the bombers and how the *Tirpitz* had disappeared in a cloud of smoke and fire. When the cloud had dispersed, only the keel remained. Small boats were heading toward the wreck from nearby bridges. Not until they mounted their bicycles did they notice the sharp pieces of metal on the ground. Shrapnel from bursting shells had landed around them. Without realizing it, they had been in mortal danger.[786]

From the beach on the western side of Tromsø, Lieutenant Commander Sommer saw the two bomber squadrons turn west and head toward the sea. He had observed at least two hits on the battleship, perhaps three. A few minutes after the first bombs hit, another explosion—much louder than the previous—was heard. Terrified, he saw turret Caesar fly into the air as if it had been a toy. Clearly some internal explosion, probably a magazine, was the cause. The *Tirpitz* listed heavily and then became completely obscured by smoke. Sommer—petrified by terror—stared at the smoke cloud, while vaguely perceiving the commander of the anti-aircraft battery ordering his men to cease fire. The noise from the aircraft engines faded away and it became almost remarkably silent.

The battleship again appeared through the smoke veil, but instead of the familiar silhouette Sommer saw the keel, not unlike a stranded whale. The extent of the tragedy at once became clear to him.[787]

Again aircraft engines were heard, but not the monotonous rumble that had gradually increased and culminated at the same time as the huge explosions. The new sound was weaker and less regular. He did not have to shade his eyes and search the sky to realize that Ehrler's fighters had belatedly arrived at the scene.

Probably it was the sight of the men clinging to the torpedo nets or trying to crawl up the slippery keel which made him react. He dashed down to the beach where he again found the harbor master.

"Quickly!" Sommer shouted. "I need a boat."

The Norwegian shook his head. "I only have one boat," he said, "and that is the doctor's boat. I can't allow you to use it."

Sommer stepped closer. "Doctor or not," he said, "I need the boat. Hundreds of men are dying out there."

The Norwegian hesitated. Probably he was torn between the natural instinct to help men in distress and the knowledge that these men had been occupying his country for more than four years. Maybe he risked unpleasant consequences if he did not help. "Well," he muttered, "come along."[788]

As the doctor's boat lacked an engine, Sommer had to row. Many other boats also headed for the wreck. Men in the water called for help, but Sommer knew it was more important to help those caught inside the wreck. He berthed at the wreck and managed to climb up the slippery hull until he reached the bilge keel. Here he encountered a large number of seamen.[789]

Sommer knew he had to cut a hole in the hull as soon as possible if any men inside were to have a chance to survive. But he needed cutting torches to get through the thick metal. He shouted at some Norwegians in a motorboat rescuing men in the water. They came closer and Sommer asked them in English to go to Tromsø and fetch cutting torches and oxygen tubes. The Norwegians did not answer. They looked at each other and disappeared toward the beach with the soaking wet sailors. Sommer succeeded in beckoning a harbor launch with a German crew. He ordered them to get the equipment quickly.[790]

The crew nodded and disappeared toward Tromsø. Sommer investigated the entire hull. A Norwegian arrived with sand, which was scattered on the hull to make it less slippery. Sommer heard faint sounds from the inside the ship, but almost an hour passed before the boat returned from Tromsø. It turned out that several oxygen tubes had been found, but only one cutting torch.

"Even this one was hard to find," one of the crew apologized. "The Norwegians are not exactly eager to help."

Sommer felt discouraged. "Well, hurry on with it. There are people down there who need our help."[791]

Sommer knew the ship well and could conclude where it was easiest to cut holes, but where should he begin with only one cutting torch available? At this moment luck aided him. Another launch arrived with Captain Krüger, the commander of the Tromsø base. Sommer yelled that he could lead the rescue effort if Krüger could bring more cutting torches. Krüger promised to come back with the equipment and the launch chugged off toward Tromsø. Moments later, the first bluish flame from the blowtorch stung Sommer in the eyes. It was instantly turned to the metal.[792]

While Sommer worked to get into the battleship, others strived to get out. When the ship capsized and the lights went out, Bernstein was temporarily stunned from shock. The world moved around him. He tumbled against various objects and was thrown off balance. Then the emergency lights were switched on. As in some kind of bizarre dream, he saw his friends struggle to keep their balance on a sloping floor with lights on it. All loose objects had become piled at the junction between this floor and the wall. In the dream he saw his only child, a son, whom he had lost a few months earlier. While the confused Bernstein stared at the vision, the child changed appearance into a girl with long hair and blue eyes. She seemed to tell him that he would get a new child, this time a girl, but first he had to find a way out from the ship. This vision—which was the only purely unreal part of everything going on around him—finally made him wake up from the shock. For a moment he could not bring himself to accept that the battleship had capsized. Something had to be wrong with his senses, and to prove it, he used a telephone receiver as a plummet. However, it merely confirmed what his senses had already told him. The battleship seemingly lay at a 45-degree angle with the starboard side facing upwards. Parts of the ship probably still protruded above the surface of the sea. The only chance of survival for Bernstein and the men with him was to reach upward to the bottom of the ship and pray that outside help could save them.[793]

Momentarily irresolute, he sat on the hatch leading down to the compartment until water streamed up through the slit between the hatch and the roof, making his pants wet. Bernstein began to climb along the upturned ladder leading to switchboard room three, while also shouting to the other three men to follow him. He had no clear idea of where the route would bring him, but he had to do something as the other men expected orders from an officer. They entered a larger compartment where some lockers had been knocked open. Breathing apparatuses and bottles with compressed air had fallen out. Bernstein told the men to bring some of these along and then continued farther down into the ship. He hoped to get into the oil tanks, which he knew were empty.[794]

While Bernstein and his group tried to reach the keel and the oil tanks, the electricians Gerlach and Piontek had struggled in the opposite direction. Unlike Bernstein, who had a fairly accurate perception of the ship's true position, the two comrades did not realize that the direction they chose brought them away from rescue. They

climbed down a ladder, which should have been vertical but was now
almost horizontal. Thereafter followed a nightmare of small compartments, doors that could not be opened, and sloping corridors that were
strenuous to climb. Gerlach lost orientation. Not until they entered the
room belonging to the ship's band, where instruments lay scattered
about, did Gerlach realize where he was. He also realized that his
comrade was no longer with him.[795]

"Piontek, where are you?" he shouted in the direction he had come
from. "Piontek?"

He shouted many times, but only heard the gurgling, creaking, and
squeaking sounds from the sunken ship. The fear of being left alone and
the urge to go back and help his friend contrasted against the dreadful
thought of being trapped forever on this doomed ship.

He had not yet made up his mind when shouts were heard and four
men rushed into the room. A brief deliberation followed and Gerlach
decided—with a heavy heart—to join them. They had only a vague
notion of how to reach the deck, and hastened past narrow passages
and debris. Several times they were forced to make detours, as doors
could not be opened. Finally, they reached a dead end. At that moment
they at last realized that the ship was laying almost upside down, and
that their headlong flight had brought them away from the surface of
the sea, rather than bringing them upwards. Considering the size of the
ship, parts of the keel ought to remain above the sea. The only chance
to survive appeared to be to reach the keel and hope that a rescue party
could cut a hole in the hull.[796]

They began to move again, but this time in the opposite direction.
A gushing rumble made them hurry even more. The sound seemed to
come from all around them. Suddenly the light went out and ice-cold
water streamed into the room. Gerlach clasped something to avoid
being washed away, as did the others, except one who was too slow.
They heard his short cries for help before he was knocked unconscious.
In the darkness they could do nothing to help him and their own
situation was just as desperate. The water rose until it reached their
waists.[797]

They thought the end was imminent. One of them had a pistol and
they agreed that it was better to die from a bullet than drown. However,
they realized that when the first man shot himself, he would drop the
gun after the shot. It would be almost impossible to find it again unless

the light came back on. Thus one of them had to shoot the others, before he shot himself.[798]

Nobody could bring himself to shoot any of the others. When the water gradually rose to their chests, they awaited the end. Between rattling teeth from the cold, one of them whispered that he wanted a cigarette. Gerlach recalled that he had a packet in his jacket. It would not be possible to light it, but he at least wanted to sense the taste of tobacco before he died. But instead of finding a cigarette packet, his numb fingers found something round and hard—a flashlight! A second later, the room became illuminated and he could see three pale and surprised faces staring at him. They were not lost yet.[799]

At the same time, Bernstein and his group had reached the oil tanks, where they managed to open the hatch and get into the empty compartment. There was still a thick, oil film on the metal, and the air was sickening to breathe, but Bernstein knew that this was their sole chance of survival. They heard somebody knock in an adjacent compartment and a few moments later they had opened a hatch leading to one of the generator rooms. They found two engineers and about 30 other men who had made their way to the keel, like Bernstein's group. Among them were several seamen from one of the starboard 15cm guns. They had striven hard to get from the magazine to the turret, only to be met by water flooding in when the ship capsized. In panic, they had turned and struggled to reach the lowest parts of the ships, finally meeting up with Bernstein's group. They believed the steam turbines would explode at any moment. One of them, a young man, was very frightened. "We will all die here, Ernst," he complained to the man closest, holding his friend firmly by the hand. "I will never see my mother again."[800]

Bernstein knew he had to do something about the young man, lest he start a general panic. The calmer they were, the less oxygen they would consume. After investigating if there was any way out of the trap, he decided that they should remain where they were.

"My friends," he said, "either we all die here or else we will all be saved. Lieutenant Commander Sommer is ashore and will do everything to save us." He explained that it was necessary to husband the oxygen, and if everybody lay down and perhaps even slept, they would consume less oxygen. They still had eight bottles of compressed air, and these would be used as the air in the tank became poorer.

"Don't use your flashlights unnecessarily. Switch them off to save the batteries."[801]

The oil tank became dark and nobody said anything. At regular intervals one of them knocked on the metal, and those who were not asleep listened for any reply. Bernstein knew that the air would gradually deteriorate if no rescue party appeared, and then they would fall asleep and never wake up again. He struggled against claustrophobia, while contemplating the British crews who had attacked in midget submarines a year before. Their situation must have been even worse in the small crafts, with an enemy above them who tried to destroy them, not save them. They had indeed been courageous, much more so than the airmen who dropped their bombs from high altitude, where they were safe from everything but a hit from the Flak. The air at once felt worse, and he ordered another oxygen bottle to be opened.[802]

In another compartment, Gerlach and his group also waited to be rescued. The unexpectedly discovered electrical torch had enabled them to find their way through the capsized ship and finally reach the keel. Numerous difficulties had been encountered, and at one moment Gerlach had to return, as two of the men had disappeared, forcing him to swim under the surface of the water through flooded compartments before he found them and led them to the forward refrigerator room. They had not been able to open the door, but had heard that there were people in the forward machine shop. There they found 12 men with one electrical torch. They tried to open the hatch to the oil tank above, but did not succeed. However, they faintly heard men walking on the hull above them and tried to communicate by knocking on the plates. Finally, they received a reply. One of the trapped men knocked a Morse Code signal: "Sixteen men. Beneath the oil tank in the forward machine shop."[803]

"We cut through the hull," was knocked from outside. "We will get you out."

They waited and suddenly a loud bang was heard. For a moment they believed the ship was again being attacked, but the sound was caused by a large chunk of steel falling into the oil tank after being cut by the blowtorches. They saw the metal become red, before a blindingly white flame appeared. However, a problem occurred. The higher pressure inside the ship caused the air to stream out at such speed that the torch was blown out. However, soon more holes were cut and the pressure was levelled out.[804]

The work was resumed, but again was interrupted. It became silent for more than 15 minutes and the men inside the hull began to fear that the rescue party had deserted them. To their utter relief, Gerlach and the others noticed that the men outside returned. The welding flames again cut through the metal and traced long lines in the plates. Another interruption followed before the work to cut through the hull was again resumed. The reason for the interruptions was that the gases from the interior had caused one of the men handling the blowtorches to lose consciousness. Another man replaced him, but soon he lost consciousness as well. The work thus had to be postponed until breathing masks had been obtained.

As air streamed out, water began to pour in. Gerlach and the other men could feel it rising along their legs. At this moment, one last man found his way to the group. Covered with oil, he had escaped a fire by crawling through a tube containing a thick bunch of electrical cables, together with dozens of rats which were at least as scared as he was. Hardly had he arrived before a large piece of metal fell into the machine shop.

Through the hole Gerlach could see the hull of the oil tank, and above and beyond it the wonderful blue sky.[805]

The Tirpitz
and the War in the Arctic

The bombers from the 9th and 617th Squadrons landed in Scotland during the afternoon of 13 November, their mission having been accomplished. One aircraft was missing, as it had been forced to land in Sweden. Another had flown to the Shetlands, after an engine had been hit by German Flak and fuel consumption had risen alarmingly. Eight bombers had to land on other fields than those they had taken off from. Among the latter was Tait's Lancaster. When he and his crew climbed down from the bomber, they were asked if they had been on a cross-country training flight.[806]

Next day, at the 5 Group morning conference, the officers present waited to see whether the outcome of Catechism might cause a temporary change in Cochrane's stern exterior. He sat down behind his desk, glanced at the report, and then said in a matter-of-fact voice: "Last night's raid ... successful. *Tirpitz* sunk! Now, about tonight's operations ... the Dortmund-Ems canal ..."[807]

But if Cochrane appeared to regard Operation Catechism as little more than a navigation exercise, the 9th and 617th had finally put an end to British fears that the *Tirpitz* would threaten Allied shipping. They had done their utmost to prevent the German battleship from breaking out onto the Atlantic—air attacks by heavy bombers, torpedo bombers, human torpedoes, midget submarines, carrier aircraft, and further operations by heavy bombers. They had initiated deception operations like Tarantula and the pre-emptive attack on St. Nazaire. After all these efforts, success was finally achieved. In the shallow water where the *Tirpitz* had capsized, her hull, which had become a grave for

326

almost 1,000 German seamen, would remain visible for many years. A Norwegian company later began to dismantle the wreck and sell it as scrap metal. The work continued well into the 1950s, when the war was already fading into the past.

In fact, when the Tallboys hit their target near Tromsø, the outcome of the Second World War had already been decided for some time. Most likely, the German defeat was already inevitable when the midget submarines penetrated into the net cage on 22 September 1943. The battleship would not participate in any operation after Sizilien. Her remaining career was characterised by German attempts to keep her battleworthy, while the British strenuously strove to damage and destroy her before she became fully operational again.

Perhaps Hitler's negative attitude toward the heavy warships made the efforts to repair the *Tirpitz* less energetic than they might otherwise have been. On the other hand, it was difficult to repair such a large warship in northern Norway, as suitable facilities were mainly absent. As is known from many other warships—not least German—long periods of maintenance and repairs were often needed even if no battle damage had been sustained. Almost always, such work was conducted at well-equipped shipyards.

Against this background, it appears unlikely that the *Tirpitz* could have significantly influenced the course of events after the summer of 1943. The outcome of the war had been effectively decided and, at most, the German battleship could hardly even have delayed it. Largely, the war was decided on the Eastern Front, where the Red Army firmly dictated the main events from 1943 onwards. Valuable goods were unloaded from the convoys that arrived in Murmansk and Archangelsk after the summer of 1943. Above all, these products enabled Stalin to speed up his advance west, as the equipment provided by the Western powers improved Soviet mobility.

At most, an active use of the *Tirpitz* would have prevented some merchant ships from reaching their destination, but when the battleship was finally destroyed, even this rather remote possibility vanished. At this stage of the war, the *Tirpitz* was no longer an important component in the German war effort. The British were not fully aware that the Germans had written off the *Tirpitz* as an offensive weapon in autumn 1944, but even so, their final efforts appear almost overzealous. Perhaps this is an example of how wars develop their own logic. When a process has begun, it tends to carry on by its own inertia.

With the destruction of the *Tirpitz*, the last German battleship was neutralized. Admittedly, the *Gneisenau* remained in Gdynia, but she lacked her heavy guns. They had been removed for use in Norway as coastal artillery. The work to fit her with new 38cm guns had been discontinued after the *Scharnhorst* was sunk. She was not a battleworthy warship, and as she lacked her heavy guns, was hardly even useful as a floating battery. In March 1945, the Germans sunk the *Gneisenau* to block the port of Gdynia as the Red Army was about to capture it. The autumn of 1944 did not only see the end of the German battle fleet. In the Pacific, the Battle of the Surigao Strait was fought on the night of 24–25 October, about three weeks before the destruction of the *Tirpitz*. This night action between American and Japanese battleships would turn out to be the last occasion when battleships fought each other. The battleship era had come to its end, although the ships were still used for coastal bombardment.

During her career, the *Tirpitz* did not receive significant modifications. Her radar equipment as well as her anti-aircraft defenses were improved, but otherwise she underwent no major changes. She remained very similar to her sister ship *Bismarck*. However, few modern battleships were significantly altered during World War II. The most important shortcomings the *Tirpitz* suffered from could not be attributed to her construction, but to the concept she was supposed to fit into.

Raeder had worked to create a powerful German Navy, and the heavy warships had consumed most of its resources. He had hoped to use them against British transoceanic shipping. The *Tirpitz* had been designed for this concept, but she was never permitted to fulfill the role Raeder had conceived for her. Except when she narrowly missed PQ12 and QP8, she never even came close to an enemy convoy. All other Allied ships retained a healthy distance from the *Tirpitz*'s heavy guns. Why did events unfold in such a way?

The *Tirpitz* was the last German battleship; in fact she was the last heavy German warship completed during the war. When she was commissioned, Hitler had adopted a strong aversion to using the heavy warships on any mission that entailed risk. The constraints resulting from Hitler's attitude did not make the German Navy officers inclined to use the warships with daring and innovation.

On the other hand, Hitler's caution may have been fostered by the events of 1939–41, when many German warships had been lost without having achieved any major triumph. Perhaps he valued a fairly intact fleet more than insignificant successes on the sea, in particular if the latter were won at high cost.

If Hitler argued along these lines he was not detached from the reality, because the mere existence of the *Tirpitz* in Norwegian fjords tied up significant Allied resources. For over three years the British made considerable efforts with all arms to destroy the German battleship. In a sense, the *Tirpitz* can serve as an example of a fleet in being. It is, however, difficult to judge if these effects on the British justified the resources spent by the Germans in building the battleship and maintaining it. Once the ship was completed, it was perhaps wise to make the most of her, but nevertheless the German program on heavy warships, at least later in the war, appears wasted.

Lack of fuel seems to have been a major constraint on German naval warfare. An ocean warfare concept of the kind envisaged by Raeder would have required substantial quantities of oil, or else the impact on the enemy would have remained slight. It is doubtful that Germany could have acquired the necessary quantities. Thus a common notion—that Germany began the war before her naval build-up was completed—can be called into question. The so-called Z-Plan, which Raeder put forward during the second half of the 1930s, envisaged a much larger fleet, but not until a decade later; that is, not reaching fruition until after 1945. The sources do not agree entirely on the composition of the German fleet according to the plan, but it was projected to encompass about 10 battleships, 12 unspecified armored ships, 4 carriers, and at least 20 cruisers. As it proved difficult to supply the small German fleet in World War II with sufficient fuel, a much larger fleet along the lines outlined in the Z-Plan would have been almost impossible to use effectively.

The fact is that the German strategic position before World War II placed her between two land powers: France and Poland. They were the most likely enemies, and against them the Germans above all needed a strong Army supported by air power. The Navy could not be expected to contribute significantly in a war against France and Poland and was consequently allotted only a minor portion of the defense budget. But it must also be remembered that the other major powers were accelerating their naval programs during this period. Great Britain, the United States, Japan, France, Italy, and even the Soviet Union had initiated large naval production programs. Clearly, it cannot be taken for granted that the German Navy would have been in a better position if the war had begun later. Other countries, particularly those with overseas possessions, would have progressed further. Most importantly, many of the other powers controlled much larger sources of fuel.

The German effort to produce heavy warships could hardly have contributed significantly to defeating any of its major enemies. Probably the conquest of Norway was the most important German success to which the Navy contributed significantly. By controlling Norway, the Germans had removed the threat against the Swedish iron ore deposits, which were very valuable to the German war economy. However, the occupation of Norway took place before the *Bismarck* and *Tirpitz* were completed.

If the expansion of the German Navy before World War II was a blunder, it was not without precursors. In the decade before World War I, the Imperial German Navy expanded considerably, even more than before World War II. In the end, the German surface fleet in World War I obtained very meager results, and it seems that Germany's expansion of its Navy before the war significantly contributed to the British decision to declare war.

The men who were caught inside the *Tirpitz*'s hull had more mundane problems to consider than naval strategy in distant waters. Bernstein's group had survived inside the sickening oil tank for more than eight hours when Sommer's men cut a hole in the hull. Fearing the oil might catch fire, Bernstein ordered some of the men to go for a few fire extinguishers he had seen in an adjacent compartment. They sprinkled the area where the welding flames cut through the plates. Soon a hole had been created, and the rescue party poured water on the edges to chill them. When Bernstein had got up through the hole and stood trembling while breathing the fresh air, Sommer approached him and asked, "Are there more men down there?"

"Yes, next to us," Bernstein replied. "They were banging and we could hear a piece of metal falling."

"They have already been saved," Sommer said. "They were inside the workshop above one of the tanks. We got them out before you."

Bernstein looked at the devastation surrounding the ship. Below him, remains of the torpedo nets floated in the oily water and small boats were picking up the bodies of dead seamen. On the beach, he could see small groups of survivors who had not yet found shelter from the cold. The German repair ship *Neumark* had been positioned alongside the battleship, as had the Norwegian pilot boat *Arngast*, on which more sophisticated welding equipment was carried. Everywhere on the keel, both rescuers and rescued congratulated each other. Bernstein recognized Sub-Lieutenant Wache, one of the engineers who had participated in the rescue work. Tears streamed down his cheeks. He did not weep over the lost comrades, but shed tears of joy over the saved.[808]

"I am sure there is another group rather close to us," Bernstein said. "I heard them knocking on the bulkheads."

"You have done enough now," Sommer said. "Take one of the boats and row ashore with your men. Get some rest. We are still working at the bow and I have to go there."[809]

The rescue work continued during the night and well into the morning, when the last survivors were brought out from the interior of the battleship. Altogether, Sommer and his men had saved 87 men from the wreck. At last he would find some rest.

When Sommer sat in the boat which brought him to Tromsø and looked at the huge keel, which resembled an enormous dead whale, he watched the sad remnants of the German efforts to create a powerful battle fleet. The efforts had been initiated at the end of the 19th century, and the results had been tested in two world wars. The man who set the program in motion was Alfred von Tirpitz, Secretary of the Navy in the Imperial German Cabinet, 1897–1916. It is ironic that the last German battleship carried his name.

The *Bismarck* had been the last German battleship endeavoring to cut off the British transatlantic trade routes and thus cripple the British economy. The *Tirpitz* had been given the less ambitious task to halt Allied Arctic convoys to the Soviet Union.

Neither of these aims had been achieved.

The scrapping of the *Tirpitz* after the war.

Notes

1   Kennedy, p. 22.
2   Earl F. Ziemke, *The German Northern Theatre of Operations 1940–1945* (Washington DC: Department of the Army Pamphlet 20-271, 1959) pp. 113–156.
3   KTB Tirpitz, 5.3.42, BA-MA RM 92/5200.
4   KTB Tirpitz, 5.3.42, BA-MA RM 92/5200.
5   Kennedy, p. 11; Peillard, p. 23–25.
2   KTB Tirpitz, 5.3.42-6.3.42, BA-MA RM 92/5200.
3   KTB Tirpitz, 5.3.42-6.3.42, BA-MA RM 92/5200.
4   KTB Tirpitz, 5.3.42-6.3.42, BA-MA RM 92/5200.
5   KTB Tirpitz, 5.3.42-6.3.42, BA-MA RM 92/5200; Schmalenbach, p. 142–163.
6   The operation that was to unfold has often been called "Sportpalast" after the war, but that name is inappropriate. There was indeed an operation called "Sportpalast": the transfer of *Admiral Scheer* and *Prinz Eugen* from Germany to Norway, which had been undertaken in February, when the *Prinz Eugen* had been hit by the torpedo from the *Trident*. However, the same communication procedures that had been used during the original "Sportpalast" were also used in the forthcoming sortie. This is possibly the cause of the confusion. Also, the Germans did not agree on a code name. In the war diary of the supreme German naval command, it was simply referred to as "Unternehmen gegen PQ-Geleitzug," i. e. Operation against PQ-convoy. However, Vice Admiral Ciliax and his staff used a code name: "Nordmeer." As Ciliax was the key actor in the enterprise, we have decided to call the operation "Nordmeer." There are two files in the German military archives which deal with Operation Sportpalast (BA-MA RM 35 I/388a and BA-MA RM 35 I/388a). They comprise hundreds of pages on the transfer of the Scheer and Prinz Eugen to Norway. However, the word "Sportpalast" does not appear in the war diary of the Tirpitz (BA-MA RM 92/5200). In the war diary of the command held by Ciliax (Befehlshaber der Schlachtschiffe, file BA-MA RM 50/182), the section on the chase of convoys

PQ12 and QP8 has been filed as a separate annex, where the name "Nordmeer" is clearly evident.

[7] KTB Tirpitz, 6.3.42, BA-MA RM 92/5200.
[8] KTB Tirpitz, 6.3.42, BA-MA RM 92/5200.
[9] KTB Tirpitz, 6.3.42, BA-MA RM 92/5200.
[10] KTB Tirpitz, 6.3.42, BA-MA RM 92/5200.
[11] KTB Tirpitz, 6.3.42, BA-MA RM 92/5200; Roskill (1956), p. 120.
[12] KTB Tirpitz, 6.3.42, BA-MA RM 92/5200.
[13] KTB Tirpitz, 6.3.42, BA-MA RM 92/5200; Roskill (1956), p. 120; Woodman, p. 68.
[14] Roskill (1956), p. 120.
[15] Woodman, p. 69.
[16] KTB Tirpitz, 6.3.42, BA-MA RM 92/5200.
[17] Schofield, p. 30; KTB Tirpitz, 7.3.42, BA-MA RM 92/5200; Brown, p. 56; Roskill (1956) p. 119.
[18] KTB Tirpitz, 7.3.42, BA-MA RM 92/5200.
[19] KTB Tirpitz, 7.3.42, BA-MA RM 92/5200.
[20] KTB Tirpitz, 7.3.42, BA-MA RM 92/5200.
[21] KTB Tirpitz, 7.3.42, BA-MA RM 92/5200.
[22] Roskill (1956) map 12; Woodman, p. 69–70.
[23] Roskill (1956) map 12, p. 120–1; Woodman, p. 72–4.
[24] Roskill (1956) map 12, p. 120–1; Woodman, p. 69–71.
[25] Roskill (1956) map 12, p. 120–1; Woodman, p. 69–71.
[26] Roskill (1956) map 12, p. 120–1; Woodman, p. 69–71; KTB Tirpitz, 7.3.42, BA-MA RM 92/5200.
[27] B = abbreviation for the German word "Beobachtungsdienst."
[28] KTB Tirpitz, 7.3.42, BA-MA RM 92/5200.
[29] Roskill (1956) map 12, p. 120–1; Woodman, p. 72–5.
[30] Roskill (1956) map 12, p. 120–1; Woodman, p. 72–5.
[31] KTB Tirpitz, 7.3.42, BA-MA RM 92/5200.
[32] KTB Tirpitz, 7.3.42, BA-MA RM 92/5200.
[33] KTB Tirpitz, 7.3.42, BA-MA RM 92/5200.
[34] KTB Tirpitz, 7.3.42, BA-MA RM 92/5200.
[35] KTB Tirpitz, 7.3.42, BA-MA RM 92/5200.
[36] Roskill (1956) map 12, p. 120–1; Woodman, p. 72–5; KTB Tirpitz, 7.3.42, BA-MA RM 92/5200.
[37] Roskill (1956) map 12, p. 120–1; Woodman, p. 72–5; KTB Tirpitz, 7.3.42, BA-MA RM 92/5200.
[38] Roskill (1956) map 12, p. 121–2; Peillard, p. 64; Woodman, p. 72–5.
[39] KTB Tirpitz, 8.3.42, BA-MA RM 92/5200.
[40] KTB Tirpitz, 8.3.42, BA-MA RM 92/5200.
[41] Roskill (1956) karta 12, sid 121-2; Woodman, sid. 74-6.
[42] KTB Tirpitz, 8.3.42, BA-MA RM 92/5200.
[43] KTB Tirpitz, 8.3.42, BA-MA RM 92/5200; Roskill (1956) map. 12, p. 121–2; Woodman, p. 74–6.

44 Roskill (1956) map 12, p. 121–2; Woodman, p. 75–7; Peillard, p. 64; Brown, p. 20.

45 Roskill (1956) map 12, p. 121–2; Woodman, p. 75–7; Peillard, p. 64.

46 Roskill (1956) map 12, p. 121–2; Woodman, p. 76–8; Peillard, p. 65.

47 KTB Tirpitz, 9.3.42, BA-MA RM 92/5200.

48 Bekker, *Verdammte See*, p. 254; Sweetman, p. 20.

49 Sweetman, s. 20.

50 Roskill (1956) map 12, p. 121–3; Sweetman, p. 20; Woodman, p. 77–8.

51 KTB Tirpitz, 9.3.42, BA-MA RM 92/5200; Bekker, *Verdammte See*, p. 254; Peillard, p. 66.

52 Peillard, p. 66.

53 KTB Tirpitz, 9.3.42, BA-MA RM 92/5200; Bekker, *Verdammte See*, p. 254; Peillard, p. 66.

54 KTB Tirpitz, 9.3.42, BA-MA RM 92/5200; Bekker, *Verdammte See*, p. 254; Peillard, p. 66.

55 KTB Tirpitz, 9.3.42, BA-MA RM 92/5200.

56 Sweetman, p. 20; Peillard, p. 66; KTB Tirpitz, 9.3.42, BA-MA RM 92/5200.

57 Roskill (1956) map 12, p. 121–3; Woodman, p. 77–9.

58 Kennedy, p. 27; Sweetman, p. 21.

59 KTB Tirpitz, 9.3.42, BA-MA RM 92/5200; Sweetman, p. 21; Roskill (1956) map 12, p. 121–3; Woodman, p. 77–9.

60 Peillard, p. 67–69; Kennedy p. 27–30; Sweetman, p. 21–22; KTB Tirpitz, 9.3.42, BA-MA RM 92/5200; Roskill (1956) map 12, p. 121–3; Woodman, p. 77–9.

61 Peillard, p. 68; Sweetman, p. 22.

62 KTB Tirpitz, 9.3.42, BA-MA RM 92/5200; Sweetman, p. 22; Roskill (1956) map 12, p. 121–3; Woodman, p. 77–9.

63 Peillard, p. 69.

64 On board the *Tirpitz*, three planes were claimed to be shot down. However, such errors are prevalent in virtually all reports on enemy losses. KTB Tirpitz, 9.3.42, BA-MA RM 92/5200; Roskill (1956) map 12, p. 121–3; Woodman, p. 77–9.

65 KTB Tirpitz, 9.3.42, BA-MA RM 92/5200.

66 KTB Tirpitz, 9.3.42, BA-MA RM 92/5200.

67 KTB Tirpitz, 9.3.42, BA-MA RM 92/5200.

68 KTB Tirpitz, 9.3.42, BA-MA RM 92/5200.

69 Roskill (1956) map 12, p. 121–3; Woodman, p. 77–9.

70 KTB Tirpitz, 9.3.42-12.3.42, BA-MA RM 92/5200.

71 KTB Tirpitz, 12.3.42-13.3.42, BA-MA RM 92/5200; Roskill (1956) map 12, p. 123.

72 The German invasion of Norway (Operation Weserübung) significantly curtailed the time the German warships could operate on the Atlantic. First, the ships were held back during the preparation of the operation. Second, during the battles in the seas around Norway, several German ships were either sunk or damaged. During the summer 1940, the German Navy had to stay on alert for the projected invasion of Britain (Operation Seelöwe). Also, several German ships required overhaul or repairs at shipyards, due to mechanical problems that

had occurred.

[73] "Umsteuerung der Heeresrüstung," Berlin 27.6.1941, Anlage zu Nr. 14511/41 g. Wa Stab Ia, von Rohden collection, National Archives, Washington DC, microfilm publication T971, Roll 47, Frames 839ff.

[74] *Führer Conferences on Naval Affairs 1939–1945* (London: Greenhill Books 1990) p. 222–5.

[75] Actually, there was a third alternative: to ship weapons, equipment, and raw materials to Soviet ports on the Pacific coast, but it was not considered by the British at this stage of the war.

[76] Woodman, p. 10.

[77] Woodman, p. 10.

[78] Woodman, pp. 10–11.

[79] Woodman, p 11.

[80] Woodman, pp 12–13.

[81] Woodman, p. 42.

[82] Woodman, p. 42; Samuelson, pp. 259–260.

[83] *Führer Conferences on Naval Affairs 1939–1945* (London: Greenhill Books 1990) pp. 225–235.

[84] *Führer Conferences on Naval Affairs 1939–1945* (London: Greenhill Books 1990) p. 237.

[85] Ibid, pp. 235–243.

[86] Ibid, pp. 246–249.

[87] Ibid, pp. 246–249.

[88] Ibid, pp. 246–249.

[89] Ibid, pp. 246–249.

[90] Ibid, pp. 246–249 & 259.

[91] Ibid, p. 259.

[92] Roskill (1956), p. 115.

[93] Roskill (1956), p. 116; KTB Tirpitz, BA-MA RM 92/5200.

[94] Sweetman, p. 15.

[95] Roskill (1956), pp. 117–8; Churchill, vol IV, p. 98; KTB Tirpitz, BA-MA RM 92/5200.

[96] Busch, pp. 37–41; Bredemeier, pp. 197–233; Schmalenbach, pp. 142–147.

[97] Woodman, pp. 60–62.

[98] *Führer Conferences on Naval Affairs 1939–1945* (London: Greenhill Books 1990) pp. 101, 243 & 265–267. The German decision of April 1940, to discontinue the work on *Graf Zeppelin*, has been criticized. However, it should not be forgotten that the basic premise—Germany's inability to win a protracted war—proved correct. As the course of the war suggests, Germany's chances of winning the war were virtually nil, at least from the moment Operation Barbarossa was halted. Efforts that were unlikely to result in useful capabilities before the autumn of 1941 could thus be seen as wasted.

[99] *Führer Conferences on Naval Affairs 1939–1945* (London: Greenhill Books 1990) pp. 265–267.

[100] Ibid, pp. 242 & 246.

[101]   Roskill (1956), p. 124; Sweetman, p. 15.
[102]   Sweetman, pp. 15–17; KTB Tirpitz, 30.1.42, BA-MA RM 92/5200.
[103]   Sweetman, pp. 18–19.
[104]   Sweetman, pp. 24–26.
[105]   Warren/Benson, p. 323.
[106]   Warren/Benson, p. 324; Jacobsen, p. 94.
[107]   Kennedy; pp. 45–46; Warren/Benson, pp. 324–325.
[108]   Warren/Benson, p. 324; Kennedy, p. 46.
[109]   Warren/Benson, p. 17.
[110]   Ford, s. 12–13.
[111]   Woodward, pp. 48–50.
[112]   Woodward, pp. 48–50.
[113]   Woodward, pp. 48–50.
[114]   Dorrian, p. 2.
[115]   Ford, p. 29.
[116]   Woodward, pp. 48–50.
[117]   Ford, p. 60.
[118]   Ford, p. 48, 60; Woodward, pp. 48–50.
[119]   Ford, p. 35; Dorrian, pp. 101–102.
[120]   Dorrian, pp. 102–103; Ford, p. 35.
[121]   Ford, p. 36.
[122]   Ford, p. 36.
[123]   Dorrian, p. 110.
[124]   HMSO No 65-38086.
[125]   Ford, p. 38.
[126]   HMSO No 65-38086; Dorrian, p. 43.
[127]   Dorrian, p. 125.
[128]   Ford, p. 39.
[129]   Dorian, p. 126.
[130]   Dorrian, p. 125.
[131]   HMSO No 65-38086; Dorrian, pp. 126–127.
[132]   Dorrian, p. 127; Kennedy, pp. 43–44.
[133]   Dorrian, pp. 126–127.
[134]   Dorrian, p. 127.
[135]   Dorrian, p. 133.
[136]   Dorrian, p. 134.
[137]   Dorrian, p. 136.
[138]   Dorrian, p. 136.
[139]   Dorrian, pp. 136–137.
[140]   Dorrian, p. 137.
[141]   Dorrian, p. 138.
[142]   Dorrian, p. 139.
[143]   Dorrian, p. 139.
[144]   Dorrian, p. 139.
[145]   Dorrian, p. 140.

146 Ford, p. 54; Dorrian, p. 140.
147 Dorrian, pp. 141–142.
148 Dorrian, p. 142; Ford, pp. 52–53.
149 Ford, p. 60.
150 Ford, p. 55; Dorrian, p. 167.
151 Ford, p. 55.
152 Ford, p. 55.
153 Ford, p. 58.
154 Ford, pp. 46–51.
155 Ford, pp. 46–51.
156 Ford, pp. 46–51.
157 Dorrian, p. 143; Ford, pp. 46–51.
158 Ford, pp. 63–68.
159 Dorrian, pp. 149–150.
160 Ford, p. 70.
161 Ford, pp. 70–71.
162 Dorrian, p. 143.
163 Dorrian, pp. 160–161.
164 Dorrian, p. 161.
165 TheHistorynet.com
166 Dorrian, pp. 168–169; HMSO No 65-38086.
167 Dorrian, pp. 199–201.
168 HMSO No 65-38086.
169 Ford, pp. 76–77.
170 Ford, p. 86.
171 Dorrian, pp. 260–261; Ford, p. 86.
172 Schuur/Martens/Kohler, pp. 81–93; *Führer Conferences on Naval Affairs 1939–1945* (London: Greenhill Books 1990) pp. 65–67 & 81–81.
173 *Führer Conferences on Naval Affairs 1939–1945* (London: Greenhill Books 1990) p. 236.
174 *The Rise and Fall of the German Air Force*, p. 113.
175 *The Rise and Fall of the German Air Force*, pp.109–113; Kriegsgliederung Luftflotte 5, 1.5.1942, BA-MA RL 7/514; Bekker, p. 257.
176 *The Rise and Fall of the German Air Force*, pp.109–113; Kriegsgliederung Luftflotte 5, 1.5.1942, BA-MA RL 7/514; Bekker, p. 257.
177 Several examples of mine laying operations are mentioned in the Luftflotte 5 war diary for the period February-March 1942, see BA-MA RL 7/493.
178 BA-MA RL 7/493; Anlage 4 zu Gruppe Nord B.Br. Nr. 460/42, 7.3.1942, BA-MA RM 35/I 140; Bekker, pp.257-8; *Führer Conferences on Naval Affairs 1939–1945* (London: Greenhill Books 1990) p. 261; Jacobsen, p.102.
179 Ibid.
180 Sweetman, pp. 26–7.
181 KTB Tirpitz, BA-MA RM 92/5200; Sweetman, p. 27.
182 Woodman, p. 83; KTB Marinegruppe Nord, 21.3.42, BA-MA RM 35 I/140.
183 Woodman, pp.84–5.

184 Woodman, pp.8–6.
185 Schofield, p. 30; Woodman, pp.86–7.
186 Woodman, p. 87; See KTB Luftflotte 5, 27 March 1942, BA-MA RL 7/493 and KTB Marinegruppe Nord, 27 March 1942, BA-MA RM 35 I/140.
187 KTB Marinegruppe Nord, 28.3.42, BA-MA RM 35 I/140.
188 KTB Marinegruppe Nord, 28–29 March 1942, BA-MA RM 35 I/140; KTB Luftflotte 5, 28–29 March 1942, BA-MA RL 7/493.
189 KTB Luftflotte 5, 28 March 1942, BA-MA RL 7/493; Roskill (1956), p. 126.
190 Roskill (1956), p. 126; Woodman pp. 89–90.
191 KTB Marinegruppe Nord, 30 March 1942, BA-MA RM 35 I/140; Roskill (1956) p. 126; Woodman, pp. 93–101.
192 KTB Marinegruppe Nord, 30–31 March 1942, BA-MA RM 35 I/140; Roskill (1956) pp. 126–7; Woodman, pp. 93–101.
193 Roskill (1956) pp. 127.
194 Roskill (1956) p. 127; Woodman, p. 103.
195 Woodman, p. 103.
196 KTB Marinegruppe Nord, 8.4.42, 9.4.42, BA-MA RM 35/I 140; Woodman, p. 105.
197 KTB Luftflotte 5, 11.4.42, BA-MA RL 7/493; Woodman p. 108.
198 KTB Luftflotte 5, 12.4.42, BA-MA RL 7/493; Woodman, p. 108.
199 KTB Luftflotte 5, 13.4.42, BA-MA RL 7/493; Woodman, p. 108.
200 Woodman, pp. 105–6.
201 KTB Luftlotte 5, 13-18.4.42, BA-MA RL 7/493; KTB Marinegruppe Nord, 11-18.4.42, BA-MA RM 35 I/140; Woodman, pp. 104–111.
202 Anlage 7 zum KTB Marinegruppe Nord v. 16.-30.4.42, BA-MA RM RM 35 I/140.
203 Kriegsgliederungen Luftflotte 5, 1.5.42, BA-MA RL 7/514.
204 Anlage 18 zum KTB Marinegruppe Nord v. 16.-30.4.42, BA-MA RM RM 35 I/140.
205 See Boris V. Sokolov, "The Role of Lend-Lease in Soviet Military Efforts, 1941–1945," *Journal of Slavic Military Studies, Vol 7, No 3 (September 1994)*, pp. 567–586.
206 Sokolov, op.cit., pp. 571–2.
207 Ibid, pp. 569–570.
208 Sokolov, p. 572.
209 Sokolov, p. 573.
210 Sokolov, pp. 574–581.
211 Sweetman, pp. 27–29.
212 Sweetman, pp. 27–31.
213 KTB Tirpitz, 27–28 April 1942, BA-MA RM 92/5200; Sweetman, pp. 30–33.
214 KTB Tirpitz, 28–29 April 1942, BA-MA RM 92/5200; Sweetman, pp. 33–35; Roskill (1956) p. 127.
215 Woodman, pp. 117–8.
216 Woodman, pp. 118–9.
217 KTB Luftflotte 5, 26 April 1942, BA-MA RL 7/493.

218 KTB Luftflotte 5, 28–30 April 1942, BA-MA RL 7/493.
219 KTB Marinegruppe Nord, 26–28 April 1942, BA-MA RM 35 I/140.
220 KTB Marinegruppe Nord, 29 April 1942, BA-MA RM 35 I/140.
221 KTB Marinegruppe Nord, 29 April 1942, BA-MA RM 35 I/140.
222 Roskill (1956), p. 128.
223 KTB Luftflotte 5, 1 May 1942, BA-MA RL 7/495; Roskill (1956), p. 128.
224 Roskill (1956), pp. 128–129.
225 Brown, p. 61; Woodman, pp. 119–120.
226 Woodman, pp. 121–122.
227 KTB Luftflotte 5, 1–4 May 1942, BA-MA RL 7/495; Roskill (1956), p. 129.
228 Roskill (1956), p. 130.
229 Roskill (1956), p. 130.
230 Roskill (1956), pp. 130–131.
231 KTB Luftflotte 5, 20–31 May 1942, BA-MA RL 7/494.
232 KTB Luftflotte 5, 20–31 May 1942, BA-MA RL 7/494.
233 Roskill (1956), p. 132.
234 Roskill (1956), p. 134.
235 KTB Tirpitz, BA-MA RM 92/5200; *Führer Conferences on Naval Affairs 1939–1945* (London: Greenhill Books 1990) p. 284.
236 Jacobsen, pp. 99–100.
237 KTB Tirpitz, BA-MA RM 92/5200; *Führer Conferences on Naval Affairs 1939–1945* (London: Greenhill Books 1990) p. 284.
238 *Führer Conferences on Naval Affairs 1939–1945* (London: Greenhill Books 1990) p. 284; Marinegruppenkommando Nord B.Br.Gkdos.Chefs. 770/42 Aop., 4.6.1942, "Operative Weisung für Einsatz der Drontheim-und Narvik-Gruppe gegen einem PQ-Geleitzug" (Deckname: Rösselsprung), BA-MA RM 35 I/142, pp. 55–65.
239 Befehlshaber der Schlachtschiffe, B.Nr. 375/42, 30.5.42, BA-MA RM 48/265.
240 *Führer Conferences on Naval Affairs 1939–1945* (London: Greenhill Books 1990) pp. 286–7.
241 Anlage zu Gruppe Nord B.Br.Gkdos.Chefs. 770/42 Aop. vom 4.6.1942, "Lagebetrachtung zum Einsatz schwerer Seestreitkräfte gegen einen PQ-Geleitzug," BA-MA RM 35 I/142, pp. 66–72.
242 KTB Marinegruppe Nord, 22.6.42, 14.43 Uhr, BA-MA RM 35 I/142.
243 KTB Marinegruppe Nord, 23.6.42, 11.52 Uhr, BA-MA RM 35 I/142.
244 Woodman, p. 191.
245 The directive was known as Marinegruppenkommando Nord B.Br.Gkdos.Chefs. 770/42 Aop., 4.6.1942, "Operative Weisung für Einsatz der Drontheim-und Narvik-Gruppe gegen einem PQ-Geleitzug (Deckname: Rösselsprung)." It can be found at Bundesarchiv-Militärarchiv, file RM 35 I/142, pp. 55-65. Se också Woodman, p. 190.
246 Woodman, pp. 187–188.
247 Jacobsen, pp. 62–63.
248 Woodman, pp. 187–188; Jacobsen, p. 63.
249 See Roskill, The War at Sea, vol II.

[250] Brown, pp. 46–7.
[251] Roskill (1956), p. 134.
[252] KTB Luftflotte 5, 26.6.42-30.6.42, BA-MA RL 7/495; KTB Luftflotte 5, 1.7.42-2.7.42, BA-MA RL 7/496.
[253] Woodman, p. 195.
[254] Brown, p. 66; Woodman, p. 196.
[255] Woodman, pp. 197 & 199.
[256] Roskill (1956), p. 136.
[257] Roskill (1956), p. 136; Woodman pp. 189–191; Jacobsen, p. 63.
[258] Woodman, pp. 195–199.
[259] Woodman, p. 197. The war diary of Marinegruppe Nord (BA-MA RM 35 I/142) for the relevant days contains nothing suggesting that the *Exford's* transmision had been noted. To the contrary, a genuine uncertainty about the position of PQ17 prevailed.
[260] Woodman, p. 198.
[261] Woodman, pp. 200–201.
[262] KTB Marinegruppe Nord, 23.6.42, 14.41 Uhr & 25.6, BA-MA RM 35 I/142.
[263] KTB Marinegruppe Nord, 26.6.42, 16.20 Uhr, 27.6.42, 16.11 Uhr och 30.6.42, 03.18 Uhr, BA-MA RM 35 I/142.
[264] KTB Marinegruppe Nord, 28.6.42, 16.38 Uhr, 29.6.42, 03.20 Uhr, BA-MA RM 35 I/142.
[265] KTB Marinegruppe Nord, 30.6.42, 02.07 Uhr & 21.17 Uhr, BA-MA RM 35 I/142.
[266] KTB Marinegruppe Nord, 30.6.42, 02.07 Uhr & 21.17 Uhr, BA-MA RM 35 I/142; KTB Luftflotte 5, 26.6.42-30.6.42, BA-MA RL 7/495.
[267] Woodman, p. 201; KTB Marinegruppe Nord, 1.7.42, 17.05 Uhr, BA-MA RM 35 I/142.
[268] KTB Marinegruppe Nord, 1.7.42, 17.05 Uhr, BA-MA RM 35 I/142.
[269] KTB Tirpitz, 1.7.42, BA-MA RM 92/5200; KTB Luftflotte 5, 1.7.42, BA-MA RL 7/496.
[270] Woodman, p. 201.
[271] Woodman, pp. 201–202.
[272] Woodman, p. 202.
[273] Woodman, p. 202. KTB Luftflotte 5, 12.7.42, "Zusammengefasster Kampfbericht über die Einsätze gegen PQ17," sid. 28, BA-MA RL 7/496.
[274] KTB Tirpitz, 2.7.42, BA-MA RM 92/5200.
[275] KTB Tirpitz, 2.7.42, BA-MA RM 92/5200.
[276] KTB Tirpitz, 2.7.42, BA-MA RM 92/5200.
[277] KTB Tirpitz, 2.7.42, BA-MA RM 92/5200.
[278] KTB Tirpitz, 2.7.42, BA-MA RM 92/5200; Roskill (1956), pp. 137–8.
[279] KTB Tirpitz, 2.7.42, BA-MA RM 92/5200.
[280] KTB Tirpitz, 3.7.42, BA-MA RM 92/5200.
[281] KTB Tirpitz, 3.7.42, BA-MA RM 92/5200.
[282] KTB Tirpitz, 3.7.42, BA-MA RM 92/5200.
[283] KTB Tirpitz, 3.7.42, BA-MA RM 92/5200.

284		KTB Tirpitz, 3.7.42, BA-MA RM 92/5200.
285		KTB Tirpitz, 3.7.42, BA-MA RM 92/5200.
286		KTB Tirpitz, 3.7.42, BA-MA RM 92/5200.
287		Roskill (1956), p. 139.
288		Roskill (1956), map after p. 136 and p. 137.
289		Schofield, p. 77; Roskill (1956), p. 137.
290		Woodman, pp. 202–3.
291		KTB Marinegruppe Nord, 3.7.42, 17.53 Uhr, BA-MA RM 35 I/142; Woodman, p. 202.
292		KTB Marinegruppe Nord, 3.7.42, 17.53 Uhr, BA-MA RM 35 I/142; Woodman, p. 202.
293		Woodman, p. 203.
294		KTB Marinegruppe Nord, 3.7.42, 16.48-17.53 Uhr, BA-MA RM 35 I/142.
295		KTB Marinegruppe Nord, 3.7.42, 16.48-17.53 Uhr, BA-MA RM 35 I/142.
296		KTB Tirpitz, 3.7.42, BA-MA RM 92/5200.
297		KTB Tirpitz, 3-4.7.42, BA-MA RM 92/5200.
298		KTB Tirpitz, 4.7.42, BA-MA RM 92/5200.
299		KTB Luftflotte 5, 4.7.42, BA-MA RL 7/496; Woodman, pp. 204–5.
300		Woodman, p. 205.
301		Woodman, p. 205.
302		Woodman, pp. 205–6.
303		Bekker, p. 266.
304		KTB Luftflotte 5, 4.7.42, BA-MA RL 7/496; Woodman, pp. 209–210.
305		Broome, p. 167; Roskill (1956), pp. 138–141; Woodman, pp. 210–212.
306		Kemp, p. 75.
307		Kemp, pp. 73–74; John Jackson, *Ultra's Arctic War, The Bletchley Archive, vol 2* (Milton Keynes: The Military Press, 2003) p. 102.
308		Kemp, p. 74.
309		Kemp, p. 75.
310		Woodman, pp. 213–5; Kemp, p. 75.
311		Kemp, p. 75.
312		Broome, p. 173.
313		Broome, p. 182–183.
314		Broome, p. 187.
315		Broome, p. 189.
316		Broome, p. 195.
317		KTB Marinegruppe Nord 4.7.42, BA-MA RM 35 I/142.
318		See for example KTB Tirpitz, 4.7.42, BA-MA RM 92/5200 & KTB Marinegruppe Nord, 4.7.42, BA-MA RM 35 I/142. Both these files indicate a position slightly to the west of Bear Island. However, at this stage, Tovey's warships were about 450 kilometers farther to the west (see Roskill, 1956, map after p. 136). At 17.00 on 4 July, an enemy battleship is still mentioned in Admiral Carls' situation report (see KTB Marinegruppe Nord, 4.7.42, BA-MA RM 35 I/142). Although an air reconnaisance report at 23.00 mentioned four cruisers and no battleship, Admiral Carls' situation report from 06.00 on 5 July

still included the presumed enemy battleship. (see KTB Marinegruppe Nord, 4.7.42-5.7.42, BA-MA RM 35 I/142).

319 KTB Marinegruppe Nord 4.7.42-5.7.42, BA-MA RM 35 I/142.
320 KTB Tirpitz, 5.7.42, BA-MA RM 92/5200; Roskill (1956) map after p. 136.
321 KTB Tirpitz, 5.7.42, BA-MA RM 92/5200.
322 KTB Tirpitz, 5.7.42, BA-MA RM 92/5200.
323 KTB Tirpitz, 5.7.42, BA-MA RM 92/5200.
324 Woodman, p. 219.
325 See for example KTB Tirpitz, 5.7.42, BA-MA RM 92/5200, where nothing suggests that a submarine had been noted.
326 KTB Tirpitz, 5.7.42, BA-MA RM 92/5200.
327 Kennedy, p. 72; KTB Tirpitz, 5.7.42-8.7.42, BA-MA RM 92/5200.
328 KTB Tirpitz, 5.7.42-8.7.42, BA-MA RM 92/5200.
329 Bekker, p. 269; KTB Luftflotte 5, BA-MA RL 7/496; Roskill (1956), map after p. 140.
330 KTB Luftflotte 5, BA-MA RL 7/496; Roskill (1956), map after p. 140.
331 Roskill (1956), map after p. 140.
332 http://www.cbrnp.com/RNP/Flower/ARTICLES/Poppy/Beardmore-1.htm
333 Roskill (1956), map after p. 140 & p. 143.
334 KTB Luftflotte 5, 12.7.42 (the concluding report on the attacks against PQ17) BA-MA RL 7/496. Consumption of ammunition had been modest, 212 tons of bombs and 61 torpedoes. However, the German stocks of torpedoes were small and they were not sufficient to repeat the effort against PQ17 if another Allied convoy had been dispatched soon afterwards.
335 Warren/Benson, p. 20; Kemp (Underwater Warriors), p. 116.
336 Warren/Benson, pp. 20–21.
337 See e.g www.ananova.com/news/story/sm_495823.html. The Polyanna story appeared too unlikely to be true and was often dismissed as a myth, but a photo of Sladen and Polyanna has been found.
338 Kemp (Underwater Warriors), pp. 116–117; Warren/Benson, pp. 21–22.
339 Warren/Benson, pp. 27–28.
340 Warren/Benson, pp. 28–29.
341 WW2 People's War, X-Craft and Operation Source, BBC, Internet.
342 Kemp (Underwater Warriors), p. 119; Warren/Benson, p. 39.
343 Warren/Benson, pp. 48–49.
344 Kemp (Underwater Warriors), p. 119.
345 Kemp (Underwater Warriors), p. 119.
346 Kemp (Underwater Warriors), p. 120; Warren/Benson, p. 54.
347 Kemp (Underwater Warriors), p. 120.
348 Except some of the auxiliary cruisers, i.e armed merchant ships sent by the Germans to raid distant waters.
349 For more on the Admiral Scheers long voyage 23 October 1940–1 april 1941 see N. Zetterling & M. Tamelander, *Bismarck* (Drexel Hill, PA: Casemate, 2009) pp. ZZZ skall föras in när vi får Bismarck.
350 Marinegruppe Nord B.Nr.g.Kdos. 850/42, 1 July 1942, i KTB Marinegruppe

Nord, BA-MA RM 35 I/142, pp. 237–244.

351   Ibid.

352   Ibid.

353   KTB Marinegruppe Nord, 15.8.42, BA-MA RM 35 I/143.

354   The directive for Operation Wunderland can be found in KTB Marinegruppe
       Nord, Anlage 18 zum KTB 1.-15.8.1942, BA-MA RM 35 I/143, p. 91.

355   KTB Marinegruppe Nord, 15.8.42, BA-MA RM 35 I/143.

356   KTB Admiral Scheer 15–30 August 1942, BA-MA RM 92/5233; Anlage Nr. 1
       zum KTB vom 1.9 bis 15.9.42, KTB Marinegruppe Nord, BA-MA RM 35 I/143,
       Bl. 213ff.

357   Anlage Nr. 1 zum KTB vom 1.9 bis 15.9.42, KTB Marinegruppe Nord, BA-MA
       RM 35 I/143, Bl. 213ff.

358   KTB Admiral Scheer 15–30 August 1942, BA-MA RM 92/5233; Anlage Nr. 1
       zum KTB vom 1.9 bis 15.9.42, KTB Marinegruppe Nord, BA-MA RM 35 I/143,
       Bl. 213ff.

359   KTB Admiral Scheer 15–30 August 1942, BA-MA RM 92/5233; Anlage Nr. 1
       zum KTB vom 1.9 bis 15.9.42, KTB Marinegruppe Nord, BA-MA RM 35 I/143,
       Bl. 213ff.

360   Roskill (1956) pp. 277–282.

361   Roskill (1956) pp. 280–281.

362   KTB Marinegruppe Nord, 6.9.42, 18.17 Uhr and 7.9.42, 23.47 Uhr, BA-MA
       RM 35 I/143.

363   KTB Marinegruppe Nord, 8.9.42, 07.36 Uhr, BA-MA RM 35 I/143.

364   KTB Marinegruppe Nord, 8.9.42, BA-MA RM 35 I/143.

365   KTB Marinegruppe Nord, 9.9.42, BA-MA RM 35 I/143.

366   Roskill (1956), p. 283.

367   Werner Klümper, "Der Einsatz des KG 26 als Torpedotraeger in Norwegen," BA-
       MA RL 10/630.

368   Initially, Klümper's unit was based on Bardufoss, but transferred to Banak on 17
       September. See KTB Luftflotte 5, 17.9.42, BA-MA RL 7/496. Elements of
       Klümpers unit had already moved to Banak, by landing there after completing
       missions.

369   Werner Klümper, "Der Einsatz des KG 26 als Torpedotraeger in Norwegen," BA-
       MA RL 10/630.

370   Bekker, p. 271; Werner Klümper, "Der Einsatz des KG 26 als Torpedotraeger in
       Norwegen," BA-MA RL 10/630.

371   Bekker, p. 271; Werner Klümper, "Der Einsatz des KG 26 als Torpedotraeger in
       Norwegen," BA-MA RL 10/630.

372   Werner Klümper, "Der Einsatz des KG 26 als Torpedotraeger in Norwegen," BA-
       MA RL 10/630.

373   Roskill (1956), p. 283; Bekker, p. 271; Kemp, p. 104.

374   Werner Klümper, "Der Einsatz des KG 26 als Torpedotraeger in Norwegen," BA-
       MA RL 10/630.

375   Roskill (1956), p. 283.

376   Roskill (1956), pp. 283–4.

377 KTB Tirpitz, 1.9.42, 9.9.42, 14.9.42, BA-MA RM 92/5200.
378 Werner Klümper, "Der Einsatz des KG 26 als Torpedotraeger in Norwegen," BA-MA RL 10/630.
379 Kemp, p. 105; Werner Klümper, "Der Einsatz des KG 26 als Torpedotraeger in Norwegen," BA-MA RL 10/630.
380 Werner Klümper, "Der Einsatz des KG 26 als Torpedotraeger in Norwegen," BA-MA RL 10/630.
381 Werner Klümper, "Der Einsatz des KG 26 als Torpedotraeger in Norwegen," BA-MA RL 10/630.
382 Kemp, p. 105.
383 Werner Klümper, "Der Einsatz des KG 26 als Torpedotraeger in Norwegen," BA-MA RL 10/630.
384 Werner Klümper, "Der Einsatz des KG 26 als Torpedotraeger in Norwegen," BA-MA RL 10/630.
385 http://www.portchicago.org
386 Werner Klümper, "Der Einsatz des KG 26 als Torpedotraeger in Norwegen," BA-MA RL 10/630.
387 KTB Luftflotte 5, 14.9.42 & 16.9.42, BA-MA RL 7/496; Werner Klümper, "Der Einsatz des KG 26 als Torpedotraeger in Norwegen," BA-MA RL 10/630. British claims on aircraft shot down and own losses can be found in Roskill (1956), pp. 283–4; Kemp, p. 106.
388 KTB Luftflotte 5, 15.9.42, BA-MA RL 7/496; Roskill (1956) p. 284.
389 Roskill (1956), pp. 284–285.
390 Roskill (1956), pp. 284–285.
391 Peillard, pp. 34–37.
392 Peillard, p. 119.
393 Saelen, p. 111.
394 Saelen, p. 111; Warren/Benson, p. 64.
395 Saelen, p. 112; Warren/Benson, p. 64.
396 Saelen, pp. 110, 112; Warren/Benson, p. 64.
397 Saelen, p. 112; Warren/Benson, p. 64.
398 Saelen, p. 112; Warren/Benson, pp. 40–42, 64.
399 Saelen, p. 112; Warren/Benson, p. 64.
400 Warren/Benson, p. 66; Saelen, p. 115.
401 Peillard, p. 124.
402 Warren/Benson, pp. 68–69.
403 Warren/Benson, pp. 69–70; Saelen, pp. 121–123; Peillard, pp. 127–128.
404 Saelen, p. 123; Peillard. p. 128.
405 Peillard, pp. 128–129.
406 Warren/Benson, pp. 71–75; Saelen, pp. 124–127; Peillard, pp. 129–132.
407 Peillard, p. 132.
408 Saelen, p. 128.
409 Saelen, p. 128–129; Peillard, pp. 119, 133.
410 Warren/Benson, p. 76–78; Saelen, p. 130–132; Peillard, p. 134–136.
411 Saelen, pp. 132–133.

412   Warren/Benson, p. 79; Saelen, pp. 133–134; Peillard, pp. 137–138.
413   Saelen, pp. 135–137; Woodward, p. 87; Peillard, pp. 138–139.
414   Peillard, p. 139.
415   Peillard, p. 140; Kemp (Underwater Warriors), p. 121.
416   Warren/Benson, p. 81; Woodward, p. 87; Peillard, p. 141; Saelen, p. 139.
417   Peillard, p. 141.
418   Saelen, p. 138.
419   Peillard, p. 143.
420   In fact, *Arthur* was subsequently found by the Germans, as her mast tops actually appeared above the water. They raised her and made use of her until the end of the war. She was subsequently returned to the person Larsen had stolen her from (Peillard, p. 143).
421   The versions describing the brief engagement differ considerably. We find Peillards' account most reliable (pp. 153–4), in particular as he had access to previous authors' accounts when he interveiwed Larsen.
422   The killing of Evans was among the charges that resulted in the death sentence imposed on Keitel at Nürnberg.
423   *Führer Conferences on Naval Affairs 1939–1945* (London: Greenhill Books 1990) pp. 294–7.
424   KTB Marinegruppe Nord, 30.9.42, BA-MA RM 35 I/143.
425   Anlage 15 zum KTB Marinegruppe Nord, 24.9.42, BA-MA RM 35 I/143.
426   Anlage 15 zum KTB Marinegruppe Nord, 17.9.42, BA-MA RM 35 I/143.
427   Kriegsgliederungen Luftflotte 5 1942, BA-MA RL 7/514; Werner Kluemper, "Der Einsatz des KG 26 als Torpedotraeger in Norwegen," BA-MA RL 10/630.
428   The German Navy had the follwoing heavy ships on 1 September 1939 (including thus in production and eventually completed during the war): The battleships *Gneisenau, Scharnhorst, Bismarck, Tirpitz*; the heavy cruisers *Admiral Hipper, Blücher* och *Prinz Eugen*; the light cruisers *Emden, Karlsruhe, Köln, Königsberg, Leipzig* och *Nürnberg*; the armored ships (also know as pocket battleships and heavy cruisers) *Deutschland* (which was renamed *Lützow* in 1940), *Admiral Scheer, Admiral Graf Spee*.
In 1939, *Admiral Graf Spee* was scuttled off Montevideo by her own crew. Also, the light crusier *Lipzig* was damaged so badly by the British submarine *Ursula*, that she never again saw active service. She was subsequently used as a training ship in the Baltic.
In 1940, the cruisers *Blücher, Köln*, and *Karlsruhe* was lost in the attack on Norway.
In 1941, the battleship *Bismarck* was lost.
In 1942, the *Gneisenau* was badly damaged and brought to Gdynia for reconstruction, which was never completed.
Thus by the autumn 1942, the German Navy had, in reality, lost three of six light crusiers, one of three heavy crusiers, one of three armored ships, and two of the four battlships. And of the ships that remained, some were undergoing repairs.
429   KTB Tirpitz, 23-24.10.42, BA-MA RM 92/5201.

430   Roskill (1956), p. 289.
431   Roskill (1956), pp. 289–290.
432   Roskill (1956) pp. 289–291.
433   Roskill (1956) p. 291; KTB Luftflotte 5 15.12.42 – 30.12.42; BA-MA RL 4/497.
434   Roskill (1956) pp. 291–2.
435   *Führer Conferences on Naval Affairs 1939–1945* (London: Greenhill Books 1990) p. 302.
436   *Führer Conferences on Naval Affairs 1939–1945* (London: Greenhill Books 1990) p. 302; Roskill (1956) pp. 289–292.
437   Woodward, pp. 95–96.
438   Brennecke (2003), pp. 228–234; Roskill (1956), pp. 291–295.
439   Brennecke (2003), pp. 228–234; Roskill (1956), pp. 291–295.
440   Brennecke (2003), pp. 228–240; Roskill (1956), pp. 291–296.
441   Brennecke (2003), pp. 234–247; Roskill (1956), pp. 291–296.
442   Brennecke (2003), pp. 234–247; Roskill (1956), pp. 291–296.
443   Brennecke (2003), pp. 239–247; Roskill (1956), pp. 291–296.
444   Brennecke (2003), pp. 246–250; Roskill (1956), pp. 294–298.
445   Brennecke (2003), pp. 246–256; Roskill (1956), pp. 294–298.
446   Roskill (1956), pp. 294–298.
447   *Führer Conferences on Naval Affairs 1939–1945* (London: Greenhill Books 1990) p. 302.
448   BA-MA, akt RW 6/v.535, pp. 5, 12 och 20.
449   B. Müller-Hillebrand, *Das Heer, vol II* (Frankfurt: Mittler & Sohn, 1956) pp. 40 & 102.
450   *Führer Conferences on Naval Affairs 1939–1945* (London: Greenhill Books 1990) p. 302.
451   KTB Tirpitz, Jan-Feb 1943, BA-MA RM 92/5201.
452   Brown, p. 29; Woodward, p. 115.
453   Brown, p. 29; Woodward, p. 115; Warren/Benson, p. 147; HMSO No 65-38204.
454   Brown, p. 29; Gallagher, p. 47; HMSO No 65-38204.
455   Kennedy, p. 94; Gallagher, pp. 26–27.
456   Gallagher, pp. 26–27.
457   HMSO No 65-38204; Gallagher, p. 41; Woodward, p. 115.
458   Gallagher, pp. 26, 36–37.
459   Brown, p. 29; Gallagher, p. 40.
460   Walker/Mellor, p. 151; Gallagher, pp. 43–44.
461   Gallagher, pp. 36–37.
462   Gallagher, pp. 43–44; Walker/Mellor, p. 151.
463   Gallagher, p. 45.
464   Warren/Benson, p. 156; Gallagher, pp. 44–45.
465   Warren/Benson, p. 150–151.
466   Kennedy, p. 95; Gallagher, p. 28.
467   Kennedy, p. 94; Gallagher, p. 29.
468   Woodward, p. 117; Jacobsen, p. 114; Gallagher, p. 49.
469   Gallagher, p. 48; HMSO No 65-38204.

470   Gallagher, pp. 48–53; HMSO No 65-38204.

471   HMSO No 65-38204; Brown, p. 29; Jacobsen, p. 115.

472   *Führer Conferences on Naval Affairs 1939–1945* (London: Greenhill Books 1990) p. 311. For more on the *Hipper*, see Jochen Brennecke, *Eismeer, Atlantik, Ostsee* (München: Pavillion Verlag, 2003).

473   *Führer Conferences on Naval Affairs 1939–1945* (London: Greenhill Books 1990) p. 311.

474   *Führer Conferences on Naval Affairs 1939–1945* (London: Greenhill Books 1990) pp. 311–2.

475   Dönitz estimated that only one third of the submarines could be in action at a given time, as one third would be travelling to or from the area where they operated, and one third would be on port or training. At this time, he had about 300 submarines at his disposal.

476   Roskill (1956), pp. 397–402.

477   KTB Tirpitz, March 1943, BA-MA RM 92/5201.

478   KTB Tirpitz, March 1943, BA-MA RM 92/5201.

479   KTB Tirpitz, March 1943, BA-MA RM 92/5201.

480   KTB Tirpitz, March 1943, BA-MA RM 92/5201.

481   KTB Tirpitz, March–May 1943, BA-MA RM 92/5201.

482   Bredemeier, pp. 245–246.

483   KTB Tirpitz, June–July 1943, BA-MA RM 92/5201.

484   KTB Tirpitz, 6.9.1943, BA-MA RM 92/5201.

485   KTB Tirpitz, 6.9.1943, BA-MA RM 92/5201.

486   KTB Tirpitz, 6.9.1943, BA-MA RM 92/5201.

487   KTB Tirpitz, 6.9.1943-7.9.1943, BA-MA RM 92/5201.

488   KTB Tirpitz, 8.9.1943, BA-MA RM 92/5201; Bredemeier, pp. 248–250.

489   KTB Tirpitz, 8.9.1943, BA-MA RM 92/5201; Bredemeier, pp. 248–250.

490   KTB Tirpitz, 8.9.1943, BA-MA RM 92/5201.

491   KTB Tirpitz, 8.9.1943, BA-MA RM 92/5201.

492   KTB Tirpitz, 8.9.1943, BA-MA RM 92/5201.

493   KTB Tirpitz, 8.9.1943, BA-MA RM 92/5201.

494   KTB Tirpitz, 8.9.1943, BA-MA RM 92/5201; KTB Scharnhorst, 8.9.1943, BA-MA RM 92/5199.

495   KTB Tirpitz, 8.9.1943, BA-MA RM 92/5201; KTB Scharnhorst, 8.9.1943, BA-MA RM 92/5199.

496   KTB Tirpitz, 8.9.1943, BA-MA RM 92/5201; Bredemeier, pp, 248–250; KTB Scharnhorst, 8.9.1943, BA-MA RM 92/5199.

497   KTB Tirpitz, 8.9.1943, BA-MA RM 92/5201.

498   KTB Tirpitz, 8.9.1943, BA-MA RM 92/5201.

499   The British, however, would re-establish their position on Svalbard, and the Germans would not make an attempt to destroy it again.

500   Bericht Wener Krux, p. 11, BA-MA RM 92/5186.

501   Kemp (Underwater Warriors), p. 146; Roskill, p. 317.

502   HMSO No 65-38204.

503   Peillard, pp. 184–185.

504 HMSO No 65-38204; Brown, p. 29; Kennedy, pp. 103–104; Gallagher, p. 58.
505 Peillard, p. 187.
506 Peillard, pp. 187–188.
507 Peillard, p. 188.
508 Peillard, pp. 188–189.
509 Peillard, pp. 188–189.
510 Brown, p. 29; Peillard, p. 191.
511 Gallagher, pp. 61–62.
512 Peillard, pp. 191–192; Gallagher, pp. 59–60.
513 Peillard, p. 192.
514 Brown, p. 30; Kemp (Underwater Warriors), pp. 146–147; Peillard, p. 194; Gallagher, p. 75.
515 HMSO No 65-38204; Brown, p. 30; Peillard, p. 194; Gallagher, p. 74; Schofield, pp. 159–160.
516 Peillard, pp. 194–195; Brown, p. 30; HMSO No 65-38204; Kemp (Underwater Warriors), p. 148; Schofield, p. 160; Gallagher, p. 75; Woodward, p. 117.
517 Kennedy, p. 99.
518 Gallagher, pp. 79–80.
519 Brown, p. 30; Bismarck-class.dk.
520 Gallagher, p. 82.
521 Gallagher, pp. 82–83.
522 HMSO No 65-38204; Schofield, pp. 160–161; Gallagher, pp. 82–83.
523 Gallagher, pp. 86–87.
524 Warren/Benson, p. 171; Kennedy, p. 100.
525 Kennedy, p. 101; Gallagher, pp. 80–81.
526 Gallagher, p. 88; Kennedy, p. 100.
527 Gallagher, p. 88.
528 Gallagher, pp. 89–90.
529 Kennedy, p. 101; Gallagher, pp. 90–91.
530 Gallagher, pp. 91–92.
531 Gallagher, p. 94.
532 Kennedy, p. 101; Gallagher, pp. 94–95.
533 Peillard, p. 214.
534 Gallagher, p. 96.
535 Kennedy, p. 123; Gallagher, p. 96.
536 HMSO No 65-38204; Schofield, p. 161; Kemp (Underwater Warriors), p. 150; Warren/Benson, p. 172; Kennedy, pp. 100–101; Gallagher, p. 96.
537 Schofield, p. 161; Gallagher, pp. 96–97.
538 Kemp (Underwater Warriors), p. 149; Jacobsen, p. 162; Gallagher, p. 103.
539 Gallagher, pp. 103–105.
540 Gallagher, pp. 103–105.
541 Kennedy, p. 104; Gallagher, p. 104.
542 Schofield, p. 161; Warren/Benson, p. 172; Kemp (Underwater Warriors), p. 151; Peillard, p. 225; Kennedy, p. 104; Gallagher, pp. 104–105.
543 Warren/Benson, p. 172; Peillard, p. 226; Gallagher, p. 106; Walker/Mellor, p.

191; Kennedy, p. 104.
544 Gallagher, p. 107.
545 Gallagher, p. 108.
546 Gallagher, p. 113.
547 Gallagher, p. 113.
548 Woodward, p. 117; Gallagher, p. 114; Kennedy, p. 104.
549 Gallagher, p. 114.
550 Woodward, p. 117.
551 Schofield, p. 161.
552 Schofield, p. 161; Walker/Mellor, pp. 170–172; Kennedy, p. 105; Warren/Benson, p. 173; WW2 People's War, X-Craft and Operation Source, BBC, Internet.
553 Kemp (Underwater Warriors), p. 150; Warren/Benson, p. 174; Kennedy, p. 105.
554 Kemp (Underwater Warriors), p. 151; Warren/Benson, p. 172; Jacobsen, p. 161.
555 Warren/Benson, pp. 174–175.
556 Jacobsen, pp. 166–167.
557 Gallagher, p. 120.
558 Peillard, p. 234; Kennedy, p. 108.
559 Schofield, p. 162; Kemp (Underwater Warriors), p. 152; Kennedy, p. 106.
560 Peillard, p. 234.
561 Woodward, p. 117; Peillard, p. 234.
562 Gallagher, p. 122.
563 Warren/Benson, p. 175; Kemp (Underwater Warriors), p. 151; Gallagher, pp. 122–123.
564 Gallagher, p. 123; Peillard, p. 228.
565 Gallagher, p. 123; Peillard, p. 228.
566 Gallagher, p. 125.
567 Kennedy, p. 108; Gallagher, pp. 127–129.
568 Peillard, p. 238; Gallagher, p. 129.
569 Peillard, p. 238; Walker/Mellor, p. 191.
570 Gallagher, p. 130.
571 Schofield, p. 163; Woodward, p. 118; Kennedy, p. 110; Gallagher, pp. 130–131; Peillard, pp. 238–239.
572 Gallagher, pp. 130–131; Peillard, pp. 238–239.
573 Gallagher, p. 133; Kennedy, p. 110.
574 Woodward, p. 118; Kennedy, p. 110.
575 Gallagher, p. 134.
576 Gallagher, pp. 134–135.
577 Peillard, p. 240.
578 Gallagher, p. 137; Peillard, p. 240.
579 Kemp (Underwater Warriors), p. 154; Schofield, p. 163; Kennedy, p. 111.
580 Woodward, p. 119; Warren/Benson, p. 179; Gallagher, p. 140.
581 Warren/Benson, p. 179; Gallagher, pp. 140–141.
582 Gallagher, p. 141; Warren/Benson, p. 179.
583 Kennedy, p. 113; Gallagher, p. 141.
584 Gallagher, p. 136.

585 Gallagher, p. 142; Walker/Mellor, p. 178.

586 Extensive efforts to find X-5 have been made, but so far she has not been found. In fact, the Kaafjord has been searched so meticulously, that it can not be excluded that Henty-Creer may have made it from the fjord and sunk somewhere else. The damage inflicted on the *Tirpitz* may also suggest that the X-5 crew managed to position their charges under the battleship's keel. However, nothing can be said with certainty, and the fate of X-5 and her crew remains one of the many unanswered questions lingering from WWII.

587 Walker/Mellor, p. 178.

588 Kennedy, p. 111; Walker/Mellor, p. 178.

589 Warren/Benson, p. 179; WW2 People's War, X-Craft and Operation Source, BBC, Internet.

590 Warren/Benson, pp. 180–181; WW2 People's War, X-Craft and Operation Source, BBC, Internet.

591 Warren/Benson, pp. 180–181; WW2 People's War, X-Craft and Operation Source, BBC, Internet.

592 Kennedy, p. 113; Warren/Benson, pp. 180–181; WW2 People's War, X-Craft and Operation Source, BBC, Internet.

593 Warren/Benson, pp. 180–181; WW2 People's War, X-Craft and Operation Source, BBC, Internet; Gallagher, p. 145.

594 Gallagher, pp. 149–150; WW2 People's War, X-Craft and Operation Source, BBC, Internet; Kennedy, p. 113.

595 Kennedy, p. 113; Gallagher, p. 150.

596 Gallagher, p. 150.

597 Warren/Benson, pp. 180–181; WW2 People's War, X-Craft and Operation Source, BBC, Internet; Gallagher, p. 150.

598 Kemp (Underwater Warriors), p. 156.

599 Kemp (Underwater Warriors), p. 155.

600 Bericht Werner Krux, pp. 5–11, BA-MA RM 92/5186.

601 Bericht Werner Krux, pp. 5–11, BA-MA RM 92/5186; KTB Tirpitz, October 1943, BA-MA RM 92/5201.

602 Woodman, pp. 335–352.

603 Woodman, pp. 348–349.

604 Woodman, pp. 352–354.

605 As we have seen, Kummetz was appointed "Befehlshaber der Kreuzer" (Commander of cruisers) in June 1942. On 19 February, the position was renamed "Befehlshaber der Kampfgruppe" (Commander of the task force).

606 Bredemeier, pp. 257–263.

607 Bredemeier, pp. 262–6; Marinegruppenkommando Nord, "Angriff auf PQ24 durch Scharnhorst am 26.12.43," BA-MA RM 35 I/219, pp. 1–11.

608 Bredemeier, pp. 262–6; Marinegruppenkommando Nord, "Angriff auf PQ24 durch Scharnhorst am 26.12.43," BA-MA RM 35 I/219, pp. 1–11.

609 Marinegruppenkommando Nord, "Angriff auf PQ24 durch Scharnhorst am 26.12.43," BA-MA RM 35 I/219, pp. 17–21.

610 Marinegruppenkommando Nord, "Angriff auf PQ24 durch Scharnhorst am

26.12.43," BA-MA RM 35 I/219, pp. 21–27.

[611] Marinegruppenkommando Nord, "Angriff auf PQ24 durch Scharnhorst am 26.12.43," BA-MA RM 35 I/219, pp. 21–27.

[612] Bredemeier, p. 268.

[613] Jacobsen (Scharnhorst), p. 153.

[614] Woodman, pp. 355–7.

[615] Woodman, pp. 356–357; Marinegruppenkommando Nord, "Angriff auf PQ24 durch Scharnhorst am 26.12.43," BA-MA RM 35 I/219, pp. 17–21.

[616] Woodman, p. 370.

[617] Bredemeier, pp. 269–270; Schuur/Martens/Koehler, pp. 133–134; Jacobsen (Scharnhorst), p. 163.

[618] Bredemeier, pp. 269–270; Schuur/Martens/Koehler, pp. 133–134.

[619] Bredemeier, pp. 264 & 274–5; www.naval-history.net.

[620] Bredemeier, pp. 275–6; Woodman, pp. 363–4; Jacobsen (Scharnhorst), p. 172.

[621] Bredemeier, pp. 276–7. KTB Scharnhorst, "Vernehmung des Matr.Gefr. Sträter (Günter) von der Scharnhorst Gefechtsstation Bb. 4. 15 cm-Turm, Ladenr.", 6. Oktober 1944, BA-MA RM 92/5199; Jacobsen (Scharnhorst), p. 183.

[622] Bredemeier, pp. 277–8.

[623] Ibid.

[624] Ibid.

[625] Jacobsen (Scharnhorst), pp. 176–177.

[626] Ibid, p. 178.

[627] Bredemeier, pp. 278–281; Woodman, pp. 365–8.

[628] Woodman, pp. 365–366; Jacobsen (Scharnhorst), pp. 184–185.

[629] Jacobsen (Scharnhorst), p. 185; Woodman, pp. 365–8; Bredemeier, pp. 280–284.

[630] Bredemeier, pp. 281–284; Schuur/Martens/Koehler, pp. 142–143.

[631] Woodman, pp. 366–368.

[632] Woodman, pp. 367–368.

[633] Jacobsen (Scharnhorst), p. 193; Bredemeier, p. 286; Woodman, pp. 368–369. Different sources give somewhat different information on when the *Duke of York* opened fire, but the variation is small. We have chosen 16.50 as a sort of average, but the differences are of minor significance.

[634] Bredemeier, pp. 286; Woodman, pp. 368–369.

[635] Jacobsen (Scharnhorst), p. 196; Woodman, p. 370.

[636] Woodman, p. 370; Jacobsen (Scharnhorst), p. 201.

[637] Jacobsen (Scharnhorst), p. 202; Woodman, p. 370.

[638] Jacobsen (Scharnhorst), p. 202.

[639] Bredemeier, pp. 288–291; Woodman, pp. 371–2; Jacobsen (Scharnhorst), p. 202.

[640] Jacobsen (Scharnhorst), p. 204; Bredemeier, pp. 288–291; Woodman, pp. 371–2.

[641] Jacobsen (Scharnhorst), pp. 205–206.

[642] Bredemeier, pp. 288–291; Woodman, pp. 371–2.

[643] KTB Scharnhorst, "Vernehmung des Matr.Gefr. Sträter (Günter) von der Scharnhorst Gefechtsstation Bb. 4. 15 cm-Turm, Ladenr.", 6. Oktober 1944, BA-MA RM 92/5199; Bredemeier, pp. 288–304; Woodman pp. 371–372.

[644] http://www.scharnhorst-class.dk/scharnhorst/history/scharnostfront.html

645   Jacobsen (Scharnhorst), p. 210.

646   KTB Scharnhorst, "Vernehmung des Matr.Gefr. Sträter (Günter) von der Scharnhorst Gefechtsstation Bb. 4. 15 cm-Turm, Ladenr.", 6. Oktober 1944, BA-MA RM 92/5199.

647   KTB Scharnhorst, "Vernehmung des Matr.Gefr. Sträter (Günter) von der Scharnhorst Gefechtsstation Bb. 4. 15 cm-Turm, Ladenr.", 6. Oktober 1944, BA-MA RM 92/5199; Bredemeier, pp. 292–307.

648   Sweetman, p. 55.

649   It was considered to start heavy bombers from British bases, drop the bombs on the *Tirpitz*, and land at Soviet air bases. Also, using U.S. bombers with greater range was considered, but the intensified Allied bombing campaign against German industrial centers prevented such schemes. The lack of accuracy also spoke against the heavy bombers. See Sweetman, p. 53.

650   Brown, p. 33; Sweetman, pp. 56–57.

651   Lewin, p. 230; Brown, p. 33.

652   Brown, p. 34.

653   fleetairarmarchive.net

654   Brown, p. 33; Bismarck-class.dk; Sweetman, p. 57.

655   Brown, pp. 33–34; Roskill, p. 358.

656   Roskill, pp. 359–360; Bismarck-class.dk; Kennedy, p. 124.

657   Sweetman, p. 62, samt bildark mellan pp. 83–84.

658   Sweetman, pp. 62-3.

659   BA-MA RM 92/5107; Peillard, karta mellan p. 167–168.

660   BA-MA RM 92/5107. VAD MER.

661   Sweetman, p. 57.

662   Sweetman, p. 62.

663   Peillard, p. 265; BA-MA RM 92/5107.

664   Peillard, p. 265; BA-MA RM 92/5107; Kennedy p. 125; Brown, p. 206.

665   Peillard, p. 265; BA-MA RM 92/5107.

666   Peillard, p. 268.

667   Brown, p. 34; Bericht Hugo Heydel, BA-MA RM 92/5244; Jacobsen, p. 213.

668   Brown, p. 34; Bericht Hugo Heydel, BA-MA RM 92/5244.

669   BA-MA RM 92/5107.

670   Sweetman, p. 63.

671   Bericht Hugo Heydel, BA-MA RM 92/5244; Kennedy, p. 125; Sweetman, p. 71; Jacobsen, p. 214.

672   Bericht Hugo Heydel, BA-MA RM 92/5244; Kennedy, p. 125; Sweetman, p. 71.

673   BA-MA RM 92/5107; Brown, p. 34; Kennedy, p. 125.

674   Bericht Hugo Heydel, BA-MA RM 92/5244; Sweetman, p. 71; Peillard, pp. 268–269.

675   Bericht Hugo Heydel, BA-MA RM 92/5244; Peillard, pp. 268–269.

676   Sweetman, p. 63.

677   BA-MA RM 92/5107; Kennedy, pp. 125–126; Peillard, p. 269; Sweetman, p. 71.

678   Bericht Hugo Heydel, BA-MA RM 92/5244.

679   Bericht Hugo Heydel, BA-MA RM 92/5244; Bismarck-class.dk; Kennedy, p. 126;

Brown pp. 34–35.

680 Sweetman, p. 63; Brown, p. 35.

681 Sweetman, p. 64.

682 Sweetman, p. 65.

683 Sweetman, p. 68.

684 Sweetman, p. 68–69.

685 Sweetman, p. 68–69.

686 Brown, p. 36; Sweetman, p. 72.

687 Kommando Schlachtschiff Tirpitz, B.Nr. 395 gKdos, "Gefechtsbericht über den Luftangriff auf Schlachtschiff Tirpitz am 3. April im Kaafjord," 13.4.44, BA-MA RM 92/5203; Bericht Werner Krux, BA-MA RM 92/5186.

688 KTB Tirpitz, 8.4.44, 12.4.44, 13.4.44, BA-MA RM 92/5202;, Bericht Werner Krux, BA-MA RM 92/5186.

689 KTB Tirpitz, 8.4.44, 12.4.44, 13.4.44, 15.4.44, 22.4.44, BA-MA RM 92/5202;, Bericht Werner Krux, BA-MA RM 92/5186.

690 KTB Tirpitz, Juni 1944, BA-MA RM 92/5202; Bericht Werner Krux, pp. 22–23, BA-MA RM 92/5186.

691 Sweetman, p. 75.

692 Brown, p. 37; Sweetman, pp. 76–77.

693 Brown, pp. 37–38; Bismarck-class.dk; Sweetman, p. 79.

694 Sweetman, pp. 77–80, 85.

695 Bismarck-class.dk; Brown, p. 38.

696 Bismarck-class.dk; Hague, p. 189.

697 Sweetman, pp. 85–86; Kemp (Convoy), p. 203; Roskill, p. 401.

698 Sweetman, p. 87.

699 Kemp (Convoy), p. 203.

700 Sweetman, p. 94.

701 Winchester, pp. 26–27.

702 Cooper, pp. 82–83.

703 Cooper, pp. 82–84.

704 Cooper, p. 83.

705 Price, p. 100; Lancastermuseum.ca; Cooper, p. 83.

706 Price, p. 100.

707 Price, pp. 100–101.

708 Cooper, p. 86.

709 Sweetman, pp. 103–106; Cooper, pp. 89–91.

710 Sweetman, pp. 103–104; Cooper, pp. 89–91.

711 Cooper, p. 92.

712 Sweetman, p. 111.

713 Woodward, p. 151; Cooper, pp. 92–93.

714 Price, p. 102; Cooper, p. 93.

715 Price, pp. 102–103; Cooper, p. 93.

716 Peillard, p. 284.

717 Cooper, pp. 93–94.

718 Cooper, p. 94.

719   Cooper, p. 94.

720   Cooper, p. 95; Bennett, p. 108; Sweetman, p. 116.

721   Cooper, pp. 95–96.

722   Cooper, p. 96.

723   KTB Tirpitz, 15.9.44, BA-MA RM 92/5202; Bericht Werner Krux, pp. 24–25; BA-MA RM 92/5186.

724   KTB Tirpitz, 15.9.44, BA-MA RM 92/5202; Bericht Werner Krux, pp. 24–25; BA-MA RM 92/5186; Ziemke (1985), pp. 387–401.

725   Sweetman, pp. 117–118.

726   Peillard, pp. 286–288.

727   Kemp (Convoy), p. 204; Jacobsen, p. 238.

728   Bericht Werner Krux, pp. 27–28, BA-MA RM 92/5186.

729   KTB Tirpitz, 15.10.44, BA-MA RM 92/5200; Bericht Werner Krux, pp. 25–26, BA-MA RM 92/5186.

730   Kemp (Convoy), p. 204.

731   Cooper, p. 105; Sweetman, pp. 126–127; Price, p. 104.

732   Bismarck-class.dk; Cooper, p. 105.

733   Bismarck-class.dk.

734   Sweetman, p. 131.

735   Bennett, p. 120.

736   Bennett, pp. 120–121.

737   Peillard, p. 292.

738   Cooper, p. 106.

739   Bryggman, pp. 15–17.

740   Bryggman, pp. 15–17; Cooper p. 106; Bennett, pp. 125–127.

741   Bryggman, pp. 15–17; Cooper p. 106; Bennett, pp. 125–127.

742   Bennett, pp. 126–127.

743   Bismarck-class.dk; Cooper, p. 105.

744   Kennedy, p. 133; Schofield, p. 203.

745   Sweetman, p. 137.

746   Kennedy, pp. 133–134; Peillard, p. 294; Sweetman, p. 138.

747   Sweetman, p. 138.

748   Sweetman, pp. 138–139; Cooper, p. 110.

749   Price, p. 105.

750   Sweetman, p. 139; Peillard, p. 295; Bismarck-class.dk; Price, p. 105.

751   Sweetman, p. 139; Peillard, p. 295; Bismarck-class.dk; Price, p. 105.

752   Peillard, p. 299.

753   Jacobsen, pp. 251–252.

754   Peillard, p. 300; Cooper, p. 115; Sweetman, p. 153; Jacobsen, p. 252.

Archival Records

A large part of the records from the German Navy survived the war and are today available at the Bundesarchiv-Militärarchiv at Freiburg (abbreviated BA-MA), including, for example, the war diary (abbreviated KTB in the notes) kept on the *Tirpitz*. We have used the following files from the Bundesarchiv-Militärarchiv when writing this book:

BA-MA RM 92/5200: War Diary of the Tirpitz 25 February 1941 – 29 September 1942.

BA-MA RM 92/5201: War Diary of the Tirpitz 30 September 1942 – 22 September 1943.

BA-MA RM 92/5202: War Diary of the Tirpitz 16 October 1943 – 12 November 1944.

BA-MA RM 92/5170: British report on the air attack 3 April 1944.

BA-MA RM 92/5203: After action report from the Tirpitz 3 April 1944

BA-MA RM 92/5204 & RM 92/5205: Miscellaneous photos from artificial fog exercises at the Kaafjord.

BA-MA RM 92/5423: Miscellaneous excerpts from the Tirpitz War Diary 16 april – 8 juli 1944.

BA-MA RM 92/5244: Various accounts written by men who served on the Tirpitz.

BA-MA RM 92/5186: Extensive technical report written by Werner Krux.

BA-MA RM 35 I/217: Miscellaneous correspondence and other documents pertaining to the Tirpitz F22 September 1943 – 5

December 1944.

BA-MA RM 35 I/388a & RM 35 I/388b: Documents, orders and other papers on the operations Sportpalast and Eisenbahn, February 1942.

BA-MA RM 35 I/219: Dokument from Marinegruppe Nord pertaining to the Scharnhorst's attack on JW55B 26 december 1943.

BA-MA RM 92/5199: War Diary of the Scharnhorst 12 March 1943 – 26 December 1943 (incomplete).

BA-MA RM 48/192: War Diary Flottenkommando 23 March 1942 – 30 April 1942.

BA-MA RM 35 I/140 War Diary Marinegruppe Nord 1 March – 30 April 1942.

BA-MA RM 35 I/142 War Diary Marinegruppe Nord 1 June – 31 July 1942.

BA-MA RM 35 I/143 War Diary Marinegruppe Nord 1 August – 30 September 1942.

BA-MA RM 48/265: Documents on operation Rösselsprung.

BA-MA RM 48/265: Dokument rörande anfallen mot PQ18.

BA-MA RL 7/493: War Diary Luftflotte 5 Februari – April 1942.

BA-MA RL 7/494 & RL 7/495: War Diary Luftflotte 5 May – June 1942.

BA-MA RL 7/496: War Diary Luftflotte 5 July – September 1942.

BA-MA RL 7/497: War Diary Luftflotte 5 October – December 1942.

BA-MA RL 7/514: Organization charts Luftflotte 5.

BA-MA RL 10/578: Documents on Kampfgeschwader 30.

BA-MA RL 10/578: Account on Kampfgeschwader 26 written by Werner Klümper.

Published Sources

Bekker, Cajus, *Hitler's Naval War*, London: Corgi Books, 1974.

Bekker, Cajus, *The Luftwaffe War Diaries*, New York: Da Capo, 1974.

Bekker, Cajus, *Verdammte See*, Framkfurt am Main: Ullstein, 2002.

Bennett, Tom, *617 Squadron: The Dambusters at War*, Wellingborough: Patrick Stevens, 1987.

Bidlingmeyer, Gerhard, *Einsatz der schweren Kriegsmarineeinheiten im ozeanischen Zufuhrkrieg*, Neckargemünd: Scharnhorst Buchkameradschaft, 1963.

Bredemeier, Heinrich, *Schlachtschiff Scharnhorst*, München: Pavillon, 2003.

Brennecke, Jochen, *Schlachtschiff Bismarck*, München: Koehlers, 1960.

Brennecke, Jochen, *Schlachtschiff Tirpitz*, München: Wilhelm Heyne Verlag, 1980.

Brennecke, Jochen, *Die Wende im U-Boot-Krieg*, Augsburg: Weltbild, 1995.

Brennecke, Jochen, *Eismeer, Atlantik, Ostsee – Die Einsätze des Schweren Kreuzers "Admiral Hipper,"* München: Pavillon, 2003.

Breyer, Siegfried, *Battleship "Tirpitz,"* West Chester, Pennsylvania: Schiffer, 1989.

Breyer, Siegfried, *The German Battleship Scharnhorst*, West Chester, Pennsylvania: Schiffer, 1990.

Broome, Jack, *Convoy is to Scatter: The Story of PQ-17*, London: Futura, 1974.

Brown, David, *Tirpitz: The Floating Fortress*, London: Arms & Armour Press, 1977.

Brown, David, *Warship Losses of World War II*, London: Arms and Armour, 1990.

Budianskij, Stephen, *Battle of Wits*, London: Penguin Books, 2000.

Busch, Fritz-Otto, *The Drama of the Scharnhorst*, London: Hale, 1991.

Cooper, Alan, *Beyond the Dams to the Tirpitz*, London: Goodall Publications, 1991.

Dorrian, James G., *Storming St Nazaire*, Barnsley: Pen & Sword, 2001.

Elfrath, U. & B. Herzog, *Schlachtschiff Bismarck – Technische Daten, Ausrüstung, Bewaffnung, panzerung, kampf und Untergang*, Friedberg: Podzun-Pallas, 1982.

Ford, Ken, *St Nazaire 1942: The Great Commando Raid*, Oxford: Osprey, 2001.

Fuehrer Conferences on Naval Affairs 1939–1945, London: Greenhill, 1990.

Gallagher, Thomas, *Against All Odds*, London: Pan Books, 1973.

Hague, Arnold, *The Allied Convoy System 1939–1945*, Ontario: Vanwell, 2000.

Jackson, John, *Ultra's Arctic War, The Bletchley Archive, Vol. 2*, Milton Keynes: The Military Press, 2003.

Jacobsen, Alf R., *Dödligt Angrepp*, Stockholm: Natur och Kultur, 2003.

Jacobsen, Alf R., *Scharnhorst*, Phoenix Mill: Sutton, 2003.

Kemp, Paul, *Convoy: Drama in Arctic Waters*, London: Cassell, 2002.

Kemp, Paul, *Underwater Warriors*, London: Brockhampton, 1999.

Kennedy, Ludovic, *Menace: Life and Death of the Tirpitz*, London: Sphere, 1981.

Lenton, H. T. & J. J. Colledge, *Warships of World War II*, London: Ian Allan, 1973.

Lewin, Ronald, *Ultra Goes to War*, London: Penguin, 2001.

von Müllenheim-Rechberg, Burkhardt, *Schlachtschiff Bismarck*, Frankfurt a. M.: Ullstein, 2002.

Peillard, Léonce, *Sink the Tirpitz*, London: Granada, 1983.

Peter, Karl, *Schlachtkreuzer Scharnhorst – Kampf und Untergang*, Berlin: Mittler & Sohn, 1951.

Price, Alfred, *Sky Warriors: Classic Air War Battles*, London: Cassell, 1998.

Raeder, Erich, *Mein Leben, Band I & II*, Tübingen: Schlichtenmeyer, 1956-1957.

Roskill, Stephen, *The Navy at War 1939–45*, London: Wordsworth, 1998.

Roskill, Stephen, *The War at Sea, Vol. II*, London: HMSO, 1954.

Saelen, Frithjof, *None but the Brave: The Story of Leif Larsen*, London: Corgi Books, 1956.

Samuelson, Lennart, *Röd koloss på larvfötter*, Stockholm: SNS, 1999.

Schmalenbach, Paul, *Kreuzer Prinz Eugen unter drei Flaggen*, Hamburg: Koehlers, 2001.

Schofield, B. B., *The Russian Convoys*, London: Pan, 1984.

Schuur, H., & R. Martens & W. Koehler, *Führungsprobleme der Marine im Zweiten Weltkrieg*, Freiburg: Rombach, 1973.

Sokolov, Boris V., "The Role of Lend-Lease in Soviet Military Efforts, 1941-1945," *Journal of Slavic Military Studies, Vol. 7, No. 3 (September 1994)*.

Sweetman, John, *Tirpitz – Hunting the Beast*, Poenix Mill: Sutton, 2000.

Tarrant, V. E., *King George V Class Battleships*, London: Arms and Armour, 1999.

von Tuleja, Thaddeus, *Deutsche Schlachtschiffe und schwere Kreuzer 1939–1945*, Freidberg: Podzun-Pallas, not dated.

Walker, Frank & Pamela Mellor, *The Mystery of X5: Lieutenant H. Henty-Creer's Attack on the Tirpitz*, London: William Kimber, 1988.

Warren, C. E. T. och James Benson, *Above Us the Waves*, London: Corgi Books, 1955.

Williamson, Gordon, *German Battleships 1939–45*, Oxford: Osprey, 2003.

Winchester, Jim, *Aircraft of World War II*, Rochester: Grange Books, 2004.

Woodman, Richard, *Arctic Convoys 1941–1945*, London: John Murray, 1995.

Woodward, David, *Tirpitz*, London: NEL Books, 1974.

Ziemke, Earl F., *The German Northern Theatre of Operations 1940–1945*, Washington DC: Department of the Army Pamphlet 20-271, 1959.

Ziemke, Earl F., *Stalingrad to Berlin*, New York: Military Heritage Press, 1985.